Richard Wright's

Native Son

A Critical Handbook

WADSWORTH GUIDES TO LITERARY STUDY

Maurice Beebe, General Editor

***ALICE'S ADVENTURES IN WONDERLAND:* A Critical Handbook**
edited by Donald Rackin, Temple University

APPROACHES TO *MACBETH*
edited by Jay L. Halio, University of Delaware

APPROACHES TO *WALDEN*
edited by Lauriat Lane, Jr., University of New Brunswick

A *BENITO CERENO* HANDBOOK
edited by Seymour L. Gross, University of Detroit

***THE BROTHERS KARAMAZOV* AND THE CRITICS**
edited by Edward Wasiolek, University of Chicago

TRUMAN CAPOTE'S *IN COLD BLOOD:* A Critical Handbook
edited by Irving Malin, City College of New York

CONRAD'S *HEART OF DARKNESS* AND THE CRITICS
edited by Bruce Harkness, Kent State University

CONRAD'S *SECRET SHARER* AND THE CRITICS
edited by Bruce Harkness, Kent State University

STEPHEN CRANE'S *MAGGIE:* Text and Context
edited by Maurice Bassan, San Francisco State College

***CRIME AND PUNISHMENT* AND THE CRITICS**
edited by Edward Wasiolek, University of Chicago

***FREEDOM AND CULTURE:* Literary Censorship in the 70s**
edited by Eleanor Widmer, with the assistance of Kingsley Widmer, San Diego State College

GOETHE'S *FAUST PART I:* Essays in Criticism
edited by John B. Vickery and J'nan Sellery, University of California at Riverside

HOMER'S *ODYSSEY:* A Critical Handbook
edited by Conny Nelson, Washington State University

JAMES JOYCE'S *DUBLINERS:* A Critical Handbook
edited by James R. Baker, San Diego State College, and Thomas F. Staley, University of Tulsa

THE *KING LEAR* PERPLEX
edited by Helmut Bonheim

LITERARY SYMBOLISM: An Introduction to the Interpretation of Literature
edited by Maurice Beebe, Temple University

MELVILLE'S *BILLY BUDD* AND THE CRITICS, Second Edition
edited by William T. Stafford, Purdue University

***OEDIPUS REX:* A Mirror for Greek Drama**
edited by Albert Cook, State University of New York

J. D. SALINGER AND THE CRITICS
edited by William F. Belcher and James W. Lee, North Texas State University

A *SCARLET LETTER* HANDBOOK
edited by Seymour L. Gross, University of Detroit

WILLIAM STYRON'S *THE CONFESSIONS OF NAT TURNER:* A Critical Handbook
edited by Melvin J. Friedman, University of Wisconsin at Milwaukee, and Irving Malin, City College, New York

SUCCESS IN AMERICA
edited by James J. Clark and Robert H. Woodward, San Jose State College

MARK TWAIN'S *THE MYSTERIOUS STRANGER* AND THE CRITICS
edited by John S. Tuckey, Purdue University

VOLTAIRE'S *CANDIDE* AND THE CRITICS
edited by Milton P. Foster, Eastern Michigan Univers

ROBERT PENN WARREN'S *ALL THE KING'S MEN* A Critical Handbook
edited by Maurice Beebe, Temple University, and Leslie Field, Purdue University

Richard Wright's

Native Son

A Critical Handbook

edited by

Richard Abcarian

San Fernando Valley State College

Wadsworth Publishing Company, Inc.
Belmont, California

L. C. Cat. Card No.: 71–126363
Printed in the United States of America
1 2 3 4 5 6 7 8 9 10–74 73 72 71 70

PREFACE

When Richard Wright's *Native Son* appeared in 1940, it received all the acclaim a great novel deserves. A selection of the Book-of-the-Month Club, it reached the top of the best-seller lists immediately and within a month had sold 250,000 copies. And the book's popular, commercial success was matched by its critical success. *Native Son* was widely and enthusiastically reviewed as the first novel that definitively exploded the white myth of the happy-go-lucky darky, cheerfully occupying his inferior station in American society. An American reality was presented with such artistic power that few critics could deny its essential truth: the shuffling and smiling of the black man, the "yes suh" and "no suh" were merely the survival reflexes that concealed what *Time* magazine called "the murderous potentialities of the whole U.S. Negro problem."

Native Son, like a ghetto in riot, flared briefly into America's consciousness, and received the literary equivalent of the Kerner Commission report. Then it was promptly forgotten, for soon after the appearance of *Native Son*, the nation was drawn into the Second World War.

With peace came the growing insistence by blacks that they be accorded their rights. Despite a history of sporadic race riots in the North, America had long viewed racism as a Southern problem. In the South, black men were denied the vote, segregated, bombed, and lynched. These brutalities provided Northern cities occasion for comfortable moral outrage that helped block out the closer realities of their own ghettos.

On the literary front, the initial critical enthusiasm for *Native Son* did not mean that Wright had won a permanent place in literary history. The most powerful critics belonged to the school of New Criticism, which was more interested in poetry than fiction and was dominated by the Jamesian principle of the delicate, well-made novel. The attitude of the New Criticism toward *Native Son* (when it remembered the novel at all) was summarized by R. P. Blackmur's condescending remark in *Language as Gesture* (1952), quoted approvingly by other critics, that "*Native Son* is one of those books in which everything is undertaken with seriousness except the writing." Having thus disposed of *Native Son*, the critics could write books such as *The American Novel and Its Tradition* and *The Novel of Violence in America* without even mentioning Wright and produce a voluminous *Literary History of the United States* in which Jack London got four pages, Hamlin Garland three, and Booth Tarkington two, while Richard Wright was mentioned only in passing.

But the sixties changed both social and literary attitudes. The Southern problem suddenly and violently became a national problem, as ghetto after ghetto exploded like a dream deferred. And there stood Bigger Thomas, a "bad nigger" determined to take by force what had been monotonously promised and regularly denied him: food, clothing, decent furniture—and his freedom, his manhood. These convulsions appalled the same uncomprehending white America that twenty years earlier had been so moved by Wright's prophetic masterpiece.

The racial upheavals of the sixties made it difficult for America to ignore the profound dimensions of its racism. One aspect of the widespread re-examination of ourselves and our history has been the realization of literary critics that the literature produced by black Americans had not received the attention it deserved. They discovered, in the words of John A. Williams, that Richard Wright is "the most important black writer, American, of all times."

This volume begins with three essays by Richard Wright that provide illuminating information about the author's life and art. The first essay, "A World View of the American Negro," was written in 1946, shortly after Wright took up residence in Paris. His description of the American Negro as a colonial subect anticipates by almost two decades the feelings of many blacks today. "The Ethics of Living Jim Crow" is a summary autobiography of Wright's early Southern years, describing in a series of sharply focused episodes the pattern of physical and psychological violence by which the South turned dignified human beings into humble niggers. (These episodes Wright incorporated into his classic autobiography of his Southern years, *Black Boy* [1945].) In "How Bigger Was Born," Wright describes the experiences, including his membership in the Communist party, out of which *Native Son* grew. He also reveals the technical and personal problems he grappled with while writing his novel. In part a sequel to "The Ethics of Living Jim Crow" the essay describes how Wright made the pilgrimage North in pursuit of the American dream, only to discover the nightmare of the urban ghetto.

Part Two is a group of the most significant and representative reviews of *Native Son*. Readers will find them interesting in a variety of ways and will no doubt be struck by their extraordinarily contemporary ring. Most of the reviews are taken from journals, as newspaper reviews tend to be brief plot summaries rather than critical analyses. The exceptions, besides the reviews from the *New York Times* and the *New York Herald Tribune*, are the reviews which appeared in the Negro *Chicago Defender* and in the Communist *New York Sunday Worker*. The latter review is particularly noteworthy both because it was a lengthy review by an important black Communist of a novel by a fellow party member and because it appeared more than a month after other newspaper reviews, indicating the party's uncertainty about how to respond to the novel. Two influential journals, the *Atlantic Monthly* and the *American Mercury,* carried sharply adverse reviews that aroused Wright to rebuttal. The rebuttals are also included in this section.

Part Three contains what seem to me some of the best and most representative critical essays on *Native Son.* They offer much formal literary analysis. But *Native Son,* a large and explosive novel about America's most burning reality, is scarcely to be contained within the confines of narrow critical formalism. The questions Wright's novel raise range from the justness of his portrayal of Negro life to the nature (and validity) of protest literature, from the psychology of the oppressed to the prospects for racial peace in America. That this is so is a tribute to the novel's specifically *artistic* power.

Indeed, the following section of related essays, selected from distinguished books by black authors, comprises a powerful supplement to and comment on the essential accuracy and enduring relevance of *Native Son.* These essays tell us much about the novel, especially about that most disturbing aspect—Wright's presentation of violence as positive and liberating. At the end, Bigger gropes his way from the murky prison of his unreflected soul to a major insight: "But, what I killed for, I *am,*" he says. If there is too much reality in his statement for America to bear, it can hardly begin to understand the insight of Bigger's modern brothers who say with Camus' rebel, "I rebel—therefore we exist."

CONTENTS

PART ONE: ESSAYS BY RICHARD WRIGHT

To Richard Wright

CONRAD KENT RIVERS

You said that your people
Never knew the full spirit of
Western Civilization.
To be born unnoticed
Is to be born black,
And left out of the grand adventure.

Miseducation, denial,
Are lost in the cruelty of oppression.
And the faint cool kiss of sensuality
Lingers on our cheeks.

The quiet terror brings on silent night.
They are driving us crazy. And our father's
Religion warps his life.

To live day by day
  Is not to live at all.

Conrad Kent Rivers (1933–1968). Poet, teacher, public relationist of Philadelphia. Worked in Chicago, Illinois and Gary, Indiana.

A World View of the American Negro

RICHARD WRIGHT

My dear Friend:

One way of describing what is happening in the world today is to say that more than a billion people who used to employ crude tools to cultivate the soil are now being taught how to use complex machines and are learning how to live in machine-made cities. This process is not simple; it manifests itself in social, psychological, economic, and cultural terms. There are many approaches to it. If one is a Marxist, one may want to dwell upon its economic aspects. If one is an anthropologist, one may be prone to depict the ritual of living involved. If one is a psychologist, one may want to study the conflict of cultures as they are reflected in personalities. If one is a sociologist, one would want to study the institutional structures as they change from one generation to another.

I am not a Communist, a Socialist, a Republican, a Catholic, a Capitalist, an Anarchist, or a Fascist. I am merely a man who is curious about the tissue and texture of human experience. By social definition, I am an American Negro and what I'll have to say will deal with Negro life in the U.S.A., not because I think that that life or its problems are of supreme importance, but because Negro life in the U.S.A. dramatically symbolizes the struggle of a people whose forefathers lived in a warm, simple culture and who are now trying to live the new way of life that dominates our time: machine-civilization and all the consequences flowing from it.

It must be understood that when I talk of American Negroes, I am talking about everybody. I'm talking about the Americans who made the Civil War and enthroned industrialism as a way of life; I'm talking about the French who made the French Revolution; the English who made the Reformation; and the Russians who flung back the Czars and

---

Reprinted from *Twice A Year* (Fall 1946–Winter 1947), No. 14–15, pp. 346–348. Published originally in the French publication *Les Nouvelle Epitres* (1947).

lifted themselves out of their feudal darkness into the Century of the Machine.

The American Negro was involved in this vast process, but with a strange difference. He did not choose when he was to break away from his simple culture. The long, sloping shores of Western Africa lent themselves to the easy access of slave traders and the Negro was snatched from his continent, transported across the Atlantic, made to raise cotton on the vast American plantations. Hence, the Negro is intrinsically a colonial subject, but one who lives not in China, India, or Africa, but next door to his conquerors, attending their schools, fighting their wars, and laboring in their factories. The American Negro problem, therefore, is but a facet of the global problem that splits the world in two: Handicraft vs. Mass Production; Family vs. the Individual; Tradition vs. Progress; Personality vs. Collectivity; the East (the colonial peoples) vs. the West (exploiters of the world).

Nowhere on earth have these extremes met and clashed with such prolonged violence as in America between Negro and white, and this fact alone endows the American Negro problem with a vital importance, for what happens between whites and blacks in America foreshadows what will happen between the colored billions of Asia and the industrial whites of the West. Indeed, the world's fate is symbolically prefigured today in the race relations of America.

The Negro problem in America is romantic and prophetic in the sense that it brings the distant and problematic into the reality of the here and now. It is historically valuable for study in that it depicts the effort of a people who in a short space of 300 years have absorbed—under conditions of violence and against great odds!—the 2,000-year old history of the Western World: for the history of the Negro in America is but the history of the Western World writ small.

Imagine a people stolen from the warm nest of their ancient living, stripped of their culture, defined in economic terms, worked for 300 years, and suddenly freed! Imagine millions of such illiterate people facing life in a nation where, in 1860, the forces of modern industry were gathering strength to leap to a climax of industrial development that would result in the construction and use of the atom bomb!

How did these people fare? What happened inside of them? What personality traits did they acquire as a result of such an experience? What kind of cultural manifestations did they express?

When one recalls that there are over a billion people on earth who have yet to make the leap from their ancient way of life to that of our industrial civilization, then the history of the American Negro becomes truly a remarkable story. Yet it is one of the least known stories in the modern world. You have heard of the Negro's jazz music, his spirituals, his folklore, his dancing . . . Well, these accomplishments, as strange as it may seem, are the least important facts that the American Negro has to offer about himself.

As the pain of the American Negro's defensive living leaves him, as he gathers more confidence in himself, he will make known to you a tale that will mirror, in a rare but familiar way, your *own* lives, your *own* hopes and aspirations, for the Negro is you, grappling with the problems of modern life against odds which you have never known, and wringing deep meaning out of them.

Sensitive Negroes in America know this, and they are fighting to tear away the sentimentality, the many misrepresentations, the white supremacy ideology which has for centuries obscured the reality of their lives. And they are slowly making known a body of experience which is no less tragic than it is glorious, no less theirs than it is mankind's. Bred in a harsh school of life, they seek to speak the language of the human heart.

As ever,

RICHARD WRIGHT

The Ethics of Living Jim Crow

RICHARD WRIGHT

I

My first lesson in how to live as a Negro came when I was quite small. We were living in Arkansas. Our house stood behind the railroad tracks. Its skimpy yard was paved with black cinders. Nothing green ever grew in that yard. The only touch of green we could see was far away, beyond the tracks, over where the white folks lived. But cinders were good enough for me and I never missed the green growing things. And anyhow cinders were fine weapons. You could always have a nice hot war with huge black cinders. All you had to do was crouch behind the brick pillars of a house with your hands full of gritty ammunition. And the first woolly black head you saw pop out from behind another row of pillars was your target. You tried your very best to knock it off. It was great fun.

I never fully realized the appalling disadvantages of a cinder environment till one day the gang to which I belonged found itself

---

engaged in a war with the white boys who lived beyond the tracks. As usual we laid down our cinder barrage, thinking that this would wipe the white boys out. But they replied with a steady bombardment of broken bottles. We doubled our cinder barrage, but they hid behind trees, hedges, and the sloping embankments of their lawns. Having no such fortifications, we retreated to the brick pillars of our homes. During the retreat a broken milk bottle caught me behind the ear, opening a deep gash which bled profusely. The sight of blood pouring over my face completely demoralized our ranks. My fellow-combatants left me standing paralyzed in the center of the yard, and scurried for their homes. A kind neighbor saw me, and rushed me to a doctor, who took three stitches in my neck.

I sat brooding on my front steps, nursing my wound and waiting for my mother to come from work. I felt that a grave injustice had been done me. It was all right to throw cinders. The greatest harm a cinder could do was leave a bruise. But broken bottles were dangerous; they left you cut, bleeding, and helpless.

When night fell, my mother came from the white folks' kitchen. I raced down the street to meet her. I could just feel in my bones that she would understand. I knew she would tell me exactly what to do next time. I grabbed her hand and babbled out the whole story. She examined my wound, then slapped me.

"How come yuh didn't hide?" she asked me. "How come yuh awways fightin'?"

I was outraged, and bawled. Between sobs I told her that I didn't have any trees or hedges to hide behind. There wasn't a thing I could have used as a trench. And you couldn't throw very far when you were hiding behind the brick pillars of a house. She grabbed a barrel stave, dragged me home, stripped me naked, and beat me till I had a fever of one hundred and two. She would smack my rump with the stave, and, while the skin was still smarting impart to me gems of Jim Crow wisdom. I was never to throw cinders any more. I was never to fight any more wars. I was never, never, under any conditions, to fight *white* folks again. And they were absolutely right in clouting me with the broken milk bottle. Didn't I know she was working hard every day in the hot kitchens of the white folks to make money to take care of me? When was I ever going to learn to be a good boy? She couldn't be bothered with my fights. She finished by telling me that I ought to be thankful to God as long as I lived that they didn't kill me.

All that night I was delirious and could not sleep. Each time I closed my eyes I saw monstrous white faces suspended from the ceiling, leering at me.

From that time on, the charm of my cinder yard was gone. The green trees, the trimmed hedges, the cropped lawns grew very meaningful, became a symbol. Even today when I think of white folks, the hard, sharp outlines of white houses surrounded by trees, lawns, and hedges are present somewhere in the background of my mind. Through the years they grew into an overreaching symbol of fear.

It was a long time before I came in close contact with white folks again. We moved from Arkansas to Mississippi. Here we had the good fortune not to live behind the railroad tracks, or close to white neighborhoods. We lived in the very heart of the local Black belt. There were black churches and black preachers; there were black schools and black teachers; black groceries and black clerks. In fact, everything was so solidly black that for a long time I did not even think of white folks, save in remote and vague terms. But this could not last forever. As one grows older one eats more. One's clothing costs more. When I finished grammar school I had to go to work. My mother could no longer feed and clothe me on her cooking job.

There is but one place where a black boy who knows no trade can get a job, and that's where the houses and faces are white, where the trees, lawns, and hedges are green. My first job was with an optical company in Jackson, Mississippi. The morning I applied I stood straight and neat before the boss, answering all his questions with sharp yessirs and nosirs. I was very careful to pronounce my *sirs* distinctly, in order that he might know that I was polite, that I knew where I was, and that I knew he was a *white* man. I wanted that job badly.

He looked me over as though he were examining a prize poodle. He questioned me closely about my schooling, being particularly insistent about how much mathematics I had had. He seemed very pleased when I told him I had had two years of algebra.

"Boy, how would you like to try to learn something around here?" he asked me.

"I'd like it fine, sir," I said, happy. I had visions of "working my way up." Even Negroes have those visions.

"All right," he said. "Come on."

I followed him to the small factory.

"Pease," he said to a white man of about thirty-five, "this is Richard. He's going to work for us."

Pease looked at me and nodded.

I was then taken to a white boy of about seventeen.

"Morrie, this is Richard, who's going to work for us."

"Whut yuh sayin' there, boy!" Morrie boomed at me.

"Fine!" I answered.

The boss instructed these two to help me, teach me, give me jobs to do, and let me learn what I could in my spare time.

My wages were five dollars a week.

I worked hard, trying to please. For the first month I got along O.K. Both Pease and Morrie seemed to like me. But one thing was missing. And I kept thinking about it. I was not learning anything and nobody was volunteering to help me. Thinking they had forgotten that

I was to learn something about the mechanics of grinding lenses, I asked Morrie one day to tell me about the work. He grew red.

"Whut yuh tryin' t' do, nigger, get smart?" he asked.

"Naw; I ain' tryin' t' git smart," I said.

"Well, don't, if yuh know whut's good for yuh!"

I was puzzled. Maybe he just doesn't want to help me, I thought. I went to Pease.

"Say, are yuh crazy, you black bastard?" Pease asked me, his gray eyes growing hard.

I spoke out, reminding him that the boss had said I was to be given a chance to learn something.

"Nigger, you think you're *white*, don't you?"

"Naw, sir!"

"Well, you're acting mighty like it!"

"But, Mr. Pease, the boss said . . ."

Pease shook his fist in my face.

"This is a *white* man's work around here, and you better watch yourself!"

From then on they changed toward me. They said good-morning no more. When I was just a bit slow in performing some duty, I was called a lazy black son-of-a-bitch.

Once I thought of reporting all this to the boss. But the mere idea of what would happen to me if Pease and Morrie should learn that I had "snitched" stopped me. And after all the boss was a white man, too. What was the use?

The climax came at noon one summer day. Pease called me to his work-bench. To get to him I had to go between two narrow benches and stand with my back against a wall.

"Yes, sir," I said.

"Richard, I want to ask you something," Pease began pleasantly, not looking up from his work.

"Yes, sir," I said again.

Morrie came over, blocking the narrow passage between the benches. He folded his arms, staring at me solemnly.

I looked from one to the other, sensing that something was coming.

"Yes, sir," I said for the third time.

Pease looked up and spoke very slowly.

"Richard, *Mr.* Morrie here tells me you called me *Pease*."

I stiffened. A void seemed to open up in me. I knew this was the show-down.

He meant that I had failed to call him Mr. Pease. I looked at Morrie. He was gripping a steel bar in his hands. I opened my mouth to speak, to protest, to assure Pease that I had never called him simply *Pease*, and that I had never had any intentions of doing so, when Morrie grabbed me by the collar, ramming my head against the wall.

"Now, be careful, nigger!" snarled Morrie, baring his teeth. "*I* heard yuh call 'im *Pease!* 'N' if yuh say yuh didn't, yuh're callin' me a *lie*, see?" He waved the steel bar threateningly.

If I had said: No, sir, Mr. Pease, I never called you *Pease*, I would have been automatically calling Morrie a liar. And if I had said: Yes, sir, Mr. Pease, I called you *Pease*, I would have been pleading guilty to having uttered the worst insult that a Negro can utter to a southern white man. I stood hesitating, trying to frame a neutral reply.

"Richard, I asked you a question!" said Pease. Anger was creeping into his voice.

"I don't remember calling you *Pease*, Mr. Pease," I said cautiously. "And if I did, I sure didn't mean . . ."

"You black son-of-a-bitch! You called me *Pease*, then!" he spat, slapping me till I bent sideways over a bench. Morrie was on top of me, demanding:

"Didn't yuh call 'im *Pease?* If yuh say yuh didn't, I'll rip yo' gut string loose with this bar, yuh black granny dodger! Yuh can't call a white man a lie 'n' get erway with it, you black son-of-a-bitch!"

I wilted. I begged them not to bother me. I knew what they wanted. They wanted me to leave.

"I'll leave," I promised. "I'll leave right *now*."

They gave me a minute to get out of the factory. I was warned not to show up again, or tell the boss.

I went.

When I told the folks at home what had happened, they called me a fool. They told me that I must never again attempt to exceed my boundaries. When you are working for white folks, they said, you got to "stay in your place" if you want to keep working.

II

My Jim Crow education continued on my next job, which was portering in a clothing store. One morning, while polishing brass out front, the boss and his twenty-year-old son got out of their car and half dragged and half kicked a Negro woman into the store. A policeman standing at the corner looked on, twirling his night-stick. I watched out of the corner of my eye, never slackening the strokes of my chamois upon the brass. After a few minutes, I heard shrill screams coming from the rear of the store. Later the woman stumbled out, bleeding, crying, and holding her stomach. When she reached the end of the block, the policeman grabbed her and accused her of being drunk. Silently, I watched him throw her into a patrol wagon.

When I went to the rear of the store, the boss and his son were washing their hands at the sink. They were chuckling. The floor was bloody and strewn with wisps of hair and clothing. No doubt I must have appeared pretty shocked, for the boss slapped me reassuringly on the back.

"Boy, that's what we do to niggers when they don't want to pay their bills," he said, laughing.

His son looked at me and grinned.

"Here, hava cigarette," he said.

Not knowing what to do, I took it. He lit his and held the match for me. This was a gesture of kindness, indicating that even if they had beaten the poor old woman, they would not beat me if I knew enough to keep my mouth shut.

"Yes, sir," I said, and asked no questions.

After they had gone, I sat on the edge of a packing box and stared at the bloody floor till the cigarette went out.

That day at noon, while eating in a hamburger joint, I told my fellow Negro porters what had happened. No one seemed surprised. One fellow, after swallowing a huge bite, turned to me and asked:

"Huh! Is tha' all they did t' her?"

"Yeah. Wasn't tha' enough?" I asked.

"Shucks! Man, she's a lucky bitch!" he said, burying his lips deep into a juicy hamburger. "Hell, it's a wonder they didn't lay her when they got through."

III

I was learning fast, but not quite fast enough. One day, while I was delivering packages in the suburbs, my bicycle tire was punctured. I walked along the hot, dusty road, sweating and leading my bicycle by the handle-bars.

A car slowed at my side.

"What's the matter, boy?" a white man called.

I told him my bicycle was broken and I was walking back to town.

"That's too bad," he said. "Hop on the running board."

He stopped the car. I clutched hard at my bicycle with one hand and clung to the side of the car with the other.

"All set?"

"Yes, sir," I answered. The car started.

It was full of young white men. They were drinking. I watched the flask pass from mouth to mouth.

"Wanna drink, boy?" one asked.

I laughed as the wind whipped my face. Instinctively obeying the freshly planted precepts of my mother, I said:

"Oh, no!"

The words were hardly out of my mouth before I felt something hard and cold smash me between the eyes. It was an empty whisky bottle. I saw stars, and fell backwards from the speeding car into the dust of the road, my feet becoming entangled in the steel spokes of my bicycle. The white men piled out and stood over me.

"Nigger, ain' yuh learned no better sense'n tha' yet?" asked the man who hit me. "Ain' yuh learned t' say *sir* t' a white man yet?"

Dazed, I pulled to my feet. My elbows and legs were bleeding.

Fists doubled, the white man advanced, kicking my bicycle out of the way.

"Aw leave the bastard alone. He's got enough," said one.

They stood looking at me. I rubbed my shins, trying to stop the flow of blood. No doubt they felt a sort of contemptuous pity, for one asked:

"Yuh wanna ride t' town now, nigger? Yuh reckon yuh know enough t' ride now?"

"I wanna walk," I said, simply.

Maybe it sounded funny. They laughed.

"Well, walk, yuh black son-of-a-bitch!"

When they left they comforted me with:

"Nigger, yuh sho better be damn glad it wuz us yuh talked t' tha' way. Yuh're a lucky bastard, 'cause if yuh'd said tha' t' somebody else, yuh might've been a dead nigger now."

IV

Negroes who have lived South know the dread of being caught alone upon the streets in white neighborhoods after the sun has set. In such a simple situation as this the plight of the Negro in America is graphically symbolized. While white strangers may be in these neighborhoods trying to get home, they can pass unmolested. But the color of a Negro's skin makes him easily recognizable, makes him suspect, converts him into a defenseless target.

Late one Saturday night I made some deliveries in a white neighborhood. I was pedaling my bicycle back to the store as fast as I could, when a police car, swerving toward me, jammed me into the curbing.

"Get down and put up your hands!" the policemen ordered.

I did. They climbed out of the car, guns drawn, faces set, and advanced slowly.

"Keep still!" they ordered.

I reached my hands higher. They searched my pockets and packages. They seemed dissatisfied when they could find nothing incriminating. Finally, one of them said:

"Boy, tell your boss not to send you out in white neighborhoods after sundown."

As usual, I said:

"Yes, sir."

V

My next job was as hall-boy in a hotel. Here my Jim Crow education broadened and deepened. When the bell-boys were busy, I was often called to assist them. As many of the rooms in the hotel were occupied by prostitutes, I was constantly called to carry them liquor and cigarettes. These women were nude most of the time. They did not bother about clothing, even for bell-boys. When you went into their rooms, you were supposed to take their nakedness for granted, as though it startled you no more than a blue vase or a red rug. Your presence awoke in them no sense of shame, for you were not regarded as human. If they were alone, you could steal sidelong glimpses at them. But if they were receiving men, not a flicker of your eyelids could show. I remember one incident vividly. A new woman, a huge, snowy-skinned blonde, took a room on my floor. I was sent to wait upon her. She was in bed with a thick-set man; both were nude and uncovered. She said she wanted some liquor and slid out of bed and waddled across the floor to get her money from a dresser drawer. I watched her.

"Nigger, what in hell you looking at?" the white man asked me, raising himself upon his elbows.

"Nothing," I answered, looking miles deep into the blank wall of the room.

"Keep your eyes where they belong, if you want to be healthy!" he said.

"Yes, sir."

VI

One of the bell-boys I knew in this hotel was keeping steady company with one of the Negro maids. Out of a clear sky the police descended upon his home and arrested him, accusing him of bastardy. The poor boy swore he had had no intimate relations with the girl. Nevertheless, they forced him to marry her. When the child arrived, it was found to be much lighter in complexion than either of the two supposedly legal parents. The white men around the hotel made a great joke of it. They spread the rumor that some white cow must have scared the poor girl while she was carrying the baby. If you were in their presence when this explanation was offered, you were supposed to laugh.

VII

One of the bell-boys was caught in bed with a white prostitute. He was castrated and run out of town. Immediately after this all the bell-boys and hall-boys were called together and warned. We were given to understand that the boy who had been castrated was a "mighty, mighty lucky bastard." We were impressed with the fact that next time the management of the hotel would not be responsible for the lives of "trouble-makin' niggers." We were silent.

VIII

One night, just as I was about to go home, I met one of the Negro maids. She lived in my direction, and we fell in to walk part of the way home together. As we passed the white night-watchman, he slapped the maid on her buttock. I turned around, amazed. The watchman looked at me with a long, hard, fixed-under stare. Suddenly he pulled his gun and asked:

"Nigger, don't yuh like it?"

I hesitated.

"I asked yuh don't yuh like it?" he asked again, stepping forward.

"Yes, sir," I mumbled.

"Talk like it, then!"

"Oh, yes, sir!" I said with as much heartiness as I could muster.

Outside, I walked ahead of the girl, ashamed to face her. She caught up with me and said:

"Don't be a fool! Yuh couldn't help it!"

This watchman boasted of having killed two Negroes in self-defense.

Yet, in spite of all this, the life of the hotel ran with an amazing smoothness. It would have been impossible for a stranger to detect anything. The maids, the hall-boys, and the bell-boys were all smiles. They had to be.

IX

I had learned my Jim Crow lessons so thoroughly that I kept the hotel job till I left Jackson for Memphis. It so happened that while in Memphis I applied for a job at a branch of the optical company. I was hired. And for some reason, as long as I worked there, they never brought my past against me.

Here my Jim Crow education assumed quite a different form. It was no longer brutally cruel, but subtly cruel. Here I learned to lie, to steal, to dissemble. I learned to play that dual role which every Negro must play if he wants to eat and live.

For example, it was almost impossible to get a book to read. It was assumed that after a Negro had imbibed what scanty schooling the state furnished he had no further need for books. I was always borrowing books from men on the job. One day I mustered enough courage to ask one of the men to let me get books from the library in his name. Surprisingly, he consented. I cannot help but think that he consented because he was a Roman Catholic and felt a vague sympathy for Negroes, being himself an object of hatred. Armed with a library card, I obtained books in the following manner: I would write a note to the librarian, saying: "Please let this nigger boy have the following books." I would then sign it with the white man's name.

When I went to the library, I would stand at the desk, hat in hand, looking as unbookish as possible. When I received the books desired I would take them home. If the books listed in the note happened to be out, I would sneak into the lobby and forge a new one. I never took any chances guessing with the white librarian about what the fictitious white man would want to read. No doubt if any of the white patrons had suspected that some of the volumes they enjoyed had been in the home of a Negro, they would not have tolerated it for an instant.

The factory force of the optical company in Memphis was much larger than that in Jackson, and more urbanized. At least they liked to talk, and would engage the Negro help in conversation whenever possible. By this means I found that many subjects were taboo from the white man's point of view. Among the topics they did not like to discuss with Negroes were the following: American white women; the Ku Klux Klan; France, and how Negro soldiers fared while there; French women; Jack Johnson; the entire northern part of the United States; the Civil War; Abraham Lincoln; U. S. Grant; General Sherman; Catholics; the Pope; Jews; the Republican Party; slavery; social equality; Communism; Socialism; the 13th and 14th Amendments to the Constitution; or any topic calling for positive knowledge or manly self-assertion on the part of the Negro. The most accepted topics were sex and religion.

There were many times when I had to exercise a great deal of ingenuity to keep out of trouble. It is a southern custom that all men must take off their hats when they enter an elevator. And especially did this apply to us blacks with rigid force. One day I stepped into an elevator with my arms full of packages. I was forced to ride with my hat on. Two white men stared at me coldly. Then one of them very kindly lifted my hat and placed it upon my armful of packages. Now the most accepted response for a Negro to make under such circumstances is to look at the white man out of the corner of his eye and grin. To have said: "Thank you!" would have made the white man *think* that you *thought* you were receiving from him a personal service. For such an act I have seen Negroes take a blow in the mouth. Finding the first alternative distasteful, and the second dangerous, I hit upon an acceptable course of action which fell safely between these two poles. I immediately—no sooner than my hat was lifted—pretended that my packages were about to spill, and appeared deeply distressed with keeping them in my arms. In this fashion I evaded having to acknowledge his service, and, in spite of adverse circumstances, salvaged a slender shred of personal pride.

How do Negroes feel about the way they have to live? How do they discuss it when alone among themselves? I think this question can be answered in a single sentence. A friend of mine who ran an elevator once told me:

"Lawd, man! Ef it wuzn't fer them polices 'n' them ol' lynch-mobs, there wouldn't be nothin' but uproar down here!"

How "Bigger" Was Born

RICHARD WRIGHT

I AM NOT SO PRETENTIOUS AS TO IMAGINE THAT IT IS POSSIBLE FOR ME TO account completely for my own book, *Native Son*. But I am going to try to account for as much of it as I can, the sources of it, the material that went into it, and my own years' long changing attitude toward that material.

In a fundamental sense, an imaginative novel represents the merging of two extremes; it is an intensely intimate expression on the part of a consciousness couched in terms of the most objective and commonly known events. It is at once something private and public by its very nature and texture. Confounding the author who is trying to lay his cards on the table is the dogging knowledge that his imagination is a kind of community medium of exchange: what he has read, felt, thought, seen, and remembered is translated into extensions as impersonal as a worn dollar bill.

The more closely the author thinks of why he wrote, the more he comes to regard his imagination as a kind of self-generating cement which glued his facts together, and his emotions as a kind of dark and obscure designer of those facts. Always there is something that is just beyond the tip of the tongue that could explain it all. Usually, he ends up by discussing something far afield, an act which incites skepticism and suspicion in those anxious for a straight-out explanation.

Yet the author is eager to explain. But the moment he makes the attempt his words falter, for he is confronted and defied by the inexplicable array of his own emotions. Emotions are subjective and he can communicate them only when he clothes them in objective guise; and how can he ever be so arrogant as to know when he is dressing up the right emotion in the right Sunday suit? He is always left with the uneasy notion that maybe *any* objective drapery is as good as *any* other for any emotion.

And the moment he does dress up an emotion, his mind is confronted with the riddle of that "dressed up" emotion, and he is left peering with eager dismay back into the dim reaches of his own incommunicable life. Reluctantly, he comes to the conclusion that to account for his book is to account for his life, and he knows that that is impossible. Yet, some curious, wayward motive urges him to supply the answer, for there is the feeling that his dignity as a living being is challenged by something within him that is not understood.

So, at the outset, I say frankly that there are phases of *Native Son* which I shall make no attempt to account for. There are meanings in my book of which I was not aware until they literally spilled out upon the paper. I shall sketch the outline of how I *consciously* came into possession of the materials that went into *Native Son*, but there will be many things I shall omit, not because I want to, but simply because I don't know them.

The birth of Bigger Thomas goes back to my childhood, and there was not just one Bigger, but many of them, more than I could count and more than you suspect. But let me start with the first Bigger, whom I shall call Bigger No. 1.

When I was a bareheaded, barefoot kid in Jackson, Mississippi, there was a boy who terrorized me and all of the boys I played with. If we were playing games, he would saunter up and snatch from us our balls, bats, spinning tops, and marbles. We would stand around pouting, sniffling, trying to keep back our tears, begging for our playthings. But Bigger would refuse. We never demanded that he give them back; we were afraid, and Bigger was bad. We had seen him clout boys when he was angry and we did not want to run that risk. We never recovered our toys unless we flattered him and made him feel that he was superior to us. Then, perhaps, if he felt like it, he condescended, threw them at us and then gave each of us a swift kick in the bargain, just to make us feel his utter contempt.

That was the way Bigger No. 1 lived. His life was a continuous challenge to others. At all times he *took* his way, right or wrong, and those who contradicted him had him to fight. And never was he happier than when he had someone cornered and at his mercy; it seemed that the deepest meaning of his squalid life was in him at such times.

I don't know what the fate of Bigger No. 1 was. His swaggering personality is swallowed up somewhere in the amnesia of my childhood. But I suspect that his end was violent. Anyway, he left a marked impression upon me; maybe it was because I longed secretly to be like him and was afraid. I don't know.

If I had known only one Bigger I would not have written *Native Son*. Let me call the next one Bigger No. 2; he was about seventeen and tougher than the first Bigger. Since I, too, had grown older, I was a little less afraid of him. And the hardness of this Bigger No. 2 was not directed toward me or the other Negroes, but toward the whites who ruled the South. He bought clothes and food on credit and would not pay for them. He lived in the dingy shacks of the white landlords and refused to pay rent. Of course, he had no money, but neither did we. We did without the necessities of life and starved ourselves, but he never would. When we asked him why he acted as he did, he would tell us (as though we were little children in a kindergarten) that the white folks had everything and he had nothing. Further, he would tell us that we were fools not to get what we wanted while we were alive in this world. We would listen and silently agree. We longed to believe and act as he did, but we were afraid. We were Southern Negroes and we were hungry and we wanted to live, but we were more willing to tighten our belts than risk conflict. Bigger No. 2 wanted to live and he did; he was in prison the last time I heard from him.

There was Bigger No. 3, whom the white folks called a "bad nigger." He carried his life in his hands in a literal fashion. I once worked as a ticket-taker in a Negro movie house (all movie houses in Dixie are Jim Crow; there are movies for whites and movies for blacks), and many times Bigger No. 3 came to the door and gave my arm a hard pinch and walked into the theater. Resentfully and silently, I'd nurse my bruised arm. Presently, the proprietor would come over and ask how things were going. I'd point into the darkened theater and say: "Bigger's in there." "Did he pay?" the proprietor would ask. "No, sir," I'd answer. The proprietor would pull down the corners of his lips and speak through his teeth: "We'll kill that goddamn nigger one of these days." And the episode would end right there. But later on Bigger No. 3 was killed during the days of Prohibition: while delivering liquor to a customer he was shot through the back by a white cop.

And then there was Bigger No. 4, whose only law was death. The Jim Crow laws of the South were not for him. But as he laughed and cursed and broke them, he knew that some day he'd have to pay for his freedom. His rebellious spirit made him violate all the taboos and consequently he always oscillated between moods of intense elation and depression. He was never happier than when he had outwitted some foolish custom, and he was never more melancholy than when brooding over the impossibility of his ever being free. He had no job, for he regarded digging ditches for fifty cents a day as slavery. "I can't live on that," he would say. Ofttimes I'd find him reading a book; he would stop and in a joking, wistful, and cynical manner ape the antics of the white folks. Generally, he'd end his mimicry in a depressed state and say: "The white folks won't let us do nothing." Bigger No. 4 was sent to the asylum for the insane.

Then there was Bigger No. 5, who always rode the Jim Crow streetcars without paying and sat wherever he pleased. I remember one morning his getting into a streetcar (all streetcars in Dixie are divided into two sections: one section is for whites and is labeled—FOR WHITES; the other section is for Negroes and is labeled—FOR COLORED) and sitting in the white section. The conductor went to him and said: "Come on, nigger. Move over where you belong. Can't you read?" Bigger answered: "Naw, I can't read." The conductor flared up: "Get out of that seat!" Bigger took out his knife, opened it, held it nonchalantly in his hand, and replied: "Make me." The conductor turned red, blinked, clenched his fists, and walked away, stammering: "The goddamn scum of the arth!" A small angry conference of white men took place in the front of the car and the Negroes sitting in the Jim Crow section overheard: "That's that Bigger Thomas nigger and you'd better leave 'im alone." The Negroes experienced an intense flash of pride and the streetcar moved on its journey without incident. I don't know what happened to Bigger No. 5. But I can guess.

The Bigger Thomases were the only Negroes I know of who consistently violated the Jim Crow laws of the South and got away with it, at least for a sweet brief spell. Eventually, the whites who restricted their lives made them pay a terrible price. They were shot, hanged, maimed, lynched, and generally hounded until they were either dead or their spirits broken.

There were many variations to this behavioristic pattern. Later on I encountered other Bigger Thomases who did not react to the locked-in Black Belts with this same extremity and violence. But before I use Bigger Thomas as a springboard for the examination of milder types, I'd better indicate more precisely the nature of the environment that produced these men, or the reader will be left with the impression that they were essentially and organically bad.

In Dixie there are two worlds, the white world and the black world, and they are physically separated. There are white schools and black schools, white churches and black churches, white businesses and black businesses, white graveyards and black graveyards, and, for all I know, a white God and a black God. . . .

This separation was accomplished after the Civil War by the terror of the Ku Klux Klan, which swept the newly freed Negro through arson, pillage, and death out of the United States Senate, the House of Representatives, the many state legislatures, and out of the public, social, and economic life of the South. The motive for this assault was simple and urgent. The imperialistic tug of history had torn the Negro from his African home and had placed him ironically upon the most fertile plantation areas of the South; and, when the Negro was freed, he outnumbered the whites in many of these fertile areas. Hence, a fierce and bitter struggle took place to keep the ballot from the Negro, for had he had a chance to vote, he would have automatically controlled the richest lands of the South and with them the social, political, and economic destiny of a third of the Republic. Though the South is politically a part of America, the problem that faced her was peculiar and the struggle between the whites and the blacks after the Civil War was in essence a struggle for power, ranging over thirteen states and involving the lives of tens of millions of people.

But keeping the ballot from the Negro was not enough to hold him in check; disfranchisement had to be supplemented by a whole panoply of rules, taboos, and penalties designed not only to insure peace (complete submission), but to guarantee that no real threat would ever arise. Had the Negro lived upon a common territory, separate from the bulk of the white population, this program of oppression might not have assumed such a brutal and violent form. But this war took place between people who were neighbors, whose homes adjoined, whose farms had common boundaries. Guns and disfranchisement, therefore, were not enough to make the black neighbor keep his distance. The white neighbor decided to limit the amount of education his black neighbor could receive; decided to keep him off the police force and out of the local national guards; to segregate him residentially; to Jim Crow him in public places; to restrict his participation in the professions and jobs; and to build up a vast, dense ideology of racial superiority that would justify any act of violence taken against him to defend white dominance; and further, to condition him to hope for little and to receive that little without rebelling.

But, because the blacks were so *close* to the very civilization which sought to keep them out, because they could not *help* but react in some way to its incentives and prizes, and because the very tissue of their consciousness received its tone and timbre from the strivings of the dominant civilization, oppression spawned among them a myriad variety of reactions, reaching from outright blind rebellion to a sweet, otherworldly submissiveness.

In the main, this delicately balanced state of affairs has not greatly altered since the Civil War, save in those parts of the South which have been industrialized or urbanized. So volatile and tense are these relations that if a Negro rebels against rule and taboo, he is lynched and the reason for the lynching is usually called "rape," that catchword which has garnered such vile connotations that it can raise a mob anywhere in the South pretty quickly, even today.

Now for the variations in the Bigger Thomas pattern. Some of the Negroes living under these conditions got religion, felt that Jesus would redeem the void of living, felt that the more bitter life was in the present the happier it would be in the hereafter. Others, clinging still to that brief glimpse of post-Civil War freedom, employed a thousand ruses and stratagems of struggle to win their rights. Still others projected their hurts and longings into more naïve and mundane forms—blues, jazz, swing—and, without intellectual guidance, tried to build up a compensatory nourishment for themselves. Many labored under hot suns and then killed the restless ache with alcohol. Then there were those who strove for an education, and when they got it, enjoyed the financial fruits of it in the style of their bourgeois oppressors. Usually they went hand in hand with the powerful whites and helped to keep their groaning brothers in line, for that was the safest course of action. Those who did this called themselves "leaders." To give you an idea of how completely these "leaders" worked with those who oppressed, I can tell you that I lived the first seventeen years of my life in the South without so much as hearing of or seeing one act of rebellion from *any* Negro, save the Bigger Thomases.

But why did Bigger revolt? No explanation based upon a hard and fast rule of conduct can be given. But there were always two factors psychologically dominant in his personality. First, through some quirk of circumstance, he had become estranged from the religion and the folk culture of his race. Second, he was trying to react to and answer the call of the dominant civilization whose glitter came to him through the newspapers, magazines, radios, movies, and the mere imposing sight and sound of daily American life. In many respects his emergence as a distinct type was inevitable.

As I grew older, I became familiar with the Bigger Thomas conditioning and its numerous shadings no matter where I saw it in Negro life. It was not, as I have already said, as blatant or extreme as in the originals; but it was there, nevertheless, like an undeveloped negative.

Sometimes, in areas far removed from Mississippi, I'd hear a Negro say: "I wish I didn't have to live this way. I feel like I want to burst." Then the anger would pass; he would go back to his job and try to eke out a few pennies to support his wife and children.

Sometimes I'd hear a Negro say: "God, I wish I had a flag and a country of my own." But that mood would soon vanish and he would go his way placidly enough.

Sometimes I'd hear a Negro ex-soldier say: "What in hell did I fight in the war for? They segregated me even when I was offering my life for my country." But he, too, like the others, would soon forget, would become caught up in the tense grind of struggling for bread.

I've even heard Negroes, in moments of anger and bitterness, praise what Japan is doing in China, not because they believe in oppression (being objects of oppression themselves), but because they would suddenly sense how empty their lives were when looking at the dark faces of Japanese generals in the rotogravure supplements of the Sunday newspapers. They would dream of what it would be like to live in a country where they could forget their color and play a responsible role in the vital processes of the nation's life.

I've even heard Negroes say that maybe Hitler and Mussolini are all right; that maybe Stalin is all right. They did not say this out of any intellectual comprehension of the forces at work in the world, but because they felt that these men "did things," a phrase which is charged with more meaning than the mere words imply. There was in the back of their minds, when they said this, a wild and intense longing (wild and intense because it was suppressed!) to belong, to be identified, to feel that they were alive as other people were, to be caught up forgetfully and exultingly in the swing of events, to feel the clean, deep, organic satisfaction of doing a job in common with others.

It was not until I went to live in Chicago that I first thought seriously of writing Bigger Thomas. Two items of my experience combined to make me aware of Bigger as a meaningful and prophetic symbol. First, being free of the daily pressure of the Dixie environment, I was able to come into possession of my own feelings. Second, my contact with the labor movement and this ideology made me see Bigger clearly and feel what he meant.

I made the discovery that Bigger Thomas was not black all the time; he was white, too, and there were literally millions of him, everywhere. The extension of my sense of the personality of Bigger was the pivot of my life; it altered the complexion of my existence. I became conscious, at first dimly, and then later on with increasing clarity and conviction, of a vast, muddied pool of human life in America. It was as though I had put on a pair of spectacles whose power was that of an x-ray enabling me to see deeper into the lives of men. Whenever I picked up a newspaper, I'd no longer feel that I was reading of the doings of whites alone (Negroes are rarely mentioned in the press unless they've committed some crime!), but of a complex struggle for life going on in my country, a struggle in which I was involved. I sensed, too, that the Southern scheme of oppression was but an appendage of a far vaster and in many respects more ruthless and impersonal commodity-profit machine.

Trade-union struggles and issues began to grow meaningful to me. The flow of goods across the seas, buoying and depressing the wages of men, held a fascination. The pronouncements of foreign governments, their policies, plans, and acts were calculated and weighed in relation to the lives of people about me. I was literally overwhelmed when, in reading the works of Russian revolutionists, I came across descriptions of the "holiday energies of the masses," "the locomotives of history," "the conditions prerequisite for revolution," and so forth. I approached all of these new revelations in the light of Bigger Thomas, his hopes, fears, and despairs; and I began to feel far-flung kinships, and sense, with fright and abashment, the possibilities of *alliances* between the American Negro and other people possessing a kindred consciousness.

As my mind extended in this general and abstract manner, it was fed with even more vivid and concrete examples of the lives of Bigger Thomas. The urban environment of Chicago, affording a more stimulating life, made the Negro Bigger Thomases react more violently than even in the South. More than ever I began to see and understand the environmental factors which made for this extreme conduct. It was not that Chicago segregated Negroes more than the South, but that Chicago had more to offer, that Chicago's physical aspect—noisy, crowded, filled with the sense of power and fulfillment—did so much more to dazzle the mind with a taunting sense of possible achievement that the segregation it did impose brought forth from Bigger a reaction more obstreperous than in the South.

So the concrete picture and the abstract linkages of relationships fed each other, each making the other more meaningful and affording my emotions an opportunity to react to them with success and understanding. The process was like a swinging pendulum, each to and fro motion throwing up its tiny bit of meaning and significance, each stroke helping to develop the dim negative which had been implanted in my mind in the South.

During this period the shadings and nuances which were filling in Bigger's picture came, not so much from Negro life, as from the lives of whites I met and grew to know. I began to sense that they had their own kind of Bigger Thomas behavioristic pattern which grew out of a more subtle and broader frustration. The waves of recurring crime, the silly fads and crazes, the quicksilver changes in public taste, the hysteria and fears—all of these had long been mysteries to me. But now I looked back of them and felt the pinch and pressure of the environment that gave them their pitch and peculiar kind of being. I began to feel with my mind the inner tensions of the people I met. I don't mean to say that I think that environment *makes* consciousness (I suppose God makes that, if there is a God), but I do say that I felt and still feel that the environment supplies the instrumentalities through which the organism expresses itself, and if that environment is warped or tranquil, the mode and manner of behavior will be affected toward deadlocking tensions or orderly fulfillment and satisfaction.

Let me give examples of how I began to develop the dim negative of Bigger. I met white writers who talked of their responses, who told me how whites reacted to this lurid American scene. And, as they talked, I'd translated what they said in terms of Bigger's life. But what was more important still, I read their novels. Here, for the first time, I found ways and techniques of gauging meaningfully the effects of American civilization upon the personalities of people. I took these techniques, these ways of seeing and feeling, and twisted them, bent them, adapted them, until they became *my* ways of apprehending the locked-in life of the Black Belt areas. This association with white writers was the life preserver of my hope to depict Negro life in fiction, for my race possessed no fictional works dealing with such problems, had no background in such sharp and critical testing of experience, no novels that went with a deep and fearless will down to the dark roots of life.

Here are examples of how I culled information relating to Bigger from my reading:

There is in me a memory of reading an interesting pamphlet telling of the friendship of Gorky and Lenin in exile. The booklet told of how Lenin and Gorky were walking down a London street. Lenin turned to Gorky and, pointing, said: "Here is *their* Big Ben." "There is *their* Westminster Abbey." "There is *their* library." And at once, while reading that passage, my mind stopped, teased, challenged with the effort to remember, to associate widely disparate but meaningful experiences in my life. For a moment nothing would come, but I remained convinced that I had heard the meaning of those words sometime, somewhere before. Then, with a sudden glow of satisfaction of having gained a little more knowledge about the world in which I lived, I'd end up by saying: "That's Bigger. That's the Bigger Thomas reaction."

In both instances the deep sense of exclusion was identical. The feeling of looking at things with a painful and unwarrantable nakedness was an experience, I learned, that transcended national and racial boundaries. It was this intolerable sense of feeling and understanding so much, and yet living on a plane of social reality where the look of a world which one did not make or own struck one with a blinding objectivity and tangibility, that made me grasp the revolutionary impulse in my life and the lives of those about me and far away.

I remember reading a passage in a book dealing with old Russia which said: "We must be ready to make endless sacrifices if we are to be able to overthrow the Czar." And again I'd say to myself: "I've heard that somewhere, sometime before." And again I'd hear Bigger Thomas, far away and long ago, telling some white man who was trying to impose upon him: "I'll kill you and go to hell and pay for it." While living in America I heard from far away Russia the bitter accents of tragic calculation of how much human life and suffering it would cost a man to live as a man in a world that denied him the right to live with dignity. Actions and feelings of men ten thousand miles from home helped me to understand the moods and impulses of those walking the streets of Chicago and Dixie.

I am not saying that I heard any talk of revolution in the South when I was a kid there. But I did hear the lispings, the whispers, the mutters which some day, under one stimulus or another, will surely grow into open revolt unless the conditions which produce Bigger Thomases are changed.

In 1932 another source of information was dramatically opened up to me and I saw data of a surprising nature that helped to clarify the personality of Bigger. From the moment that Hitler took power in Germany and began to oppress the Jews, I tried to keep track of what was happening. And on innumerable occasions I was startled to detect, either from the side of the Fascists or from the side of the oppressed, reactions, moods, phrases, attitudes that reminded me strongly of Bigger, that helped to bring out more clearly the shadowy outlines of the negative that lay in the back of my mind.

I read every account of the Fascist movement in Germany I could lay my hands on, and from page to page I encountered and recognized familiar emotional patterns. What struck me with particular force was the Nazi preoccupation with the construction of a society in which there would exist among all people (*German* people, of course!) *one* solidarity of ideals, *one* continuous circulation of fundamental beliefs, notions, and assumptions. I am not now speaking of the popular idea of regimenting people's thought; I'm speaking of the implicit, almost unconscious, or pre-conscious, assumptions and ideals upon which whole nations and races act and live. And while reading these Nazi pages I'd be reminded of the Negro preacher in the South telling of a life beyond this world, a life in which the color of men's skins would not matter, a life in which each man would know what was deep down in the hearts of his fellow man. And I could hear Bigger Thomas standing on a street corner in America expressing his agonizing doubts and chronic suspicions, thus: "I ain't going to trust nobody. Everything is a racket and everybody is out to get what he can for himself. Maybe if we had a true leader, we could do something." And I'd know that I was still on the track of learning about Bigger, still in the midst of the modern struggle for solidarity among men.

When the Nazis spoke of the necessity of a highly ritualized and symbolized life, I could hear Bigger Thomas on Chicago's South Side saying: "Man, what we need is a leader like Marcus Garvey. We need a nation, a flag, an army of our own. We colored folks ought to organize into groups and have generals, captains, lieutenants, and so forth. We ought to take Africa and have a national home." I'd know, while listening to these childish words, that a white man would smile derisively at them. But I could not smile, for I knew the truth of those simple words from the facts of my own life. The deep hunger in those childish ideas was like a flash of lightning illuminating the whole dark inner landscape of Bigger's mind. Those words told me that the civilization which had given birth to Bigger contained no spiritual sustenance, had created no culture which could hold and claim his allegiance and faith, had sensitized him and had left him stranded, a free agent to roam the streets of our cities, a hot and whirling vortex of undisciplined and unchannelized impulses. The results of these observations made me feel more than ever estranged from the civilization in which I lived, and more than ever resolved toward the task of creating with words a scheme of images and symbols whose direction could enlist the sympathies, loyalties, and yearnings of the millions of Bigger Thomases in every land and race. . . .

But more than anything else, as a writer, I was fascinated by the similarity of the emotional tensions of Bigger in America and Bigger in Nazi Germany and Bigger in old Russia. All Bigger Thomases, white and black, felt tense, afraid, nervous, hysterical, and restless. From far away Nazi Germany and old Russia had come to me items of knowledge that told me that certain modern experiences were creating types of personalities whose existence ignored racial and national lines of demarcation, that these personalities carried with them a more universal drama-element than anything I'd ever encountered before; that these personalities were mainly imposed upon men and women living in a world whose fundamental assumptions could no longer be taken for granted: a world ridden with national and class strife; a world whose metaphysical meanings had vanished; a world in which God no longer existed as a daily focal point of men's lives; a world in which men could no longer retain their faith in an ultimate hereafter. It was a highly geared world whose nature was conflict and action, a world whose limited area and vision imperiously urged men to satisfy their organisms, a world that existed on a plane of animal sensation alone.

It was a world in which millions of men lived and behaved like drunkards, taking a stiff drink of hard life to lift them up for a thrilling moment, to give them a quivering sense of wild exultation and fulfillment that soon faded and let them down. Eagerly they took another drink, wanting to avoid the dull, flat look of things, then still another, this time stronger, and then they felt that their lives had meaning. Speaking figuratively, they were soon chronic alcoholics, men who lived by violence, through extreme action and sensation, through drowning daily in a perpetual nervous agitation.

From these items I drew my first political conclusions about Bigger: I felt that Bigger, an American product, a native son of this land, carried within him the potentialities of either Communism or Fascism. I don't mean to say that the Negro boy I depicted in *Native Son* is either a Communist or a Fascist. He is not either. But he is product of a dislocated society; he is a dispossessed and disinherited man; he is all of this, and he lives amid the greatest possible plenty on earth and he is looking and feeling for a way out. Whether he'll follow some gaudy, hysterical leader who'll promise rashly to fill the void in him, or whether he'll come to an understanding with the millions of his kindred fellow workers under trade-union or revolutionary guidance depends upon the future drift of events in America. But, granting the emotional state, the tensity, the fear, the hate, the impatience, the sense of exclusion, the ache for violent action, the emotion and cultural hunger, Bigger Thomas, conditioned as his organism is, will not become an ardent, or even a lukewarm, supporter of the *status quo*.

The difference between Bigger's tensity and the German variety is that Bigger's, due to America's educational restrictions on the bulk of her Negro population, is in a nascent state, not yet articulate. And the difference between Bigger's longing for self-identification and the Russian principle of self-determination is that Bigger's, due to the effects of American oppression, which has not allowed for the forming of deep ideas of solidarity among Negroes, is still in a state of individual anger and hatred. Here, I felt, was *drama!* Who will be the first to touch off these Bigger Thomases in America, white and black?

For a long time I toyed with the idea of writing a novel in which a Negro Bigger Thomas would loom as a symbolic figure of American life, a figure who would hold within him the prophecy of our future. I felt strongly that he held within him, in a measure which perhaps no other contemporary type did, the outlines of action and feeling which we would encounter on a vast scale in the days to come. Just as one sees when one walks into a medical research laboratory jars of alcohol containing abnormally large or distorted portions of the human body, just so did I see and feel that the conditions of life under which Negroes are forced to live in America contain the embryonic emotional prefigurations of how a large part of the body politic would react under stress.

So, with this much knowledge of myself and the world gained and known, why should I not try to work out on paper the problem of what will happen to Bigger? Why should I not, like a scientist in a laboratory, use my imagination and invent test-tube situations, place Bigger in them, and, following the guidance of my own hopes and fears, what I had learned and remembered, work out in fictional form an emotional statement and resolution of this problem?

But several things militated against my starting to work. Like Bigger himself, I felt a mental censor—product of the fears which a Negro feels from living in America—standing over me, draped in white, warning me not to write. This censor's warnings were translated into my own thought processes thus: "What will white people think if I draw the picture of such a Negro boy? Will they not at once say: 'See, didn't we tell you all along that niggers are like that? Now, look, one of their own kind has come along and drawn the picture for us!' " I felt that if I drew the picture of Bigger truthfully, there would be many reactionary whites who would try to make of him something I did not intend. And yet, and this was what made it difficult, I knew that I could not write of Bigger convincingly if I did not depict him as he *was:* that is, resentful toward whites, sullen, angry, ignorant, emotionally unstable, depressed and unaccountably elated at times, and unable even, because of his own lack of inner organization which American oppression has fostered in him, to unite with the members of his own race. And would not whites misread Bigger and, doubting his authenticity, say: "This man is preaching hate against the whole white race"?

The more I thought of it the more I became convinced that if I did not write of Bigger as I saw and felt him, if I did not try to make him a living personality and at the same time a symbol of all the larger things I felt and saw in him, I'd be reacting as Bigger himself reacted: that is, I'd be acting out of *fear* if I let what I thought whites would say constrict and paralyze me.

As I contemplated Bigger and what he meant, I said to myself: "I must write this novel, not only for others to read, but to free *myself* of this sense of shame and fear." In fact, the novel, as time passed, grew upon me to the extent that it became a necessity to write it; the writing of it turned into a way of living for me.

Another thought kept me from writing. What would my own white and black comrades in the Communist party say? This thought was the most bewildering of all. Politics is a hard and narrow game; its policies represent the aggregate desires and aspirations of millions of people. Its goals are rigid and simply drawn, and the minds of the majority of politicians are set, congealed in terms of daily tactical maneuvers. How could I create such complex and wide schemes of associational thought and feeling, such filigreed webs of dreams and politics, without being mistaken for a "smuggler of reaction," "an ideological confusionist," or "an individualistic and dangerous element"? Though my heart is with the collectivist and proletarian ideal, I solved this problem by assuring myself that honest politics and honest feeling in imaginative representation ought to be able to meet on common healthy ground without fear, suspicion, and quarreling. Further, and more importantly, I steeled myself by coming to the conclusion that whether politicians accepted or rejected Bigger did not really matter; my task, as I felt it, was to free myself of this burden of impressions and feelings, recast them into the image of Bigger and make him *true*. Lastly, I felt that a right more immediately deeper than that of politics or race was at stake; that is, a *human* right, the right of a man to think and feel honestly. And especially did this personal and human right bear hard upon me, for temperamentally I am inclined to satisfy the claims of my own ideals rather than the expectations of others. It was this obscure need that had pulled me into the labor movement in the beginning and by exercising it I was but fulfilling what I felt to be the laws of my own growth.

There was another constricting thought that kept me from work. It deals with my own race. I asked myself: "What will Negro doctors, lawyers, dentists, bankers, school teachers, social workers and business men, think of me if I draw such a picture of Bigger?" I knew from long and painful experience that the Negro middle and professional classes were the people of my own race who were more than others ashamed of Bigger and what he meant. Having narrowly escaped the Bigger Thomas reaction pattern themselves—indeed, still retaining traces of it within the confines of their own timid personalities—they would not relish being publicly reminded of the lowly, shameful depths of life above which they enjoyed their bourgeois lives. Never did they want people, especially *white* people, to think that their lives were so much touched by anything so dark and brutal as Bigger.

Their attitude toward life and art can be summed up in a single paragraph: "But, Mr. Wright, there are so many of us who are *not* like Bigger. Why don't you portray in your fiction the *best* traits of our race, something that will show the white people what we have done in *spite* of oppression? Don't represent anger and bitterness. Smile when a white person comes to you. Never let him feel that you are so small that what he has done to crush you has made you hate him! Oh, above all, save your *pride!*"

But Bigger won over all these claims; he won because I felt that I was hunting on the trail of more exciting and thrilling game. What Bigger meant had claimed me because I felt with all of my being that he was more important than what any person, white or black, would say or try to make of him, more important than any political analysis designed to explain or deny him, more important, even, than my own sense of fear, shame, and diffidence.

But Bigger was still not down upon paper. For a long time I had been writing of him in my mind, but I had yet to put him into an image, a breathing symbol draped out in the guise of the only form of life my native land had allowed me to know intimately, that is, the ghetto life of the American Negro. But the basic reason for my hesitancy was that another and far more complex problem had risen to plague me. Bigger, as I saw and felt him, was a snarl of many realities; he had in him many levels of life.

First, there was his personal and private life, that intimate existence that is so difficult to snare and nail down in fiction, that elusive core of being, that individual data of consciousness which in every man and woman is like that in no other. I had to deal with Bigger's dreams, his fleeting, momentary sensations, his yearning, visions, his deep emotional responses.

Then I was confronted with that part of him that was dual in aspect, dim, wavering, that part of him which is so much a part of *all* Negroes and *all* whites that I realized that I could put it down upon paper only by feeling out its meaning first within the confines of my own life. Bigger was attracted and repelled by the American scene. He was an American, because he was a native son; but he was also a Negro nationalist in a vague sense because he was not allowed to live as an American. Such was his way of life and mine; neither Bigger nor I resided fully in either camp.

Of this dual aspect of Bigger's social consciousness, I placed the nationalistic side first, not because I agreed with Bigger's wild and intense hatred of white people, but because his hate had placed him, like a wild animal at bay, in a position where he was most symbolic and explainable. In other words, his nationalist complex was for me a concept through which I could grasp more of the total meaning of his life than I could in any other way. I tried to approach Bigger's *snarled* and *confused* nationalist feelings with *conscious* and *informed* ones of my own. Yet, Bigger was not nationalist enough to feel the need of religion or the folk culture of his own people. What made Bigger's social consciousness most complex was the fact that he was hovering unwanted between two worlds—between powerful America and his own stunted place in life—and I took upon myself the task of trying to make the reader feel this No Man's Land. The most that I could say of Bigger was that he felt the *need* for a whole life and *acted* out of that need; that was all.

Above and beyond all this, there was that American part of Bigger which is the heritage of us all, that part of him which we get from our seeing and hearing, from school, from the hopes and dreams of our friends; that part of him which the common people of America never talk of but take for granted. Among millions of people the deepest convictions of life are never discussed openly; they are felt, implied, hinted at tacitly and obliquely in their hopes and fears. We live by an idealism that makes us believe that the Constitution is a good document of government, that the Bill of Rights is a good legal and humane principle to safeguard our civil liberties, that every man and woman should have the opportunity to realize himself, to seek his own individual fate and goal, his own peculiar and untranslatable destiny. I don't say that Bigger knew this in the terms in which I'm speaking of it; I don't say that any such thought ever entered his head. His emotional and intellectual life was never that articulate. But he knew it emotionally, intuitively, for his emotions and his desires were developed, and he caught it, as most of us do, from the mental and emotional climate of our time. Bigger had all of this in him, dammed up, buried, implied, and I had to develop it in fictional form.

There was still another level of Bigger's life that I felt bound to account for and render, a level as elusive to discuss as it was to grasp in writing. Here again, I had to fall back upon my own feelings as a guide, for Bigger did not offer in his life any articulate verbal explanations. There seems to hover somewhere in that dark part of all our lives, in some more than in others, an objectless, timeless, spaceless element of primal fear and dread, stemming, perhaps, from our birth (depending upon whether one's outlook upon personality is Freudian or non-Freudian!), a fear and dread which exercises an impelling influence upon our lives all out of proportion to its obscurity. And, accompanying this *first fear,* is, for the want of a better name, a reflex urge toward ecstasy, complete submission, and trust. The springs of religion are here, and also the origins of rebellion. And in a boy like Bigger, young, unschooled, whose subjective life was clothed in the tattered rags of American "culture," this primitive fear and ecstasy were naked, exposed, unprotected by religion or a framework of government or a scheme of society whose final faiths would gain his love and trust; unprotected by trade or profession, faith or belief; opened to every trivial blast of daily or hourly circumstance.

There was yet another level of reality in Bigger's life: the impliedly political. I've already mentioned that Bigger had in him impulses which I had felt were present in the vast upheavals of Russia and Germany. Well, somehow, I had to make these political impulses felt by the reader in terms of Bigger's daily actions, keeping in mind as I did so the probable danger of my being branded as a propagandist by those who would not like the subject matter.

Then there was Bigger's relationship with white America, both North and South, which I had to depict, which I had to make known once again, alas; a relationship whose effects are carried by every Negro, like scars, somewhere in his body and mind.

I had also to show what oppression had done to Bigger's relationships with his own people, how it had split him off from them, how it had baffled him; how oppression seems to hinder and stifle in the victim those very qualities of character which are so essential for an effective struggle against the oppressor.

Then there was the fabulous city in which Bigger lived, an indescribable city, huge, roaring, dirty, noisy, raw, stark, brutal; a city of extremes: torrid summers and sub-zero winters, white people and black people, the English language and strange tongues, foreign born and native born, scabby poverty and gaudy luxury, high idealism and hard cynicism! A city so young that, in thinking of its short history, one's mind, as it travels backward in time, is stopped abruptly by the barren stretches of wind-swept prairie! But a city old enough to have caught within the homes of its long, straight streets the symbols and images of man's age-old destiny, of truths as old as the mountains and seas, of dramas as abiding as the soul of man itself! A city which has become the pivot of the Eastern, Western, Northern, and Southern poles of the nation. But a city whose black smoke clouds shut out the sunshine for seven months of the year; a city in which, on a fine balmy May morning, one can sniff the stench of the stockyards; a city where people have grown so used to gangs and murders and graft that they have honestly forgotten that government can have a pretense of decency!

With all of this thought out, Bigger was still unwritten. Two events, however, came into my life and accelerated the process, made me sit down and actually start work on the typewriter, and just stop the writing of Bigger in my mind as I walked the streets.

The first event was my getting a job in the South Side Boys' Club, an institution which tried to reclaim the thousands of Negro Bigger Thomases from the dives and the alleys of the Black Belt. Here, on a vast scale, I had an opportunity to observe Bigger in all of his moods, actions, haunts. Here I felt for the first time that the rich folk who were paying my wages did not really give a good goddamn about Bigger, that their kindness was prompted at bottom by a selfish motive. They were paying me to distract Bigger with ping-pong, checkers, swimming, marbles, and baseball in order that he might not roam the streets and harm the valuable white property which adjoined the Black Belt. I am not condemning boys' clubs and ping-pong as such; but these little stopgaps were utterly inadequate to fill up the centuries-long chasm of emptiness which American civilization had created in these Biggers. I felt that I was doing a kind of dressed-up police work, and I hated it.

I would work hard with these Biggers, and when it would come time for me to go home I'd say to myself, under my breath so that no one could hear: "Go to it, boys! Prove to the bastards that gave you these games that life is stronger than ping-pong. . . . Show them that full-blooded life is harder and hotter than they suspect, even though that life is draped in a black skin which at heart they despise. . . ."

They did. The police blotters of Chicago are testimony to how *much* they did. That was the only way I could contain myself for doing a job I hated; for a moment I'd allow myself, vicariously, to feel as Bigger felt—not much, just a little, just a *little*—but, still, there it was.

The second event that spurred me to write of Bigger was more personal and subtle. I had written a book of short stories which was published under the title of *Uncle Tom's Children.* When the reviews of that book began to appear, I realized that I had made an awfully naïve mistake. I found that I had written a book which even bankers' daughters could read and weep over and feel good about. I swore to myself that if I ever wrote another book, no one would weep over it; that it would be so hard and deep that they would have to face it without the consolation of tears. It was this that made me get to work in dead earnest.

Now, until this moment I did not stop to think very much about the plot of *Native Son.* The reason I did not is because I was not for one moment ever worried about it. I had spent years learning about Bigger, what had made him, what he meant; so, when the time came for writing, *what had made him and what he meant* constituted my plot. But the far-flung items of his life had to be couched in imaginative terms, terms known and acceptable to a common body of readers, terms which would, in the course of the story, manipulate the deepest held notions and conviction of their lives. That came easy. The moment I began to write, the plot fell out, so to speak. I'm not trying to oversimplify or make the process seem oversubtle. At bottom, what happened is very easy to explain.

Any Negro who has lived in the North or the South knows that times without number he has heard of some Negro boy being picked up on the streets and carted off to jail and charged with "rape." This thing happens so often that to my mind it had become a representative symbol of the Negro's uncertain position in America. Never for a second was I in doubt as to what kind of social reality or dramatic situation I'd put Bigger in, what kind of test-tube life I'd set up to evoke his deepest reactions. Life had made the plot over and over again, to the extent that I knew it by heart. So frequently do these acts recur that when I was halfway through the first draft of *Native Son* a case paralleling Bigger's flared forth in the newspapers of Chicago. (Many of the newspaper items and some of the incidents in *Native Son* are but fictionalized versions of the Robert Nixon case and rewrites of news stories from the *Chicago Tribune.*)* Indeed, scarcely was *Native Son* off the press before Supreme Court Justice Hugo L. Black gave the nation a long and vivid account of the American police methods of handling Negro boys.

Let me describe this stereotyped situation: A crime wave is sweeping a city and citizens are clamoring for police action. Squad cars cruise the Black Belt and grab the first Negro boy who seems to be unattached and homeless. He is held for perhaps a week without charge or bail, without the privilege of communicating with anyone,

---

* The Robert Nixon case is discussed in Keneth Kinnamon's essay, included in Part Two of this anthology, "*Native Son:* The Personal, Social, and Political Background."

including his own relatives. After a few days this boy "confesses" anything that he is asked to confess, any crime that handily happens to be unsolved and on the calendar. Why does he confess? After the boy has been grilled night and day, hanged up by his thumbs, dangled by his feet out of twenty-story windows, and beaten (in places that leave no scars—cops have found a way to do that), he signs the papers before him, papers which are usually accompanied by a verbal promise to the boy that he will not go to the electric chair. Of course, he ends up by being executed or sentenced for life. If you think I'm telling tall tales, get chummy with some white cop who works in a Black Belt district and ask him for the lowdown.

When a black boy is carted off to jail in such a fashion, it is almost impossible to do anything for him. Even well-disposed Negro lawyers find it difficult to defend him, for the boy will plead guilty one day and then not guilty the next, according to the degree of pressure and persuasion that is brought to bear upon his frightened personality from one side or the other. Even the boy's own family is scared to death; sometimes fear of police intimidation makes them hesitate to acknowledge that the boy is a blood relation of theirs.

Such has been America's attitude toward these boys that if one is picked up and confronted in a police cell with ten white cops, he is intimidated almost to the point of confessing anything. So far removed are these practices from what the average American citizen encounters in his daily life that it takes a huge act of his imagination to believe that it is true; yet, this same average citizen, with his kindness, his American sportsmanship and good will, would probably act with the mob if a self-respecting Negro family moved into his apartment building to escape the Black Belt and its terrors and limitations. . . .

Now, after all of this, when I sat down to the typewriter, I could not work; I could not think of a good opening scene for the book. I had definitely in mind the kind of emotion I wanted to evoke in the reader in that first scene, but I could not think of the type of concrete event that would convey the motif of the entire scheme of the book, that would sound, in varied form, the note that was to be resounded throughout its length, that would introduce to the reader just what kind of an organism Bigger's was and the environment that was bearing hourly upon it. Twenty or thirty times I tried and failed; then I argued that if I could not write the opening scene, I'd start with the scene that followed. I did. The actual writing of the book began with the scene in the pool room.

Now, for the writing. During the years in which I had met all of those Bigger Thomases, those varieties of Bigger Thomases, I had not consciously gathered material to write of them; I had not kept a notebook record of their sayings and doings. Their actions had simply made impressions upon my sensibilities as I lived from day to day, impressions which crystallized and coagulated into clusters and configurations of memory, attitudes, moods, ideas. And these subjective states, in turn, were automatically stored away somewhere in me. I was not even aware of the process. But, excited over the book which I had set myself to write, under the stress of emotion, these things came surging up, tangled, fused, knotted, entertaining me by the sheer variety and potency of their meaning and suggestiveness.

With the whole theme in mind, in an attitude almost akin to prayer, I gave myself up to the story. In an effort to capture some phase of Bigger's life that would not come to me readily, I'd jot down as much of it as I could. Then I'd read it over and over, adding each time a word, a phrase, a sentence until I felt that I had caught all the shadings of reality I felt dimly were there. With each of these rereadings and rewritings it seemed that I'd gather in facts and facets that tried to run away. It was an act of concentration, of trying to hold within one's center of attention all of that bewildering array of facts which science, politics, experience, memory, and imagination were urging upon me. And then, while writing, a new and thrilling relationship would spring up under the drive of emotion, coalescing and telescoping alien facts into a known and felt truth. That was the deep fun of the job: to feel within my body that I was pushing out to new areas of feeling, strange landmarks of emotion, tramping upon foreign soil, compounding new relationships of perceptions, making new and—until that very split second of time!—unheard-of and unfelt effects with words. It had a buoying and tonic impact upon me; my senses would strain and seek for more and more of such relationships; my temperature would rise as I worked. That is writing as I feel it, a kind of significant living.

The first draft of the novel was written in four months, straight through, and ran to some 576 pages. Just as a man rises in the mornings to dig ditches for his bread, so I'd work daily. I'd think of some abstract principle of Bigger's conduct and at once my mind would turn it into some act I'd seen Bigger perform, some act which I hoped would be familiar enough to the American reader to gain his credence. But in the writing of scene after scene I was guided by but one criterion: to tell the truth as I saw it and felt it. That is, to objectify in words some insight derived from my living in the form of action, scene, and dialogue. If a scene seemed improbable to me, I'd not tear it up, but ask myself: "Does it reveal enough of what I feel to stand in spite of its unreality?" If I felt it did, it stood. If I felt that it did not, I ripped it out. The degree of morality in my writing depended upon the degree of felt life and truth I could put down upon the printed page. For example, there is a scene in *Native Son* where Bigger stands in a cell with a Negro preacher, Jan, Max, the State's Attorney, Mr. Dalton, Mrs. Dalton, Bigger's mother, his brother, his sister, Al, Gus, and Jack. While writing that scene, I knew that it was unlikely that so many people would ever be allowed to come into a murderer's cell. But I wanted those people in that cell to elicit a certain important emotional response from Bigger. And so the scene stood. I felt that what I wanted that scene to say to the reader was *more important than its surface reality or plausibility.*

Always, as I wrote, I was both reader and writer, both the conceiver of the action and the appreciator of it. I tried to write so that, in the same instant of time, the objective and subjective aspects of Bigger's life would be caught in a focus of prose. And always I tried to *render, depict,* not merely to tell the story. If a thing was cold, I tried to make the reader *feel* cold, and not just tell about it. In writing in this fashion, sometimes I'd find it necessary to use a stream of consciousness technique, then rise to an interior monologue, descend to a direct rendering of a dream state, then to a matter-of-fact depiction of what Bigger was saying, doing, and feeling. Then I'd find it impossible to say what I wanted to say without stepping in and speaking outright on my own; but when doing this I always made an effort to retain the mood of the story, explaining everything only in terms of Bigger's life and, if possible, in the rhythms of Bigger's thought (even though the words would be mine). Again, at other times, in the guise of the lawyer's speech and the newspaper items, or in terms of what Bigger would overhear or see from afar, I'd give what others were saying and thinking of him. But always, from the start to the finish, it was Bigger's story, Bigger's fear, Bigger's flight, and Bigger's fate that I tried to depict. I wrote with the conviction in mind (I don't know if this is right or wrong; I only know that I'm temperamentally inclined to feel this way) that the main burden of all serious fiction consists almost wholly of character-destiny and the items, social, political, and personal, of that character-destiny.

As I wrote I followed, almost unconsciously, many principles of the novel which my reading of the novels of other writers had made me feel were necessary for the building of a well-constructed book. For the most part the novel is rendered in the present; I wanted the reader to feel that Bigger's story was happening *now,* like a play upon the stage or a movie unfolding upon the screen. Action follows action, as in a prize fight. Wherever possible, I told of Bigger's life in close-up, slow-motion, giving the feel of the grain in the passing of time. I had long had the feeling that this was the best way to "enclose" the reader's mind in a new world, to blot out all reality except that which I was giving him.

Then again, as much as I could, I restricted the novel to what Bigger saw and felt, to the limits of his feeling and thoughts, even when I was conveying *more* than that to the reader. I had the notion that such a manner of rendering made for a sharper effect, a more pointed sense of the character, his peculiar type of being and consciousness. Throughout there is but one point of view: Bigger's. This, too, I felt, made for a richer illusion of reality.

I kept out of the story as much as possible, for I wanted the reader to feel that there was nothing between him and Bigger; that the story was a special *première* given in his own private theater.

I kept the scenes long, made as much happen within a short space of time as possible; all of which, I felt, made for greater density and richness of effect.

In a like manner I tried to keep a unified sense of background throughout the story; the background would change, of course, but I tried to keep before the eyes of the reader at all times the forces and elements against which Bigger was striving.

And, because I had limited myself to rendering only what Bigger saw and felt, I gave no more reality to the other characters than that which Bigger himself saw.

This, honestly, is all I can account for in the book. If I attempted to account for scenes and characters, to tell why certain scenes were written in certain ways, I'd be stretching facts in order to be pleasantly intelligible. All else in the book came from my feelings reacting upon the material, and any honest reader knows as much about the rest of what is in the book as I do; that is, if, as he reads, he is willing to let his emotions and imagination become as influenced by the materials as I did. As I wrote, for some reason or other, one image, symbol, character, scene, mood, feeling evoked its opposite, its parallel, its complimentary, and its ironic counterpart. Why? I don't know. My emotions and imagination just like to work that way. One can account for just so much of life, and then no more. At least, not yet.

With the first draft down, I found that I could not end the book satisfactorily. In the first draft I had Bigger going smack to the electric chair; but I felt that two murders were enough for one novel. I cut the final scene and went back to worry about the beginning. I had no luck. The book was one-half finished, with the opening and closing scenes unwritten. Then, one night, in desperation—I hope that I'm not disclosing the hidden secrets of my craft!—I sneaked out and got a bottle. With the help of it, I began to remember many things which I could not remember before. One of them was that Chicago was overrun with rats. I recalled that I'd seen many rats on the streets, that I'd heard and read of Negro children being bitten by rats in their beds. At first I rejected the idea of Bigger battling a rat in his room; I was afraid that the rat would "hog" the scene. But the rat would not leave me; he presented himself in many attractive guises. So, cautioning myself to allow the rat scene to disclose *only* Bigger, his family, their little room, and their relationships, I let the rat walk in, and he did his stuff.

Many of the scenes were torn out as I reworked the book. The mere rereading of what I'd written made me think of the possibility of developing themes which had been only hinted at in the first draft. For example, the entire guilt theme that runs through *Native Son* was woven in *after* the first draft was written.

At last I found out how to end the book; I ended it just as I had begun it, showing Bigger living dangerously, taking his life into his hands, accepting what life had made him. The lawyer, Max, was placed in Bigger's cell at the end of the novel to register the moral—or what *I* felt was the moral—horror of Negro life in the United States.

The writing of *Native Son* was to me an exciting, enthralling, and even a romantic experience. With what I've learned in the writing of this book, with all of its blemishes, imperfections, with all of its unrealized potentialities, I am launching out upon another novel, this time about the status of women in modern American society. This book, too, goes back to my childhood just as Bigger went, for, while I was storing away impressions of Bigger, I was storing away impressions of many other things that made me think and wonder. Some experience will ignite somewhere deep down in me the smoldering embers of new fires and I'll be off again to write yet another novel. It is good to live when one feels that such as that will happen to one. Life becomes sufficient unto life; the rewards of living are found in living.

I don't know if *Native Son* is a good book or a bad book. And I don't know if the book I'm working on now will be a good book or a bad book. And I really don't care. The mere writing of it will be more fun and a deeper satisfaction than any praise or blame from anybody.

I feel that I'm lucky to be alive to write novels today, when the whole world is caught in the pangs of war and change. Early American writers, Henry James and Nathaniel Hawthorne, complained bitterly about the bleakness and flatness of the American scene. But I think that if they were alive, they'd feel at home in modern America. True, we have no great church in America; our national traditions are still of such a sort that we are not wont to brag of them; and we have no army that's above the level of mercenary fighters; we have no group acceptable to the whole of our country upholding certain humane values; we have no rich symbols, no colorful rituals. We have only a money-grubbing, industrial civilization. But we do have in the Negro the embodiment of a past tragic enough to appease the spiritual hunger of even a James; and we have in the oppression of the Negro a shadow athwart our national life dense and heavy enough to satisfy even the gloomy broodings of a Hawthorne. And if Poe were alive, he would not have to invent horror; horror would invent him.

PART TWO: REVIEWS OF *NATIVE SON*

For Richard Wright

ZACK GILBERT

Many times I felt the anger
And the pain,
But not until I read
Your *Native Son*
Did I know it raw and real.
Your prose, a living
Breathing thing
Reached into the guts,
Into the bowels.
It tampered with the blood
And blew the brain.
I'm glad I suffered
From this shocking force,
This strong, black push and power.
I'm glad you made me
Ice and stone
For this mad time,
This troubled, acid hour.

Book-of-the-Month Club News

HENRY SEIDEL CANBY

THIS POWERFUL AND SENSATIONAL NOVEL IS VERY DIFFICULT TO DESCRIBE so as to convey its real purpose and its real strength. But it is important to describe it accurately, because it is certainly the finest novel as yet written by an American Negro—not that it was chosen by the Book-of-the-Month Club just because it was written by a Negro. It would have been chosen for its deep excitement and intense interest whether written by white, yellow, or black. Yet, nevertheless, this is a novel which only a Negro could have written; whose theme is the mind of the Negro we see every day; whose emotion is the emotion of that native born American under the stress of a social situation difficult in the extreme; whose point and purpose are not race war or propaganda of any kind, but to show how a "bad nigger" is made from human material that might have become something very different.

Superficially, *Native Son* is a crime story, adventurous, exciting, often terrible—with two murders, a chase and a gun fight over the roofs of Chicago, a trial, and what might have been, but was not, a rape. It is the old story of a man hunted down by society. But the reader will get through only a few chapters before he realizes that there is something different in this story. Bigger—and we all know Bigger—is no persecuted black saint. His family is a good family, as tenement families go; but he is a bad actor from the first. He is mean; he is a coward; he is on occasion liar, thief, and bully. There is no sentimentalism in the writer who created Bigger, and made him chauffeur in the family of a wealthy philanthropist who spent some of the money wrung from Negro tenements on benefits for the race. Bigger is headed toward jail from the first chapter. When Mary Dalton, the flighty daughter of the philanthropist, asks Bigger to help along her intrigue with her Communist lover (also a negrophile), he has no compunctions. But he did not mean to kill her, he did not want to kill her, though he hated patronizing whites. Had her blind mother not come in at the fatal moment, the girl would have slept off her drunkenness, and Bigger would never have got beyond petty crime. With a skill which any master of the detective story might envy, Mr.

Reprinted from the *Book-of-the-Month Club News* (February 1940), 2–3. Reprinted by permission of the Book-of-the-Month Club, Inc.

Wright builds his book on the inevitable and terrifying results of an unpremeditated killing; the burning of the body; the false accusations; the murder of Bigger's Negro girl friend, lest she implicate him; the capture; the trial in which Mr. Max, the defending lawyer, pleads unsuccessfully the cause of a race driven toward crime, against a district attorney needing notoriety for his next election. And finally comes Bigger's confession—not of the murder which was not a murder, and of the rape which was not a rape, but of the obscure inarticulate causes which made him hate, and made him try to make up for his sense of inferiority by aggressive acts against the society in which he lived.

All this highly complicated story is handled with competence by Mr. Wright in a swift narrative style proceeding by staccato dialogue and with rapidly mounting suspense. The characters, too, are fully realized. There is a deadly satire in the portraits of the young radicals—Mary who is killed, and Jan, the Communist, who chooses Bigger to work on, not realizing that this kind of political pity is more offensive to a Negro than color prejudice. And the mob itself is a character, stirred up by sensational newspapers, getting bloodthirsty, wanting to lynch—the mob whose threatening roar is always in the background of the book and of the Negro's mind. Yet even in its characters this is not a vindictive book. Bigger dies without hate for anything, except the obscure circumstances which compelled him to be what he was. Max, his lawyer, with the ancient wisdom of the Jews, pleads for him on the broad basis of an America in grave danger from a conflict of races which only a deeper-going justice can ameliorate. Even the Negro evangelist who tries to bring back Bigger to the emotional religion which has helped so many men and women of his race, is presented with sympathy and pathos.

Indeed, two statements may be made with safety by the most conservative critic about this remarkable novel. No reader, however harrowed by its frank brutalities, will be able to stop in its engrossing story, which coils and mounts until a tale of crude violence broadens into a human tragedy. And no white man—and, I suspect, few Negroes—will finish this narrative without an enlargement of imagination toward the psychological problems of the Negroes in our society—and an appreciable extension of sympathy. This will hold, I prophesy, for South as well as North. Indeed, I suspect that this book and its probings will be less of a surprise to, and more readily understood by, Southerners than by Northerners. Mr. Wright himself was born and educated in Mississippi, and has lived his later life in the North. It is not the ex-slave of the South, or the almost-like-a-white-man Negro of the North, but the essential Negro-in-America of both, that he gets into Bigger and his book.

Let me repeat, this novel is no tract or defense plea. Like *Grapes of Wrath,* it is a fully realized story of unfortunates, uncompromisingly realistic, and quite as human as it is Negro. To the growing list of artistic achievements of a high quality, by a race which is, perhaps, singularly gifted in art, *Native Son* must surely be added, with a star for notable success.

Introduction to the First Edition of *Native Son*

DOROTHY CANFIELD FISHER

HOW TO PRODUCE NEUROSES IN SHEEP AND PSYCHOPATHIC UPSETS IN RATS and other animals has been known to research psychologists for so long that accounts of these experiments have filtered out to us, the general public, through books and periodicals. The process seems to be a simple one: the animal is trained to react in certain ways to certain stimuli, and then is placed in a situation in which these reactions are impossible. After making a number of attempts to go on reacting as he has been trained to, each attempt blocked, the frustration produces a nervous breakdown. His actions become abnormal, quite different from what is natural to him in health. The sheep, by definition gregarious, becomes solitary and morose, he will neither mingle with his fellows nor eat nor drink as he usually does, nor react in a normal manner to any stimuli, even the simplest and most familiar. The rat continues madly to dash his head against the locked door until, bruised and bleeding, he has battered himself to exhaustion, almost to death.

The National Youth Commission, of which Mr. Owen D. Young is Chairman, includes, among its projects for research into the condition of American youth, an investigation as to what is offered Negro Youth by the U. S. A. The first statement made in a report recently sent in to the Commission by the specialists assigned to this field, reads:

> The four area research studies just completed by the staff of the American Youth Commission concerned with an analysis of the minority status of Negro youth present conclusive evidence that large percentages of Negro youth by virtue of their combined handicap of racial barriers and low social position subtly reflect in their own personality-traits minor or major distortions or deficiencies which compound their problem of personality adjustment in American society. More specifically, the research studies have revealed: That being a Negro in most cases not only means living in the presence of severe physical limitation, but, more important for personality

development, also means living in an intimate culture *whose incentives, rewards, and punishments prevent the development of that type of personal standards, attitudes, and habits which the general community deems desirable.*

In other words, our American society creates around all youth (as every society does) a continual pressure of suggestion to try to live up to the accepted ideals of the country—such ordinary, traditional, taken-for-granted American ideals as to fight injustice fearlessly; to cringe to no man; to choose one's own life work; to resist with stout-hearted self-respect affronts to decent human dignity, whether one's own or others'; to drive ahead toward honestly earned success, all sails spread to the old American wind blowing from the Declaration of Independence. But our society puts Negro youth in the situation of the animal in the psychological laboratory in which a neurosis is to be caused, by making it impossible for him to try to live up to those never-to-be-questioned national ideals, as other young Americans do.

Native Son is the first report in fiction we have had from those who succumb to these distracting cross-currents of contradictory nerve-impulses, from those whose behavior-patterns give evidence of the same bewildered, senseless tangle of abnormal nerve-reactions studied in animals by psychologists in laboratory experiments.

It is not suprising that this novel plumbs blacker depths of human experience than American literature has yet had, comparable only to Dostoievski's revelation of human misery in wrong-doing.

I do not at all mean to imply that *Native Son* as literature is comparable to the masterpieces of Dostoievski (although I think there is no one single effect in Dostoievski finer than the last page of *Native Son* in which—just before he dies, not having yet lived—the stultified Negro boy is born at last into humanity and makes his first simple, normal human response to a fellow-man). What I mean to say is only that the author of this book, as has no other American writer, wrestles with utter sincerity with the Dostoievski subject—a human soul in hell because it is sick with a deadly spiritual sickness.

This is really all I have to say about this absorbing story of a "bad Negro," except to warn away from it, urgently, those who do not like to read books which harrow them up. It can be guaranteed to harrow up any human heart capable of compassion or honest self-questioning.

Yet, perhaps, it would be well to add two more short comments. One is to remind the reader that Bigger's mother and sister, although subjected to exactly the same psychological cross-currents as he, are not bad but good—the hymn-singing, submissive, all-enduring, religious, affront-swallowing yes-massa-ing Negroes, so heartily approved by white people looking for cheap help "to do their work for them." They are, as much as Bigger, in accordance with the experiments in psychological laboratories. For not all sheep fall into bewildered nervous breakdowns, not all rats become psychotic. Some—are they the ones which are placid? or insensitive?—simply take what comes to them, without losing their normal appetite for living. There is no sounder stroke of realism in *Native Son* than the portrait of Bigger's sweet-natured, infinitely patient, unrebelling door-mat of a mother.

The other point I would like to make is that the author shows genuine literary skill in the construction of his novel in giving so few pages to show us in concrete detail the exact ways in which American society constantly stimulates the powerful full-blooded human organism to action, which is as constantly forbidden to him by our mores.

Mr. Wright does not prove to us, in one realistic incident after another, taken from the childhood and youth of his hero, that the outlets to native power which would have been open to any white boy were closed to Bigger. He knows he does not need to prove this. With a bold stroke of literary divination, he assumes that every one of his American readers will know all that without being told. And he is right. We do.

New York Times

CHARLES POORE

RICHARD WRIGHT'S *Native Son,* AN ENORMOUSLY STIRRING NOVEL OF crime and punishment, is published this morning. It is a story to trouble midnight and the noon's respose, as Mr. Eliot once said about another matter, and to haunt the imagination many days.

It was widely praised long before publication. Indeed, few other recent novels have been preceded by more advance critical acclamation, or lived up to the expectations they aroused so well. Mr. Wright is a Negro. His novel concerns a young Negro, Bigger Thomas, who twice commits murder before your eyes, and the whole dark background of his crimes. It is an extraordinarily difficult task he has undertaken—on the Dostoievskian scale—and the praise is soundly based on his accomplishment as a novelist.

Edward Weeks, editor of *The Atlantic Monthly,* calls *Native Son* "a performance of great talent—powerful, disturbing, unquestionably authentic." We'll question the authenticity of Bigger Thomas's ability to discuss the wider implications of his tragic destiny so expertly. But that is another matter. Henry Seidel Canby calls it "the finest novel yet written by an American Negro,"—which it is, without a doubt. It would be a fine novel no matter who wrote it: though, to perpetrate an

---

Irish bull in all sincerity, only a Negro could have written *Native Son.* In a special introduction, Dorothy Canfield Fisher makes the parallel with Dostoievsky, observes that this novel "can be guaranteed to harrow up any human heart capable of compassion or honest self-questioning," and shows how the story of Bigger Thomas bears out the studies in racial barriers carried out by the American Youth Commission under the chairmanship of Owen D. Young.

The praise has been cumulative. It gathered while *Native Son* awaited publication after it had been chosen (with Conrad Richter's "The Trees," which will be reviewed here tomorrow) by the Book-of-the-Month Club for March. Finally, we are told that the Guggenheim awards committee read *Native Son* in manuscript, and, on the strength of its strength, gave Mr. Wright—whose earlier book of stories, *Uncle Tom's Children,* was also a prizewinner—one of its fellowships.

Mr. Wright drives his story forward at a furious yet skillfully controlled pace. The full drama is unfolded in just about two weeks. There is first of all the prophetic killing of a rat in the room where Bigger, his mother, his sister and his brother live in quarreling, desperate squalor. Then Bigger, who has a bad name as a braggart living by shady devices, goes out to meet the poolroom gang [his] environment provides. He plans a hold-up he is afraid to carry out. To hide his cowardice he terrorizes one of his friends.

You see his character. That is the point. Mr. Wright is champion of a race, not defender of an individual wrongdoer. Bigger gets a job as chauffeur in the house of Mr. Dalton, who is a philanthropist toward Negroes and owner of many Negro tenements. Mary Dalton, the daughter of the house, and her friend Jan, a supernally noble radical, make him drink with them. Through an accident, Bigger kills Mary Dalton. That is the first murder.

There is a gruesome dismemberment to hide the crime. Bigger thinks of demanding money, and makes his girl, Bessie, help him. His crime is discovered. After that there is the flight, the second murder, deliberate and brutal, the man-hunt spreading terror over the whole South Side, then the spectacular capture and the day of reckoning in court for all concerned.

It is a long time since we've read a new novelist who had such command of the technique and resources of the novel. Mr. Wright's method is generally Dreiserian; but he has written his American tragedy in a notably firm prose. He knows how to tell a story. He knows how to develop a character, how to show influences playing on a man or a situation. Reflection blends into action. Accents and intonations are caught. Ideas are dramatized with concrete and inescapable images. And dialogue goes crackling down the page.

Bigger is a symbol. But, as we have suggested, he is able to express what he symbolizes more fluently than seems natural, considering how clearly Mr. Wright has made us see his life. There is a constant, probing inquiry into the state of the world that creates people like Bigger Thomas. We do not doubt it. We cannot. But we can and do doubt that it could flow so coherently through Bigger's mind. It's better left to the lawyer's summation in the court-room scene.

Native Son is, in truth, one of those compelling books to which people pay the uneasy tribute of saying their picture is impressive but overdrawn. That places Richard Wright in very good company—from Charles Dickens to John Steinbeck. After all, we do not lack stories of quaint Negro life.

Apart from the ideas that give it volume, force and scope, *Native Son* has some magnificently realized scenes: in the early part, where Bigger, a stranger and afraid, as Housman said, in a world he never made, gropes for freedom from the walls that hold him; in the flight across the roofs and the stand high over the world, in the jail where processions of people come to see him, at the inquest and in the howling mob outside the court. The measure in which it shakes a community is the measure of its effectiveness.

Saturday Review of Literature

JONATHAN DANIELS

FOR TERROR IN NARRATIVE, UTTER AND COMPELLING, THERE ARE FEW PAGES in modern American literature which will compare with this story of the few little days which carried Bigger Thomas, Negro from Mississippi in Chicago, from bullying cowardice through murder to the position of black fiend against the hating world hunted across rooftops in the snow. It is authentic, powerful writing, about a young Negro driven by his cramped destiny to crime, but only flung up by accident and anger as quarry for roaring fury. But I doubt that Bigger Thomas proves any more about the Negro than he does about the world. Man's inhumanity to man did not begin in Mississippi. It did not end with Bigger Thomas in Chicago. What Mr. Wright has written again and wonderfully well, in terms of a member of his own race, is the very ancient story of all criminals who have advanced through the cruel caprices of environment into the frenzy of unequal enmity against a continually imperfect world. Undoubtedly, however, with the wise choice of an unpopular symbol Mr. Wright has pointed in the case of

---

Reprinted from the *Saturday Review of Literature*, XXI (March 2, 1940), 5.

the Negro the place where with deepest unreason we shape the criminal we kill.

The story of Bigger Thomas is the story of a rat. He may be, as Dorothy Canfield Fisher suggests in a brief introduction to the stirring story, the blocked and frenzied rat in the psychopathic laboratory of the world. He is also what a good many of us call a rat when we speak of the Bigger Thomases who recur in our civilization. In his story of Bigger's crimes and flight Mr. Wright does not make him anything else. Indeed, to begin with, he emphasizes the boy's furtive and ugly cowardice better in his attack on a Negro member of his petty pool-room gang than in any act against the surrounding and constricting white world.

Nevertheless Mr. Wright skillfully delivers our sympathies to Bigger. We feel the constricting white world around him. We share his sullen timidity as he enters the rich white world as chauffeur. We resent with him the insensitive fraternizing of the communist Jan Erlone and the rich radical Mary Dalton, for whose accidental murder after an evening of drinking he died. We stand in terror with him across the slow questioning hours beyond Mary's disappearance. And we run with him when the remnants of Mary Dalton's bones are found in the ashes of the furnace where he burned her. Our fear is even on his side when he follows accidental murder with a deliberate attempt to extort money by a kidnapping note to the rich and conventionally kind parents of the girl he killed—as it is when he kills his own colored sweetheart in the frenzy of flight. The cowardice as well as the sympathy which is in us all runs with the rat. We are all caught; the holes we might flee into are stopped. And the police and the mob which come in roaring search behind sirens and shouting represent the wild fury of our own world.

In the almost aching narrative which carries Bigger to his capture, Mr. Wright has written his story with an objectivity which is irresistible. He is the story-teller and the story-teller alone, though one who shocks our minds and squeezes our hearts. And beyond that flight Bigger's story goes on with power in the ordered violence of the law's processes. But even though skillfully written, the preaching comes, the tract emerges. In the satire both of the brutally ambitious district attorney and of the brutally sensational journalism, as well as in the almost mystical plea for Bigger's life by the wise radical Jewish lawyer who would identify Bigger's crime with the guilt of us all, there is a slowing of pace toward solemnity and almost—not quite—to sentimentality.

As a Southerner I may suspect, but I think this book is better as a headlong, hard-boiled narrative than as any preaching about race relations in America, North or South. Certainly no sensible Southerner will deny the authenticity of Mr. Wright's picture of the plight of his race. But not only Negro boys in pool rooms and slums in Chicago feel caught and find a distorted manhood in violence. The rules of an insensitive world may be more binding, more hope-denying among them. But every order creates its rats and rebels and every civilization—so far in existence—deserves them. Bigger Thomas, for Vermont, for Mississippi, for Chicago, is a symbol of man's failure and, in his fear of contemplating it, the object of his frenzy, his cruelty, and his hate. He is not pretty. But he is the child of our living in this land.

New Yorker

CLIFTON FADIMAN

RICHARD WRIGHT'S *Native Son* IS THE MOST POWERFUL AMERICAN NOVEL to appear since *The Grapes of Wrath.* It has numerous defects as a work of art, but it is only in retrospect that they emerge, so overwhelming is its central drive, so gripping its mounting intensity. No one, I think, except the most unconvertible Bourbons, the completely callous, or the mentally deficient, can read it without an enlarged and painful sense of what it means to be a Negro in the United States of America seventy-seven years after the Emancipation Proclamation. *Native Son* does for the Negro what Theodore Dreiser in *An American Tragedy* did a decade and a half ago for the bewildered, inarticulate American white. The two books are similar in theme, in technique, in their almost paralyzing effect on the reader, and in the large, brooding humanity, quite remote from special pleading, that informs them both. *Native Son,* as Henry Seidel Canby says in his illuminating comment printed on the jacket, "is certainly the finest novel as yet written by an American Negro." True enough, and it is a remarkable novel no matter how much or how little melanin its author happens to have in his skin.

Bigger Thomas is a twenty-year-old black boy, living with his mother and sister in one room in a Chicago tenement. Bigger is, when the story opens, already a "bad nigger" with a reform school past. Dimly he knows why he is bad, morose, a thief, a bully. It is because the pressure of his environment makes it difficult for him to be anything else. Were his temperment more malleable, he might become totally passive, like his mother and sister. Were he endowed with shrewdness, or talent, he might rise in the social scale, as a small and brilliant percentage of his race is doing. But something in him demands an outlet other than mechanical, reflex living, other than the simple pieties of a consolatory religion. As Dorothy Canfield Fisher

---

Reprinted from *The New Yorker,* XVI (March 2, 1940), 52–53.

makes clear in her fine introduction, society holds out to him a picture of what the American citizen should be—independent, decent, courageous—and then prevents him from doing anything toward the realization of these ideals. The result of this frustration is a neurosis. The result of Bigger's neurosis is, as so often happens, the most horrible violence. Dimly, Bigger feels all this. "He knew that the moment he allowed what his life meant to enter fully into his consciousness, he would either kill himself or somebody else."

This surly, half-maddened, groping Negro is given a chauffeur's job in the home of the Negrophile Daltons, Chicago millionaires, "liberals," nice people. Within twenty-four hours he has unpremeditatedly murdered young Mary Dalton, stuffed her corpse into the furnace, and is ready to understand the real meaning of his life. This Bigger is a stupid fool; he does everything calculated to get himself caught; he murders again, this time his woman, Bessie. But his stupidities are not only the effect of his rudimentary intelligence; they are the almost inevitable blind reactions of the neurotic rat, a rat cornered by a society it fears and cannot understand. "To Bigger and his kind white people were not really people; they were a sort of great natural force, like a stormy sky looming overhead, or like a deep swirling river stretching suddenly at one's feet in the dark."

Caught after a breathtaking fight and chase over the rooftops of a block of Chicago tenements, Bigger is imprisoned and brought to trial. He is defended by Max, a labor lawyer, through whose compassionate eyes we are made to see, very slowly, the larger implications of Bigger's monstrous deeds. There is a long scene in the prison in which he tries to explain to Max why he did what he did, and an even more extraordinary one in which Max traces before the court the jungle tangle of motives that have made Bigger the murderer he unquestionably is. There is no hope for Bigger. He is sentenced to death. With the electric chair but a few days away, Bigger thinks out his life, a life which has not yet begun, which has not been permitted to begin. "I hurt folks 'cause I felt I had to; that's all. They was crowding me too close: they wouldn't give me no room. . . . I didn't know I was really alive in this world until I felt things hard enough to kill for 'em." That last sentence, quite terrible, one feels, is not an "excuse" for Bigger, but it is an indictment of a society, itself fearful, blind, and groping, which has not yet learned how not to produce Biggers, whether white or black. Max, no sentimentalist, no Negrophile, sums it up in court when he says, "He has murdered many times, but there are no corpses . . . This Negro boy's entire attitude toward life is a *crime!*"

Mr. Wright is too explicit. He says many things over and over again. His characterizations of upper-class whites are paper-thin and confess unfamiliarity. I think he overdoes his melodrama from time to time. He is not a finished writer. But the two absolute necessities of the first-rate novelist—passion and intelligence—are in him. That he received the most rudimentary schooling, that for most of his life he has been an aimless itinerant worker are interesting facts but of no great moment in judging his book.

Native Son is no whining plea for "generosity," nor is it a bellicose proletarian tract. Mr. Wright has obviously been deeply affected by the labor movement, but he does not base the argument of his horrifying story upon any facile thesis of economic determinism. He goes deeper than that, often into layers of consciousness where only Dostoevski and a few others have penetrated, into the recess of "a human soul in hell because it is sick with a deadly spiritual sickness," if I may quote Mrs. Fisher once more.

The comparison with *An American Tragedy* comes to my mind again for the two books are hewn out of the same block and indeed tell almost the same story, with a half-accidental murder as the central episode in both cases. Dreiser's book is greater, more monumental, more controlled, more knowledgeable, but *Native Son* is apt to have much the same effect on any reader who is not afraid to go through its dark and bloody pages. I say "afraid" advisedly, for this is strong meat. It is not merely a book but a deep experience.

New York Herald Tribune

MILTON RUGOFF

IT IS DIFFICULT TO WRITE TEMPERATELY OF A BOOK WHICH ABOUNDS IN such excitement, in so much that is harrowing, and in so profound an understanding of human frailty. The first extraordinary aspect of *Native Son* is that it approaches the tragedy of a race not through an "average" member but through a criminal who commits such atrocities as are dealt with only in the most sensational tabloids. Addressing a world which will not perhaps be affected by anything less, this book speaks with a voice of horror calculated to pierce even the thickest skin.

As a story it is above all unflaggingly exciting. For almost from the moment we meet him there hovers around Bigger Thomas an air of suppressed violence and emotional tension of the most ominous sort. Whether in the rat-infested tenement where he lives with his mother, brother and sister or among his pals in the pool parlor, he is like a vessel that keeps boiling over, and promises, some day when clamped too tight, to explode. Bigger Thomas is 250 years of Negro frustration incarnate. He is filled with fear and uncertainty for himself, and with hate for the white men around him. Instinctively he learns that the one

---

Reprinted from the *New York Herald Tribune Books* (March 3, 1940), 5.

thing that can give him confidence and a sense of power is the act of transgression. The bolder it is, the more adequate.

But this states in static terms what *Native Son* presents with a dramatic intensity that is almost feverish. When Bigger boils over at first he merely snarls at his nagging long-suffering mother, or abuses a crony. When he explodes, when all the pent-up fear and hate of his own dark life and all his racial memory erupts, he commits the most heinous deed that an American black can commit. The explosion comes the first night that he goes as chauffeur to the Daltons. Once he has struck out successfully at his white enemies, Bigger undergoes every emotional extreme from exultation and catharsis to quaking dread.

What follows is sensational in the extreme. Whirled in a maelstrom of warring instincts, Bigger burns the body, frantically tries sending a ransom note, and then flees when the girl's bones are discovered. His visit to his sweetheart—violence now is the only way he can stave off terror—and his mad flight through abandoned tenements and over snow-covered roof tops with the whole inflamed city howling at his heels is not meant for queasy stomachs.

There is much here that may be simply the excitement of violence or the fascination of the morbid, but in the end each act is traced to a significant reflex, and all these, finally, to the social set-up that conditioned it. Like a diver locked with an octopus, Wright wrestles on and on with the chaos that is Bigger's reaction to life, until he has laid bare every fibre and nerve and, at the last, its very heart. Although from the first page we are kept vividly aware of Bigger as the inevitable product of his environment, it is in the last third of the book, in the events that follow his capture—the lurid trial and his defense by a radical attorney—that *Native Son* graduates from one individual's pathology to the whole tragedy of the Negro spirit in a white world.

The aftermath of Bigger's superhuman exertions is apathy; he spurns even religion because he knows it as something meant to lull his people into submission. The one who finally reaches him is the Jewish lawyer who comes to his aid. Against the travesty which is the state's case, the lawyer's defense is an attempt to show how society made Bigger what he is. Through his tongue, *Native Son* strikes with all its strength. It does not beg; it indicts. It hits even those like the Daltons who give millions to Negroes; for even they sanction discrimination. It bends no knees, it asks no pity; it seeks to scourge.

Part of Wright's triumph is that we know without being told that fathoms beneath Bigger's terrifying public personality lies a core of trembling flesh within which rots the seed of the man who might have been. Once, in a quite wonderful scene, this comes to the surface—facing the chair and surprised out of himself by the lawyer's plea for him, Bigger breaks through the great wall of his mute pain and reaches out to his defender in the most moving of human gestures. Elsewhere one may feel that a novel which relies too heavily on frantic excitement and abnormal situations cannot reach the largest emotions, that high tragedy cannot be wrought from horror and hate alone. However, in such a scene—and there are several almost as good—the impact is overwhelming.

The faults of the book should be recognized; it is more than once guilty of melodrama, adding artificial excitement to a sufficiency of the natural kind; it heaps up complications beyond the reader's powers of assimilation; occasionally the plot skates on thin ice; and several times Bigger's confusion seems to baffle even his creator—but in the end these all seem easy to overlook, negligible imperfections on the surface of an extraordinary story movingly told. If the tests of a memorable novel are that it engage the reader completely, move him profoundly and constitute a revelatory intellectual experience, then *Native Son* will not soon be forgotten.

New Masses

SAMUEL SILLEN

THE TREMENDOUS POWER OF *Native Son* HAS ITS ULTIMATE SOURCE IN A revolutionary vision of life. It is, in the most profound sense, a philosophical novel, a creative affirmation of the will to live and to transform life. Wright has often said that the discovery of *meaning* in the suffering of an oppressed group dooms the social order that is responsible for the suffering. His novel is a dramatization of the tortured search for values by which Bigger Thomas is to struggle, live, and die. Every arrangement of a class society conspires to maim Bigger for refusing to submit without challenge. The overbearing environment which engenders his suffering mutilates the forms of his protest and aspiration. But if the process of discovery is tragic, it is also, in the end, emancipatory; and if Bigger is condemned to die at the moment he has learned to live, our own minds have been flooded with meaning. A bold conception of human dignity gives this novel its stature. The episodes of violence, the sensitive notations of life in a segregated community, and the subtle documentation of a social machine which grinds down human personality, are important only in so far as they materialize this conception.

Only a courageous novelist would have attempted so difficult a theme. Only a supremely gifted one could have executed it so perfectly. For Bigger Thomas, externally, is the stereotyped monster of a

---

Reprinted from *New Masses,* XXXIV (March 5, 1940), 24–25. Reprinted by permission.

lynch-inciting press. So far as the police record is concerned, he is the murderer of Mary Dalton, the daughter of his wealthy white "benefactor." He is a "brutish sex-slayer." His Negro mistress is the victim of his "primitive blood-lust." His trial for murder is the subject for horrified editorials in the Jackson (Miss.) *Daily Star* and gory news columns in the Chicago *Tribune*. This is explosive material. And it does explode—in the faces of the stereotype makers. The police record is here turned into its opposite, an indictment not of an individual but of a brutal and discriminatory order.

Bigger Thomas is not a "sex-slayer" at all. He is a fear-ridden boy whose attitude of iron reserve is a wall between himself and a world which will not allow him to live and grow. A deepening sense of hysteria has accompanied the blacking of his normal impulses. "Playing white" with his friends on a Chicago street corner is a grim substitute for living white, for living in a world, that is, where one may presumably be an aviator, or a President or a millionaire or whatever one wants to be. Bigger acts tough toward his poverty-stricken family, sensing that if he allows the shame and misery of their lives to invade his consciousness his own fear and despair will become intolerable. The victim of movie-inspired fantasies, he cannot find a possible order or meaning in his relations to other people. He does not know, at the beginning of the novel, that his crushed existence is part of a much larger pattern which includes Negroes *and* whites.

The events which lead to Bigger's unintentional smothering of Mary, his burning of the body, his flight from the police, and his murder of his mistress, Bessie, who he fears will betray him, create a sense of dramatic excitement that catches us up in the tensions and rhythms of Bigger's life. Though he did not plan Mary's murder, Bigger accepts it as his own act. Like Dmitry Karamazov, who felt guilty because in his heart he had wished his father's death, Bigger feels that he has killed many times before, "only on those other times there had been no handy victim or circumstance to make visible or dramatic his will to kill." The murders give him a sense of *creation*. He feels that they have given a focus to the chaotic circumstances of his existence. The acceptance of moral guilt makes Bigger feel free for the first time.

But such a commitment to life was doomed to disillusion. After his capture, Bigger realizes that he is as defenseless in the face of death as he had been in the face of life: "a new pride and a new humility would have to be born in him, a humility springing from a new identification with some part of the world in which he lived, and this identification forming the basis for a new hope that would function in him as pride and dignity." Having renounced fear and flight, he must possess a conception of man's fate which will enable him to die. He cannot respect the submissive path of religion which his mother and Reverend Hammond urge him to follow. He must have an affirmative idea. And he discovers its spirit in the Labor Defender lawyer, Mr. Max, and the young Communist, Jan Erlone.

In an essay published two years ago, Richard Wright declared that "If the sensory vehicle of imaginative writing is required to carry too great a load of didactic material, the artistic sense is submerged." He might have added that when the artistic sense is submerged, the didactic material becomes ineffective. In *Native Son,* as in the stories of *Uncle Tom's Children,* he has skillfully avoided the danger. Idea and image are remarkably integrated. Only a critic whose esthetic senses are blunted or whose social prejudices are unalterable will attempt to shout this novel down with the old cry of "propaganda." And yet, like *The Grapes of Wrath,* it will jar men and women out of their routine ways of looking at life and sweep them toward a new conception of the way things are and the way they ought to be.

But an effort will undoubtedly be made by some people to distort the plain meaning of the book in order to bolster their own bigotry. The reader must be warned against the blurb by Henry Seidel Canby which appears on the jacket of the book, and I hope that the publishers will be persuaded to withdraw it as a gross and vicious misrepresentation. Canby describes Jan Erlone, the Communist, as a "negrophile"! He suspects that the book will be "less of a surprise to, and more readily understood by, Southerners than by Northerners." He relishes the "deadly satire in the portraits of the young radicals—Mary who is killed, and Jan, the Communist, who chooses Bigger to work on, not realizing that this kind of political pity is more offensive to a Negro than color prejudice."

This is the most blatant stuff I have ever read. It angles the novel away from itself to the very stereotype which the novel demolishes. For the plain fact is that the radicals, Mr. Max and Jan Erlone, are the only ones who make Bigger aware of his dignity as a human being. To be sure, this does not happen overnight. To be sure, Jan makes an initial blunder in treating Bigger as a comrade before Bigger has learned to believe in the very existence of comradeship. But if one reads the novel in its full sweep one cannot mistake the overwhelming significance of Bigger's final remark: "Tell . . . Tell Mister . . . Tell Jan hello." It is, at last, a dropping of the Mister, an affirmation of that solidarity with other human beings in which only Jan and Max have taught him to believe.

It is difficult to think of an American novel that provides a more brilliant analysis of the interplay of social and psychological factors in experience. Wright has fused the valid elements in the naturalistic and psychological traditions, and the result is something quite new. For lack of a better phrase, "dramatic realism" will do. Structurally, the novel is divided into three sections corresponding to the three acts of a play. The action is not chopped up into chapters; it moves in a long sweep toward three climaxes. The tonal unity and psychological tension which we associate with an intense drama can be sustained only with great difficulty in fiction. As a sheer achievement in structural craftsmanship, *Native Son* is worth careful study. There is nothing wayward, either in detail or in mood. It is the work of a writer who feels his material deeply and authentically at the same time that he can view it from an ideological perspective.

What this perspective is, Wright has explained elsewhere. The Marxist analysis of society, he holds, "creates a picture which, when placed before the eyes of the writer, should unify his personality, buttress him with a tense and obdurate will to change the world. And, in turn, this changed world will dialectically change the writer. Hence, it is through a Marxist conception of reality and society that the maximum degree of freedom in thought and feeling can be gained for the Negro writer. Further, this dramatic Marxist vision, when consciously grasped, endows the writer with a sense of dignity which no other vision can give. Ultimately, it restores to the writer his lost heritage, that is, his role as a creator of the world in which he lives, and as a creator of himself." *Native Son* is his first full-length embodiment of this conception in the warm and living terms of fiction. It is a first novel, but it places Richard Wright, incontrovertibly, in the first ranks of American literature in our time. There is no writer in America of whom one can say more confidently: He is the creator of our better world and our greater art.

Commonweal

EDWARD SKILLEN, JR.

It is nearly twenty years since Theodore Dreiser published his bulky *American Tragedy*, an indictment of America's heartless worship of money and business success. Environment was meant to be the real villain in his rough-hewn tale of crime and inevitable punishment. However he produced a rather different effect. His hero Clyde Griffiths's sense of guilt was developed so painstakingly and he seemed so normal an individual that the reader came to identify himself individually with Clyde and feel personally guilty of the crime.

Richard Wright has followed a strikingly similar pattern in *Native Son*. In this case it is more difficult for the reader to identify himself with young Bigger Thomas, who, by the time the story opens, is in a highly pathological state. Besides, the environment of South Side Chicago's Negro district is far more vicious, more potent for evil, than Clyde Griffiths' smaller mid-western factory town. Finally, Mr. Wright handles the problems of style with far greater ease than Mr. Dreiser.

Reprinted from *Commonweal*, XXXI (March 8, 1940), 438.

Except for the defense attorney's long speech toward the end of the book—a wholly unnecessary pointing of the moral—*Native Son* fairly races along both in narrative and dialogue. So Mr. Wright really does succeed in making environment the principal villain in this new American Tragedy.

Even compared with Dreiser this volume is strong meat. From the moment a giant black rat steals into the Thomas family's one-room flat, on the opening pages, till Bigger in his death cell bids his attorney farewell on page 359, *Native Son* is a "shocker." It is brutal, frank, sordid. It is no book for adolescents or for squeamish adults. But this brutality is skillfully subordinated to a wider purpose.

To be sure most Americans are no longer ignorant that the Negro over here is a victim of the most unjust discrimination. Many have heard, for instance, that in some parts of Harlem people sleep in three shifts in order to meet the high rents. Negroes have to pay the piper since they are barred from other sections of Manhattan. Lynching in the South and border states and the mental-emotional outlook that violence manifests are also widely known. But from most of us these situations are as far removed as a Chinese flood or the inhumanities of a French penal colony in the Guianas. Yet the problem is at our very doors.

Mr. Wright makes it real by reducing it to very simple human terms. When young Bigger Thomas goes to work for a wealthy family which might eventually have helped him, he already is a problem case. He is a member of a poolroom gang that has not yet pulled off a major crime but might well do so any day. He regularly has illicit relations with a young waitress. And deep in his breast rankles a burning resentment against the white race which seems to thwart his ambitions at every turn and keeps his family in abject misery. He cannot bear to face his true situation squarely.

What makes *Native Son* doubly tragic is that Bigger's first victim is a white girl who is sincerely trying to be his friend, to treat him as a fellow human being. Mary's sweetheart is a communist who also tries to befriend Bigger to the very end. Her mother, who is blind, loves to encourage Negroes to study and get ahead. The only poetic justice is that Mary's father was one of the landlords whose exorbitant rents cause such widespread misery in Chicago, New York and in all the other cities where Negroes are so harshly segregated.

The very first night of his new job Bigger finds that he has accidentally killed Mary Dalton. The story then rushes through a series of other crimes to Bigger's arrest and conviction with a sort of grim inevitability. Again it is highly reminiscent of the even more acute sense of impending doom that comes upon Dreiser's Clyde Griffiths, who knows and makes the readers of the *American Tragedy* painfully aware that nothing will save him from the chair.

Here and there Richard Wright gives hints as to the way out of the tragic situation he has epitomized so stirringly in Bigger Thomas.

Boys' clubs and ping pong tables he holds in contempt; palliatives such as settlement houses do not provide the answer either for the injustices to his race. Religion appears in his pages as well-meaning but futile. Some new social system—not necessarily the Marxist one—is implicitly his prescription. As is so often the case in real life, only the communists in this novel succeed in convincing the Negro that they sincerely believe and act on the principle of the brotherhood of man.

There is one final reason that this startling book provides such a challenge to all Americans. Bigger knew that he, like many innocent lynch victims, would be presumed guilty as a matter of course if he was apprehended under suspicious circumstances. To be looked upon as ignorant, lazy, shiftless, vicious, subhuman by a white master race was what enraged him most. His deepest satisfaction is to know at the very end something that might have saved him six months earlier, that one white man really accepts him on equal terms as a man. Is that an impossible prescription for a starter?

Chicago Defender

ANOTHER ALEXANDRE DUMAS HAS RISEN IN THE NEW WORLD. NOT THE Dumas of the *Three Musketeers* and the *Count of Monte Cristo,* important and popular though he be, but the younger Dumas whose *Lady of the Camelias* shook the whole structure of the French society. Just as he, through the pages of a vibrant, realistic novel, had exposed to full view the shocking aberrations and unmitigated strictures of the social organism of his time, so has Richard Wright in his *Native Son* paraded before the eyes of an indolent, indifferent public the organic weaknesses of the American social order.

Though Dumas' novels, as literary critics are fond of saying, are classed in the category of sociological theses, shocking as they are to the senses of polite society, they nevertheless must be considered in the light of the romantic striving of an artist whose sole aim is the faithful reproduction upon the canvas of the spasms of a world in agony. The result is a picture, well painted, beautifully executed, revealing the delicate touch of an artist with consummate skill; drawing sympathy, exciting admiration but conveying no definitive compelling message.

In *Native Son,* Richard Wright has done more than painting a distressful, lurid picture of contemporary America. He has subjected to

---

Reprinted from the *Chicago Defender* (March 16, 1940), 22. Reprinted by permission.

microscopic examination the panorama of the social, economic and political disparities that deter the cultural integration of the black minority into American society. With the deftness and precision of the experienced surgeon whose scalpel cuts through dead tissues in order better to excise a malignant tumor, Mr. Wright has gone into the very matrix of our social organization.

The demented university student, in *Native Son*, expresses much of the plight of the Race when he says that he will tell the President of the United States that

> you make us live in such crowded conditions on the South side that one out of every ten of us is insane! I'll tell 'im that you dump all the stale foods into the Black Belt and sell them for more than you can get anywhere else! I'll tell 'im you tax us, but you won't build hospitals! I'll tell 'im the schools are so crowded that they breed perverts! I'll tell 'im you hire us last and fire us first!

Though uttered by a disordered mind, these lines reflect some of the basic issues which confront us not only in Chicago but all over America—issues that are verbalized often more violently by the sane among us. Their presence may well be responsible for the chronic neurosis which manifests itself in uncontrolled emotional reactions.

As Dorothy Canfield Fisher, who wrote a preface for the book, explained:

> Our American society creates around all youth a continual pressure of suggestion to try to live up to the accepted ideals of the country—such ordinary, traditional, taken-for-granted American ideals as to fight injustice fearlessly; to cringe to no man; to choose one's own life work; to resist with stout-hearted self-respect affronts to decent human dignity, whether one's own or others'; to drive ahead toward honestly earned success, all sails spread to the old American wind blowing from the Declaration of Independence. But our society puts Negro youth in the situation of the animal in the psychological laboratory in which a neurosis is to be caused by making it impossible for him to try to live up to those never-to-be-questioned national ideals as other young Americans do.
>
> *Native Son* is the first report in fiction we have had from those who succumb to these distracting cross-currents of contradictory nerve-impulses, from those whose behavior-patterns give evidence of the same bewildered, senseless tangle of abnormal nerve-reactions studied in animals by psychologists in laboratory experiments. It is not surprising that this novel plumbs blacker depths of human experience than American literature has yet had, comparable only to Dostoievski's revelation of human misery in wrong-doing.

Dostoievski's *Crime and Punishment* deals with the universally unchanging and unchangeable human instinct; Dreiser's *American Tragedy* is the representation of a social complex that has not disturbed greatly the conscience of our present generation. But Wright's

Native Son is neither an experimental nor a philosophic novel. It is a penetrating, realistic, clinical examination of a raw, open wound which is yet bleeding.

While the critics are in unanimity in proclaiming Richard Wright a novelist of the first magnitude, we, who belong to the world of social proscription, of frustrated hopes, of organized discrimination out of which came Bigger Thomas—the main character of the book—fervently hope that *Native Son* shall not only focus attention upon the evils which are visited upon us, but that it shall, by the very urgency of its message, transform a rotten social, economic system into a living democracy for all.

Nation

MARGARET MARSHALL

THE NEGRO IN AMERICA IS CONFRONTED BY TWO ATTITUDES. HE IS TREATED either as an inferior and an outcast or as the member of an oppressed race who is therefore owed special consideration by "enlightened" whites. These opposite attitudes are in fact the two sides of the same coin of race prejudice, since both deny to the man who happens to be colored his standing as a human being—to be accepted or rejected as such in his relations with other human beings. This is the real tragedy of the black man in America, and this is the basic theme of *Native Son* by Richard Wright.

With a boldness entirely justified by the result Mr. Wright has chosen for his "hero," not a sophisticated Negro who at least understands his predicament and can adapt himself to it, but a "bad nigger," a "black ape," who is only dimly aware of his extra-human status and therefore completely at the mercy of the impulses it generates. Bigger Thomas, a twenty-year-old colored boy, lives with his family—a meek, religious mother and sister, and a younger brother who worships him—in a grisly tenement room on the South Side of Chicago. Bigger hangs out at pool halls with a gang of friends who go in for petty robbery and spend their idle hours planning "jobs" and talking about white folks, about cars and airplanes and all the symbols of power in free America which are forever flaunted yet pretty consistently forbidden to 11,000,000 of its "native sons."

In the first part of the book one gets a picture of a dark world inclosed by a living white wall to which the black inhabitants react

Reprinted from the *Nation*, CL (March 16, 1940), 367–368.

according to their natures. Bigger's mother and sister are humble; Bigger and his friends are resentful; all feel powerless and afraid of the white world, which exploits, condescends to, and in turn fears the race it has segregated. Against this psychological and social backdrop, which hangs over the reader like an overcast sky, the terrible story of Bigger unrolls. He is removed from the WPA to be given a job as chauffeur and handyman in the establishment of a rich white real-estate operator who owns the tenement in which the Thomas family lives but who has contributed millions to Negro philanthropies. Bigger's first task is to drive Mary, the daughter of the house, to a lecture. Instead she orders him to take her to a rendezvous, with her lover, Jan, a Communist, whose views she shares after the romantic fashion of the college revolutionist. In their "proletarian" exuberance Mary and Jan insist that Bigger eat and drink with them. Bigger, who is terrified of "reds" and regards the strange friendliness of Jan and Mary as only another expression of white scorn, sullenly complies. At the end, drunk and confused and frightened, he carries the girl, who cannot walk, to her room; and out of fear, when her blind mother enters, he smothers her to prevent an outcry and his own discovery. From there on the sands run out fast. Faced with the evidence of his unpremeditated murder he burns Mary's body. Then, driven by an inexplicable sense of power and release which his crime has given him, he evolves a stupid scheme for extracting ransom money, forcing his girl Bessie to act as his accomplice. When suspicion falls upon him, he kills Bessie in order to protect himself. After a police hunt during which race feeling rises and innocent Negroes are persecuted for his crime, Bigger is caught and tried while troops guard him from the anger of the mob. A Communist lawyer, Max, takes up his defense but pleads in vain, and Bigger is condemned to death.

The tale is sheer melodrama, but it is no Grand Guignol in black and white. For Mr. Wright has laid bare, with a ruthlessness that spares neither race, the lower depths of the human and social relationship of blacks and whites; and his ruthlessness so clearly springs not from a vindictive desire to shock but from a passionate—and compassionate—concern with a problem obviously lying at the core of his own personal reality that while the reader may recoil he cannot escape from the conviction that this problem is part of his reality as well. It is not pleasant to feel at the end that one is an accessory to the crimes of Bigger Thomas; but that feeling is impressive evidence of the power of Mr. Wright's indictment with its cutting and accurate title of *Native Son*.

As narrative, the story of Bigger Thomas carries its own dreadful fascination. Bigger's world is made real and terrifying; the theme is developed with such passion and honesty—Mr. Wright plays so directly upon the sense of guilt that is inevitably part of the white American's attitude toward his black fellow-citizens—that the critical faculties tend to be held in abeyance while one reads his book. Only afterward does one take stock of its defects as a work of art. And here, too, it is Mr. Wright who forces one's hand, for he would be the first to scorn indulgence.

The defects have to do with characterization and style. Aside from Bigger, the characters are too lightly sketched. Bigger's friends are real; the girl and her father are not; the Communist lawyer, Max, is only a voice, though a stirring one. In the case of Bigger Mr. Wright has not solved the admittedly difficult problem of projecting in terms of an ignorant and confused, though intelligent, Negro boy the forces that motivate his actions. As a result the author often ascribes to Bigger thoughts of which he is plainly incapable. The situation is saved because Bigger's behavior is authentic and because Mr. Wright's analysis of the roots of that behavior is so patently true.

Mr. Wright's style often reminds one of a stream "riled" by a heavy storm. Its element of Biblical rhetoric is not out of place since it is part of the colloquial heritage of the Negro in America, but there is in addition a bookish quality, often encountered in the self-educated writer, which should be weeded out. Mr. Wright's boldness in choosing to develop his theme through the story of a "bad nigger" is all to the good, but his flair for the melodramatic could bear curbing.

These defects cannot be described as minor, but they are extenuated by the wealth of evidence in *Native Son* that they can be overcome by a writer whose talent and seriousness are apparent on every page, who displays a maturity of thought and feeling beside which the eloquence of *The Grapes of Wrath* grows pale. And Mr. Wright's youth demonstrates once more that maturity is not necessarily a matter of years.

New Republic

MALCOLM COWLEY

Native Son IS THE MOST IMPRESSIVE AMERICAN NOVEL I HAVE READ SINCE *The Grapes of Wrath*. In some ways the two books resemble each other: both deal with the dispossessed and both grew out of the radical movement of the 1930's. There is, however, a distinction to be drawn between the motives of the two authors. Steinbeck, more privileged than the characters in his novel, wrote out of deep pity for them, and the fault he had to avoid was sentimentality. Richard Wright, a Negro, was moved by wrongs he had suffered in his own person, and what he had to fear was a blind anger that might destroy the pity in him, making him hate any character whose skin was whiter than his own. His first book, *Uncle Tom's Children,* had not completely avoided that fault. It was a collection of stories all but one of which had the same pattern: a Negro was goaded into killing one or more white men and was killed in turn, without feeling regret for himself or his victims. Some of the stories I found physically painful to read, even though I admired them. So deep was the author's sense of the indignities heaped on his race that one felt he was revenging himself by a whole series of symbolic murders. In *Native Son* the pattern is the same, but the author's sympathies have broadened and his resentment, though quite as deep, is less painful and personal.

The hero, Bigger Thomas, is a Negro boy of twenty, a poolroom loafer, a bully, a liar and a petty thief. "Bigger, sometimes I wonder why I birthed you," his pious mother tells him. "Honest, you the most no-countest man I ever seen in all my life." A Chicago philanthropist tries to help the family by hiring him as chauffeur. That same night Bigger kills the philanthropist's daughter—out of fear of being discovered in her room—and stuffs her body into the furnace. This half-accidental crime leads to others. Bigger tries to cast the blame for the girl's disappearance on her lover, a Communist; he tries to collect a ransom from her parents; after the body is found he murders his Negro mistress to keep her from betraying him to the police. The next day he is captured on the snow-covered roof of a South Side tenement, while a mob howls in the street below.

In the last part of the book, which is also the best, we learn that the case of Bigger Thomas is not the author's deepest concern. Behind it is another, more complicated story he is trying hard to explain, though the words come painfully at first, and later come in a flood that almost sweeps him away. "Listen, you white folks," he seems to be saying over and over. "I want to tell you about all the Negroes in America. I want to tell you how they live and how they feel. I want you to change your minds about them before it is too late to prevent a worse disaster than any we have known. I speak for my own people, but I speak for America too." And because he does speak for and to the nation, without ceasing to be a Negro, his book has more force than any other American novel by a member of his race.

Bigger, he explains, had been trained from the beginning to be a bad citizen. He had been taught American ideals of life, in the schools, in the magazines, in the cheap movie houses, but had been denied any means of achieving them. Everything he wanted to have or do was reserved for the whites. "I just can't get used to it," he tells one of his poolroom buddies. "I swear to God I can't. . . . Every time I think

---

about it I feel like somebody's poking a red-hot iron down my throat."

At the trial, his white-haired Jewish lawyer makes a final plea to the judge for mercy. "What Bigger Thomas did early that Sunday morning in the Dalton home and what he did that Sunday night in the empty building was but a tiny aspect of what he had been doing all his life long. He was *living*, only as he knew how, and as we have forced him to live. . . . The hate and fear which we have inspired in him, woven by our civilization into the very structure of his consciousness, into his blood and bones, into the hourly functioning of his personality, have become the justification of his existence. . . . Every thought he thinks is potential murder."

This long courtroom speech, which sums up the argument of the novel, is at once its strongest and its weakest point. It is strongest when Mr. Max is making a plea for the American Negroes in general. "They are not simply twelve million people; in reality they constitute a separate nation, stunted, stripped and held captive *within* this nation." Many of them—and many white people too—are full of "balked longing for some kind of fulfilment and exultation"; and their existence is "what makes our future seem a looming image of violence." In this context, Mr. Max's talk of another civil war seems not so much a threat as an agonized warning. But his speech is weakest as a plea for the individual life of Bigger Thomas. It did not convince the judge, and I doubt that it will convince many readers.

It is not that I think Bigger "deserved" the death sentence for his two murders. Most certainly his guilt was shared by the society that condemned him. But when he killed Mary Dalton he was performing the first free action in his whole fear-tortured life; he was accepting his first moral responsibility. That is what he tried so hard to explain to his lawyer. "I ain't worried none about them women I killed. . . . I killed 'em 'cause I was scared and mad. But I been scared and mad all my life and after I killed that first woman, I wasn't scared no more for a little while." And when his lawyer asks him if he ever thought he would face the electric chair, "Now I come to think of it," he answers, "it seems like something like this just had to be." If Mr. Max had managed to win a life sentence for Bigger Thomas, he would have robbed him of his only claim to human courage and dignity. But that Richard Wright makes us feel this, while setting out to prove something else—that he makes Bigger Thomas a human rather than a racial symbol—shows that he wrote an even better novel than he had planned.

Phylon

JOSEPH H. JENKINS, JR.

In a few short hours a simply curious reader may discover in the three hundred-odd pages of Richard Wright's second book, the novel, *Native Son,* how Bigger Thomas, a twenty-year-old black boy from Mississippi, managed within only seven days to threaten a playmate with a knife, kill the daughter of his white employer, bash in the head of his Negro girl as she slept, led detectives, police, and a fire company a hot chase over Chicago South Side rooftops, and finally earn the penalty of death. Such is a brief external record of a Negro youth's crime and punishment. Seekers after thrills may thus be more than fairly rewarded for their time and pains.

But that is not all the astute writer, far from being a mere sensation-monger, has put into this book.

Among intelligent men and women of good will today it is no longer the considered opinion that individual men are alone accountable for misdemeanors and atrocities committed. They recognize a criminal other than a wayward human being who may now and again wield a deadly instrument, brandish an incendiary torch, or cast aside from the insistent promptings of strange and wild passions those inhibitions sanctioned by society in its own interest. They hold society itself *particeps criminis,* if not, indeed, often the very instigator—society, that amorphous, ill-regulated, insensate body within or outside of which all must live. Society also has its own record of crime—and no mean or scanty one—against its constituent members in the long account of deprivations forced upon the helpless, of fatuous antagonisms created and maintained among men and women who need and want peace and security, and of the exploitation of the consequent maladjustments. The fit punishment for these atrocities is a ruinous waste of the resources of society in not only material goods, but human life and spirit as well, together with ultimate confinement in discord, confusion, loss of hope, and final destruction.

In *Native Son* society is the real criminal. Bigger is only a small sore, however annoying, upon the social body, symptomatic of a chronic malady pervading the whole system. As the disease of inhumanity discloses itself in the variedly corrupt lives of many people

---

Reprinted from *Phylon,* I (Second Quarter 1940), 195–197. Reprinted by permission of the publisher.

...terminedly circumstanced and judged, in the United States prejudice against the Negro, fatedly delimiting his world, induced the peculiar morbidity instanced in the case of Bigger Thomas. Debarred from the proper world in which to live and move and have his being, Bigger was driven to a sullen fear of the alien normal world open to privileged, white human beings. Exclusion brought on fear, so that out of pathetic necessity he might—had he been permitted full opportunity to learn these words—with a more fundamental justification than Macbeth have said,

> I am cabin'd, cribb'd
> confined, bound in
> To saucy doubts and fears.

For Bigger's fear of what he did not and could never hope to understand was the mainspring of his action. His fear had no medium of expression but active hate; his hate worked itself out in that destruction during which he finally came to find self-fulfillment as a free agent. The desire to live, not to be denied in his case, sought and found a satisfactory realization in destroying everything it touched. Insolently it asserted itself. The anomaly of his circumstances Bigger felt keenly, however much his stunted intelligence failed to comprehend the gross abnormality of his plight.

Mr. Wright, himself Mississippi-born, has no such difficulty. He comprehends well enough. With surgeon-like dispassion and skill he probes delicately but firmly into the character of Bigger to discover the real nature of this abnormal growth upon the social body, this wayward human being. He reveals the anomaly as but a single manifestation of the monstrous irony inherent in the conditions of a social order wherein, as the lawyer for the defense outspokenly and eloquently asserts, most men are often lost and at cross-purposes with the acerbated relations existing between Negroes and whites in the United States, it makes the reader conscious of a larger, wider area of festered human life including all society. Mr. Wright has such keen insight, such sound judgment, such a great spirit as enabled him to produce what is perhaps the best book on the race problem so far written. He has understanding; he has wisdom.

Already *Uncle Tom's Children* has indicated the appearance of a very good writer. Now *Native Son* sets Mr. Wright forth as an excellent writer, who can marshal incidents of compelling verisimilitude into a clear, swift, steady narrative and work those incidents into a tissue of symbols charged with extended meaning in the world of his novel—as, for example, in the business of the crosses and in the coffee-drinking scene, when the Dalton household receives the reporters in the cellar. One may cavil at the too near approach some of the incidents make to the melodramatic, and the unrestrained irrelevant pleasure the author seemed to take in writing a discourse on democracy rather than making an authentic defense attorney speak. But the book as a whole is a notable piece of literary work treating an important perilous subject with courage, objectivity, and searching profundity. The Book-of-the-Month Club exercised its customary discerning taste in selecting this novel for its members.

Appreciative readers, after completing *Native Son,* will find themselves eagerly interested in what still finer work further development will doubtless enable Mr. Wright to achieve.

Journal of Negro History

J. D. JEROME

Native Son HAS BEEN RECEIVED AS ONE OF THE GREATEST AMERICAN novels. A few reviewers have mentioned as defects a tendency toward melodrama, artificial excitement, excessive complications, and here and there weakness in the plot. With such matters, however, we are primarily concerned in supplying an estimate from the point of view of the historian.

This novel is historical in more than one sense. The book deals with an important present-day situation which is deeply rooted in the past and the success with which the book has met the test is epoch-making. The status of the Negro treated in this book has been so long neglected by the American people until it has been thus suddenly forced upon public attention as has been the author himself who has rapidly pushed up from obscurity through relief channels to an outstanding position in the public eye. While the book shows how inhuman man may become to man in America, this same America offers, nevertheless, a great opportunity for the lowest of the lowly to rise from poverty to fame.

What the book deals with is not an unfamiliar theme. The method by which attention has been focused upon the problem, however, is something new. The Negroes who heretofore had the same theme have not shown the imagination and the dramatic ability of Richard Wright. He has sufficient sense of humor and a sympathetic touch with the life of which he is a part to portray things as they are rather than lose his audience by ebullitions of sentiment. Heretofore most Negro writers have dealt with the exceptional colored Americans who have contrived to rise above their surroundings. Here the portrayal is that of the

---

Reprinted from the *Journal of Negro History,* XXV (April 1940), 251–252.

underprivileged Negro constituting the main problem in the American social order.

Briefly told, the book says that the American race prejudice is responsible for this social order which produces the atmosphere out of which emerges Bigger Thomas, who ends his career as the lowest of the lowest down, a most tremendous liability of the social order. The custom has been to wreak vengeance upon the Negroes thus depraved and upon other members of the race to which they belong, but the responsibility in the case lies with the American people themselves. Here is what they have permitted to come about when a policy of equality and justice for all might have worked out otherwise. Now, what will the people do about it?

Interracial Review

THEOPHILUS LEWIS

A DOZEN TIMES A YEAR, MORE OR LESS, THE POLICE ARE CONFRONTED WITH an astoundingly ghoulish murder, the motive for which eludes sane comprehension. While the authorities search for clues the city editors have a field day. The papers publish horrendous details of the crime, and describe the movements of the police as they follow the trail of the fiend, lose it, pick it up again, and finally corner the quarry, regaling the public with the excitement of a vicarious man hunt.

In *Native Son,* the thrill of the newspaper crime story is stepped up to high voltage and the point of view reversed. Instead of following the maneuvers of the police as they close in on the criminal, the reader is made privy to the mental and emotional processes of the murderer as he skulks and dodges to escape the tentacles of the law. It is an experience that will not be quickly forgotten.

The technique of the novel follows the journalistic pattern so closely that its plot might be the literal transcription of any one of half a hundred horror stories recently played up in the newspapers. Bigger Thomas has a subnormal mentality that cannot adjust itself to the inequalities of life. He feels that race prejudice bars him from all the larger activities of society, shuts him up in a dark and cramping corner, from which he can see the glory and gaiety of the world but cannot participate in them. As a consequence he harbors an ingrowing hate and suspicion of white people. The author does not explain that if Bigger had been white he would have fear just as bitter toward some

---

Reprinted from *Interracial Review,* XIII (April 1940), 64–65. Reprinted by permission of the publisher.

other inequality, and we have no right to ask him to. It is the author's privilege to select the materials that serve his purpose best. He has given us a plausible, no, convincing reason for Bigger's conduct and that is all we can fairly demand of him.

The narrative opens when Bigger, a Chicago reliefer, is on the eve of getting a job, his first after a long period of idleness. His employer is a real-estate magnate who, with his blind wife, is benevolently interested in Negro welfare; so interested, indeed, that he has contributed several millions of dollars for eleemosynary work among Negroes. Their daughter is a Red sympathizer, and her sweetheart is an active Communist. All of them are bent on helping Bigger reach a normal and active adjustment to society, although the younger people have more specific and radical ideas in mind. But Bigger, whose mind has been conditioned to hate and distrust the white world, is perplexed and alarmed by the attitude of these friendly white people, and he suspects their motives. He is like an animal caught in a snare, as dangerous to a man who wants to release it as it is to one who intends its destruction.

When Bigger finds himself in a perilous situation, he murders his employer's daughter, hacks off her head and shoves head and torso into the furnace. The reader who likes thrills in his fiction will find plenty here, for the narrative omits none of the grisly details. There are as many shivers in these pages as one will find in half a score of vampire mysteries. And more are to follow.

The effect of his crime on Bigger, after the first shock of fright, is to cause a tremendous expansion of his rage. He is no longer a puny victim of the white world, he is its enemy. The white world cannot ignore him now. It must exert its wits and strength to discover and punish him, while he stands at bay guarding his secret. As his feeling of self importance mounts, he concludes that while outwitting the white world he can lay it under tribute. Forthwith he decides to make his employers believe their daughter has been kidnaped and pay ransom for her return. As he needs a confederate in that venture, Bigger confides his scheme to his girl friend who reluctantly consents to join in the plot.

But the murder is discovered at an embarrassing moment, and Bigger's thoughts turn from ransom to escape. Aware that his girl friend knows he is implicated in the crime, he fears that she may betray him. To forestall that danger, he kills her—by the comparatively humane method of braining her with a brick and pitching her out of a fourth-floor window into an areaway, where she freezes to death in the snow. But the murder is out now. The police are on his trail and the hue and cry rises to crescendo.

In the depiction of Bigger's chase and capture the reader discovers the peak passages of the book. With delectable irony, the author describes a town gone wild. Instead of sending out two or three detectives to arrest Bigger—a force ample for the job—the police make a show of his pursuit. They deploy riot squads, get out their gas bombs, deputize swarms of special officers and conscript the aid of the fire department. The States Attorney, ham actor that he is, steps into the floodlight to announce that he will make Bigger's swift punishment a warning to other potential murderers. While the law is making an ass of itself, the newspapers go to town plastering the community with inflammatory headlines that incite public clamor and boost circulation. As the crime is too atrocious to be exaggerated, the papers enhance its horror by embroidering it with superstitions culled from the folklore of race prejudice. The mature reader will find grim humor here. That an underprivileged boy who is none too bright should commit a senseless crime is not astonishing. That his crime could throw a huge civilized city off balance into tumultuous hysteria, making its officials and editors act the part of clowns and procurers. . . . That decreases one's respect for the "superior" race.

As Bigger is rushed to inevitable doom, his defense is undertaken by a humanitarian lawyer, a sort of fictional Clarence Darrow or Samuel Deibowitz, who pleads that the crime is a psychological end product of race prejudice. The plea does not impress the court, nor is it likely to impress the reader who has advanced beyond the belief that race friction is a comparatively simple problem. Indeed, even the naive reader is likely to remember the gruesome murders and the exciting chase long after he has forgotten the evils of race prejudice to which the author attributes the crime, while those who believe Negro character is essentially primitive or bestial will feel that the book confirms their opinion.

To that serious weakness one might add several minor technical flaws. Nevertheless, in point of style and general craftsmanship it is one of the strongest novels written by a Negro author.

The Crisis

JAMES W. IVY

ON THE SURFACE THIS IS MERELY ANOTHER SENSATIONAL CRIME STORY, but at bottom is much more than that; it is a profound and searching analysis of the mind of the American Negro and a penetrating study of the tragic position of the Negro in American life. *Native Son* is Dostoevskian in its sweep and significance and tugs at the very guts of the reader. No one can read this story and continue to be complacent

Reprinted from *The Crisis*, XLVII (April 1940), 122. Reprinted by permission of The Crisis Publishing Company.

about the position of the Negro in American society. It churns up the emotions and performs the cleansing effects of the catharsis of Greek tragedy. Bigger Thomas is a creation worthy to rank with Raskolnikov or one of the Brothers Karamazov.

The center of the story is Bigger Thomas, the twenty-year-old black boy who is killed ostensibly for killing a white girl, but really because he is a social misfit. Bigger is the victim of social injustice and that deeper malignity of race prejudice. He is no saint and the author does not sentimentalize him, but he is just as much a victim of his environment as was Clyde Griffith. He is the perfect "bad nigger" of Chicago's South Side living in a mouldy and decaying one-room tenement with his sister, his brother, and his pious mother. His instincts are bad and he snarls all through breakfast. The author paints this in an almost artistically perfect first scene where Bigger kills a rat with a skillet. Begging a quarter from his mother Bigger joins his pals in a shady poolroom to plan the holdup of a delicatessen. But Bigger is a coward and picks a fight with one of his pals to hide his blue funk. He is furious because he knows that Gus knows that he (Bigger) is afraid. Gus is afraid too; but Bigger is equally as afraid.

That same afternoon he goes to take a job as a chauffeur with Mr. Dalton of Drexel Boulevard, where the relief people have sent him. Mr. Dalton is a philanthropist who has made some of his millions out of rotting South Side tenements, but he returns part of his tainted gains to Negroes in charity contributions. Mrs. Dalton likes to send her Negro chauffeurs to night school, and the daughter, Mary, is a radical flirting with Communism. At eight o'clock Bigger is supposed to drive Mary to the university to a lecture, but Mary directs him to a rendezvous with her Communist lover Jan. Then they direct Bigger to a South Side Negro restaurant, and later they order him to drive around the park while Mary and Jan drink and make love on the back seat. It is a very drunk Mary that Bigger returns to her bedroom at two that morning, but before he can get out, the blind Mrs. Dalton comes in to see her daughter and Bigger smothers Mary in a pillow to keep her from speaking of his presence. If Mrs. Dalton had known that he was there, she would have suspected him of rape, and Bigger knows this. He has unwittingly killed the girl; so he puts her body in a trunk, takes it down to the basement, and burns it. But her head won't fit in the furnace and he has to chop it off with a hatchet. He now turns on the exhaust fan to clear the basement of the odor of burning flesh.

The next morning Mary is missing, but since she had planned to go to Detroit no one thinks her absence unusual. But in the meantime, Bigger knows that with the first suspicion of foul play he is going to be the suspect; therefore, he plans to pin the crime on Jan. He also figures that he can collect kidnap money on the pretense that Mary is alive, and takes his girl Bessie into the plot. Mary's bones are discovered in the ashes of the furnace and Bigger flees.

He takes Bessie along because he can't afford to leave her behind.

But when he finds that she is a burden, he batters her head in with a brick and tosses her body down the airshaft of an empty building. After a brief roof-top chase, he is soon caught and brought to trial. He is tried in an atmosphere of mob hysteria and race hate. Though defended by the able Jewish lawyer, Max, he is found guilty and condemned to the chair.

In a part of his last confession Bigger admits that he has never "felt a sense of wholeness" in his entire life, and this is the tragedy of his life as it is of the members of his race caught in the hot desert of the white man's prejudice. There are many Bigger Thomases in actual life; one of their snarls is, "I'll go to hell for a white man any day." Almost every American Negro is frustrated, but he escapes from reality through socially more acceptable means: excessive religiousness, Uncle Tomism, jazz, back-to-Africa movements, Father Divineism, "research," and various other futile doings. Most of the personality-traits of the American Negro are to be explained through the deep frustrations which he suffers in American life. His often strange illogic, intense emotionalism, and sudden and fretful switches from Pollyannaism to cynical fatalism are explicable on these grounds. Anything to escape from consciousness of the galling realities surrounding his position in America.

Native Son is undoubtedly the greatest novel written by an American Negro. In fact, it is one of the best American novels, and Mr. Wright is one of the great novelists of this generation.

New York Sunday Worker

BEN DAVIS, JR.

Native Son HAS, OVERNIGHT, BECOME A LITERARY WORK OF NATIONAL interest and discussion in which varied opinions are expressed by people in all walks of life. That the reactions to the book have differed, even among Communists, is not surprising. My own conclusions, set forth in this review, were arrived at only after lengthy consideration, based upon reading and re-reading the book.

It is clear, however, that *Native Son* is the most powerful and important novel of 1940. It deals with the life of the Negro people. The fact that it projects the role of the Communist Party, even though in a confused manner and in a distorted form, gives it great political as well as literary consequence. It is an achievement in the world of

---

Reprinted from the *New York Sunday Worker* (April 14, 1940), 4, 6. Reprinted by permission.

letters and, despite its shortcomings, is a document of positive social significance.

With *Native Son,* Richard Wright, the Negro author, already known and recognized for his literary talent by his earlier writings, notably *Uncle Tom's Children,* has leaped forward into the front rank of American novelists. Bourgeois critics are compelled to compare the book with such a modern classic as John Steinbeck's *The Grapes of Wrath* and with such a generally accepted work as Theodore Dreiser's *An American Tragedy.* The very literary excellence of the book once more attests the deep cultural genius of the Negro people, expressing their ability to produce artists who can articulate their most bitter oppression and their burning aspirations.

Through slum-bred Bigger Thomas, the author has taken an unemployed Negro youth with frustrated desires for opportunity, traced him through the labyrinth of horrible crimes into which he is forced and entrapped by his white capitalist oppressors, and shows to this youth and to the world that the Communist Party is the only organization profoundly interested in relieving the terrible plight of the Negro people.

Wright runs into many difficulties—serious and sometimes unconquered difficulties—in trying to achieve his objective, but the objective is nonetheless there. He wants to show the most degrading oppression of the Negro—what capitalism can do to a human being, and he tries to show the road that leads to victory. The first he accomplishes through the most superlative and realistic craftsmanship. The latter he does not fully achieve but even here he reflects the fact that the Communist Party is the only organization which can give the ray of light to penetrate the swamp of degradation into which the Negro people have been hurled.

Native Son has a value, first, in that it brings relentlessly to the fore in the form of a realistic novel, the existence of special oppression of the Negro people as a nation. Even in the "best" of novels, the oppression and aspirations of the Negro people are either understressed, distorted or wholly glossed over. But Wright has made use of the art of fiction to burn this problem and responsibility for it deep into the conscience of the American people.

The book is a terrific indictment of capitalist America, which deliberately robs vast Negro communities and holds them in subjection in "Southsides" and "Harlems," under appalling conditions of misery and discrimination, of childhood and adulthood without opportunity; of blockings of the main social highway and of forced detours to criminal by-ways. Bigger Thomas is the product of this special and bitter national oppression and, again and again, he finds himself caught in its web. The very beginning of the book—a picture of Bigger and his whole family battling a giant slum rat—is symbolic of the capitalist monster which devours the Negro people with peculiar relish. Wright does this picture with a marvelous bit of stark writing.

Bigger, Gus, and their pals, like millions of unemployed youths today, find themselves in a dead end, imprisoned by a social system which attempts to hold open only one door to them—the door to crime. But in the process capitalism is digging its own grave, and it tries to keep barred another door which the Communist Party alone hails the Negro people and white workers to enter. That door leads to struggle against capitalism. *Native Son*, at least, cracks that door.

A wall of discrimination exists around the aviation school which Bigger wants to attend; the disruptive factor of poverty and want reaches into Bigger's own family life to impair and strain relations which should be normally warm, human and sympathetic. The almost inconceivable wretchedness of the poor Negro—worse than even the squalor of the poor white—is drawn by Wright in all its rawness. Many of those who are shocked by the crimes into which Bigger is driven by an anti-Negro social system, are too often unshocked by the unendurable conditions under which Negroes are compelled to live.

The pious mask of the white, richman "benefactor" of the Negroes, is abruptly torn off. In Mr. Dalton, the millionaire philanthropist—who typically came into his money through his heiress wife—we have what the bourgeoisie prides itself upon, the "well-disposed, upright and kindly friend" of all the Negroes.

One cannot fail to see that this very Mr. Dalton is a part of that white ruling class whose subjection of the Negro it tries to "atone" for with unctuous and ineffectual gifts. He, the donor of philanthropic sums and ping-pong tables to Negro institutions; he, the "Christian-hearted" employer of the wayward Negro boy, is exposed as the wealthy landlord of the slum houses in which these derelict boys and their crowded families are compelled to live—at rentals considerably in excess of what is mulcted even from poor whites.

Mr. Dalton virtually burglarizes Negro tenants because it is the "custom," and he cannot reduce the rents on the overcrowded Chicago Southside because that would be "unethical" toward his fellow landlords. Bigger himself is the victim of this widespread "ethical custom" of the realty owners. As Max, Bigger's lawyer, says to Mr. Dalton at the coroner's inquest in one of the most penetrating passages in the book:

"So, the profits you take from the Thomas family in rents, you give back to them to ease the pain of their gouged lives and to salve the ache of your own conscience?"

Mr. Dalton tries to explain away the forced Jim-Crow ghettos by saying the Negroes are "happier together," only to be ripped to pieces in cross-examination by Bigger's counsel, who points out the ghetto is "more profitable." Mr. Dalton has to admit that he gives no jobs to any of the Negroes his philanthropy and ping-pong tables "help to educate." In baring the false tissue of white ruling class philanthropy and the hideous double-bookkeeping of capitalism, Wright makes one of the best contributions of the book. There's scarcely a Negro in America who cannot see in Mr. Dalton, the class of hypocritical Carnegies,

Fords and Rockefellers, who are the very causes of the unemployment, poverty and misery among the Negro people, which their million-dollar gifts are falsely alleged to cure.

Exposed too—and with magnificent writing—are the mechanics of the state machinery that sets in motion, in collaboration with the press, the mob violence which accompanies Bigger's trial. However, this is not a typical case, for like Scottsboro, the typical lynch trial is where the Negro is completely and wholly innocent. Neither do I.L.D. attorneys in life, plead their clients guilty. Nevertheless, the mob scene in the book does show how the state apparatus seizes upon individual cases to terrorize entire Negro communities, to whip up hysteria for persecution of the Communist Party and labor unions.

This mob hysteria is still a technique of the capitalist class, as just witnessed in the brutal lynch hysteria against the Negroes on the Maryland Eastern Shore in Show Hill. But more and more, as a result of the courageous fight of the Communist Party and the I.L.D. in Scottsboro and in other cases—and as a result of the great CIO recruiting drives particularly in the South—the state machinery finds it more difficult to whip up its "democratic citizens" mobs, even in the South. It is these courageous activities which made Wright see the light.

Now the tendency is for lynchings to be perpetrated by local officials through underground and dead of night gangs, as in the recent Atlanta floggings. These Klan bands very seldom choose to face the wrath of the community. Twenty unreported lynchings in Mississippi last year mark the new technique which must be taken into account in the up-to-date treatment of the lynching evil. The strong and still developing labor and progressive movement in Chicago would make it difficult indeed for such a mob to take over as in *Native Son.*

In his characterization it is clear that Wright deliberately chose Bigger Thomas, and developed him into a dangerous criminal, to make his indictment of capitalism airtight. He certainly did not pick the average unemployed Negro youth, who does not become a rapist, a murderer, and fall into the pitfall of crime, as Bigger did despite the intense pressure on the average youth exerted by his white ruling class oppressors. In fact one of the serious weaknesses of the book, particularly in the third part, is that the author overwrites Bigger into a symbol of the whole Negro people, a native son to the Negro people.

The bourbon enemies of the Negro people will try to seize upon this weakness to further their slanders against the whole Negro people despite the fact that the book as a whole says the contrary. It is, of course, inevitable that where they do not see the light some of the Negroes are forced to take the path of the anti-social criminal but the overwhelming majority are responding to the changed attitude of large sections of white labor as a consequence of Communist and other progressive struggles. One does not find this latter Negro majority in the book in more than a suggestive form.

It is nevertheless a source of dramatic power to the book that

Wright chooses a Bigger instead of a more moderate, and less spectacular average Negro as protagonist. The average white person has been taught through the press and radio, through lying history books and whatnot, that the Bigger Thomases are typical of the Negroes. As Jim, one of Bigger's pals says after Bigger is found out:

"We's all dogs in they sight! Youh gotta stan' up 'n' fight these folks . . . We's all murderers t'them . . ."

And the book has sought to take that very bourbon conception of the Negro to use it as a boomerang against the same capitalist bourbons.

Thus does Wright speak to America in terms of the kind of Negro which they have been taught exists. America must listen because Wright talks to them in their own personal medium, and on their own grounds. A picture of the hundreds of thousands of Negroes who are swelling progressive ranks accepting at last the proffered hand of white workers for their freedom, might not reach this America so poignantly, for capitalist propaganda has taught that these Negroes are unreal, "not typical" or, at best, "an exception." Wright has not permitted this excuse to be used.

It cannot be contended successfully that Bigger is a natural killer, a born monster whose criminal bent is inherent. Bigger begins with the same aspirations as any other American youth. He says repeatedly that this "white world" has "everything" and he and his people nothing. When he and his pals "play white" that symbolizes the inaccessibility of the good things of life to them as Negroes. They are driven into petty thievery for money that jobs, not available to them, would provide.

Bigger had ambitions, as he told Max, his lawyer:

"I wanted to be an aviator once. But they wouldn't let me go to the school where I was suppose' to learn it. They built a big school and then drew a line around it and said that nobody could go to it but those who lived within the line. That kept all the colored boys out.

". . . I wanted to be in the army once . . . Hell, it's a Jim-Crow army. All they want a black man for is to dig ditches. And in the navy, all I can do is wash dishes and scrub floors."

Battered down in his every desire and wanting to fight instead of submit, is there any wonder that Bigger views with admiration Japan's bloody "conquering" of China, or the necessity of a "Hitler" to save the Negro people with fire and sword? Did he not get his slanderous impression of Communists from the movies? Is this not life itself for a crushed member of an oppressed people who sees no one to whom he can turn? Does Bigger not express a natural distrust of those reactionary Negro leaders who have so often betrayed their people to the white ruling class, when he tells Max:

"Aw, hell Mr. Max. They (Negro leaders) wouldn't listen to me. They rich, even though the white folks treat them almost like they do me. They almost like white people, when it comes to guys like me.

They say guys like me make it hard for them to get along with white folks."

Even in the introspection of Bigger—which is sometimes baffling and mystical—he is brought face to face with this "hostile white world" which he is trying to defeat and which is constantly trying to strangle his very existence. Here is no "dumb brute" as the capitalist class tries to make of the most undeveloped Negro, but a living, thinking being, trying to reason out his way to freedom, equality and opportunity, and who becomes lost before he finds the way. It is true that Wright's explanation of Bigger's murders as "creation" is somewhat mystical, but it is even more true that Bigger's desire for creation symbolizes the desire of an oppressed nation to live its own life, to express its own creation, in art, culture, and in its full nationhood.

The contrast of splendor, opulence and power in the white ruling class (which Bigger erroneously attributed to the undifferentiated "white world"), especially in a city like Chicago, as compared to the bleak misery of the Negro hovels, is a contradiction which would naturally whet Bigger's creative impulses even more. The urge to "be somebody" and measure shoulders with this "white world" pushes Bigger desperately onward.

Throughout his hair-raising plot, Wright definitely brings each crisis in Bigger's short life, each major event back to its cause in the capitalist social structure. That is the essential unity and strength of the plot and weaves through the entire book. Bigger accidentally kills Mary Dalton because he finds himself in a circumstance in which discovery means sure death, probably lynching for him. The life of any Negro found in such an ambiguous situation under capitalist society with a white woman, though the question of intimacy were never involved, wouldn't be worth a dime. Bigger knew this, and in trying to save himself, accidentally killed.

It seems however, that it would not have injured Wright's general purpose and structural unity if the victim had not been Mary, but some other person entirely disconnected with the labor and progressive movement. There is a touch of unreality here, in that it permits of the impression that had it not been for Bigger's contact with Communists, however untypical these Communists were, he would not have been forced to kill.

The particularly brutal murder and rape of Bessie, Bigger's sweetheart, is traceable to a certain callousness Bigger acquired in his effort to free himself of the capitalist "justice" closing in on him. He feared revelation of the ransom plot. To divert suspicion he implicates the Communists in the ransom note. Bessie too—who cannot be regarded as typical of Negro women servants—is dragged by Bigger into the maelstrom of the anti-Negro "white world," because Bigger needs her in his plan to defeat this hostile white capitalist state. But every single Negro character, including Bigger's own family, is pretty much beaten and desperate—utterly devoid of a smattering of the progressive developments among the Negro people, and in a city like Chicago where the Negroes are so politically articulate. That situation is rather unconvincing, and strains the realism of the artistic medium.

This is where the book falls into one of its most serious errors. Bigger is exaggerated into a symbol of the whole Negro people. It is true that Bigger symbolizes the plight of the Negro, but he does not symbolize the attitude of the entire Negro people toward that plight. Therefore, because no other character in the book portrays the Negro masses, the tendency becomes that the reader sees Bigger and no distinction whatever between him and the masses who are finding the correct way out despite capitalism.

The book could have, for example, made of Bigger's mother a strong woman typical of Negro womanhood of today. And it seems only natural that through some of Bigger's pals or in some other way the progressiveness and the constructive power of the Negro masses could have been brought forward more distinctly.

There is little that directly shows the power of the Negro people, although the book as a whole assumes the existence of the Negro mass as a background. Yet that power is historically present and is evident today in political struggle. It is shown in cultural achievement and in the developing alliance between the Negro people and white workers in the advancing Negro liberation movement. The white masses also are left out, except in the mob scene, which gives an incomplete and untruthful picture by omitting trends among white workers and progressives in the fight for Negro rights. John L. Lewis typified this in his recent address in Washington for the right of the Negroes and poor whites to vote in the South. The problem of including the mass psychology is a difficult literary one, it must be admitted, since a novel must deal with individual characters, but this is bound to be hammered out in the development of fiction of social consciousness. In this case the failure of the book to bring forward clearly the psychology of the Negro mass will find the capitalist enemies of the Negro trying to attribute Bigger's attitude to the whole Negro people.

Since it is clear that Bigger is a product of brutal national oppression, it is correct to defend him, and to hold guilty the capitalist oppressors who drove him to crime. It is very easy to defend a class conscious white worker or Negro. But to give up Bigger, to abandon him, is to condone the system which crushed his social aspirations and enmeshed him in crime. To give him up—the most oppressed—is to give up the thousands of dead-end white youths who are driven to crime daily.

The role of the Communists is projected by the book through characters who are not typical and who reflect distorted ideas which are far from adequately expressing the policies of the Communist Party. But our Party shares the condemnation of such attitudes and such dilettante types even though ruling class enemies will seize upon Jan and Mary and present them as typical of all Communists and

Party sympathizers. The Communist Party, in life, ruthlessly burns out such chauvinist ideas. The patronizing attitude of Jan and Mary led Bigger to include them in his "hostile white world."

But notwithstanding these shortcomings, the book portrays the Communist Party as the main and only force having an understanding of the difficulties of the Negro people and of the relation of these difficulties to the rest of society. The book would have been immeasurably strengthened with a Communist character more typical of the Communist Party. But even as it is, the Party is that force which comes to the defense of Bigger, and tries to instill into him the self-confidence and understanding of the way out.

Certain passages in Max's speech show an understanding of the responsibility of capitalism for Bigger's plight, even though Max's otherwise distorted defense brief must be categorically rejected as an example of the working class defense policies of the Communist Party or the I.L.D. Max well says in his speech to the jury:

> The hunt for Bigger Thomas served as an excuse to terrorize the entire Negro population, to arrest hundreds of Communists, to raid labor union headquarters and workers organizations. Indeed, the tone of the press, the silence of the church, the attitude of the prosecution and the stimulated temper of the people are of such a nature as to indicate that more than revenge is being sought upon a man who has committed a crime.
>
> What is the cause of all this high feeling and excitement? . . . Were labor unions and workers halls raided solely because a Negro committed a crime? . . . Your Honor, you know that this is not the case! Negroes, workers and labor unions were hated as much yesterday as they are today. Crimes of even greater brutality and horror have been committed in this city. Gangsters have killed and have gone free to kill again. But none of that brought forth an indignation to equal this. Your Honor, that mob did not come here of its own accord! It was incited! Who then fanned this latent hate into fury?
>
> The State Attorney knows, for he promised the Loop bankers that if he were re-elected demonstrations for relief would be stopped! The Governor of the State knows, for he has pledged the Manufacturers Association that he would use troops against workers who went out on strike! The Mayor knows, for he told the merchants of the city that the budget would be cut down, that no new taxes would be imposed to satisfy the clamor of the masses of the needy.
>
> There is guilt in the rage that demands that this man's life be snuffed out quickly! There is fear in the heat and impatience which impels the action of the mob congregated upon the streets beyond that window! All of them—the mob and the mobsters: the wire-pullers and the frightened; the leaders and the pet vassals—know and feel that their lives are built upon a historical deed of wrong against many people, people from whose lives they have bled their leisure and their luxury!

But Max represents the type of so-called legal defense which the Communist Party and the I.L.D. have been fighting, dating from

Scottsboro. Some of his speech is mystical, unconvincing, and expresses the point of view held not by the Communists but by those reformist betrayers who are being displaced by the Communists. He accepts the idea that Negroes have a criminal psychology as the book erroneously tends to symbolize in Bigger. He does not challenge the false charge of rape against Bigger, though Bigger did not rape Mary, and though this is the eternal bourbon slander flung against Negroes. He does not deal with the heinous murder of Bessie, tending to accept the bourbon policy that crimes of Negroes against each other don't matter and are not cut from the same capitalist cloth.

Worst of all, he pleads Bigger guilty to both rape and murder of Mary, though it was plain that the killing of Mary was accidental. He argues that Bigger, and by implication the whole Negro mass, should be held in jail to protect "white daughters" though capitalism is plainly the guilty criminal which threatens poor white womanhood as well as Negro. He states that Bigger's existence is a "crime against the state," when really the capitalist state is a crime against Bigger. Max should have argued for Bigger's acquittal in the case, and should have helped stir the political pressure of the Negro and white masses to get that acquittal. From Max's whole conduct the first business of the Communist Party or of the I.L.D. would have been to chuck him out of the case.

The difficulty is that the book tries to answer the powerful actions of misguided Bigger, with words instead of with powerful counteractions drawn from life. The defense of the Biggers, of the slum-oppressed Negro people, is primarily the work of the Communist Party among the masses, fighting for decent housing, for jobs, for the organization of the Negro workers into unions, against lynch justice, and for the day to day needs of the Negroes. A Communist is not seen in action in the book—the Communists in life would have been fighting for better conditions for Bigger families, against Dalton's high rentals.

The main center of Communist activity is not in the courts—as indispensably important as that is—but in the communities among the people. The Communists appear to have come into the plot accidentally, and not out of community struggles, as in life. And in presenting only white Communists, the book omits the great role which the Negroes play in the Party—from top to bottom—as the best instrument to fight for the full liberation of their people. What political party in the United States has a Negro leadership? None other save the Communist. To omit this great historic fact, is to permit the misconception that the Communist Party is something "foreign" to the Negro people.

However, in seeking to save Bigger, whom the State prosecutor refers to as a "black thing," the Communist Party in the book was attempting to defend a people all of whom are "black things" to the vicious white ruling class. It is through the taking of his defense by the Communist Party, that Bigger finally gets a ray of understanding, not quite of the Communist Party, but of the fact that his allies include whites as well as blacks who will fight with him against the common capitalist enemy. This is perhaps the meaning of Bigger's last goodbye to Max:

"Tell . . . Tell Mister . . . Tell Jan hello . . ."

Wright has done a brilliant and courageous job, with bold initiative. He, himself, is part of that great progressive Negro mass which is barely suggested in the book. He is an example of the creative genius of the Negro, the ability of an oppressed people to overcome all obstacles. Our Party joins with the Negro people in rejoicing over his magnificent artistry, as a native son of his people and of America. Wright is young, and *Native Son* projects for him a potential future rich in development, and historic in achievement.

Atlantic Monthly

DAVID L. COHN

RICHARD WRIGHT, A MISSISSIPPI-BORN NEGRO, HAS WRITTEN A BLINDING and corrosive study in hate. It is a novel entitled *Native Son.* The race hatred of his hero, Bigger Thomas, is directed with equal malevolence and demoniac intensity toward *all* whites, whether they are Mary Dalton, the moony Negrophile whom he murdered, or the vague white men who seemed to bar his youthful ambition to become an aviator or join the navy. This book has far-reaching qualities of significance above and beyond its considerable virtues as a novel, because Mr. Wright elects to portray his hero not as an individual merely but as a symbol of twelve million American Negroes.

Bigger is very young. His exact age is not stated, but we are told he is too young to vote, and he is therefore under twenty-one. Although his life has hardly begun, his career and hopes for the future have been blasted by the Negro-hating whites of Chicago. On page 14 of *Native Son,* Bigger and his friend Gus are watching an airplane above the city. 'I *could* fly a plane if I had a chance,' Bigger says. 'If you wasn't black and if you had some money and if they'd let you go to that aviation school, you *could* fly a plane,' Gus answers, And time after time, throughout the length of this book, Bigger bitterly complains that he is denied access to the broad, glittering world which the whites monopolize for themselves to the exclusion of Negroes. Toward

---

Reprinted from the *Atlantic Monthly,* CLXV (May 1940), 659–661.

the end of the novel (p. 302), Bigger, in jail for murdering a white girl and his Negro mistress, says: 'I ain't asking nobody to be sorry for me . . . I'm black. *They don't give black people a chance*' (my italics). Bigger's crimes and his fate in the electric chair, the author makes clear to us, are consequently to be laid at the door of white society.

In the speech of Bigger's lawyer at his trial, one finds the fullest summation of Mr. Wright's point of view toward the Negro question in America, and the most explicit statement of his use of Bigger as a symbol of the oppressed Negro. 'This boy,' says lawyer Max, 'represents but a tiny aspect of the problem whose reality sprawls over a third of a nation. . . . Multiply Bigger Thomas twelve million times, allowing for environmental and temperamental variations . . . and you have the psychology of the Negro people. . . . Taken collectively, they are not simply twelve million; in reality they constitute a separate nation, stunted, stripped, and held captive *within* this nation, devoid of political, social, economic and property rights.'

Mr. Wright might have made a more manly and certainly more convincing case for his people if he had stuck to fact. In all of the non-Southern states, Negroes have complete political rights, including the suffrage, and even in the South Negro suffrage is constantly being extended. So powerful, indeed, is the Negro vote, and so solidly is it cast en bloc in Negro-populous Eastern and Midwestern states, that in closely contested Presidential elections the Negro vote may decide who shall become President of the United States. Hence the scramble of both parties for the Negro vote. Nowhere in America save in the most benighted sections of the South, or in times of passion arising from the committing of atrocious crime, is the Negro denied the equal protection of the laws. If he is sometimes put in jail for no reason at all in Memphis, so too are whites put in jail for no reason at all in Pittsburgh. This is the unjust fate, not of the Negro alone, but of the poor, the obscure, and the inarticulate everywhere, regardless of pigmentation. The ownership, also, of more than a billion dollars' worth of property by Negroes in the South alone, and the presence of prosperous Negro business concerns throughout the country, are some refutation of the sweeping statement that Negroes are denied property rights in this country.

Through the mouth of Bigger's lawyer we are told in unmistakable terms that the damming up of the Negro's aspirations, and the denial to him of unrestricted entry into the whole environment of the society in which he is cast, may lead Negroes, in conjunction with others, toward a new civil war in America. Mr. Wright seems to have completely forgotten the unparalleled phenomenon—unique in the world's history—of the *first* American Civil War, in which millions of white men fought and killed one another over the issue of the black slave. If it be granted that the original enslavement of Negroes was a crime against justice, then it must also be granted that its bloody expiation was filled with enough death and destruction to satisfy even the most hate-consumed Negro. But it doesn't seem to satisfy Mr. Wright. A second civil war must begin where the first one left off in order to bring about the eventual freeing of the Negro minority, even if it means the destruction of the society of the majority. Justice and understanding are to come through the persuasive snouts of machine guns.

Bigger's lawyer is a Jew. As a member of a race which has known something of oppression,—not for three centuries, the length of the Negro's residence in America, but for more than twenty centuries in nearly every country of the world,—he pleads extenuation for his client both on broad grounds of justice and on the ground that white society drove Bigger to crime by repressing him. If repression of the members of a minority drives them to slay members of the majority, it would follow that the principal occupation of Jews in Tsarist Russia, Poland, Rumania, and other bitterly anti-Semitic countries would have been to use their oppressors as clay pigeons. Jewish revolutionists there have been, indeed, but over the whole sweep of two thousand years of dark Jewish history the mass of these people, enduring greater oppression than Negroes knew here even in slavery, created within the walls of their ghettos an intense family and communal life and constructed inexhaustible wells of spiritual resource. They used their talents and energies as best they could, serene in the belief either that a Messiah would ultimately come and deliver them out of bondage into the Promised Land or that justice would ultimately triumph. Mr. Wright uses a Jewish lawyer as his mouthpiece, but he has learned nothing from Jewish history, nor gleaned anything of the spirit of that group whom Tacitus called 'a stubborn people.'

It is beyond doubt that Negroes labor under grave difficulties in America; that economic and social discrimination is practised against them; that opportunities open to whites are closed to blacks. It is also beyond doubt that the position, if not the status, of the Negro is constantly improving in the United States. The evidence on this point is overwhelming. But there is one hard and inescapable fact which must be courageously faced. The social structure of America, despite many racial admixtures, is Anglo-Saxon. And nowhere on earth—save in isolated instances—do whites and Negroes in Anglo-Saxon communities intermingle socially or intermarry. And so long as this is a fact, neither the Negro—and this is what completely escapes Mr. Wright—*nor the white man* will function as a full-fledged personality. It could easily be demonstrated that Southern whites living in the presence of masses of Negroes, and maintaining at least tolerable racial relations through the exercise of exquisite, intuitive tact on both sides, suffer aberrations and distortions of the spirit only slightly less severe than those suffered by Negroes.

It is no fault of the Negro or of the present generation of whites that the Negro is here. But the preaching of Negro hatred of whites by

Mr. Wright is on a par with the preaching of white hatred of Negroes by the Ku Klux Klan. The position, moreover, of a minority struggling toward the sun must be gauged at any given time by its relative rather than its absolute state, and in accordance with this postulate it is clear that the Negro's lot in America is constantly being ameliorated.

It is highly significant of the whole hate-headlong point of view of Mr. Wright that he has chosen to make his hero so hopelessly despairing of making a good life for himself because of white repressions, that he drives him to crime and execution when his adult life has hardly begun. Contrast this with the experience of the Jews in England, who were first granted full civil rights only after five centuries of living in the country.

Mr. Wright obviously does not have the long view of history. He wants not only complete political rights for his people, but also social equality, and he wants them now. Justice demands that every right granted to others shall be granted to Negroes, but men are not gods. A hard-headed people will be conscious of the Pauline law of expediency: 'All things are lawful unto me, but all things are not expedient.'

Justice or no justice, the whites of America simply will not grant to Negroes at this time those things that Mr. Wright demands. The Negro problem in America is actually insoluble; all profound, complex social problems are insoluble, and only a politically naïve people will believe otherwise. In the meanwhile, recognition by both sides that the question is insoluble, followed by tempered, sincere efforts to make the best of the situation within its frame of reference, will produce the most equitable results for both. Hatred, and the preaching of hatred, and incitement to violence can only make a tolerable relationship intolerable.

Even Abraham Lincoln did not envisage a time when the Negro question would be solved upon Mr. Wright's terms. In 1862 he said to a Negro delegation who called on him:

> You and we are different races. . . . But even when you cease to be slaves you are yet far from being placed on an equality with the white race. . . . The aspiration of men is to enjoy equality with the best when free, but on this continent not a single man of your race is made the equal of a single man of ours. . . . Go where you are treated best, and the ban is still upon you.

And Mr. Wright's hero kills and dies in Mr. Lincoln's state of Illinois.

I Bite the Hand That Feeds Me

RICHARD WRIGHT

I WANT TO REPLY TO MR. DAVID L. COHN, WHOSE ARTICLE CRITICIZED MY novel, *Native Son,* in the May issue of the *Atlantic Monthly.* In the eyes of the average white American reader, his article made it more difficult for a Negro (child of slaves and savages!) to answer a cultured Jew (who had two thousand years of oppression to recommend him in giving advice to other unfortunates!) than an American white. Indeed, Mr. Cohn writes as though he were recommending his 'two thousand years of oppression' to the Negroes of America! No, thank you, Mr. Cohn. I don't think that we Negroes are going to have to go through with it. We might perish in the attempt to avoid it; if so, then death as men is better than two thousand years of ghetto life and seven years of Herr Hitler.

The Negro problem in America is *not* beyond solution. (I write from a country—Mexico—where people of all races and colors live in harmony and without racial prejudices or theories of racial superiority. Whites and Indians live and work and die here, always resisting the attempts of Anglo-Saxon tourists and industrialists to introduce racial hate and discrimination.) Russia has solved the problem of the Jews and that of all her other racial and national minorities. Probably the Soviet solution is not to Mr. Cohn's liking, but I think it is to the liking of the Jews in Russia and Biro-Bidjan. I accept the Russian solution. I am proletarian and Mr. Cohn is bourgeois; we live on different planes of social reality, and we see Russia differently.

'He [Wright] wants not only complete political rights for his people, but also social equality, and he wants them now.' Certainly I want them now. And what's wrong with my wanting them now? What guarantee have we Negroes, if we were 'expedient' for five hundred years, that America would extend to us a certificate stating that we were civilized? I am proud to declaim—as proud as Mr. Cohn is of his two thousand years of oppression—that at no time in the history of American politics has a Negro stood for anything but the untrammeled rights of human personality, *his* and *others.*

Mr. Cohn implies that as a writer I should look at the state of the Negro through the lens of relativity, and not judge his plight in an

---

Reprinted from the *Atlantic Monthly,* CLXV (June 1940), 826–828.

absolute sense. That is precisely what, as an artist, I try *not* to do. My character, Bigger Thomas, lives and suffers in the real world. Feeling and perception, from moment to moment, are absolute, and if I dodged my responsibility as an artist and depicted them as otherwise I'd be a traitor, not to my race alone, but to *humanity*. An artist deals with aspects of reality different from those which a scientist sees. My task is not to abstract reality, but to enhance its value. In the process of objectifying emotional experience in words—paint, stone, or tone—an artist uses his feelings in an immediate and absolute sense. To ask a writer to deny the validity of his sensual perceptions is to ask him to be 'expedient' enough to commit spiritual suicide for the sake of politicians. And that I'll *never* consent to do. No motive of 'expediency' can compel me to elect to justify the ways of white America to the Negro; rather, my task is to weigh the effects of our civilization upon the personality, as it affects it *here* and *now*. If, in my weighing of those effects, I reveal rot, pus, filth, hate, fear, guilt, and degenerate forms of life, must I be consigned to hell? (Yes, Bigger Thomas hated, but he hated because he *feared*. Carefully, Mr. Cohn avoided all mention of that fact. Or does Mr. Cohn feel that the 'exquisite, intuitive' treatment of the Negro in America does not inspire fear?) I wrote *Native Son* to show what manner of men and women our 'society of the majority' breeds, and my aim was to depict a character in terms of the living tissue and texture of daily consciousness. And who is responsible for his feelings, anyway?

Mr. Cohn, my view of history tells me this: *Only the strong are free*. Might may not make right, but there is no 'right' nation without might. That may sound cynical, but it is nevertheless true. If the Jew has suffered for two thousand years, then it is mainly because of his religion and his other-worldliness, and he has only himself to blame. The Jew had a choice, just as the Negro in America has one. We Negroes prefer to take the hint of that great Jewish revolutionist, Karl Marx, and look soberly upon the facts of history, and organize, ally ourselves, and fight it out. Having helped to build the 'society of the majority,' we Negroes are not so dazzled by its preciousness that we consider it something holy and beyond attack. We know our weakness and we know our strength, and we are not going to fight America *alone*. We are not so naïve as that. The Negro in America became politically mature the moment he realized that he could not fight the 'society of the majority' alone and organized the National Negro Congress and threw its weight behind John L. Lewis and the CIO!

I urge my race to become strong through *alliances*, by joining in common cause with other oppressed groups (and there are a lot of them in America, Mr. Cohn!), workers, *sensible* Jews, farmers, declassed intellectuals, and so forth. I urge them to master the techniques of political, social, and economic struggle and cast their lot with the millions in the world today who are fighting for freedom, crossing national and racial boundaries if necessary.

The unconscious basis upon which most whites excuse Negro

oppression is as follows: (1) the Negro did not have a culture when he was brought here; (2) the Negro was physically inferior and susceptible to diseases; (3) the Negro did not resist his enslavement. These three falsehoods have been woven into an ideological and moral principle to justify whatever America wants to do with the Negro, and, whether Mr. Cohn realizes it or not, they enable him to say 'the Negro problem in America is actually insoluble.'

But there is not one ounce of history or science to support oppression based upon these assumptions.

The Negro (just as the Mexican Indian today) possessed a rich and complex culture when he was brought to these alien shores. He resisted oppression. And the Negro, instead of being physically weak, is tough and has withstood hardships that have cracked many another people. This, too, is history. Does it sound strange that American historians have distorted or omitted hundreds of records of slave revolts in America?

We Negroes have no religion that teaches us that we are 'God's chosen people'; our sorrows cannot be soothed with such illusions. What culture we did have when we were torn from Africa was taken from us; we were separated when we were brought here and forbidden to speak our languages. We possess no remembered cushion of culture upon which we can lay our tired heads and dream of our superiority. We are driven by the nature of our position in this country into the thick of the struggle, whether we like it or not.

In *Native Son* I tried to show that a man, bereft of a culture and unanchored by property, can travel but one path if he reacts positively but unthinkingly to the prizes and goals of civilization; and that one path is emotionally blind rebellion. In *Native Son* I did not defend Bigger's actions; I explained them through depiction. And what alarms Mr. Cohn is not what I say Bigger *is*, but what I say *made* him what he is. Yes, white boys commit crimes, too. But would Mr. Cohn deny that the social pressure upon Negro boys is far greater than that upon white boys? And how does it materially alter the substance of my book if white boys do commit murder? Does not Mr. Cohn remember the Jewish boy who shot the Nazi diplomat in Paris a year or two ago? No Jewish revolutionist egged that boy to do that crime. Did not the Soviet officials, the moment they came into power, have to clean up the roaming bands of Jewish and Gentile youth who lived outside of society by crime, youth spawned by the Czar's holy belief that social, racial, and economic problems were 'actually insoluble'?

Now, let me analyze more closely just how much and what kind of hate is in *Native Son*. Loath as I am to do this, I have no choice. Mr. Cohn's article, its tone and slant, convince me more than anything else that I was *right* in the way I handled Negro life in *Native Son*. Mr. Cohn says that the burden of my book was a preachment of hate against the white races. It was not. No *advocacy* of hate is in that book. *None!* I wrote as objectively as I could of a Negro boy who hated and feared whites, hated them because he feared them. What

Mr. Cohn mistook for my advocacy of hate in that novel was something entirely different. In every word of that book are *confidence, resolution,* and the *knowledge* that the Negro problem can and will be solved *beyond* the frame of reference of thought such as that found in Mr. Cohn's article.

Further in his article Mr. Cohn says that I do not understand that oppression has harmed whites as well as Negroes. Did I not have my character, Britten, exhibit through page after page the aberrations of whites who suffer from oppression? Or, God forbid, does Mr. Cohn *agree* with Britten? Did I not make the mob as hysterical as Bigger Thomas? Did I not ascribe the hysteria to the same origins? The entire long scene in the furnace room is but a depiction of how warped the whites have become through their oppression of Negroes. If there had been *one* person in the Dalton household who viewed Bigger Thomas as a human being, the crime would have been solved in half an hour. Did not Bigger himself know that it was the denial of his personality that enabled him to escape detection so long? The one piece of incriminating evidence which would have solved the 'murder mystery' was Bigger's humanity, and the Daltons, Britten, and the newspaper men could not see or admit the living clue of Bigger's humanity under their very eyes! More than two thirds of *Native Son* is given over to depicting the very thing which Mr. Cohn claims 'completely escapes' me. I wonder how much of my book escaped *him.*

Mr. Cohn says that Bigger's age is not stated. It is. Bigger himself tells his age on page 42. On page 348 it is stated again in the official death sentence.

Mr. Cohn wonders why I selected a Negro *boy* as my protagonist. To any writer of fiction, or anyone acquainted with the creative process, the answer is simple. Youth is the turning point in life, the most sensitive and volatile period, the state that registers most vividly the impressions and experiences of life; and an artist likes to work with sensitive material.

Catholic World

REVEREND JOSEPH MCSORLEY

THIS BOOK-OF-THE-MONTH CLUB STORY—WHOLLY FICTITIOUS—DESCRIBES the criminal career of a psychopathic Negro youth who has been stunted mentally and morally by the environment in which White America forces the members of his race to live; and most of the book

Reprinted from the *Catholic World,* CLI (May 1940), 243–244. Reprinted by permission of the publisher.

is taken up with the thoughts and impulses provoked in Bigger Thomas by endless repression and frustration. He is bestial, treacherous, utterly unlovable, with no redeeming trait—a typical product of the policy which wealthy, cultured, liberty-loving America has consistently pursued in dealing with the Blacks. Barring obscurities and exaggerations, the author's work has been well done to this extent that he gives us a striking and, indeed, a profoundly moving picture. What purpose he had in mind, however, the reader will find it difficult to surmise.

The story will impress reasonable people with an acute sense of our common responsibility for the present condition of the Negro in America. But that impression might much better have been produced by some other means. In so far as this tale may be taken to represent actual conditions, it will have the effect of spreading and deepening distrust of the Negro. Granted that our society is criminally responsible for having taken an attitude toward the black man which tends to turn him into a savage moron, brooding on his wrongs, merely waiting his chance to rape and kill—and there is at least some truth in this assumption—what is the logical deduction? First of all of course that we should acknowledge our guilt and then undertake to co-operate intelligently with the Negro in his attempt to rise to a higher level. But meanwhile, what? Why if Mr. Wright's description is true to life, then every healthy young Negro male must be regarded with justifiable suspicion and carefully barred from the opportunities of crime which are open to the average American citizen. In a word, the argument has been carried far too far.

It was easy to see that this book would be a best seller. Immediately its transcendental merits were proclaimed by that chorus of critics who in respect of faultless timing and perfect unison are superior even to a symphony orchestra. Nevertheless, discriminating people will regard the book as a wordy presentation of a familiar, irrefutable thesis. Wordy because something like 360 pages lie between the prospective reader and the last line of the book. And not capable of refutation, because our treatment of the Negro has been obviously as unintelligent as it has been brutal and the futile throwing of crumbs from the tables of well-meaning white people easily produces new misery and new crime. Incidentally, the wholly admirable character in Mr. Wright's cast is the Communist lawyer Max, and the sole hope of lasting improvement for the Negro is contained in Mr. Max's program.

American Mercury

BURTON RASCOE

CONCERNING NO NOVEL IN RECENT TIMES, WITH THE POSSIBLE EXCEPTION of *The Grapes of Wrath,* have the reviewers in general displayed a more utterly juvenile confusion of values than they have shown in their ecstatic appraisal of Richard Wright's *Native Son.* The only way I can account for the cataclysmic impact this novel made upon their brains is by deducing that they have kept themselves virginally aloof from the sort of reading which daily gives millions of us the stimulation and catharsis of pity and terror in the tabloids and in the magazine fiction professionally described as the "pulps." To this may be added the further deduction that, so hysterical have the strains of the times made many of us, these good people, the reviewers, go easily haywire about anything which looks to them like a social document exposing "conditions."

Sanely considered, it is impossible for me to conceive of a novel's being worse, in the most important respects, than *Native Son.* It has many technical excellences. They are such as any Street & Smith editor would applaud, or as Walter B. Pitkin, in his writing classes at Columbia, would grade as A-1. But the editors for Street & Smith, and Mr. Pitkin, would probably say very sensibly that there are faults in this novel which even a tyro in fiction should not be guilty of. Let me enumerate some of them:

(1) If there is a moral message to be emphasized, that message should be made implicit in the consistent action and dialogue of the novel. It should not be in the form of a running commentary by the author, particularly not when the author is very confused about what he wants to prove.

(2) If a character is conceived as being inarticulate and dumb about the economic and social forces which have (in your mind) been responsible for his social and moral delinquency, it is an artistic error to portray that character, at times, as being fully conscious of the "conditions" which have mentally and emotionally crippled him. It is an elementary principle not only of art but of moral law, of legal principle, and of common sense, that, if you are aware of yourself and of the factors under which you live, you are, *yourself,* responsible for what you do and you must accept that responsibility. Mr. Wright has

---

Reprinted from the *American Mercury,* L (May 1940), 113–116.

Bigger Thomas, the hero of his story, commit two murders on the appalling theory that he is justified in so doing because, as ecstatic reviewers assure us, "he knows religion as something meant to lull people into submission" and because Bigger feels "powerless and afraid of the white world, which exploits, condescends to, and in turn fears the race it has segregated." (The quotes are, respectively, from Milton Rugoff in the New York *Herald Tribune* and Margaret Marshall in the *Nation.*)

(3) It is a violation of a fundamental esthetic principle—sanctioned from Aristotle on down—to portray a character in speech, thought or action in a way not consistent with what you, the writer, might conceivably do in similar circumstances and in similar conditions.

Recently I witnessed a *reductio ad absurdum* of Mr. Wright's fundamental thesis in *Native Son.* Mr. Wright was a luncheon guest, in New York, of a club whose membership comprises men who have achieved a degree of importance in the creative arts—writers, musicians, painters, illustrators, engineers, editors, etc. Mr. Wright was introduced eulogistically by Mr. William Chenery, editor of *Collier's,* who dwelt upon the young novelist's accomplishment as a writer who had achieved best-sellerdom. There was no reference, condescending or otherwise, to the guest's color.

Mr. Wright had been told that, as the club's guest, he need not make any speech unless he felt like doing so. He is a handsome young man; his face is fine, kind and intelligent. It was a spontaneous tribute to him and to the success he had attained that the club gave him an ovation such as it has rarely given to anyone but artists like Pablo Casals and Jascha Heifetz. Mr. Wright was, on this occasion (though he may not have realized it), an embodied refutation of his theme in *Native Son.* He was the only black man there, surrounded by white people. Yet they were all rejoicing in his success, eager to do him honor—even if there were many, of course, who had not read his book.

They were not, even unconsciously, trying to make things so difficult for Mr. Wright that he would have artistic or any other justification if he should choose to murder the first two debutantes he met after leaving the luncheon. Mr. Wright must have had some intimations of this anomaly—this contrast between himself and his fictional hero—when he arose to speak. In response to the spontaneous acclaim, he got up to say a few words. He was doubtless confused and embarrassed. Good writers, and Mr. Wright in his best vein is decidedly good, are rarely good speakers. He faltered, as most of us do who have not been trained to speak in public, and in his confusion he said, with the nicest air of camaraderie—as if to say "Come up and see me some time": "I hope you will all have a chance to meet Bigger Thomas."

I don't know what others who had read *Native Son* felt about the author's hope, but I for one shuddered. Bigger Thomas, in the novel, is a murderer because (so his creator tells us) he resents the white race. Bigger murders a rich white girl who is sentimentally interested in "the Negro problem" and whose family has contributed millions to alleviate conditions among the poor in the Negro quarters of Chicago. Bigger also murders his Negro mistress. He indulges in this slaughter not because of anything these poor, misguided women, white and black, have done to him, since they haven't harmed him at all, but because (Mr. Wright argues) all of us who happen to have white skins instead of black have made Bigger what he is.

In the midst of the hurrahing I rise to assert that I think the moral in *Native Son* is utterly loathsome and utterly insupportable as a "message." When I carefully examine all the evidence Mr. Wright offers to prove that Bigger Thomas should have become a murderer and that the guilt lies on our own heads, I remain emphatically unconvinced. I can't see that Bigger Thomas had anything more to contend with, in childhood and youth, than I had or than dozens of my friends had. Their lives and mine have not been velvety but we do not want to kill people because of this. And I have known fine priests, fine rabbis, fine Protestant ministers (black and white) whose "conditional environment" was even worse than this "conditional environment" which Mr. Wright would have us believe makes murderers out of Negro men.

Mr. Wright is as much an American as you are or I am. We Americans are constitutionally for the underdog, so long as it does not seriously interfere with the business at hand of getting along. It is quite the thing now, among our intellectuals, to contend that whites have given the Negroes a dirty deal, forgetting that whites have given themselves a dirty deal also. These intellectuals deplore Hitler, Stalin and Mussolini on psychopathic grounds, but they are unable to see that by their own logic Bigger Thomas is just a small-scale Negro Hitler. Or a Negro Stalin or Mussolini. The partiality of these dictators for bloodletting also can be traced to conditional environment. If I am supposed to start grieving over what I have done to Hitler and Stalin in their hard early life, I won't take any.

And the same applies to Bigger. This is also to serve notice that despite all the eloquence Bigger's lawyer and Wright's reviewers bring to Bigger's defense, if I were on the jury I would vote to hang Bigger. Bigger, I have been amply convinced, wouldn't hesitate two minutes to shoot me or his lawyer or his author, even if we were going about business and paying him no mind. I don't like the idea of being shot, even fictionally, just because my color is not like Bigger's. I wouldn't like it even if I knew that all the Bigger Thomases think I am somehow responsible because life hasn't been cushy for them. I'm just unreasonable in these matters of murder, where I'm the murderee.

Mr. Wright, one may note, is doing very well. A lot of white writers with talent doubtless are wishing they were making as much money as he is making. But they are not envious of him, nor do they begrudge his success in the least. They hope he prospers. For myself, I hope that now he has got *Native Son* out of his system, he will use his talents to more sensible ends. He is one of the two writers, white or black, who have ever had the ear to catch and transliterate Negro speech correctly. The other writer is Louis Paul, who is white.

Rascoe-Baiting

RICHARD WRIGHT

SIR:

Mr. Burton Rascoe's review of my book, *Native Son,* under the heading *Negro Novel and White Reviewers,* certainly introduces some brand new and unheard of principles into American literary criticism. What in God's name has "He is a handsome young man; his face is fine and intelligent . . ." got to do with the merits or shortcomings of a novel? I had hoped that the *Mercury*'s review of *Native Son* would be as objective as my treatment of Bigger, but I suppose that's hoping for too much from the *Mercury* these days.

Mr. Rascoe hopes that now, with *Native Son* out of my system, I'll give some sweetness and light. No, not yet. I'll be dishing out this for quite some time to come. Understated in Mr. Rascoe's review is this attitude: "Why in the world does a Negro writer want to bother with such stuff when he can write differently and be liked for it and paid for it?" The answer is simply this: I don't choose to. I prefer to write out of the background of my experience in an imaginative fashion. I don't prefer to streamline my stuff to what the public will like. It is no fault of mine that *Native Son* is selling; it was not written to sell, but to convey in terms of words an American-Negro experience of life. Too often when a Negro writes something which wins a prize, or sells, and which carries in it a note of protest, a white reviewer rises to ask: "What is he yelling about? He's making money, isn't he?" Has the *Mercury* fallen that low?

Following his personal line, Mr. Rascoe implied that I tried to insult the members of the Dutch Treat Club. What rot! I don't think a single person in that audience misunderstood my remarks (not a speech!) to the extent that Mr. Rascoe did. When I attended that luncheon my book had been off the press for about two weeks; I knew that very few of those present had read it. I took the occasion to remark that I hoped that they would meet Bigger Thomas if they had the time; that is, I expressed my hope that they would read the book. Only a "Negro-baiter" could twist such a statement and make it mean something else.

As an artist I reserve the right to depict the actions of people I do not agree with, Aristotle to the contrary! After reading Mr. Rascoe's review, I wondered why he did not reprint Buckley's speech and let it stand as his view; it would have been more clean-cut and honest. Yes; while writing the book I realized that Max's speech would be "utterly loathsome" to many people. That is why Max said:

> Of all things, men do not like to feel that they are guilty of wrong, and if you make them feel guilty, they will try desperately to justify it on any grounds; but failing that, and seeing no immediate solution that will set things right without too much cost to their lives and property, they will kill that which evoked in them the condemning sense of guilt. . . .

Does not this fall in line with Mr. Rascoe's statement that "We Americans are constitutionally for the underdog, so long as it does not seriously interfere with the business at hand of getting along"? I know that and that is why I wrote as I did. Max's speech anticipated every point raised by Mr. Rascoe. Read the book again, Mr. Rascoe, and pay close attention to Max's speech, which was directed toward men of your attitude. And remember that the author wrote that book, in the words of Max, as "a test symbol" to determine if 100 per cent Americans would feel "utterly loathsome" when confronted with one of their own historical mistakes! *Mr. Rascoe ran true to form!*

RICHARD WRIGHT

(Note: *Nowhere in his review did Mr. Rascoe imply that this novelist "insulted" anyone. Neither can we find in it the remotest suggestion of "Negro-baiting."*—Editor, *American Mercury*)

Opportunity

STERLING A. BROWN

A BOOK-OF-THE-MONTH CLUB SELECTION, ITS FIRST EDITION SOLD OUT within three hours, a quarter million copies called for within six weeks, Richard Wright's *Native Son* is a literary phenomenon. Magazines have run articles about it after the first reviews. It is discussed by literary

---

From *Opportunity*. Reprinted by permission of the author.

critics, scholars, social workers, journalists, writers to the editor, preachers, students, and the man in the street. It seems important to the reviewer that debates on *Native Son* may be heard in grills and "juke-joints" as well as at "literary" parties, in the deep South as well as in Chicago, among people who have not bothered much to read novels since Ivanhoe was assigned in high school English.

One commentator writes that the book "has torn the surface veneer from a condition which is awakening the conscience of the entire nation." Only the future can decide whether the revelations in *Native Son* awaken the conscience of the nation; according to history that conscience is not easily aroused. But, if such a great and difficult task could be achieved by a single book, *Native Son* is that book.

Richard Wright is, of course, not the first Negro to compound bitterness and wisdom eloquently, nor the first to see the terrible effects of frustration. He is the first, however, to give a psychological probing of the consciousness of the outcast, the disinherited, the generation lost in the slum jungles of American civilization. Mr. Wright has urged that novelists should have perspective and an integrated vision of their material. In *Native Son* he gives such a philosophical novel. With a narrative skill all of his own, with what he has elsewhere called "the potential cunning to steal into the inmost recesses of the human heart," with a surprising mastery of the techniques of fiction, tested in the past as well as the present, Mr. Wright has struck with tremendous impact. Earlier writers have likewise struck out; sometimes their blows were powerful; sometimes they were scattered, or glanced off, or missed altogether.

In one of Mr. Wright's short stories, Big Boy left "home"—a community in the deep South where white violence erupted spasmodically and where Negroes lived in a slow paralysis of fear. In Chicago Bigger meets with forces as destructive, but unlike Big Boy, he cannot leave this home. Daily, as with so many of his fellows on the Southside, or in Harlem, or in Philadelphia, Washington, Atlanta, Birmingham—wherever you choose by insult, indignity, and injury, now petty, now gross, always constant—the iron is driven into Bigger's soul. The first scene, where Bigger and Buddy corner a rat and smash it with a skillet, sets the tone for the grim sequence. *Native Son* would be distinguished if for no other reason than the social realism with which Chicago's Southside is presented. Here are the rickety "kitchenette" flats, which produce such exorbitant returns for the realtors' little investment that the human wastage does not count. Here are the dives, the poolrooms, the ineffectual boys' clubs where crimes are planned. The crushed products of this environment—although slightly sketched, for Bigger gets the lion's share—are quite convincing: Bigger's gang of Jack, G. H., and Gus; Buddy the brother (the last two are brilliantly characterized); the tragic kid Vera, sensitive to the quick, gentle-hearted and doomed; Mrs. Thomas who seeks escape through religion but cannot find it there; and Bigger's sweetheart Bessie: "She worked long hours, hard and hot hours seven days a week, with only Sunday afternoons off; and when she did get off she wanted fun, hard and fast fun, something to make her feel that she was making up for the starved life she led."

The narrative drive of this novel from the killing of the rat, through the two murders, the flight, to the capture on the tenement roof is amazing. In contrast, the last section slows down. This is to be expected, but there is likewise some repetitiousness. *Native Son* is naturally compared to Dreiser's *An American Tragedy*, but there are great differences, and one of these involves technique. A naturalist, Dreiser piles detail upon detail to gain verisimilitude; but Wright, seeking truth to a reality beyond naturalism, makes use of the devices of the symbolic novel, as do such writers as Steinbeck, Faulkner, Caldwell and Dos Passos. He compresses a great deal in small space and time: for instance, a philanthropist interested in Negro education, a politician riding to power on Negro baiting, representatives of a sensational press, the overzealous young Communist Jan, and Mary, the victim of the accidental murder; the older, more understanding Communist lawyer, Max, a Negro preacher; these and other symbolic personages cross Bigger's tragic path. With so much compression, verisimilitude is sometimes sacrificed. The hiding of the girl's body, the delay in discovering the crime, the ease with which the kidnapping note is delivered are details not completely convincing. From melodrama (even though of such a high order) some losses are as inevitable as the sure gains.

But Mr. Wright's greatest achievement is not his description of a setting, as revelatory as that is, nor his conduct of narrative, as thrilling as that is, but his characterization of Bigger Thomas. It took courage to select as hero, a wastrel, a sneak thief, a double-killer. Most writers of minority groups select as heroes those who disprove stereotypes. Here is the "bad nigger" set down without squeamishness, doing all that the "bad nigger" is supposed to do. But that is merely the start. Mr. Wright sees all around this "bad nigger" and through him, and we get the interpretative realism that shows how inevitable it was that he should get that way. Here in brief compass we see a youngster who could have been, should have been, so much more, stunted and twisted into a psychopathic hater, feeling free and important only after a murder, exercising his new power in concocting a kidnapping plot absurdly fashioned after the movies which, with the poolrooms, were his chief educators. Mr. Wright uses more than once the symbol of the rat, now cornered, now dashing into a hole, and Bigger's concept of the meeting ground between whites and Negroes as a No Man's Land. "What can I do? They got me," he asked. He knew that they had had him for a long time.

The lawyer, Max, in a profound speech (less a courtroom plea for life imprisonment than a philosophical statement of the tragic race problem) says: "Multiply Bigger Thomas twelve million times, allowing for environmental and temperamental variations, and for those

Negroes who are completely under the influence of the church, and you have the psychology of the Negro people." Max's statement is considered to be Richard Wright's. If this point is debated one should give full weight to the words: "allowing for environmental and temperamental variations." David Cohn in the current *Atlantic Monthly* considers *Native Son* "a blinding and corrosive study in hate," and lectures the author, reminding him of the Civil War "in which millions of white men fought and killed one another over the issue of the black slaves." This seems to miss the point of the novel, especially the fine closing. Other critics disagree with Mr. Cohn; Henry Seidel Canby in the Book-of-the-Month Club News, for instance, says that "this is not a vindictive book." Among so much else, Mr. Wright has established authentically and powerfully that hatred exists among the kicked around, the dispossessed. It is a further indication of the Negro's position in America that this inevitable fact, known so well by Negroes, recorded often by social scientists but never before so forcefully by our creative writers, has caused such perturbation. *Native Son* should silence many of the self-appointed white "interpreters" of the Negro, who, writing from a vantage (?) point above and outside of the race, reveal the Negro as one peculiarly endowed to bear the burdens and suffer the shame without rancor, without bitterness, and without essential humanity.

PART THREE: CRITICAL ESSAYS

The Ballad of Bigger Thomas

E. CURMIE PRICE

Bigger than your doubt, Thomas,
the sensible world beats its head
against city streets, trying
to make sense of your existential act.

Now that we're talking debts,
let's admit it; Camus' Meursault
owes something to Wright's Thomas,
who taught them *all* the exaltation
of violence in a contingent world.

Oh yes, yes; I've heard of Sartre,
Genet, and the absurd; just yesterday,
however, lost in Native Son, I had put
my fist through a gray world before I knew it.

Call it instinct, mammoth expectations.
Bigger Thomas rides again along
the tributes of my thoughts.

Native Son: The Personal, Social, and Political Background

KENETH KINNAMON

IN THE FICTION OF SOCIAL PROTEST, OF WHICH RICHARD WRIGHT'S *Native Son* (1940) is surely an outstanding example, the *donnée* has an interest almost equal to that of the artistic treatment. If the concern is with the relation of literature to society, one must not be content merely to grant the novelist his materials and concentrate on his fictional technique; one must examine carefully the factual substance on which the novelist's imagination operates. If this task is preliminary to literary criticism in the strict sense, it is necessary if that criticism is not to be impressionistic or narrowly aesthetic. An examination of Wright's fiction reveals that customarily he drew from personal experience and observation, the condition of the society about him, and his theoretic concerns. In *Native Son*, these elements may be identified respectively as certain episodes in Wright's life in Mississippi and Chicago, the social circumstances of urban Negroes and the Nixon trial, and Communist ideology.

Charles I. Glicksberg is speaking hyperbolically when he asserts that "Richard Wright is Bigger Thomas—one part of him anyway. Bigger Thomas is what Richard Wright, had circumstances worked out differently, might have become."[1] Nevertheless, there is some truth in the assertion, and not merely in the general sense, according to the formulation of James Baldwin, that "no American Negro exists who does not have his private Bigger Thomas living in the skull."[2] The general similarities between Wright at the age of twenty and the fictional protagonist of *Native Son* are obvious enough: both are Mississippi-born Negroes who migrated to Chicago; both live with their mother in the worst slums of the Black Belt of that city; both are

[1] "The Furies in Negro Fiction," *The Western Review*, XIII (Winter, 1949), 110.

[2] "Many Thousands Gone," *Partisan Review*, XVIII (November–December, 1951), 678. This essay is reprinted in James Baldwin, *Notes of a Native Son* (Boston, 1955), pp. 24–45.

From *Phylon*, XXX (Spring 1969), 66–72. Reprinted by permission.

motivated by fear and hatred; both are rebellious by temperament; both could explode into violence.

More specific likenesses were recovered from Wright's subconscious by Dr. Frederic Wertham, the eminent psychiatrist. When Wright, as a boy of fifteen, worked for a white family named Bibbs in Jackson, Mississippi, his duties included chopping wood, carrying coal, and tending the fire. The pretty young daughter of the family generally was kind to him within the limits of Southern custom, but when, on one occasion, he chanced upon her in her bedroom while she was dressing, "she reprimanded him and told him to knock before entering a room." The diffident and fearful young Negro handyman, the amiable white girl, the sexually significant situation—these elements, transmuted, found their way into *Native Son*. The name of the wealthy white family for whom Bigger works in the novel, *Dalton*, may itself bear an unconscious symbolic import. In the Chicago hospital where he worked as an orderly in 1931, Wright learned of Daltonism.[3] In their fashion, the Daltons in the novel strive toward color blindness, though they fall tragically short of achieving it.

Essentially, Bigger Thomas is a conscious composite portrait of a number of individual Negroes Wright had observed over the years. In that remarkable exercise in self-examination, *How "Bigger" Was Born*, Wright sketched five such Bigger prototypes he had known in the South. All of them were rebellious defiers of the jim crow order, and all of them suffered for their insurgency: "They were shot, hanged, maimed, lynched, and generally hounded until they were either dead or their spirits broken." In Chicago, especially when Wright worked at the South Side Boys' Club in the middle thirties, he observed other examples of the Bigger Thomas type—fearful, restless, moody, frustrated, alienated, violent youths struggling for survival in the urban jungle.[4]

The slum conditions of the South Side so vividly portrayed in *Native Son* had been the daily reality of a decade in Wright's life (1927–1937). He had lived in a cramped and dirty flat with his aunt, mother, and brother. He had visited hundreds of similar dwellings while working as an insurance agent.[5] The details of the Chicago

[3] Waldemar Kaempffert, "Science in Review: An Author's Mind Plumbed for the Unconscious Factor in the Creation of a Novel," *The New York Times*, September 24, 1944, Sec. 4, p. 11. This article asserts that the Bibbs girl loaned Wright money for his junior high school graduation suit, but Wright's autobiographical *Black Boy: A Record of Childhood and Youth* (New York, 1945) says that her mother did so (p. 156). Dr. Wertham comments briefly on his experiment with Wright in "The Dreams That Heal," his introduction to *The World Within: Fiction Illuminating Neuroses of Our Time*, ed. by Mary Louise Aswell (New York, 1947), xxi.

[4] *How "Bigger" Was Born* (New York, 1940), pp. 6, 28–29. See also Wright's pamphlet *The Negro and Parkway Community House* (Chicago, 1941).

[5] The main source for this period of the novelist's life is Richard Wright, "Early Days in Chicago," *Cross-Section 1945*, ed. by Edwin Seaver (New York,

environment in the novel have a verisimilitude that is almost photographic. The "Ernie's Kitchen Shack" of the novel, located at Forty-Seventh Street and Indiana Avenue, for example, is a slight disguise for an actual restaurant called "The Chicken Shack," 4647 Indiana Avenue, of which one Ernie Henderson was owner.[6] Similar documentary accuracy is observed throughout the book.

Aside from wide personal experience, moreover, Wright was becoming increasingly more interested in sociology at the time he was writing *Native Son*. The caseworker for the Wright family in Chicago was Mary Wirth, the wife of Louis Wirth of the University of Chicago, who was in the process of conducting an enormous research project on the urban ecology of the city. In Wirth's office Wright examined the files of the project and met Horace R. Cayton, a Negro research associate who was himself to become a distinguished sociologist and a warm friend of the novelist.[7] Sociological concepts, quite as much as Marxist theories, are apparent in the novel, especially in the final part.

In New York, too, where he moved in May, 1937, Wright became intimately acquainted with the conditions of Negro ghettos. Not only did he live for almost a year in Harlem, but as a participant in the Federal Writers' Project of New York City, he wrote the Harlem sections of *New York Panorama* (1938) and *New York City Guide* (1939), two volumes in the American Guide Series. He also served during the last five months of 1937 as chief Harlem correspondent for the *Daily Worker*, contributing forty signed articles as well as numerous brief, unsigned dispatches. A fourth of the signed articles deal with hardships of life in Harlem. In one of these Wright reported on a hearing conducted by the New York State Temporary Commission on Conditions Among Urban Negroes. The questioning of Henry Dalton about his real estate policies by Boris Max in the last part of *Native Son* draws directly from this article.[8]

As if to confirm Wright's notions about the Bigger type and society's attitude toward him, when the writer "was halfway through the first draft of *Native Son* a case paralleling Bigger's flared forth in the newspapers of Chicago."[9] This case involved Robert Nixon and

1945), pp. 306–42. This essay is reprinted, with minor changes, as "The Man Who Went to Chicago" in Wright's *Eight Men* (Cleveland and New York, 1961), pp. 210–50.

[6] Advertisement, *The Chicago Defender*, January 8, 1938, p. 3.

[7] Horace R. Cayton, *Long Old Road* (New York, 1965), pp. 247–48. Cayton gives further details in a symposium on Wright included in *Anger and Beyond: The Negro Writer in the United States*, ed. by Herbert Hill (New York, 1966), pp. 196–97. Having written the finest fictional portrayal of the South Side, Wright was the inevitable choice of Cayton and St. Clair Drake to write the introduction to their classic sociological treatise on the area, *Black Metropolis* (1945).

[8] "Gouging, Landlord Discrimination Against Negroes Bared at Hearing," *Daily Worker*, December 15, 1937, p. 6. Cf. *Native Son* (New York, 1940), pp. 276–79. Parenthetical page references in the text are to this edition.

[9] *How "Bigger" Was Born*, pp. 30–31.

Earl Hicks, two young Negroes with backgrounds similar to that of Bigger. According to the first of a long series of highly sensationalistic articles in the *Chicago Tribune,* on May 27, 1938, Mrs. Florence Johnson "was beaten to death with a brick by a colored sex criminal . . . in her apartment."[10] Nixon and Hicks were arrested soon after and charged with the crime. Though no evidence of rape was adduced, the *Tribune* from the beginning called the murder a sex crime and exploited fully this apparently quite false accusation.[11] Nixon was chosen for special attack, perhaps because he was darker and ostensibly less remorseful than Hicks. He was referred to repeatedly as the "brick moron," "rapist slayer," "jungle beast," "sex moron," and the like. His race was constantly emphasized. The casual reader of *Native Son* might consider the newspaper article which Bigger reads in his cell early in Book Three greatly exaggerated in its racism;[12] in point of fact, it is an adaptation of an actual piece in the *Tribune.* Although Nixon came from "a pretty little town in the old south—Tallulah, La.," the *Tribune* reporter wrote, "there is nothing pretty about Robert Nixon. He has none of the charm of speech or manner that is characteristic of so many southern darkies." The reporter proceeded to explain:

> That charm is a mark of civilization, and so far as manner and appearance go, civilization has left Nixon practically untouched. His hunched shoulders and long, sinewy arms that dangle almost to his knees; his outthrust head and catlike tread all suggest the animal.
>
> He is very black—almost pure Negro. His physical characteristics suggest an earlier link in the species.
>
> Mississippi river steamboat mates, who hire and fire roustabouts by the hundreds, would classify Nixon as a jungle Negro. They would hire him only if they were sorely in need of rousters. And they would keep close watch on him. This type is known to be ferocious and relentless in a fight. Though docile enough under ordinary circumstances, they are easily aroused. And when this happens the veneer of civilization disappears.

> As he talked yesterday Nixon's dull eyes lighted only when he spoke of food. They feed him well at the detective bureau, he said. He likes coconut

[10] "Sift Mass of Clews for Sex Killer," *Chicago Daily Tribune,* May 28, 1938, p. 1.

[11] David H. Orro, a Negro reporter, wrote that police stated that Nixon and Hicks were "bent upon committing a sex crime," but that "authorities were unable to state whether the woman had been sexually attacked." " 'Somebody Did It,' So 2 Youths Who 'Might Have Done It' Are Arrested," *The Chicago Defender,* May 28, 1938, p. 24. The date as printed is an error; this is actually the issue of June 4, 1938.

[12] Hubert Creekmore, the white novelist from Mississippi, charged that "the press is shown as chiefly concerned with unsubtle inspiration of hatred and intolerance. The manner and content of these newspapers exceed belief. Again Mr. Wright makes them present incidents and ideas which reflect his own mind rather than an editor's mind or the public mind." "Social Factors in *Native Son,*" *University of Kansas City Review,* VIII (Winter, 1941), 140.

pie and strawberry pop. It was after a generous meal of these refreshments that he confessed two of his most shocking murders. . . . These killings were accomplished with a ferocity suggestive of Poe's "Murders in the Rue Morgue"—the work of a giant ape.

Again the comparison was drawn between Nixon and the jungle man. Last week when he was taken . . . to demonstrate how he had slain Mrs. Florence Johnson, mother of two small children, a crowd gathered and there were cries of: "Lynch him! Kill him!"

Nixon backed against a wall and bared his teeth. He showed no fear, just as he has shown no remorse.[13]

The article concludes by quoting from a letter from the Louisiana sheriff of Nixon's home parish: "It has been demonstrated here that nothing can be done with Robert Nixon. Only death can cure him."[14]

This remedy was applied almost exactly a year after the murder of Mrs. Johnson. During this year the case became something of a local *cause célebrè*. The Chicago police quickly accused Nixon of a number of other murders, and the Los Angeles police did the same.[15] Early in the case the International Labor Defense became interested, providing Attorney Joseph Roth, white, to aid Negro lawyers in representing Nixon and Hicks.[16] Public emotion ran very high, stimulated by the lurid treatment given the case by the *Tribune*. A week after the crime the Illinois House of Representatives "approved a bill sponsored by State's Attorney Thomas J. Courtney of Cook County to curb moronic attacks." In debate on this bill, Nixon was mentioned prominently.[17] A complicated series of confessions and repudiations, charges of police brutality, and dramatic outbursts of violence[18] preceded the trial,

[13] Charles Leavelle, "Brick Slayer Is Likened to Jungle Beast," *Chicago Sunday Tribune*, June 5, 1938, Sec. 1, p. 6. Cf. *Native Son*, pp. 238–40.

[14] Leavelle, *op. cit.*

[15] "Science Traps Moron in 5 Murders," *Chicago Daily Tribune*, June 3, 1938, p. 1.

[16] "Robert Nixon Attacked by Irate Hubby," *The Chicago Defender*, June 11, 1938, p. 6.

[17] "Pass Courtney Moron Bill In Heated Debate," *Chicago Daily Tribune*, June 8, 1938, p. 1.

[18] When Nixon and Hicks were taken by police to the scene of the crime, a hostile, lynch-minded mob required police control. Then "a dramatic incident occurred just as the police were about to leave with their prisoners. Elmer Johnson, the bereaved husband . . . drove up with his two children, and his brother-in-law, John Whitton. . . . Johnson said nothing, but Whitton clenched his fists and shouted, 'I'd like to get at them.' Police hurried the prisoners away." "2 Accuse Each Other in Brick Killing," *Chicago Daily Tribune*, May 30, 1938, p. 2. Perhaps Elmer Johnson was merely waiting for a better opportunity for, at the inquest he attacked the handcuffed Nixon savagely before police intervened. Shortly after this attack, Nixon attempted to retaliate. Johnson explained his intention to a reporter: "I hoped to hit him hard enough so his head would fly back and his skull would be cracked against the wall." "Beats Slayer of Wife; Own Life Menaced," *Chicago Daily Tribune*, June 8, 1938, p. 3. See also "Robert Nixon Attacked By Irate Hubby," p. 6. Cf. the incident in *Native Son* in which Bigger is attacked at the inquest (p. 265).

which began in late July under Judge John C. Lewe after attorneys for the youths won a change of venue because of the prejudiced atmosphere.[19] The trial itself, despite some apparently contradictory evidence, was very brief, lasting just over a week before the jury reached a verdict of guilty on the first ballot after only one hour of deliberation. The death sentence was imposed on Nixon.[20] By this time, however, leaders of the Chicago Negro community were thoroughly aroused. The National Negro Congress, which had been providing legal representation for the two youths, continued its efforts on their behalf, including the sponsorship of a fund-raising dance.[21] Prominent Chicago Negro clergymen joined the struggle to save Nixon.[22] With the aid of such support, together with some irregularities in the evidence presented by the state, Nixon was able to win several stays of execution, but his struggle ceased in the Cook County electric chair three minutes after midnight, June 16, 1939.[23]

By the time Nixon was finally executed, Wright had completed *Native Son.* He did not need to wait the outcome of legal appeals and maneuvers to know the "Fate" (his title for Book Three of the novel) of Robert Nixon or of his fictional counterpart, Bigger Thomas. In any event, Wright's use of the Nixon case was that of a novelist, not that of an historian or journalist. He adapted whatever seemed useful to his fictional purpose, changing details as he wished. He followed the facts of the case fairly closely in his account of the newspaper treatment of Bigger Thomas. The inquest and trial scenes, also, resemble in certain respects their factual prototypes. Among the more significant distortions of Nixon material are those relating to Wright's polemic intent as a communist writer.

In the Nixon case the role of the International Labor Defense and its representative, Attorney Joseph Roth, was small and initiatory; it was soon replaced by the National Negro Congress. In *Native Son,* however, Wright magnifies the role of this organization (changing its name slightly to "Labor Defenders") and its radical Jewish attorney, Boris Max, who is made Bigger's sole lawyer. Another change illustrates even more vividly Wright's shift of emphasis in transforming fact to fiction. One of the murders for which Chicago police elicited confessions, later repudiated, from Nixon was that of a Mrs. Florence Thompson Castle a year before the murder of Mrs. Johnson. According to a newspaper report, in his account of this crime Nixon "told of

[19] "Brick Slayer's Trial Assigned To Judge Lewe," *Chicago Daily Tribune,* July 19, 1938, p. 6.

[20] "Guilty of Murder Gets Death In Chair," *Chicago Daily Tribune,* August 5, 1938, p. 3.

[21] "Dance Profits To Aid Nixon, Hicks," *The Chicago Defender,* August 20, 1938, p. 5.

[22] "Nixon Plea To Be Given To Governor," *The Chicago Defender,* October 15, 1938, p. 6.

[23] "Nixon Dies In Chair," *The Chicago Defender,* June 17, 1939, pp. 1–2.

picking up a lipstick belonging to Mrs. Castle and scrawling on the dresser mirror these words: 'Black Legion.' "[24] When Bigger in the novel wishes to divert suspicion to an extremist group, he selects leftists rather than fascists, signing the kidnap note to the Daltons in such a way as to implicate the Communist Party (p. 151).

As a fervent party member, Wright maintained a thoroughly communistic point of view in *Native Son*. The courtroom arguments of Max in the final section, of course, are patently leftist. He equates racial and class prejudice, both being based on economic exploitation (pp. 326–27). He repeats the basic party concept of the times regarding the collective status of Negroes in America: "Taken collectively, they are not simply twelve million people; in reality they constitute a separate nation, stunted, stripped, and held captive *within* this nation, devoid of political, social, economic, and property rights" (p. 333). He discerns in Bigger a revolutionary potentiality (pp. 337–38). Not all of Max's courtroom speech reflects so directly communist doctrine, but none of it is inconsistent with the party line on racial matters.

Communist material is obvious enough in the final section of the novel, but it is often implicit elsewhere. Early in Book One, for example, while Bigger and his friend Gus are loafing on the street they amuse themselves by "playing white," assuming roles of the white power structure. The youths are themselves nonpolitical, but the white activities Wright has them imitate are precisely those which he and other communists viewed as typical of the American capitalist system: warfare, high finance, and political racism (pp. 15–17). For Bigger's mother, religion is clearly presented as an opiate, as it is generally for the Negro masses. To accept the consolations of Christianity, Bigger comes to recognize, would be to lay "his head upon a pillow of humility and [give] up his hope of living in the world" (p. 215). The first movie that Bigger and a friend see in Book One, *The Gay Woman*, presents a Hollywood stereotype of a communist as a wild-eyed bomb thrower (pp. 27–28). Indeed, prejudice against communists is frequently depicted in the novel. On the other hand, party members Jan Erlone[25] and Boris Max are idealized portraits of selfless, noble, dedicated strivers toward the new social order.

These, then, are the main elements that went into the composition of *Native Son*. Much of the powerful sense of immediacy felt by the reader of the novel derives from the genesis of the work in the author's personal experience and observation. Though one may have reservations about the validity of Wright's communist ideological orientation, it provided him with an intellectual instrument with which to render meaningful the personal and social materials of the novel. The nice

[24] "Brick Moron Tells of Killing 2 Women," *Chicago Sunday Tribune*, May 29, 1938, p. 5.

[25] Wright may have taken the first name from that of Jan Wittenber, a white friend who was active in the Chicago John Reed Club and served as secretary of the Illinois State International Labor Defense.

balance of subjective and objective elements in *Native Son* prevents the work from becoming either a purely personal scream of pain, on the one hand, or a mere ideological tract on the other. Whatever verdict one may finally reach about the artistic merits of *Native Son,* one must take into account the personal, social, and political materials out of which it grew.

Negro Fiction in America

CHARLES I. GLICKSBERG

THE NEGRO NOVELIST MAY BE UNAWARE OF THE FORCES IN HIS CULTURE that conspire to make him a *Negro* writer, but whether he is aware of them or not his destiny is at work in the material he selects, the attitudes he adopts, the interpretation he imposes on life, the problems which seem to him of most vital importance, the very shape and significance of the language he uses. Though he may strive to think and write in terms of individuals, regardless of their "race" or color, the pressure of discrimination inevitably turns him into a figure of protest. The hostility which he and his people encounter almost everywhere in the American environment is matched by a style that is tormented, a neurotic alternation of sadism and masochism, self-pity and exalted pride, humility and furious aggression. To the horror that encompasses him on every side he replies with an agonized cry of protest.

From 1865 to 1900 Negro writers of fiction were in a quandary: they were not sure what they were doing or how they should do it. What point of view should they assume? Should they treat the Negro as a kind of picturesque and delightfully droll primitive as he stood pictured in the pages of Southern novels about life on the old plantation? Should they perhaps discard their obsession with color and create fiction about the white world? Or should they, as a last resort, create stories that would present the Negro people in a true light and thus counteract the pernicious influence of race prejudice and social and economic discrimination? Actually, at one time and another, all three strategies were tried, but it was the third solution that proved most fruitful and rewarding.

Not until after World War I did this literature of protest emerge in full force. A challenging and forthright treatment of the racial problem is given in James Weldon Johnson's *The Autobiography of an Ex-*

Charles I. Glicksberg, "Negro Fiction in America," *South Atlantic Quarterly,* XLV (October 1946), 478–488. Reprinted by permission of Duke University Press and the author.

Colored Man. Though the author attempts to tell a story, he is for the most part studying American society and revealing the miserable plight of his people: their hurts and resentments, their aspirations and defeats, the unhappy effects of a hierarchy of class differences based on color. Every Negro is forced to view life through the perspective of "color." For this very reason, too, as Johnson is careful to point out, the Negroes remain a mystery to the whites, who do not know what the colored people think and feel, what goes on behind their mask of accommodation. Worthy of note also is the novelist's observation that the black man is involved in a struggle in which he must fight passively, yet his passive resistance is highly effective, since the Southern whites must use up their best energies to combat the danger they sense all around them. The main difficulty of the race question, the author concludes, "does not lie so much in the actual condition of the blacks as it does in the mental attitudes of the whites; and a mental attitude, especially one not based on truth, can be changed more easily than actual conditions. . . . In a word, the difficulty of the problem is not so much due to the facts presented as to the hypothesis assumed for its solution." This is plain speaking and straight thinking, but unfortunately James Weldon Johnson, so richly gifted in various ways, was not a novelist.

In the same militant tradition, but less didactic in tone, is *The Walls of Jericho,* by Rudolph Fisher, a curious blend of lyricism and documentary writing, a mixture of pungent satire and genuine love of the Negro folk, with the satiric element growing stronger and stronger until it dominates the book. The narrative portions, dealing with "the low life" of Harlem, its quarrels and recreations, its social affairs and church functions, are done with rare humor, insight, and imagination. But the story contains overtones of a deeper meaning. The Negroes have learned from sad experience that they must band together against the common enemy. The whites—even the benevolent whites who wish to "uplift" the Negro race from savagery and stupor and sin—regard the Negro people as born to serve. Hence for Negroes solidarity is the law of survival. Fisher also punctures the myth of the Negro as an uninhibited child of Nature, primitive and orgiastic.

Zora Neale Hurston's *Jonah's Gourd Vine* is not only an interesting revelation of Negro character and Negro life but also one of the few novels replete with rich elements of folklore and racial humor. Behind the plot one discerns how the people live, their ignorance and poverty and hopelessness, their religiosity and their Adamic earthiness. There are some things about the Negro character which Negroes do not want the race-conscious whites to know, but Miss Hurston has no scruple about making them known. Unlike most contemporary Negro novelists, she refuses to make the race problem loom all important in her work. She is writing fiction, not propaganda. Art is not to be confused with sociology. When asked how she could write without being deeply influenced by the cruel injustice her people suffered in the United States, she replied: "I have ceased to think in terms of race; I think only in terms of individuals. . . . I am not interested in the *race* problem, but I am interested in the problems of *individuals,* white ones and black ones."

Such detachment and unconcern on the part of Negro novelists is rare. The nearer we come to our own time, the more uncompromising is the attitude of the author. Indeed, the evolution of Negro fiction in the last three decades is marked by a steadily increasing emphasis on race consciousness, an emphasis which finds its most violent expression in the work of Richard Wright. All the bitterness of a frustrated race wells up in the satirical short stories included in *The Ways of White Folks,* by Langston Hughes. How lacking in subtlety and understanding are these white people! Throughout the stories there is thrust upon the reader the picture of two conflicting worlds: white and black. *Not Without Laughter* tries to put into words the rankling bitterness that fills the hearts of many Negroes. Many conform to the pressure of socioeconomic necessity, others find consolation in a religion that preaches love and forgiveness and the bliss of life everlasting in the other world, but a rebellious group remains that will not give in. Harriet, one of the rebels in *Not Without Laughter,* hates the whites with uncontrolled fury. She tells her mother and sister: "You just take whatever white folks give you—*coon* to your face, and nigger behind your backs—and don't say nothing. You run to some white person's back door for every job you get, and then they pay you one dollar for five dollars' worth of work, and fire you whenever they get ready." On every side there is the same story of the shameless exploitation of black labor.

Hager, the mainstay of her family, refuses to abandon her dream that love, not hate, will eventually solve the racial problem. When you get old, she says, "you knows they ain't no sense in gettin' mad an' sourin' yo' soul with hatin' peoples. White folks is white folks, an' colored folks is colored, an' neither one of 'em is bad as t'other make out." When the Negro repays hate with interest he suffers the hate within himself and his heart festers like an open wound. To her listening grandson she says: "Honey, there ain't no room in de world fo' hate, white folks hatin' niggers, an' niggers hatin' white folks. There ain't no room in this world fo' nothin' but love, Sandy, chile. That's all they's room fo'—nothin' but love."

But the others have undergone experiences that belie her forgiving words; their minds are scarred with ugly memories: Negroes assaulted, driven out of the country, horribly lynched. Sandy gradually begins to understand the implications of being a Negro in a white-dominated world, and there are times when his heart brims over with molten hate. "Being colored is like being born in the basement of life, with the door to the light locked and barred—and the white folks live upstairs. They don't want us up there with them, even when we're respectable." Though the point is stressed that it is poverty which keeps the Negro people down, Hughes is not writing a thesis novel. He shows us how his people live, the experiences they pass through, the feelings they harbor within. There is only one hope he appears to hold out: the manacles of the mind must be broken; with the hammer of knowledge must his people break down the doors locked against them.

Though J. Saunders Redding's *No Day of Triumph* is autobiographical rather than fictional, it sheds a brilliant light on the crucial problem that the Negro writer must face. The journey on which he started was essentially a metaphysical quest for a people, a history. Early in childhood he made the discovery that there were classes among the Negro people who, having taken over the attitude of ridicule attaching to blackness, had become victims of their own "color complex." While he was in college the sense of alienation pressed in upon him strongly—he was rejected. "I raged with secret hatred and fear. I hated and feared the whites. I hated and feared and was ashamed of Negroes." Then he met a Jew (significantly enough, the Jew also plays a part in *Native Son*) who pointed out to him that he couldn't escape by sinking within himself and ignoring social reality. One must find communal roots, a home where the spirit can feel free. Isolation had to be broken down and vital contact established. Then it was that Redding began his wandering, his search for a people, for a relationship that would restore his integrity and give meaning and purpose to his life.

Richard Wright in *Native Son* gave us the first portrait of the frustrated Negro in all his four-dimensional complexity: hate-filled, economically helpless, moved by aggressive impulses that he cannot control. The story, Wright assures us, points its own moral. As a novelist in the naturalistic tradition all he is concerned with is to portray the truth of Bigger's character in interaction with his environment. Yet, apart from the interpretation which pervades the novel and gives it thematic unity, the author introduces introspections, interior monologue, and analyses which read suspiciously like argument. Bigger Thomas was deliberately chosen as a symbol of the Negro race. Though he had not raped Mary Dalton, he was guilty of "rape" of a different kind: the irresistible urge to strike back when he was forced against a wall by the horde of ruthless white enemies. He committed rape, we are told, "every time he looked into a white face." Many times in the past, before the actual murder, he had, in thought, killed viciously, vengefully. Now by killing he had faced the meaning of his life, discovering his painfully split personality, his want of wholeness, the contradition in his nature between thought and feeling, aspiration and consummation, will and deed, ideal and reality. His life was a chaos. Only under the stress of hatred could he succeed in resolving this internal conflict.

Native Son is a powerful psychological study of the crippling effects of the process of alienation in our society. A black pariah, Bigger was excluded by virtue of his color from merging organically with the men and women around him. The traumatic shock of the murder he had committed made him realize for the first time the nature of his relations with the people around him. Now he could feel, whereas before he was like one under an anesthetic, insensitive to pain, dead to desire. All his actions, confused as they were, sprang from a longing to be a meaningful part of this world, to merge, to belong. As he sat there in the cell brooding darkly on the past, he yearned for some redeeming symbol which would exorcise the sense of being black and despised so that he might overcome the fear of dying. But the contempt meted out to him and his people went too deep for such exorcism; it had become an integral part of him, so that at the end it was not only introjected but lived. All about him was the malevolent, relentless hate of the whites: hate that pursued him everywhere, even when he was alone. He therefore hated himself, his race, all he was and all he would ever be. *Native Son* is the first poignant and convincing creative embodiment, in the form of a novel, of the deadly hatred that, however rationalized or disguised, poisons the relations between the whites and Negroes.

Richard Wright was unfortunate, yet driven by creative necessity, in selecting Bigger Thomas as the protagonist of his novel. It was an act of courage. No Negro novelist had ever undertaken so vast, so ambitious, so challenging a theme. Wright placed himself under a tremendous handicap in trying to make Bigger seem human in spite of everything he is and does. Wright's attempt to tell a story and at the same time to drive home a sociological moral lands him in numerous difficulties. He resolves his problem neatly enough. The first section, "Fear," depicts the sordid ghetto area in which Bigger lives like a trapped animal, the skein of circumstances that constantly thwarts his impulses to reach out for human contact and fulfilment and that finally culminates in the act of murder. The second section, "Flight," moves swiftly; and yet the camera lens is steadily fixed on Bigger's inner perturbations, the jungle drama of his passionate yet darkened mind. He kills again. The last section, "Fate," offers Wright the opportunity he had been seeking of vindicating the Bigger Thomases of his race, presenting Bigger as a symbol of thirteen million folk who walk in darkness, breeding the poison of murderous hatred against the white oppressor. Now we can see Bigger alone in his cell, fighting the shadows of guilt in his own mind, making the painful effort to understand himself and his relation to the world. Despite the melodramatic tempo and intensity of the first two sections, they but serve to lead up to the heart of the novel: Bigger's self-realization at the end that his act was inevitable. This was his fate: to kill and to die.

Richard Wright is playing with dynamite. He is holding a loaded pistol at the head of the white world while he mutters between clenched teeth: "Either you grant us equal rights as human beings or else this is what will happen." It is dangerous doctrine to pour into the susceptible minds of frustrated young Negro readers, who are resentful enough as it is. The notion that by violence they can free themselves from their burden of fear and hatred may act as an explosive incentive to further aggression. When Max, the Communist lawyer, argues that in this murder trial every American Negro is being tried, the words belong to Max, but the voice is that of Richard Wright. Crime and race do not go together. Bigger deserves death as surely as any murderer ever did, even if he struck out blindly, not knowing what he was doing. False is the realization which grows upon him in prison that he knew well enough what he was doing, that he had been guilty of killing all his life long. Bigger is the victim of racial prejudice, but murder is certainly not the solution for this problem. It is sheer nonsense to insist that the act of killing made Bigger free, made him feel that his actions were important. Why should murder be the most satisfying and effectual mode of release? Max argues that Negroes are different. Unlike other elements in the population, native and foreign-born, they are not people; "in reality they constitute a separate nation, stunted, stripped, and held captive *within* this nation, devoid of political, social, economic, and property rights." Society filled Bigger Thomas, prototype of millions of others like him, with violent emotions of hate and fear which were rooted in his consciousness. His personality is diseased to such a point that he can justify his existence only by releasing the pent-up aggression within his being. Max stresses this element in Bigger's character and, as before, the words come out of the mouth of the lawyer, but the voice is that of Richard Wright.

This is the picture of not only a split, but a paranoiac, personality obsessed with an acute persecutory complex. There is, to be sure, a measure of truth in the portrayal, which falls within the school of realism typified by Dreiser's *The American Tragedy*. This is the hostile physical and psychological environment in which the Negro moves and has his being. But that Bigger Thomas should turn into a killer—that strains the sinews of belief, especially when we consider that he has been made a symbol of his race. Bigger's halting *apologia pro vita sua*—"But what I killed for, I am! It must've been pretty deep in me to make me kill!"—is out of keeping with Bigger's character. The scheme of motivation breaks down. We see all too clearly the hand of the propagandist dictating the conclusion.

Native Son is important as a landmark in American fiction, not because a Negro wrote it or because it treats of the racial problem. It is important in its own right because, regardless of the theme, it is an imaginative novel that tells a story and solves its problem in aesthetically satisfying terms, achieving a synthesis of the private and the public, translating feelings and states of mind, psychic crises and spiritual suffering, into objective acts and an organically constructed plot. Despite its inflammatory ending, it is no propaganda tract for the times.

In "How 'Bigger' Was Born," Wright affords us some revealing clues to the genesis of the novel and the way the character of Bigger developed in his own mind. There were two factors in Bigger's personality which precipitated his fateful revolt: his sense of alienation from the folk culture of his race and his urgent desire to belong to the life which had rejected him. Extremely significant for Wright's intellectual development was his study of Marxism and his interest in the labor movement. He made the liberating discovery that Bigger Thomas had counterparts in the white world; the oppressed were not always black. Such a realization enabled Wright to behold Bigger's personality and his life in a wider perspective. The Negroes were no longer a peculiar, victimized people, but an integral part of a vast world struggle, a struggle for life, in which everyone, white or black, was involved. The issue was no longer Negroes against whites.

But ideology alone could not be of much assistance in the writing of a novel. Wright needed concrete experiences, living personalities and vital incidents, and these he found in Chicago. The massive pressure of the environment—what a powerful force it is in molding the lives of people! But he was not adapting the doctrine of dialectical materialism to his fictional cosmos. The problem—no one in fiction had yet undertaken the precise kind of problem he had set himself—was far too complex for that. Was it not the duty of society to find out what produced such warped characters as Bigger Thomas and to alter the conditions which brought them into being? What saved Richard Wright from racial fanaticism was the discovery that Bigger Thomas was a world-wide character. The fearful, frustrated, hysterically aggressive personality type did not conform to any national or racial stereotype; it could be found everywhere. Bigger Thomas, an American product, shaped by his environment, carried within him, Wright says, "the potentialities of either Communism or Fascism. I don't mean to say that the Negro boy I depicted in *Native Son* is either a Communist or a Fascist. He is not either. But he is a product of a dislocated society; he is a dispossessed and disinherited man; he is all of this, and he lives amid the greatest plenty on earth and he is looking for a way out."

Another shaping influence was the determination to portray Bigger as he was and as his creator truly saw him, without fearfully considering what the whites would say in the way of condemnation. He had to free himself as a writer from the inhibiting weight of fear and shame. The writing of the novel became a necessity, an act of creative liberation, a promise of new life and fulfilment. Then, too, he had to free himself from the worry of what the leaders of his own race would say, their resentment that such an ugly and repulsive character should be held up as typical of the Negro race. Wright clung firmly to his vision of the truth, concentrating on the task of showing Bigger living in the Negro slums of Chicago. Though Bigger Thomas was an American, a native son, he was an American with a difference, a Negro nationalist since his aspirations to be an American were denied him. The nationalistic emphasis came first, Wright decided, because that corresponded most truly with Bigger's fierce hatred of the whites and because that hatred served most conspicuously as a symbol of the Negro race in America.

The cumulative weight of hatred and horror in *Native Son* is, however, too great to be borne. This is the essential defect of the book. The killing is the result of an accident, though Wright labors earnestly to convince us (and he convinces Bigger) that the murder is the breaking point of years of frustration, the culmination of a lifetime of brooding hatred. What is more, Bigger is almost subhuman, a type that is irresponsible, primitive, without pity or remorse. How then can he serve as a fitting symbol of the oppressed Negro race? Is he worth all this toil of analysis and tortured introspection? Richard Wright might argue that Bigger represents a distinct type. Yes, but of what? The killer among Negroes? That all Negroes, if thus deprived of the opportunity to lead a self-respecting life of social fulfilment, will take to murder and possibly shake the civilized world to its foundation? If that is Wright's intention, he has chosen the wrong means and the wrong material for the embodiment of his idea.

Black Boy, Wright's autobiography, gives us the clue to the feelings, the experiences, the motivations, that went into the making of Bigger Thomas and *Native Son*. Hunger and humiliation, physical suffering and spiritual torture, fear and hatred, form the heart of the book. It gives us a searching study of the effects of racial terrorism in all its forms on a sensitive being. Wright has tried to be honest with himself, to conceal nothing, to tell the truth as he lived it during his formative years. What stands out vividly is his hatred, his determination to break away from the South. He was a rebel who won freedom of the mind and finally emancipation for his body. Reflecting on the Negro character, Wright notes how it has been betrayed into acting against its real nature. The Negroes in the South had become stunted, insensible to joy or pain, living like beasts of burden. He found them, not passionate and elemental, but abject and pitiable creatures. "I saw that what had been taken for our emotional strength was our negative confusion, our flights, our fears, our frenzy under pressure."

The result of his boyhood experiences was to instil in him a neurotic feeling of terror in the presence of the whites so that he trembled when they were near. His imagination, his personality, was permanently affected by it. The more Wright heard about what the whites did to his people, the more his sense of powerlessness and blind vindictive rage increased. Like Bigger Thomas, he invented fantasies of violent retaliation. He too would kill in turn. These fantasies (note the repetition of this motif: murder as salvation) gave him the moral courage to go on living. Later he pens this confession: "In a peculiar sense, life had trapped me in a realm of emotional rejection; I had not embraced insurgency through choice."

Richard Wright, by virtue not only of his indubitable talent but far more of his flaming passion of revolt, has become the acknowledged leader of a group of Negro writers who espouse the cause of racial insurgency. Ishmaelites because of their color, they will accept and act out their fate. They will make an end of compromise and appeasement. And so they spend their creative energies in rebelling against the yoke clamped tight around their neck. They will cut themselves off from all white contamination. The Negro for the Negroes! Thus is generated the cult of racial solidarity which, paradoxically enough, if carried to an extreme, results in cultural segregation.

The Negro writer thus constructs his own psychological prison. He creates two dangerous abstractions: whites and blacks. The former is the enemy to be shunned, derided, hated at all costs, fought to a finish. The latter is to be exalted: they have been nothing, they shall be all. The race war is on, and it is waged in an atmosphere of hatred countered by the passion of love for all suffering black folk. The danger of such a movement, like the doctrine of the class war, is that it simplifies and distorts the social reality of which the Negro is a part. It makes the Negro writer a victim of the same shallow stereotypes that he resents in the whites. All this omits the fundamental consideration, of which Richard Wright is intellectually aware but which is submerged in his creative processes, that the whites are not as his inflamed imagination makes them out to be, that the white world is divided against itself. He is saved from racial chauvinism by his understanding that the race problem is but one aspect of the more inclusive and more complex socioeconomic problem, but in *Native Son* only the Communists are shown to be friends of the oppressed Negro and enlightened champions of human freedom.

Race consciousness in contemporary Negro fiction is inevitable. *Native Son* will encourage the birth of novels by Negro writers which will picture realistically the fate of the Negro in a white society that brutally forces him to assume a degraded caste-status. They will underline the imperative need for racial solidarity. Uncompromising in substance and militant in tone, they will usher in a literature of protest, a literature of self-discovery. Negro writers will increasingly turn to the life of their own people for inspiration and in doing so discover a fruitful source of race pride and remarkable potentialities for creative growth. The only danger is that they may forget that this expression of militancy, understandable as it is, does not solve their creative problem, for Negro writing does not fall within a unique cultural pattern. It has been influenced by the same influences that shaped the work of other writers. While trying to picture the No Man's Land in which the Negro must live, wandering like an outcast between two worlds, Negro writers must also remember that they are American by birth and heritage. At present it may seem like a contradiction, but it shadows forth a profound truth, a goal to strive for: the ultimate aim of Negro literature is to destroy itself, to become an indivisible part of American literature. That consummation will take place only when the social order has been so reconstructed as to permit Negroes to partake of the fruits of American democracy. Then hate will give way to love, rejection to brotherhood, and a new *Native Son* will be written. Until that time comes, the Negro writer has no choice but to declare open warfare on a world which denies his humanity.

The Promise of Democracy in Richard Wright's *Native Son*

EDWIN BERRY BURGUM

RICHARD WRIGHT IS ONE OF THE LATEST AND MOST INTRANSIGENT REPresentatives of a literary movement among our submerged nationalities that has been developing since the turn of the century as the literary analogy to the extension of our democratic ideals within the sphere of practical life.

The disappearance of the frontier around 1890 is usually accepted as the opening of a new period in our history when we became aware of the presence of minority races and underprivileged workers. From this time until the First World War a movement of 'muckraking' and reformism gathered impetus in the area of politics and business. It was very largely negative in nature, an attack upon graft and corruption, and only incidentally sympathetic to the common man who was their victim. The movement in fiction reflected these characteristics in the work of Frank Norris and Upton Sinclair; except that the nature of fiction demanded and secured a greater emphasis on the human suffering. But it is noteworthy that the literary movement as it gathered momentum in the new century shifted to a positive emphasis. In the work of novelists like Willa Cather, Theodore Dreiser, and Sherwood Anderson, and poets like Vachel Lindsay and Carl Sandburg, we no longer see Anglo-Saxon writers bemoaning the misfortunes of the poor and the foreigners, but writers still Anglo-Saxon by birth or thoroughly assimilated to Anglo-Saxon attitudes of temperament beginning to find in the foreign stock qualities superior to their own. Whether these foreigners are workers or farmers, such writers admire their self-reliance, their endurance, their zest for living, in implicit contrast to the lack of these qualities in the dominant Puritan bourgeois stock. Even after the First World War, writers like Ernest Hemingway and Dos Passos carried over this interest in the social and cultural values of common people of other stocks than their own, but infused a new note

---

Edwin Berry Burgum, "The Promise of Democracy in Richard Wright's *Native Son*," in *The Novel and the World's Dilemma* [1947] (New York: Russell & Russell, 1963).

of conscious envy or sense of inferiority on their own part. The man of foreign birth who had first been commiserated for his unfortunate economic position was not admired for his preservation of the more vital values of personality which the more prosperous native stock had sacrificed. I am here not concerned with the validity of these judgments, but only with their significance as denoting the rise in prestige of the foreign born in the eyes of certain native writers. It would be idle to claim that these writers represented the major tendency in our literature. But they were there to encourage the minorities themselves.

The thirties marked the coming of age of these submerged nationalities in the historical development of an independent American culture. When Van Wyck Brooks as a literary critic wrote *America's Coming of Age* in 1917, he was thinking only of Anglo-Saxon America. But no sooner, it would seem, had our Anglo-Saxon writers succeeded in throwing off their deference to English precedents (gaining the strength to do so through their new kinship to non-Anglo-Saxon America), than these other racial elements in American society demanded their share in the new culture. They began to point out their contribution to the national pattern. At first, through autobiography or sociological writing, in the work of Jacob Riis, Mary Antin, and Randolph Bourne, but later on, by the mid-twenties, in literature also, Americans of foreign birth began to make themselves felt, not as converts to the dominant Anglo-Saxon attitudes, but as modifiers of them. These new writers were now insisting upon their contribution to the newly forming pattern of national culture.

Within its limits, which they gladly accepted, they began to express in literary form the idioms they are introducing into the national language and to present with affectionate detail those idiosyncrasies of personality by which some of our Anglo-Saxon writers were already intrigued. Building upon this real but partial acceptance into the literary community, validated as it now was by the holding of political office and the possession of some economic power, these minority peoples could now, for the first time, express their awareness of the meaning of democracy and of the dignity of their share in it. But at the same time they could not fail to be acutely conscious of the partial character of their attainment. What had been achieved only made them the more cognizant of the long road ahead to anything like a real equality of opportunity and prestige. Their confidence in their potentialities as part of the amalgamation of a truly inclusive culture was contaminated by the knowledge that they had been forced to fight every inch of the way and a suspicion that the tolerance of the dominant Anglo-Saxon would lessen the more he found he had to tolerate.

The particular social relationship of the particular people to the Anglo-Saxon control determined the precise blend of suspicion and confidence in the literary expression.

The Negro, who has been treated worst of all despite a Civil War that ended in his specific emancipation, could not fall prey to any delusion of democracy, however personally prosperous. He could not share the optimism of other minorities in our society that their partial acceptance was either a temporary blot upon the escutcheon of our ideals or only part of the neglect of the working class in general. If self-assertion seemed to be winning acceptance for other minority groups, he could only conclude that his traditional policy of trust and co-operation was wrong. He developed a hatred of his old submissive self and a greater hatred for the whites who pretended to love and admire him in proportion as he remained without dignity. The Negro, once given a taste of dignity, drew the lesson that he had only himself to depend upon, and developed an inner core of tenacious resentment as he became aware that he was victim of the most glaring hypocrisy of all.

The new Negro, taught at length by our liberal tradition to trust himself and to expect equality, is alert for any manifestation of its spuriousness and is ready to die in shame or violence rather than submit any longer to the indignities of the past. His intransigence, it must be confessed, can hardly be palatable even to philanthropic whites. We must guard against a retreat into fear when we make the startling discovery that the roles have been reversed. It is no longer we whites who are in the position of granting equality if we please, but the Negroes who are wresting it from us whether we please or not. Such is the first shock that we get from Wright's novels. We are shaken once and for all from our complacency. If we are foolish and reactionary, we shall react by terror. If we are wise, we shall recognize that we have brought this impasse upon ourselves. But, above all, we shall become convinced that the impasse exists, and cannot be conjured away. This is the way the modern Negro feels. He is on the point of rebellion when he is mistreated. He is watchful for hypocrisy, scornful of the insufficiency of the good intention, determined not to sell his birthright for the small change of petty concessions. The Negro today feels that the gulf is absolute between the white skin and the black, save for two exceptions. They will trust those whites who stand shoulder to shoulder with them in a common fight to escape poverty and ignorance. They will trust those whites who risk a similar poverty and suffering to aid them in their own escape.

And so the new Negro literature, at its best when it is least influenced by white modes of feeling, is more bitter than that of any other minority group. This bitterness, turned inward and warped into melancholy during the period of the blues, becomes more and more direct in expression until it reaches an explosive violence, scarcely to be restrained, in Wright's fiction. Though neglected by white readers until the 'thirties, the new movement was actually earlier under way than the expression of other groups. Beginning about the year 1900 (as the *Negro Caravan* suggests), with the stories of Charles W. Chesnutt (whose work was at first taken for that of a white writer), it became a vigorous school early in the twenties, when the magazine *Opportunity* was founded and Claude MacKay and Langston Hughes were beginning to attract attention. This later work, especially the poetry, carried into esthetic expression the idioms and cadences of Negro speech, and reflected Negro sentiments in such genuine detail that its Negro origin could never have been mistaken. But though often written in a tone of aggressive resentment, its themes are usually a grim exposure of suffering to which the Negro helplessly submits rather than a narration of his revolt.

Richard Wright, therefore, had the advantage of an already developing tradition of Negro literature of protest. His greatness is to be found in the honesty and the power with which he transfers into fiction these convictions of the new Negro where they presented themselves in their most direct and least sophisticated form, unmodified by bourgeois standards, either Negro or white. In most of Wright's short stories, for instance, the Negro is an uneducated poor farmer or sharecropper of the deep South, living in rigid ostracism apart from the white world. A few stories in which the Negroes have found a common basis of feeling and action with poor whites who know something about Communism are an exception. In most of them, the possibility of equality with whites, or even of any sort of co-operation with them, is beyond the limit of experience. But these men have nevertheless caught the contagious spirit of democracy as it has been sweeping through the masses of the nation generally. All of his Negroes are psychologically convinced that they are men with rights. When his young Negro is caught by a white swimming in a forbidden pond, he talks back, defying the segregation. When the white starts to shoot him, he grabs the pistol and kills. Even though he has to flee north, he carries with him a determined spirit without regret. The Negro who has spent years trying to enlarge his small farm and become prosperous like a white farmer, when he finds his ambition frustrated, discovers his mistake in accepting bourgeois ideals and destroys everything. When such men are put upon, their spontaneous reaction is no longer to cringe, but to fight back; and when the fight proves futile, they prefer to die rather than submit. They are simple persons in the terms of formal education, but circumstances have forced upon them an intensity of emotional conflict which is more like the stuff of classical tragedy than any other quarter of American life can present.

Native Son translates into a metropolitan environment such a temperament where the conflicts become more complex and cause the breakdown of the personality. It is an environment, also, paradoxically, where constructive contact with whites becomes a possibility. The novel treats of the difficulties of such a contact for both parties. For we must remember that, if the short stories were written to reveal the new Negro to whites, *Native Son* endeavors to disclose both to each other.

The first reaction of the white reader is probably an awareness of his own inadequacy in such a situation. It dawns upon him that he is probably only a variant of the Daltons in his good intentions toward the Negroes. If he has taken pride in his practice of equality, in his magnanimous freedom from prejudices, he begins to see how, from the Negro's point of view, he must have appeared as sentimentally patronizing as the informality of Jan and Mary. He begins to recognize that barriers of suspicion and prejudice do not drop on both sides when he wills it. There are two persons concerned in a relationship of equality; for equality, where individuals are involved, is a form of friendship, and friendship is a reciprocal activity.

Normally, the establishment of friendships is facilitated by the existence of a larger framework of common class or group beliefs and interests. When, in place of this preliminary awareness of common attitudes, the opposite exists, an awareness of hostile ones, the winning of friendship becomes a gradual process. Each side must assure the other that he is an exception to the group to which he would normally belong. It therefore becomes an instance of obtuseness and arrogance, of indifference to the individuality of the other person, when we assume in him an automatic response of delighted receptivity to our advances. Despite Mary's sophistication and Jan's radical beliefs, they have not realized that to Bigger Thomas they are no more individuals than Bigger is to them. When they make advances to him, it is not to him as individual, but to him as Negro, indeed, to him as a Negro of the old school, grateful for whatever charity a white may offer. If they do not see that they are treating him as a type, they cannot be expected to see how inevitably he at the same time is treating them as a different type. Bigger knows nothing of their radical theories. All he knows is that Mary is the sort of girl who is likely to get him into trouble with both whites and blacks, and ultimately with Jan himself, since she is his lover. When they insist upon his eating with them in a Negro café habituated by his friends, they seem to think he ought to appreciate this evidence of their democracy. They do not realize either that to his friends in the café his presence will seem a disloyalty to his race, evidence of his having sold out to the whites, or that his own wishes in the matter have been completely ignored. Their equality therefore becomes an act of racial superiority through the very compulsions they mistakenly think are causing its breakdown. The meaning of social equality has never been as adequately defined in a novel.

Our delusion, however, regarding the nature of equality is but one example of the larger problem of the actual limitation of our horizons. Direct experience is the intensest authentication of abstract statement. There is no financial depression in the effective sense of the phrase, as a determinant of man's immediate relationships with others, if his income and normal associations afford him a way of life bereft of emotional participation in deprivation, lacking any approximation of equality with the deprived, in pain or renunciation or spiritual suffocation. The prosperous, therefore, in all sincerity conclude that the underprivileged who complain are exaggerating, since their own circumstances do not set up a similar compulsion to rebel. Whatever lies beyond the horizon of close personal contacts becomes an abstraction. The poor man who is habitually seen from the window of a limousine is an allegorical man who is defined not in terms that he would himself understand, but those selected by the specific relationship between the two classes, which is to the profit of the person making the judgment. Similarly, the millionaire in his limousine is an abstraction to the man who never meets one in the subway. No amount of education or personal cleverness can overcome these limitations which testify to the authority of direct relationships within the group. Whatever is without the group is distorted, unknown and therefore frightening, or not worth knowing and complacently ignored. Only thus can history explain the psychology of fascists, who are certainly neither stupid nor illiterate.

When one's abstract views are contrary to the movement of history, this distortion is of what is essential in the unexperienced. But where it is precisely the essential or typical which is rightly known, the ignorance of the nonessential tends rather to guarantee the escape from a waste of effort upon the irrelevant. The essential, under such circumstances, is not distorted, but embodied instead in the large simple pattern of allegory. If, in other words, what falls without our immediate experience is always allegory, this allegory may be either a distortion of reality or only a simplified, larger-than-life presentation of it. In the latter case, one will not be in error in the long run, but he will make regrettable mistakes in specific actions. But it remains true, all the same, that even when a theory of society which history is proving to be valid is accepted by the group, whatever passes beyond the horizon of the group will be known only in an abstract way, symbolically, and will remain unknown or distorted in detail. The union worker, we may assume, knows the capitalist more accurately as a type than the employer his worker, because his first-hand experience and superior understanding of social conditions affords him a valid insight into his general character. Each, nevertheless, will inflate the specific image of the other to an extent that will make it seem improbable to the other person. The sociological value of fiction is that it provides a partial solution of this dilemma. If it is constructed on the proper abstract basis, it pushes our horizon beyond the limits of our effective experiences, and provides a more authentic understanding of the individual. It is the particular value of *Native Son* that this service, which in most novels is only a by-product of the nature of fiction, becomes the conscious purpose that determines its method.

The conflicts that form the plot of *Native Son* take their particular form from the characters' ignorance of these limitations, just as Wright's firm hand in their delineation is a consequence of his awareness of them. Bigger Thomas, the Negro boy, weighed down by his illiteracy, is no more ignorant of the individuality of the rich philanthropists, the Daltons, than they are of his. They recognize him as a type, the underprivileged adolescent who has been in trouble with the police, and are prepared to treat him according to a formula which seems enlightened to them, rehabilitation through a job as their chauffeur in an atmosphere of kindly intentions. They fail to recognize that their theory is the approach of private charity which the Negro people are no longer willing to accept; and that, despite Bigger's apparent humility, circumstances have fashioned him into its incorrigible opponent. They know Bigger more specifically than he them, but their specific knowledge is worse than useless since it is used to justify an untenable premise. Bigger, on the other hand, who cannot be said to know the Daltons with any specificity, is right in his general view of them. For him they are allegorical figures from another world, millionaires who live sumptuously on rents torn from the poor Negroes of a segregated district. In this fundamental matter his underprivileged station has afforded him a superior insight. He senses their inconsistency and unfairness in attempting to conceal from themselves and the Negro population by the small benefactions of charity the monstrous oppression from which they draw an income, huge by comparison. Despite his illiteracy, then, Bigger's awareness of his relationship to the Daltons is more sound than theirs of him.

But Wright takes the errors of the Daltons for granted. He is concerned, rather, with the fact that Bigger, though his insights are basically more sound than the Daltons', cannot use them constructively. Sensing shame and futility in his mother's consolation from a religion that demands submission to misery and the renunciation of any hope for a better life, what might have been a healthy inner need to act is perverted by the sort of action his environment provides. At the outset, Wright keys his novel to this interpretation. Bigger kills the rat that has been frightening the women folks, and then frightens them the more by flaunting its dead body in their faces. His courage is that overcompensation for fear called bravado. It passes beyond the needs of the situation and defeats its own end here as in later crises in the novel. Its source is his acceptance of the ideals of the white race as they have penetrated his ghetto. Flying an airplane symbolizes the freedom and mastery of the white race he would like to share. Knowing that he cannot, his helplessness creates an inner state of fear which (as it has transformed his healthy impulse of courage into bravado) sets up the direct motivation of hatred, and transforms what might have been a healthy social activity into petty thievery. But, to this uneducated boy, hatred for the whites is too remote and turns inward. It vents itself upon his family with their misguided notion that decency is rewarded, upon his black neighbors from whom his gang steals, upon the gang for the pettiness of its objectives, and upon himself for his inability to attain more grandiose ends. When he accepts the job with the Daltons, it is to escape these pressures which he hates. But they have all the same been furnishing him with the uneasy stability of belonging to some grouping. In his new environment he is alone in a white world, which becomes the more formidable since he cannot treat it with the unalloyed hatred it seems to him to deserve. The apparent kindliness of the Daltons obscures the simplicity of their allegorical meaning and intensifies his inner conflicts by introducing an element of intellectual doubt to add to his fear.

Behind Wright's narrative is the unspoken assumption that Negroes must have some organization for common protest that shall enable them to bring the abstract objective into productive relationship to the specific situation, that will afford understanding and guidance in the specific situations as they arise. In its absence, as riots in the Negro sections of our large cities have shown, an inevitable demand will spend itself in anarchistic violence to the defeat of its profound and laudable intention. For Negroes, *Native Son* is a warning that there is no alternative to right organization except the futility of individual violence into which Bigger is led.

Alone with these whites, whom Bigger fears but is no longer so sure he should hate, his fear and hatred rise into a crescendo as the situation feeds his incompetence with more serious temptations. When it becomes part of his duty to put the drunken daughter of the Daltons to bed, the strain between abstract knowledge and ignorance of the immediate situation reaches the breaking point. His fear that he may be thought by her parents to be planning her rape would have been unjustified had he known the Daltons as individuals. But it is valid both as a generalization of the white world and as a temptation her previous freedom with her lover seemed to be proffering him. In his state of excitement his handling of this difficult situation defeats his intention. He smothers to death the girl he does not wish to be charged with raping. His motives here and elsewhere are quite different from those of Dostoevsky's Roskolnikov, to whom he has been wrongly compared.

His trial of constructive action has been a failure. What follows up to his arrest is the tale of one savage, misguided act after another. But Bigger has become blind to their savagery. His uncertain groping for some valid avenue of self-fulfilment before the murder now gives way to the authority of his excitement. He enters a world of paranoiac fantasy, in which his acts of frenzy seem to him not so much the clever concealment of his initial mistake as the unfolding of a grandiose plan of conquest. He has lost his sense of belonging with anybody, black or white, and his need to belong with anybody. His act of murder seems to him to have released immense potentialities that had lain imprisoned within his personality. While he is actually running away from pursuit in desperation, he conceives himself to be a Tamberlaine capable of reducing the whole world to the prostrate state it had imposed upon him and he has now escaped. He seems now to be flying the forbidden airplane above a remote and impotent world.

But this picture of his immediate reaction to his crime cannot be isolated from his subsequent attitudes. After his arrest he reverts to an apathy of complete worthlessness. His arrest and the white crowds howling for his lynching puncture his fantasy and restore him to the only contact with reality he has ever known. As long as he lacks a fraternal mechanism for its transformation, it is the only contact with reality the underprivileged Negro of our day can ever know: the certainty that there is nobody in our society who is worse treated. Now Bigger no longer possesses the illusion of power in individual hatred. He has reverted to the animal docility of slavehood. His self-respect reawakens when he finds a single man who understands him, and by understanding him enables him at last to bridge the gulf between the abstract and the particular. In the long final section of the novel his Jewish Communist lawyer repeats for him the therapeutic service David performed for the distraught Saul of Browning's poem.

Bigger, it is true, understands very little of the content of these discussions. But the lawyer's patience and kindliness of intention in conducting them are enough to convince him of their central meaning. It is enough that they are taking place in such a milieu. Through this elementary fact Bigger comes to feel that there is one man in the world who understands him better than he understands himself, and can bring to the surface of his consciousness that longing to be of some value to himself and to society which the distortions of his hatred had concealed. So starved and twisted has been his former emotional life, that this simple experience of a single friendship takes on the proportions of a sufficient achievement for a lifetime. He cannot conceive of a further goal to live for. The lawyer embodies that principle of equality which Bigger has been unable to articulate, though he reacted against Mary Dalton's mistaken bohemian notion of it that Jan had shared. Max's willingness to endure criticism for defending him and a social ostracism similar to his own has put them on a common basis of understanding. And from this common basis Bigger is able to see for the first time that he is not alone in his struggle and his torment.

Bigger Thomas is of course not a typical Negro. Some of his actions, like the slaying of the rat, are symbolic presentations of his personal traits. But though Bigger himself is an individual and not a symbolic figure, the reader accepts him as representative of other men unlike him in various respects. As often happens in contemporary fiction, the extreme disorders of personality which he exhibits are only an exaggeration of the latent characteristics of apparently more normal persons. In a world where there is scarcely a man so illiterate as not to be aware of our publicized ideals of democracy and apply them directly to his own circumstances, Bigger's hatred is shared in varying degrees by every Negro and every worker, and indeed by every individual who feels deprived of a chance to fulfill his potentialities. The only differences are in the depth to which the hatred is buried, the adequateness with which it is controlled, or in the extent to which it is diluted by compensations. Other characters besides Bigger turn out to be examples of this common hatred with the variety of qualifications I have just mentioned.

For a time, it is true, we do not get this impression. We follow Bigger's activities so closely that we share his collapse after his arrest. But in place of the apathy into which he falls, we recoil with loathing from a sudden recognition that we have been identifying ourselves too closely with his fantasies. His murders now stand forth in all their gruesome tabloid clarity. At this point, Wright introduces the insincere rhetoric of the district attorney and the white mob's demand for lynching. They reawaken our sympathy for Bigger, and bring home to us the relation between his depravity and the dominant social pressures which constantly verbalize the principles of justice and democracy but deny any adequate application of them. As though to prove that such hypocrisy does not merely produce Biggers in the black race but corrupts our whole social fabric, we become aware that this white mob is only concealing its affinity with what is vicious in Bigger by seeking from his lynching a similar paranoid satisfaction of its own frustration. Our loathing of the mob cancels out our reaction against Bigger, and our disgust turns toward the deplorable social system which is responsible for both of them. Bigger's hatred of the whites is itself a variant of the common insecurity of the common man in our culture.

Fortunately, there are forces at work to avert catastrophe in our national life. The demand for Negro labor in time of war, the growing acceptance of Negroes by the trade unions, the appearance of Negroes in the top ranks of virtually every cultural and intellectual profession, the committees on fair employment practices are but a few of the justifications for optimism. Wright might have chosen as his theme the conflict between these two groups of forces, and resolved it in an atmosphere of confidence that history cannot reverse itself and progress is inevitable. But if treated generally, with the stress on the social forces, a distortion of the good intention into sentimentality would be likely. If, on the other hand, the stress were on individual relationships, a powerful and beautiful novel might be written. But it would fail to give the right impression of the general state of affairs. Or it would become a novel not of the Negro people but of proletarian life, whites and blacks working together towards a common end, to the neglect, emotionally, of the racial element altogether.

Wright, on the contrary, has preferred to accept the general situation as it is today. He makes his reader intellectually aware of the economic and political forces at work. But he focuses our attention upon their effect on the individual personality. Desirous above all of banishing our complacency, he is not interested in the rosy promise of the future. He knows that this promise will not be valid unless whites are stimulated to action by a sense of guilt and blacks are guided by some better plan than anarchistic individualism. And so he translates the underlying social forces into their specific exhibition in the relationships of individuals. But he does not neglect the case for hope. Just as he depicts the crisis as the immediate consequence of wrong personal relationships, he seeks to show that the promise of the future depends immediately and specifically upon the capacity for making the right ones. Doubtless this capacity itself is contingent upon a plausible philosophical view of the general situation. But the important point Wright is making is that this general view needs to be written into the very structure of the personality as a capacity for friendship. The relation between Bigger and his lawyer, Max, to which the end of the book is devoted, is intended to serve as prototype of the proper constructive relationship between men generally.

Wright's accomplishment, unfortunately, is not as good as his intention. Though he conveys some impression of what he means, he is confused and repetitious in presenting the case for hope. This is in part the result of a change in method. Up to this point in the narrative, he has been following the general plan of Dreiser's *American Tragedy*. Using an objective method to reveal the subjective state of their hero's personality, on the theory of the influence of environment, both authors have tended to pile up an unnecessary quantity of substantiating detail. But Dreiser's trial scene is monotonous rather than confused. He continues to use the same technique. Wright, on the contrary, departs at this point from Dreiser's method and no longer follows the external probabilities of the situation. The character of Max's plea to the court can hardly be justified. His public speeches would never convince a jury, since they are only projections of his private conversations with Bigger in his cell. Even though during the entire novel we have been interested in Bigger's inner life, we have seen it largely through the frank interpretations of the author, without distortion of the probabilities of everyday life either in the action or the dialogue. Both are now distorted. What the lawyer says becomes ambiguous, and where he says it unlikely. The objective method is superseded by a symbolic one. Wright is no longer the detached commentator but allows his personality to merge with that of the lawyer. This change of technique was doubtless dictated by Wright's desire to involve his audience in a direct emotional appeal. He is addressing them symbolically when Max addresses the court symbolically, as though he were still clarifying Bigger's mind. His intention, if successful, would have brought the book to a crescendo of hope for the future, as Max and Bigger, the author, the court, and the readers merge in a common understanding of friendship and equality. But since Wright is unable to put his message in the clear detail of the earlier sections of the book, the effect is not that of the concluding speech in *Waiting for Lefty*, but of a sudden plunge into Dostoievsky. Wright begins to share the confusions and even something of the hysteria, the negative aspects of which he has been elucidating.

The tone of the book changes. What had given *Native Son* its refreshing atmosphere of sanity was the awareness its objective method assured, that the author had been untouched by the maladies he described. The characters, the situations, our whole social fabric, we had realized with consternation, are parallel to the decadence of Russia before the Revolution, which Dostoievsky exposed so thoroughly, and so obviously shared. Wright, like Dreiser, had stood aloof from the terrible deeds of his characters. But when he turns to the case for hope, the ambiguity of his statement is no more convincing than the frank mysticism of Dostoievsky. That social orientation towards the common man, which alone permits a genuine approach to groups beyond our immediate experience, has been clarified. But the clarification is a deduction the reader skims from the restless surface of its vague restatement. One feels that Wright has not understood Max much better than Bigger has done; and Bigger has surely not got the essence of what he was trying to say at all. From Max's fervid proffer of friendship he has drawn no further aid than the recovery of his self-esteem, and no further meaning than the dogged return to his original delusion (though it is now held in a spirit of tranquillity, as though his life had achieved a constructive aim) that his act of murder was an escape from oppression. It was easier, apparently, for Dostoievsky to accept the mystic belief of Christianity, that part of man is innately good and at war with his innately evil impulses, than for Wright to hunt with the aid of psychology for the ray of hope veiled in the depths of social decay. The anxious verbosity of Max's pleas evokes the suspicion that Wright, against his intention, shares that counterpart of the social neurosis he describes, which is the unconscious fear that hope itself is a fantasy.

Perhaps in a world where grounds for hatred are so valid, even so talented an author may be forgiven if he cannot present with equal skill the case for love and understanding. We may expect that among all our national minorities the Negro will be the last to do so, and that he will do so first in those areas of the working class where genuine friendships can be taken for granted. But as the Negro sees the white world yielding before the pressure of his merit as well as his demands, his psychology will change. He will then know that he has won a place of dignity in the American society, and the newest Negro literature is likely to be the story of his positive achievement.

Many Thousands Gone

JAMES BALDWIN

IT IS ONLY IN HIS MUSIC, WHICH AMERICANS ARE ABLE TO ADMIRE ONLY because a protective sentimentality limits their understanding of it, that the Negro in America has been able to tell his story. It is a story which otherwise has yet to be told and which no American is prepared to hear. As is the inevitable result of things unsaid, we find ourselves until today oppressed with a dangerous and reverberating silence; and the story is told, compulsively, in symbols and signs, in hieroglyphics; it is revealed in Negro speech and in that of the white majority and in their different frames of references. The ways in which the Negro has affected the American psychology is betrayed in our popular culture and in our morality; in our estrangement from him is the depth of our estrangement from ourselves. We cannot ask: what do we *really* feel about him?—such a question merely opens the gates on chaos. What we really feel about him is involved with all that we feel about everything, about everyone, about ourselves.

The story of the Negro in America is the story of America—or, more precisely, it is the story of Americans. It is not a very pretty story: the story of a people is never very pretty. The Negro in America, gloomily referred to as that shadow which lies athwart our national life, is far more than that. He is a series of shadows, self-created, intertwining, which now we helplessly battle. One may say that the Negro in America does not really exist except in the darkness of our minds.

This is why his history and his progress, his relationship to all other Americans, has been kept in the social arena. He is a social and not a personal or a human problem; to think of him is to think of statistics, slums, rapes, injustices, remote violence; it is to be confronted with an endless cataloguing of losses, gains, skirmishes; it is to feel virtuous, outraged, helpless, as though his continuing status among us were somehow analogous to disease—cancer, perhaps, or tuberculosis—which must be checked, even though it cannot be cured. In this arena the black man acquires quite another aspect from that which he has in life. We do not know what to do with him in life; if he

---

breaks our sociological and sentimental image of him we are panic-stricken and we feel ourselves betrayed. When he violates this image, therefore, he stands in the greatest danger (sensing which, we uneasily suspect that he is very often playing a part for our benefit); and, what is not always so apparent but is equally true, we are then in some danger ourselves—hence our retreat or our blind and immediate retaliation.

Our dehumanization of the Negro then is indivisible from our dehumanization of ourselves: the loss of our own identity is the price we pay for our annulment of his. Time and our own force act as our allies, creating an impossible, a fruitless tension between the traditional master and slave. Impossible and fruitless because, literal and visible as this tension has become, it has nothing to do with reality.

Time has made some changes in the Negro face. Nothing has succeeded in making it exactly like our own, though the general desire seems to be to make it blank if one cannot make it white. When it has become blank, the past as thoroughly washed from the black face as it has been from ours, our guilt will be finished—at least it will have ceased to be visible, which we imagine to be much the same thing. But, paradoxically, it is we who prevent this from happening; since it is we who, every hour that we live, re-invest the black face with our guilt; and we do this—by a further paradox, no less ferocious—helplessly, passionately, out of an unrealized need to suffer absolution.

Today, to be sure, we know that the Negro is not biologically or mentally inferior; there is no truth in those rumors of his body odor or his incorrigible sexuality; or no more truth than can be easily explained or even defended by the social sciences. Yet, in our most recent war, his blood was segregated as was, for the most part, his person. Up to today we are set at a division, so that he may not marry our daughters or our sisters, nor may he—for the most part—eat at our tables or live in our houses. Moreover, those who do, do so at the grave expense of a double alienation; from their own people, whose fabled attributes they must either deny or, worse, cheapen and bring to market; from us, for we require of them, when we accept them, that they at once cease to be Negroes and yet not fail to remember what being a Negro means: to remember, that is, what it means to us. The threshold of insult is higher or lower, according to the people involved, from the boot-black in Atlanta to the celebrity in New York. One must travel very far, among saints with nothing to gain or outcasts with nothing to lose, to find a place where it does not matter—and perhaps a word or a gesture or simply a silence will testify that it matters even there.

For it means something to be a Negro, after all, as it means something to have been born in Ireland or in China, to live where one sees space and sky or to live where one sees nothing but rubble or nothing but high buildings. We cannot escape our origins, however hard we try, those origins which contain the key—could we but find it—to all that we later become. What it means to be a Negro is a good deal more than this essay can discover; what it means to be a Negro in America can perhaps be suggested by an examination of the myths we perpetuate about him.

Aunt Jemima and Uncle Tom are dead, their places taken by a group of amazingly well-adjusted young men and women, almost as dark, but ferociously literate, well-dressed and scrubbed; who are never laughed at, who are not likely ever to set foot in a cotton or tobacco field or in any but the most modern of kitchens. There are others who remain in our odd idiom, 'underprivileged'; some are bitter and these come to grief; some are unhappy, but, continually presented with the evidence of a better day soon to come, are speedily becoming less so. Most of them care nothing whatever about race. They want only their proper place in the sun and the right to be left alone, like any other citizen of the republic. We may all breathe more easily. Before, however, our joy at the demise of Aunt Jemima and Uncle Tom approaches the indecent, we had better ask whence they sprang, how they lived? Into what limbo have they vanished?

However inaccurate our portraits of them were, these portraits do suggest, not only the conditions but the quality of their lives and the impact of this spectacle on our consciences. There was no one more forbearing than Aunt Jemima, no one stronger or more pious or more loyal or more wise; there was, at the same time, no one weaker or more faithless or more vicious and certainly no one more immoral. Uncle Tom, trustworthy and sexless, needed only to drop the title "Uncle" to become violent, crafty and sullen, a menace to any white woman who passed by. They prepared our feast tables and our burial clothes; and if we could boast that we understood them, it was far more to the point and far more true that they understood us. They were, moreover, the only people in the world who did; and not only did they know us better than we knew ourselves, but they knew us better than we knew them. This was the piquant flavoring to the national joke, it lay behind our uneasiness as it lay behind our benevolence: Aunt Jemima and Uncle Tom, our creations, at the last evaded us; they had a life—their own, perhaps a better life than ours—and they would never tell us what it was. At the point where we were driven most privately and painfully to conjecture what depths of contempt, what heights of indifference; what prodigies of resilience, what untamable superiority allowed them so vividly to endure, neither perishing, nor rising up in a body to wipe us from the earth, the image perpetually shattered and the word failed. The black man in our midst carried murder in his heart, he wanted vengeance. We carried murder too, we wanted peace.

In our image of the Negro breathes the past we deny, not dead but living yet and powerful, the beast in our jungle of statistics. It is this which defeats us, which continues to defeat us, which lends to inter-racial cocktail parties their rattling, genteel, nervously smiling air: in any drawing room at such a gathering the beast may spring, filling the air with flying things and an unenlightened wailing. Wherever the problem touches there is confusion, there is danger. Wherever the Negro face appears a tension is created, the tension of a silence filled with things unutterable. It is a sentimental error, therefore, to believe that the past is dead; it means nothing to say that it is all forgotten, that the Negro himself has forgotten it. It is not a question of memory. Oedipus did not remember the thongs that bound his feet, nevertheless the marks they left testified to that doom toward which his feet were leading him. The man does not remember the hand that struck him, the darkness that frightened him, as a child; nevertheless, the hand and the darkness remain with him, indivisible from himself forever, part of the passion that drives him wherever he thinks to take flight.

The making of an American begins at that point where he himself rejects all other ties, any other history; and himself adopts the vesture of his adopted land. This problem has been faced by all Americans throughout our history—in a way it *is* our history—and it baffles the immigrant and sets on edge the second generation until today. In the case of the Negro the past was taken from him whether he would or no; yet to forswear it was meaningless and availed him nothing, since his shameful history was carried, quite literally, on his brow. Shameful; for he was heathen as well as black and would never have discovered the healing blood of Christ had not we braved the jungles to bring him these glad tidings. Shameful; for, since our role as missionary had not been wholly disinterested, it was necessary to recall the shame from which we had delivered him in order more easily to escape our own. As he accepted the alabaster Christ and the bloody cross—in the bearing of which he would find his redemption, as, indeed, to our outraged astonishment, he sometimes did—he must, henceforth, accept that image we then gave him of himself: having no other and standing, moreover, in danger of death should he fail to accept the dazzling light thus brought into such darkness. It is this quite simple dilemma that must be borne in mind if we wish to comprehend his psychology.

However we shift the light which beats so fiercely on his head, or *prove*, by victorious social analysis, how his lot has changed, how we have both improved, our uneasiness refuses to be exorcized. And nowhere is this more apparent than in our literature on the subject—'problem' literature when written by whites, 'protest' literature when written by Negroes—and nothing is more striking than the tremendous disparity of tone between the two creations. *Kingsblood Royal* bears, for example, almost no kinship to *If He Hollers Let Him Go*, though the same reviewers praised them both for what were, at bottom, very much the same reasons. These reasons may be suggested, far too briefly but not at all unjustly, by observing that the presupposition is in both novels exactly the same: black is a terrible color with which to be born into the world.

Now the most powerful and celebrated statement we have yet had of what it means to be a Negro in America is unquestionably Richard Wright's *Native Son.* The feeling which prevailed at the time of its publication was that such a novel, bitter, uncompromising, shocking, gave proof, by its very existence, of what strides might be taken in a free democracy; and its indisputable success, proof that Americans were now able to look full in the face without flinching the dreadful facts. Americans, unhappily, have the most remarkable ability to alchemize all bitter truths into an innocuous but piquant confection and to transform their moral contradictions, or public discussion of such contradictions, into a proud decoration, such as are given for heroism on the field of battle. Such a book, we felt with pride, could never have been written before—which was true. Nor could it be written today. It bears already the aspect of a landmark; for Bigger and his brothers have undergone yet another metamorphosis; they have been accepted in baseball leagues and by colleges hitherto exclusive; and they have made a most favorable appearance on the national screen. We have yet to encounter, nevertheless, a report so indisputably authentic, or one that can begin to challenge this most significant novel.

It is, in a certain American tradition, the story of an unremarkable youth in battle with the force of circumstance; that force of circumstance which plays and which has played so important a part in the national fables of success or failure. In this case the force of circumstance is not poverty merely but color, a circumstance which cannot be overcome, against which the protagonist battles for his life and loses. It is, on the surface, remarkable that this book should have enjoyed among Americans the favor it did enjoy; no more remarkable, however, than that it should have been compared, exuberantly to Dostoevsky, though placed a shade below Dos Passos, Dreiser and Steinbeck; and when the book is examined, its impact does not seem remarkable at all, but becomes, on the contrary, perfectly logical and inevitable.

We cannot, to begin with, divorce this book from the specific social climate of that time: it was one of the last of those angry productions encountered in the late 'twenties and all through the 'thirties dealing with the inequities of the social structure of America. It was published one year before our entry into the last world war—which is to say, very few years after the dissolution of the W.P.A. and the end of the New Deal and at a time when bread lines and soup kitchens and bloody industrial battles were bright in everyone's memory. The rigors of that unexpected time filled us not only with a genuinely bewildered and despairing idealism—so that, because there at least was *something* to fight for, young men went off to die in Spain—but also with a genuinely bewildered self-consciousness. The Negro, who had been during the magnificent 'twenties a passionate and delightful primitive, now became, as one of the things we were most self-conscious about, our most oppressed minority. In the 'thirties, swallowing Marx whole, we discovered the Worker and realized—I should think with some relief—that the aims of the Worker and the aims of the Negro were one. This theorem—to which we shall return—seems now to leave rather too much out of account; it became, nevertheless, one of the slogans of the "class struggle" and the gospel of the New Negro.

As for this New Negro, it was Wright who became his most eloquent spokesman; and his work, from its beginning, is most clearly committed to the social struggle. Leaving aside the considerable question of what relationship precisely the artist bears to the revolutionary, the reality of man as a social being is not his only reality and that artist is strangled who is forced to deal with human beings solely in social terms; and who has, moreover, as Wright had, the necessity thrust on him of being the representative of some thirteen million people. It is a false responsibility (since writers are not congressmen) and impossible, by its nature, of fulfillment. The unlucky shepherd soon finds that, so far from being able to feed the hungry sheep, he has lost the wherewithal for his own nourishment: having not been allowed—so fearful was his burden, so present his audience!—to recreate his own experience. Further, the militant men and women of the 'thirties were not, upon examination, significantly emancipated from their antecedents, however bitterly they might consider themselves estranged or however gallantly they struggled to build a better world. However they might extol Russia, their concept of a better world was quite helplessly American and betrayed a certain thinness of imagination, a suspect reliance on suspect and badly digested formulae, and a positively fretful romantic haste. Finally, the relationship of the Negro to the Worker cannot be summed up, nor even greatly illuminated, by saying that their aims are one. It is true only insofar as they both desire better working conditions and useful only insofar as they unite their strength as workers to achieve these ends. Further than this we cannot in honesty go.

In this climate Wright's voice first was heard and the struggle which promised for a time to shape his work and give it purpose also fixed it in an ever more unrewarding rage. Recording his days of anger he has also nevertheless recorded, as no Negro before him had ever done, that fantasy Americans hold in their minds when they speak of the Negro: that fantastic and fearful image which we have lived with since the first slave fell beneath the lash. This is the significance of *Native Son* and also, unhappily, its overwhelming limitation.

Native Son begins with the *Brring!* of an alarm clock in the squalid Chicago tenement where Bigger and his family live. Rats live there too, feeding off the garbage, and we first encounter Bigger in the act of killing one. One may consider that the entire book, from that harsh *Brring!* to Bigger's weak "Good-by" as the lawyer, Max, leaves him in the death cell, is an extension, with the roles inverted, of this chilling metaphor. Bigger's situation and Bigger himself exert on the mind the same sort of fascination. The premise of the book is, as I take it, clearly conveyed in these first pages: we are confronting a monster created by the American republic and we are, through being made to share his experience, to receive illumination as regards the manner of his life and to feel both pity and horror at his awful and inevitable doom. This is an arresting and potentially rich idea and we would be discussing a very different novel if Wright's execution had been more perceptive and if he had not attempted to redeem a symbolical monster in social terms.

One may object that it was precisely Wright's intention to create in Bigger a social symbol, revelatory of social disease and prophetic of disaster. I think, however, that it is this assumption which we ought to examine more carefully. Bigger has no discernible relationship to himself, to his own life, to his own people, nor to any other people—in this respect, perhaps, he is most American—and his force comes, not from his significance as a social (or anti-social) unit, but from his significance as the incarnation of a myth. It is remarkable that, though we follow him step by step from the tenement room to the death cell, we know as little about him when this journey is ended as we did when it began; and, what is even more remarkable, we know almost as little about the social dynamic which we are to believe created him. Despite the details of slum life which we are given, I doubt that anyone who has thought about it, disengaging himself from sentimentality, can accept this most essential premise of the novel for a moment. Those Negroes who surround him, on the other hand, his hard-working mother, his ambitious sister, his poolroom cronies, Bessie, might be considered as far richer and far more subtle and accurate illustrations of the ways in which Negroes are controlled in our society and the complex techniques they have evolved for their survival. We are limited, however, to Bigger's view of them, part of a deliberate plan which might not have been disastrous if we were not also limited to Bigger's perceptions. What this means for the novel is that a necessary dimension has been cut away; this dimension being the relationship that Negroes bear to one another, that depth of involvement and unspoken recognition of shared experience which creates a way of life. What the novel reflects—and at no point interprets—is the isolation of the Negro within his own group and the resulting fury of impatient scorn. It is this which creates its climate of anarchy and unmotivated and unapprehended disaster; and it is this climate, common to most Negro protest novels, which has led us all to believe that in Negro life there exists no tradition, no field of manners, no possibility of ritual or intercourse, such as may, for example, sustain the Jew even after he has left his father's house. But the fact is not that the Negro has no tradition but that there has as yet arrived no sensibility sufficiently profound and tough to make this tradition articulate. For a tradition expresses, after all, nothing more than the long and painful experience of a people; it comes out of the battle waged to maintain their integrity or, to put it more simply, out of their struggle to survive. When we speak of the Jewish tradition we are speaking of centuries of exile and persecution, of the strength which endured and the sensibility which discovered in it the high possibility of the moral victory.

This sense of how Negroes live and how they have so long endured is hidden from us in part by the very speed of the Negro's public progress, a progress so heavy with complexity, so bewildering and kaleidoscopic, that he dare not pause to conjecture on the darkness which lies behind him; and by the nature of the American psychology which, in order to apprehend or be made able to accept it, must undergo a metamorphosis so profound as to be literally unthinkable and which there is no doubt we will resist until we are compelled to achieve our own identity by the rigors of a time that has yet to come. Bigger, in the meanwhile, and all his furious kin, serve only to whet the notorious national taste for the sensational and to reinforce all that we now find it necessary to believe. It is not Bigger whom we fear, since his appearance among us makes our victory certain. It is the others, who smile, who go to church, who give no cause for complaint, whom we sometimes consider with amusement, with pity, even with affection—and in whose faces we sometimes surprise the merest arrogant hint of hatred, the faintest, withdrawn, speculative shadow of contempt—who make us uneasy; whom we cajole, threaten, flatter, fear; who to us remain unknown, though we are not (we feel with both relief and hostility and with bottomless confusion) unknown to them. It is out of our reaction to these hewers of wood and drawers of water that our image of Bigger was created.

It is this image, living yet, which we perpetually seek to evade with good works; and this image which makes of all our good works an intolerable mockery. The 'nigger,' black, benighted, brutal, consumed with hatred as we are consumed with guilt, cannot be thus blotted out. He stands at our shoulders when we give our maid her wages, it is his hand which we fear we are taking when struggling to communicate with the current 'intelligent' Negro, his stench, as it were, which fills our mouths with salt as the monument is unveiled in honor of the latest Negro leader. Each generation has shouted behind him, *Nigger!* as he walked our streets; it is he whom we would rather our sisters did not marry; he is banished into the vast and wailing outer darkness whenever we speak of the 'purity' of our women, of the 'sanctity' of our homes, of 'American' ideals. What is more, he knows it. He is indeed the 'native son': he is the 'nigger.' Let us refrain from inquiring at the moment whether or not he actually exists; for we *believe* that he exists. Whenever we encounter him amongst us in the flesh, our faith is made perfect and his necessary and bloody end is executed with a mystical ferocity of joy.

But there is a complementary faith among the damned which involves their gathering of the stones with which those who walk in the light shall stone them; or there exists among the intolerably degraded the perverse and powerful desire to force into the arena of the actual those fantastic crimes of which they have been accused, achieving their vengeance and their own destruction through making the nightmare real. The American image of the Negro lives also in the Negro's heart; and when he has surrendered to this image life has no other possible reality. Then he, like the white enemy with whom he will be locked one day in mortal struggle, has no means save this of asserting his identity. This is why Bigger's murder of Mary can be referred to as an "act of creation" and why, once this murder has been committed, he can feel for the first time that he is living fully and deeply as a man was meant to live. And there is, I should think, no Negro living in America who has not felt, briefly or for long periods, with anguish sharp or dull, in varying degrees and to varying effect, simple, naked and unanswerable hatred; who has not wanted to smash any white face he may encounter in a day, to violate, out of motives of the cruelest vengeance, their women, to break the bodies of all white people and bring them low, as low as that dust into which he himself has been and is being trampled; no Negro, finally, who has not had to make his own precarious adjustment to the 'nigger' who surrounds him and to the 'nigger' in himself.

Yet the adjustment must be made—rather, it must be attempted, the tension perpetually sustained—for without this he has surrendered his birthright as a man no less than his birthright as a black man. The entire universe is then peopled only with his enemies, who are not only white men armed with rope and rifle, but his own far-flung and contemptible kinsmen. Their blackness is his degradation and it is their stupid and passive endurance which makes his end inevitable.

Bigger dreams of some black man who will weld all blacks together into a mighty fist, and feels, in relation to his family, that perhaps they had to live as they did precisely because none of them had ever done anything, right or wrong, which mattered very much. It is only he who, by an act of murder, has burst the dungeon cell. He has made it manifest that *he* lives and that his despised blood nourishes the passions of a man. He has forced his oppressors to see the fruit of that oppression: and he feels, when his family and his friends come to visit him in the death cell, that they should not be weeping or frightened, that they should be happy, *proud* that he has dared, through murder and now through his own imminent destruction, to redeem their anger and humiliation, that he has hurled into the spiritless obscurity of their lives the lamp of his passionate life and death. Henceforth, they may remember Bigger—who has died, as we may conclude, for them. But they do not feel this; they only know that he has murdered two women and precipitated a reign of terror; and that now he is to die in the electric chair. They therefore weep and are honestly frightened—for which Bigger despises them and wishes to 'blot' them out. What is missing in his situation and in the representation of his psychology—which makes his situation false and his psychology incapable of development—is any revelatory apprehension of

Bigger as one of the Negro's realities or as one of the Negro's roles. This failure is part of the previously noted failure to convey any sense of Negro life as a continuing and complex group reality. Bigger, who cannot function therefore as a reflection of the social illness, having, as it were, no society to reflect, likewise refuses to function on the loftier level of the Christ-symbol. His kinsmen are quite right to weep and be frightened, even to be appalled: for it is not his love for them or for himself which causes him to die, but his hatred and his self-hatred; he does not redeem the pains of a despised people, but reveals, on the contrary, nothing more than his own fierce bitterness at having been born one of them. In this also he is the "native son," his progress determinable by the speed with which the distance increases between himself and the auction-block and all that the auction-block implies. To have penetrated this phenomenon, this inward contention of love and hatred, blackness and whiteness, would have given him a stature more nearly human and an end more nearly tragic; and would have given us a document more profoundly and genuinely bitter and less harsh with an anger which is, on the one hand, exhibited and, on the other hand, denied.

Native Son finds itself at length so trapped by the American image of Negro life and by the American necessity to find the ray of hope that it cannot pursue its own implications. This is why Bigger must be at the last redeemed, to be received, if only by rhetoric, into that community of phantoms which is our tenaciously held ideal of the happy social life. It is the socially conscious whites who receive him—the Negroes being capable of no such objectivity—and we have, by way of illustration, that lamentable scene in which Jan, Mary's lover, forgives him for her murder; and, carrying the explicit burden of the novel, Max's long speech to the jury. This speech, which really ends the book, is one of the most desperate performances in American fiction. It is the question of Bigger's humanity which is at stake, the relationship in which he stands to all other Americans—and, by implication, to all people—and it is precisely this question which it cannot clarify, with which it cannot, in fact, come to any coherent terms. He is the monster created by the American republic, the present awful sum of generations of oppression; but to say that he is a monster is to fall into the trap of making him subhuman and he must, therefore, be made representative of a way of life which is real and human in precise ratio to the degree to which it seems to us monstrous and strange. It seems to me that this idea carries, implicitly, a most remarkable confession, that is, that Negro life is in fact as debased and impoverished as our theology claims; and, further, that the use to which Wright puts this idea can only proceed from the assumption—not entirely unsound—that Americans, who evade, so far as possible, all genuine experience, have therefore no way of assessing the experience of others and no way of establishing themselves in relation to any way of life which is not their own. The privacy or obscurity of Negro life makes that life capable, in our imaginations, of producing anything at all; and thus the idea of Bigger's monstrosity can be presented without fear of contradiction, since no American has the knowledge or authority to contest it and no Negro has the voice. It is an idea, which, in the framework of the novel, is dignified by the possibility it promptly affords of presenting Bigger as the herald of disaster, the danger signal of a more bitter time to come when not Bigger alone but all his kindred will rise, in the name of the many thousands who have perished in fire and flood and by rope and torture, to demand their rightful vengeance.

But it is not quite fair, it seems to me, to exploit the national innocence in this way. The idea of Bigger as a warning boomerangs not only because it is quite beyond the limit of probability that Negroes in America will ever achieve the means of wreaking vengeance upon the state but also because it cannot be said that they have any desire to do so. *Native Son* does not convey the altogether savage paradox of the American Negro's situation, of which the social reality which we prefer with such hopeful superficiality to study is but, as it were, the shadow. It is not simply the relationship of oppressed to oppressor, of master to slave, nor is it motivated merely by hatred; it is also, literally and morally, a *blood* relationship, perhaps the most profound reality of the American experience, and we cannot begin to unlock it until we accept how very much it contains of the force and anguish and terror of love.

Negroes are Americans and their destiny is the country's destiny. They have no other experience besides their experience on this continent and it is an experience which cannot be rejected, which yet remains to be embraced. If, as I believe, no American Negro exists who does not have his private Bigger Thomas living in the skull, then what most significantly fails to be illuminated here is the paradoxical adjustment which is perpetually made, the Negro being compelled to accept the fact that this dark and dangerous and unloved stranger is part of himself forever. Only this recognition sets him in any wise free and it is this, this necessary ability to contain and even, in the most honorable sense of the word, to *exploit* the 'nigger' which lends to Negro life its high element of the ironic and which causes the most well-meaning of their American critics to make such exhilarating errors when attempting to understand them. To present Bigger as a warning is simply to reinforce the American guilt and fear concerning him, it is most forcefully to limit him to that previously mentioned social arena in which he has no human validity, it is simply to condemn him to death. For he has always been a warning, he represents the evil, the sin and suffering which we are compelled to reject. It is useless to say to the courtroom in which this heathen sits on trial that he is their responsibility, their creation, and his crimes are theirs; and that they ought, therefore, to allow him to live, to make articulate to himself behind the walls of prison the meaning of his existence. The meaning of his existence has already been most adequately expressed, nor does anyone wish, particularly not in the name of democracy, to think of it any more; as for the possibility of articulation, it is this possibility which above all others we most dread. Moreover, the courtroom, judge, jury, witnesses and spectators, recognize immediately that Bigger is their creation and they recognize this not only with hatred and fear and guilt and the resulting fury of self-righteousness but also with that morbid fullness of pride mixed with horror with which one regards the extent and power of one's wickedness. They know that death is his portion, that he runs to death; coming from darkness and dwelling in darkness, he must be, as often as he rises, banished, lest the entire planet be engulfed. And they know, finally, that they do not wish to forgive him and that he does not wish to be forgiven; that he dies, hating them, scorning that appeal which they cannot make to that irrecoverable humanity of his which cannot hear it; and that he *wants* to die because he glories in his hatred and prefers, like Lucifer, rather to rule in hell than serve in heaven.

For, bearing in mind the premise on which the life of such a man is based, *i.e.*, that black is the color of damnation, this is his only possible end. It is the only death which will allow him a kind of dignity or even, however horribly, a kind of beauty. To tell this story, no more than a single aspect of the story of the 'nigger,' is inevitably and richly to become involved with the force of life and legend, how each perpetually assumes the guise of the other, creating that dense, many-sided and shifting reality which is the world we live in and the world we make. To tell his story is to begin to liberate us from his image and it is, for the first time, to clothe this phantom with flesh and blood, to deepen, by our understanding of him and his relationship to us, our understanding of ourselves and of all men.

But this is not the story which *Native Son* tells, for we find here merely, repeated in anger, the story which we have told in pride. Nor, since the implications of this anger are evaded, are we ever confronted with the actual or potential significance of our pride; which is why we fall, with such a positive glow of recognition, upon Max's long and bitter summing up. It is addressed to those among us of good will and it seems to say that, though there are whites and blacks among us who hate each other, we will not; there are those who are betrayed by greed, by guilt, by blood lust, but not we; we will set our faces against them and join hands and walk together into that dazzling future when there will be no white or black. This is the dream of all liberal men, a dream not at all dishonorable, but, nevertheless, a dream. For, let us join hands on this mountain as we may, the battle is elsewhere. It proceeds far from us in the heat and horror and pain of life itself where all men are betrayed by greed and guilt and blood-lust and where no one's hands are clean. Our good will, from which we yet expect such power to transform us, is thin, passionless, strident: its roots, examined, lead us back to our forebears, whose assumption it was that the black man, to become truly human and acceptable, must first become like us. This assumption once accepted, the Negro in America can only acquiesce in the obliteration of his own personality, the distortion and debasement of his own experience, surrendering to those forces which reduce the person to anonymity and which make themselves manifest daily all over the darkening world.

Black Boys and Native Sons

IRVING HOWE

JAMES BALDWIN FIRST CAME TO THE NOTICE OF THE AMERICAN LITERARY public not through his own fiction but as author of an impassioned criticism of the conventional Negro novel. In 1949 he published in *Partisan Review* an essay called "Everybody's Protest Novel," attacking the kind of fiction, from *Uncle Tom's Cabin* to *Native Son*, that had been written about the ordeal of the American Negroes; and two years later he printed in the same magazine "Many Thousands Gone," a tougher and more explicit polemic against Richard Wright and the school of naturalistic "protest" fiction that Wright represented. The protest novel, wrote Baldwin, is undertaken out of sympathy for the Negro, but through its need to present him merely as a social victim or a mythic agent of sexual prowess, it hastens to confine the Negro to the very tones of violence he has known all his life. Compulsively re-enacting and magnifying his trauma, the protest novel proves unable to transcend it. So choked with rage has this kind of writing become, it cannot show the Negro as a unique person or locate him as a member of a community with its own traditions and values, its own "unspoken recognition of shared experience which creates a way of life." The failure of the protest novel "lies in its insistence that it is [man's] categorization alone which is real and which cannot be transcended."

Like all attacks launched by young writers against their famous elders, Baldwin's essays were also a kind of announcement of his own intentions. He wrote admiringly about Wright's courage ("his work was an immense liberation and revelation for me"), but now, precisely because Wright had prepared the way for all the Negro writers to come, he, Baldwin, would go further, transcending the sterile categories of "Negro-ness," whether those enforced by the white world or

---

From *A World More Attractive: A View of Modern Literature and Politics* by Irving Howe (New York: Horizon Press, 1963), 98–110. Reprinted by permission of the author. "Black Boys and Native Sons" appeared originally in *Dissent* (Autumn 1963).

those defensively erected by the Negroes themselves. No longer mere victim or rebel, the Negro would stand free in a self-achieved humanity. As Baldwin put it some years later, he hoped "to prevent myself from becoming *merely* a Negro; or even, merely a Negro writer." The world "tends to trap and immobilize you in the role you play," and for the Negro writer, if he is to be a writer at all, it hardly matters whether the trap is sprung from motives of hatred or condescension.

Baldwin's rebellion against the older Negro novelist who had served him as a model and had helped launch his career, was not of course an unprecedented event. The history of literature is full of such painful ruptures, and the issue Baldwin raised is one that keeps recurring, usually as an aftermath to a period of "socially engaged" writing. The novel is an inherently ambiguous genre: it strains toward formal autonomy and can seldom avoid being a public gesture. If it is true, as Baldwin said in "Everybody's Protest Novel," that "literature and sociology are not one and the same," it is equally true that such statements hardly begin to cope with the problem of how a writer's own experience affects his desire to represent human affairs in a work of fiction. Baldwin's formula evades, through rhetorical sweep, the genuinely difficult issue of the relationship between social experience and literature.

Yet in *Notes of a Native Son,* the book in which his remark appears, Baldwin could also say: "One writes out of one thing only—one's own experience." What, then, was the experience of a man with a black skin, what *could* it be in this country? How could a Negro put pen to paper, how could he so much as think or breathe, without some impulsion to protest, be it harsh or mild, political or private, released or buried? The "sociology" of his existence formed a constant pressure on his literary work, and not merely in the way this might be true for any writer, but with a pain and ferocity that nothing could remove.

James Baldwin's early essays are superbly eloquent, displaying virtually in full the gifts that would enable him to become one of the great American rhetoricians. But these essays, like some of the later ones, are marred by rifts in logic, so little noticed when one gets swept away by the brilliance of the language that it takes a special effort to attend their argument.

Later Baldwin would see the problems of the Negro writer with a greater charity and more mature doubt. Reviewing in 1959 a book of poems by Langston Huges, he wrote: "Hughes is an American Negro poet and has no choice but to be acutely aware of it. He is not the first American Negro to find the war between his social and artistic responsibilities all but irreconcilable." All but irreconcilable: the phrase strikes a note sharply different from Baldwin's attack upon Wright in the early fifties. And it is not hard to surmise the reasons for this change. In the intervening years Baldwin had been living through some of the experiences that had goaded Richard Wright into rage and driven him into exile; he too, like Wright, had been to hell and back, many times over.

II

Gawd, Ah wish all them white folks was dead.

The day *Native Son* appeared, American culture was changed forever. No matter how much qualifying the book might later need, it made impossible a repetition of the old lies. In all its crudeness, melodrama and claustrophobia of vision, Richard Wright's novel brought out into the open, as no one ever had before, the hatred, fear and violence that have crippled and may yet destroy our culture.

A blow at the white man, the novel forced him to recognize himself as an oppressor. A blow at the black man, the novel forced him to recognize the cost of his submission. *Native Son* assaulted the most cherished of American vanities: the hope that the accumulated injustice of the past would bring with it no lasting penalties, the fantasy that in his humiliation the Negro somehow retained a sexual potency—or was it a childlike good-nature?—that made it necessary to envy and still more to suppress him. Speaking from the black wrath of retribution, Wright insisted that history can be a punishment. He told us the one thing even the most liberal whites preferred not to hear: that Negroes were far from patient or forgiving, that they were scarred by fear, that they hated every moment of their suppression even when seeming most acquiescent, and that often enough they hated *us,* the decent and cultivated white men who from complicity or neglect shared in the responsibility for their plight. If such younger novelists as Baldwin and Ralph Ellison were to move beyond Wright's harsh naturalism and toward more supple modes of fiction, that was possible only because Wright had been there first, courageous enough to release the full weight of his anger.

In *Black Boy,* the autobiographical narrative he published several years later, Wright would tell of an experience he had while working as a bellboy in the South. Many times he had come into a hotel room carrying luggage or food and seen naked white women lounging about, unmoved by shame at his presence, for "blacks were not considered human beings anyway . . . I was a non-man . . . I felt doubly cast out." With the publication of *Native Son,* however, Wright forced his readers to acknowledge his anger, and in that way, if none other, he wrested for himself a sense of dignity as a man. He forced his readers to confront the disease of our culture, and to one of its most terrifying symptoms he gave the name of Bigger Thomas.

Brutal and brutalized, lost forever to his unexpended hatred and his fear of the world, a numbed and illiterate black boy stumbling into a murder and never, not even at the edge of the electric chair, breaking through to an understanding of either his plight or himself, Bigger Thomas was a part of Richard Wright, a part even of the James

Baldwin who stared with horror at Wright's Bigger, unable either to absorb him into his consciousness or eject him from it. Enormous courage, a discipline of self-conquest, was required to conceive Bigger Thomas, for this was no eloquent Negro spokesman, no admirable intellectual or formidable proletarian. Bigger was drawn—one would surmise, deliberately—from white fantasy and white contempt. Bigger was the worst of Negro life accepted, then rendered a trifle conscious and thrown back at those who had made him what he was. "No American Negro exists," Baldwin would later write, "who does not have his private Bigger Thomas living in the skull."

Wright drove his narrative to the very core of American phobia: sexual fright, sexual violation. He understood that the fantasy of rape is a consequence of guilt, what the whites suppose themselves to deserve. He understood that the white man's notion of uncontaminated Negro vitality, little as it had to do with the bitter realities of Negro life, reflected some ill-formed and buried feeling that our culture has run down, lost its blood, become febrile. And he grasped the way in which the sexual issue has been intertwined with social relationships, for even as the white people who hire Bigger as their chauffeur are decent and charitable, even as the girl he accidentally kills is a liberal of sorts, theirs is the power and the privilege. "We black and they white. They got things and we ain't. They do things and we can't."

The novel barely stops to provision a recognizable social world, often contenting itself with cartoon simplicities and yielding almost entirely to the nightmare incomprehension of Bigger Thomas. The mood is apocalyptic, the tone superbly aggressive. Wright was an existentialist long before he heard the name, for he was committed to the literature of extreme situations both through the pressures of his rage and the gasping hope of an ultimate catharsis.

Wright confronts both the violence and the crippling limitations of Bigger Thomas. For Bigger white people are not people at all, but something more, "a sort of great natural force, like a stormy sky looming overhead." And only through violence does he gather a little meaning in life, pitifully little: "he had murdered and created a new life for himself." Beyond that Bigger cannot go.

At first *Native Son* seems still another naturalistic novel: a novel of exposure and accumulation, charting the waste of the undersides of the American city. Behind the book one senses the molding influence of Theodore Dreiser, especially the Dreiser of *An American Tragedy* who knows there are situations so oppressive that only violence can provide their victims with the hope of dignity. Like Dreiser, Wright wished to pummel his readers into awareness; like Dreiser, to overpower them with the sense of society as an enclosing force. Yet the comparison is finally of limited value, and for the disconcerting reason that Dreiser had a white skin and Wright a black one.

The usual naturalistic novel is written with detachment, as if by a scientist surveying a field of operations; it is a novel in which the writer withdraws from a detested world and coldly piles up the evidence for detesting it. *Native Son,* though preserving some of the devices of the naturalistic novel, deviates sharply from its characteristic tone: a tone Wright could not possibly have maintained and which, it may be, no Negro novelist can really hold for long. *Native Son* is a work of assault rather than withdrawal; the author yields himself in part to a vision of nightmare. Bigger's cowering perception of the world becomes the most vivid and authentic component of the book. Naturalism pushed to an extreme turns here into something other than itself, a kind of expressionist outburst, no longer a replica of the familiar social world but a self-contained realm of grotesque emblems.

That *Native Son* has grave faults anyone can see. The language is often coarse, flat in rhythm, syntactically overburdened, heavy with journalistic slag. Apart from Bigger, who seems more a brute energy than a particularized figure, the characters have little reality, the Negroes being mere stock accessories and the whites either "agit-prop" villains or heroic Communists whom Wright finds it easier to admire from a distance than establish from the inside. The long speech by Bigger's radical lawyer Max (again a device apparently borrowed from Dreiser) is ill-related to the book itself: Wright had not achieved Dreiser's capacity for absorbing everything, even the most recalcitrant philosophical passages, into a unified vision of things. Between Wright's feelings as a Negro and his beliefs as a Communist there is hardly a genuine fusion, and it is through this gap that a good part of the novel's unreality pours in.

Yet it should be said that the endlessly-repeated criticism that Wright caps his melodrama with a party-line oration tends to oversimplify the novel, for Wright is too honest simply to allow the propagandistic message to constitute the last word. Indeed, the last word is given not to Max but to Bigger. For at the end Bigger remains at the mercy of his hatred and fear, the lawyer retreats helplessly, the projected union between political consciousness and raw revolt has not been achieved—as if Wright were persuaded that, all ideology apart, there is for each Negro an ultimate trial that he can bear only by himself.

Black Boy, which appeared five years after *Native Son,* is a slighter but more skillful piece of writing. Richard Wright came from a broken home, and as he moved from his helpless mother to a grandmother whose religious fanaticism (she was a Seventh-Day Adventist) proved utterly suffocating, he soon picked up a precocious knowledge of vice and a realistic awareness of social power. This autobiographical memoir, a small classic in the literature of self-discovery, is packed with harsh evocations of Negro adolescence in the South. The young Wright learns how wounding it is to wear the mask of a grinning niggerboy in order to keep a job. He examines the life of the Negroes and judges it without charity or idyllic compensation—for he already knows, in his heart and his bones, that to be oppressed means to lose out on human possibilities. By the time he is seventeen, preparing to leave for Chicago, where he will work on a WPA project, become a member of the Communist Party, and publish his first book of stories called *Uncle Tom's Children,* Wright has managed to achieve the beginnings of consciousness, through a slow and painful growth from the very bottom of deprivation to the threshold of artistic achievement and a glimpsed idea of freedom.

III

Baldwin's attack upon Wright had partly been anticipated by the more sophisticated American critics. Alfred Kazin, for example, had found in Wright a troubling obsession with violence:

> If he chose to write the story of Bigger Thomas as a grotesque crime story, it is because his own indignation and the sickness of the age combined to make him dependent on violence and shock, to astonish the reader by torrential scenes of cruelty, hunger, rape, murder and flight, and then enlighten him by crude Stalinist homilies.

The last phrase apart, something quite similar could be said about the author of *Crime and Punishment;* it is disconcerting to reflect upon how few novelists, even the very greatest, could pass this kind of moral inspection. For the novel as a genre seems to have an inherent bias toward extreme effects, such as violence, cruelty and the like. More important, Kazin's judgment rests on the assumption that a critic can readily distinguish between the genuine need of a writer to cope with ugly realities and the damaging effect these realities may have upon his moral and psychic life. But in regard to contemporary writers one finds it very hard to distinguish between a valid portrayal of violence and an obsessive involvement with it. A certain amount of obsession may be necessary for the valid portrayal—writers devoted to themes of desperation cannot keep themselves morally intact. And when we come to a writer like Richard Wright, who deals with the most degraded and inarticulate sector of the Negro world, the distinction between objective rendering and subjective immersion becomes still more difficult, perhaps even impossible. For a novelist who has lived through the searing experiences that Wright has there cannot be much possibility of approaching his subject with the "mature" poise recommended by high-minded critics. What is more, the very act of writing his novel, the effort to confront what Bigger Thomas means to him, is for such a writer a way of dredging up and then perhaps shedding the violence that society has pounded into him. Is Bigger an authentic projection of a social reality, or is he a symptom of Wright's "dependence on violence and shock?" Obviously both; and it could not be otherwise.

For the reality pressing upon all of Wright's work was a nightmare of remembrance, everything from which he had pulled himself out, with an effort and at a cost that is almost unimaginable. Without the terror of that nightmare it would have been impossible for Wright to summon the truth of the reality—not the only truth about American Negroes, perhaps not even the deepest one, but a primary and inescapable truth. Both truth and terror rested on a gross fact which Wright alone dared to confront: that violence is a central fact in the life of the American Negro, defining and crippling him with a harshness few other Americans need suffer. "No American Negro exists who does not have his private Bigger Thomas living in the skull."

Now I think it would be well not to judge in the abstract, or with much haste, the violence that gathers in the Negro's heart as a response to the violence he encounters in society. It would be well to see this violence as part of an historical experience that is open to moral scrutiny but ought to be shielded from presumptuous moralizing. Bigger Thomas may be enslaved to a hunger for violence, but anyone reading *Native Son* with mere courtesy must observe the way in which Wright, even while yielding emotionally to Bigger's deprivation, also struggles to transcend it. That he did not fully succeed seems obvious; one may doubt that any Negro writer can.

More subtle and humane than either Kazin's or Baldwin's criticism is a remark made by Isaac Rosenfeld while reviewing *Black Boy:* "As with all Negroes and all men who are born to suffer social injustice, part of [Wright's] humanity found itself only in acquaintance with violence, and in hatred of the oppressor." Surely Rosenfeld was not here inviting an easy acquiescence in violence; he was trying to suggest the historical context, the psychological dynamics, which condition the attitudes all Negro writers take, or must take, toward violence. To say this is not to propose the condescension of exempting Negro writers from moral judgment, but to suggest the terms of understanding, and still more, the terms of hesitation for making a judgment.

There were times when Baldwin grasped this point better than anyone else. If he could speak of the "unrewarding rage" of *Native Son,* he also spoke of the book as "an immense liberation." Is it impudent to suggest that one reason he felt the book to be a liberation was precisely its rage, precisely the relief and pleasure that he, like so many other Negroes, must have felt upon seeing those long-suppressed emotions finally breaking through?

The kind of literary criticism Baldwin wrote was very fashionable in America during the post-war years. Mimicking the Freudian corrosion of motives and bristling with dialectical agility, this criticism approached all ideal claims, especially those made by radical and naturalist writers, with a weary skepticism and proceeded to transfer the values such writers were attacking to the perspective from which they attacked. If Dreiser wrote about the power hunger and dream of success corrupting American society, that was because he was really infatuated with them. If Farrell showed the meanness of life in the Chicago slums, that was because he could not really escape it. If Wright portrayed the violence gripping Negro life, that was because he was really obsessed with it. The word "really" or more sophisticated equivalents could do endless service in behalf of a generation of intellectuals soured on the tradition of protest but suspecting they might be pigmies in comparison to the writers who had protested. In reply, there was no way to "prove" that Dreiser, Farrell and Wright were not contaminated by the false values they attacked; probably, since they were mere mortals living in the present society, they were contaminated; and so one had to keep insisting that such writers were nevertheless presenting actualities of modern experience, not merely phantoms of their neuroses.

If Bigger Thomas, as Baldwin said, "accepted a theology that denies him life," if in his Negro self-hatred he "*wants* to die because he glories in his hatred," this did not constitute a criticism of Wright unless one were prepared to assume what was simply preposterous: that Wright, for all his emotional involvement with Bigger, could not see beyond the limitations of the character he had created. This was a question Baldwin never seriously confronted in his early essays. He would describe accurately the limitations of Bigger Thomas and then, by one of those rhetorical leaps at which he is so gifted, would assume that these were also the limitations of Wright or his book.

Still another ground for Baldwin's attack was his reluctance to accept the clenched militancy of Wright's posture as both novelist and man. In a remarkable sentence appearing in "Everybody's Protest Novel," Baldwin wrote, "our humanity is our burden, our life; we need not battle for it; we need only to do what is infinitely more difficult—that is, accept it." What Baldwin was saying here was part of the outlook so many American intellectuals took over during the years of a post-war liberalism not very different from conservatism. Ralph Ellison expressed this view in terms still more extreme: "Thus to see America with an awareness of its rich diversity and its almost magical fluidity and freedom, I was forced to conceive of a novel unburdened by the narrow naturalism which has led after so many triumphs to the final and unrelieved despair which marks so much of our current fiction." This note of willed affirmation—as if one could *decide* one's deepest and most authentic response to society! —was to be heard in many other works of the early fifties, most notably in Saul Bellow's *Adventures of Augie March.* Today it is likely to strike one as a note whistled in the dark. In response to Baldwin and Ellison, Wright would have said (I virtually quote the words he used in talking to me during the summer of 1958) that only through struggle could men with black skins, and for that matter, all the oppressed of the world, achieve their humanity. It was a lesson, said Wright with a touch of bitterness yet not without kindness, that the younger writers would have to learn in their own way and their own time. All that has happened since, bears him out.

One criticism made by Baldwin in writing about *Native Son,* perhaps because it is the least ideological, remains important. He complained that in Wright's novel "a necessary dimension has been cut away; this dimension being the relationship that Negroes bear to one another, that depth of involvement and unspoken recognition of shared experience which creates a way of life." The climate of the book, "common to most Negro protest novels . . . has led us all to believe that in Negro life there exists no tradition, no field of manners, no possibility of ritual or intercourse, such as may, for example, sustain the Jew even after he has left his father's house." It could be urged, perhaps, that in composing a novel verging on expressionism Wright need not be expected to present the Negro world with fullness, balance or nuance; but there can be little doubt that in this respect Baldwin did score a major point: the posture of militancy, no matter how great the need for it, exacts a heavy price from the writer, as indeed from everyone else. For "Even the hatred of squalor / Makes the brow grow stern / Even anger against injustice / Makes the voice grow harsh . . ." All one can ask, by way of reply, is whether the refusal to struggle may not exact a still greater price. It is a question that would soon be tormenting James Baldwin, and almost against his will.

The World and the Jug

RALPH ELLISON

What runs counter to the revolutionary convention is, in revolutionary histories, suppressed more imperiously than embarrassing episodes in private memoirs, and by the same obscure forces. . . .

—Andre Malraux

First, three questions: Why is it so often true that when critics confront the American as *Negro* they suddenly drop their advanced critical armament and revert with an air of confident superiority to quite primitive modes of analysis? Why is it that sociology-oriented critics seem to rate literature so far below politics and ideology that they would rather kill a novel than modify their presumptions concerning a given reality which it seeks in its own terms to project? Finally, why is it that so many of those who would tell us the meaning of Negro life never bother to learn how varied it really is?

These questions are aroused by "Black Boys and Native Sons," an essay by Irving Howe, the well-known critic and editor of *Dissent,* in the Autumn 1963 issue of that magazine. It is a lively piece, written with something of the Olympian authority that characterized Hannah Arendt's "Reflections on Little Rock" in the Winter 1959 *Dissent* (a dark foreshadowing of the Eichmann blowup). And in addition to a hero, Richard Wright, it has *two* villains, James Baldwin and Ralph Ellison, who are seen as "black boys" masquerading as false, self-deceived "native sons." Wright himself is given a diversity of roles (all conceived by Howe): He is not only the archetypal and true-blue black boy—the "honesty" of his famous autobiography established this for Howe—but the spiritual father of Ellison, Baldwin and all other Negroes of literary bent to come. Further, in the platonic sense he is his own father and the culture hero who freed Ellison and Baldwin to write more "modulated" prose.

Howe admires Wright's accomplishments, and is frankly annoyed by the more favorable evaluation currently placed upon the works of the younger men. His claims for *Native Son* are quite broad:

> The day [it] appeared, American culture was changed forever . . . it made impossible a repetition of the old lies . . . it brought into the open . . . the fear and violence that have crippled and may yet destroy our culture . . . A blow at the white man, the novel forced him to recognize himself as an oppressor. A blow at the black man, the novel forced him to recognize the cost of his submission. *Native Son* assaulted the most cherished of American vanities: the hope that the accumulated injustices of the past would bring with it no lasting penalties, the fantasy that in his humiliation the Negro somehow retained a sexual potency . . . that made it necessary to envy and still more to suppress him. Speaking from the black wrath of retribution, Wright insisted that history can be a punishment. He told us the one thing even the most liberal whites preferred not to hear: that Negroes were far from patient or forgiving, that they were scarred by fear, that they hated every moment of their suppression even when seeming most acquiescent, and that often enough they hated *us,* the decent and cultivated white men who from complicity or neglect shared in the responsibility of their plight.

There are also negative criticisms: that the book is "crude," "melodramatic" and marred by "claustrophobia" of vision, that its characters are "cartoons," etc. But these defects Howe forgives because of the book's "clenched militancy." One wishes he had stopped there. For, in his zeal to champion Wright, it is as though he felt it necessary to stage a modern version of the biblical myth of Noah, Ham, Shem and Japheth (based originally, I'm told, on a castration ritual), with first Baldwin and then Ellison acting out the impious role of Ham:

Baldwin by calling attention to Noah-Wright's artistic nakedness in his famous essays, "Everybody's Protest Novel" (1949) and "Many Thousands Gone" (1951); Ellison by rejecting "narrow naturalism" as a fictional method, and by alluding to the "diversity, fluidity and magical freedom of American life" on that (for him at least) rather magical occasion when he was awarded the National Book Award. Ellison also offends by having the narrator of *Invisible Man* speak of his life (Howe either missing the irony or assuming that *I* did) as one of "infinite possibilities" while living in a hole in the ground.

Howe begins by attacking Baldwin's rejection in "Everybody's Protest Novel" of the type of literature he labeled "protest fiction" (*Uncle Tom's Cabin* and *Native Son* being prime examples), and which he considered incapable of dealing adequately with the complexity of Negro experience. Howe, noting that this was the beginning of Baldwin's career, sees the essay's underlying motive as a declaration of Baldwin's intention to transcend "the sterile categories of 'Negroness' whether those enforced by the white world or those defensively erected by the Negroes themselves. No longer mere victim or rebel, the Negro would stand free in a self-achieved humanity. As Baldwin put it some years later, he hoped to 'prevent himself from becoming merely a Negro; or even, merely, a Negro writer.' " Baldwin's elected agency for self-achievement would be the novel—as it turns out, it was the essay *and* the novel—but the novel, states Howe, "is an inherently ambiguous genre: it strains toward formal autonomy and can seldom avoid being public gesture."

I would have said that it is *always* a public gesture, though not necessarily a political one. I would also have pointed out that the American Negro novelist is himself "inherently ambiguous." As he strains toward self-achievement as artist (and here he can only "integrate" and free himself), he moves toward fulfilling his dual potentialities as Negro and American. While Howe agrees with Baldwin that "literature and sociology are not one and the same," he notes nevertheless that, "it is equally true that such statements hardly begin to cope with the problem of how a writer's own experience affects his desire to represent human affairs in a work of fiction." Thus Baldwin's formula evades "through rhetorical sweep, the genuinely difficult issue of the relationship between social experience and literature." And to Baldwin's statement that one writes "out of one thing only—one's own experience" (I would have added, for the novelist, this qualification: one's own experience as understood and ordered through one's knowledge of self, culture and literature) Howe, appearing suddenly in blackface, replies with a rhetorical sweep of his own:

> What, then, was the experience of a man with a black skin, what *could* it be here in this country? How could a Negro put pen to paper, how could he so much as think or breathe, without some impulsion to protest, be it harsh or mild, political or private, released or buried? . . . The 'sociology'

of his existence forms a constant pressure on his literary work, and not merely in the way this might be true of any writer, but with a pain and ferocity that nothing could remove.

I must say that this brought a shock of recognition. Some 12 years ago, a friend argued with me for hours that I could not possibly write a novel because my experience as a Negro had been too excruciating to allow me to achieve that psychological and emotional distance necessary to artistic creation. Since he "knew" Negro experience better than I, I could not convince him that he might be wrong. Evidently Howe feels that unrelieved suffering is the only "real" Negro experience, and that the true Negro writer must be ferocious.

But there is also an American Negro tradition which teaches one to deflect racial provocation and to master and contain pain. It is a tradition which abhors as obscene any trading on one's own anguish for gain or sympathy; which springs not from a desire to deny the harshness of existence but from a will to deal with it as men at their best have always done. It takes fortitude to be a man and no less to be an artist. Perhaps it takes even more if the black man would be an artist. If so there are no exemptions. It would seem to me, therefore, that the question of how the "sociology of his existence" presses upon a Negro writer's work depends upon how much of his life the individual writer is able to transform into art. What moves a writer to eloquence is less meaningful than what he makes of it. How much, by the way, do we know of Sophocles' wounds?

One unfamiliar with what Howe stands for would get the impression that when he looks at a Negro he sees not a human being but an abstract embodiment of living hell. He seems never to have considered that American Negro life (and here he is encouraged by certain Negro "spokesmen") is, for the Negro who must live it, not only a burden (and not always that) but also a *discipline*—just as any human life which has endured so long is a discipline teaching its own insights into the human condition, its own strategies of survival. There is a fullness, even a richness here; and here *despite* the realities of politics, perhaps, but nevertheless here and real. Because it is *human* life. And Wright, for all of his indictments, was no less its product than that other talented Mississippian, Leontyne Price. To deny in the interest of revolutionary posture that such possibilities of human richness exist for others, even in Mississippi, is not only to deny us our humanity but to betray the critic's commitment to social reality. Critics who do so should abandon literature for politics.

For even as his life toughens the Negro, even as it brutalizes him, sensitizes him, dulls him, goads him to anger, moves him to irony, sometimes fracturing and sometimes affirming his hopes; even as it shapes his attitudes toward family, sex, love, religion; even as it modulates his humor, tempers his joy—it *conditions* him to deal with his life and with himself. Because it is *his* life and no mere abstraction in someone's head. He must live it and try consciously to grasp its complexity until he can change it; must live it *as* he changes it. He is no mere product of his socio-political predicament. He is a product of the interaction between his racial predicament, his individual will and the broader American cultural freedom in which he finds his ambiguous existence. Thus he, too, in a limited way, is his own creation.

In his loyalty to Richard Wright, Howe considers Ellison and Baldwin guilty of filial betrayal because, in their own work, they have rejected the path laid down by *Native Son,* phonies because, while actually "black boys," they pretend to be mere American writers trying to react to something of the pluralism of their predicament.

In his myth Howe takes the roles of both Shem and Japheth, trying mightily (his face turned backward so as not to see what it is he's veiling) to cover the old man's bare belly, and then becoming Wright's voice from beyond the grave by uttering the curses which Wright was too ironic or too proud to have uttered himself—at least in print:

> In response to Baldwin and Ellison, Wright would have said (I virtually quote the words he used in talking to me during the summer of 1958) that only through struggle could men with black skins, and for that matter, all the oppressed of the world, achieve their humanity. It was a lesson, said Wright, with a touch of bitterness yet not without kindness, that the younger writers would have to learn in their own way and their own time. All that has happened since bears him out.

What, coming 18 years after *Native Son* and 13 years after World War II, does this rather limp cliché mean? Nor is it clear what is meant by the last sentence—or is it that today Baldwin has come to out-Wrighting Richard? The real questions seem to be: How does the Negro writer participate *as a writer* in the struggle for human freedom? To whom does he address his work? What values emerging from Negro experience does he try to affirm?

I started with the primary assumption that men with black skins, having retained their humanity before all of the conscious efforts made to dehumanize them, especially following the Reconstruction, are unquestionably human. Thus they have the obligation of freeing themselves—whoever their allies might be—by depending upon the validity of their own experience for an accurate picture of the reality which they seek to change, and for a gauge of the values they would see made manifest. Crucial to this view is the belief that their resistance to provocation, their coolness under pressure, their sense of timing and their tenacious hold on the ideal of their ultimate freedom are indispensable values in the struggle, and are at least as characteristic of American Negroes as the hatred, fear and vindictiveness which Wright chose to emphasize.

Wright believed in the much abused idea that novels are

"weapons"—the counterpart of the dreary notion, common among most minority groups, that novels are instruments of good public relations. But I believe that true novels, even when most pessimistic and bitter, arise out of an impulse to celebrate human life and therefore are ritualistic and ceremonial at their core. Thus they would preserve as they destroy, affirm as they reject.

In *Native Son* Wright began with the ideological proposition that what whites think of the Negro's reality is more important than what Negroes themselves know it to be. Hence Bigger Thomas was presented as a near-subhuman indictment of white oppression. He was designed to shock whites out of their apathy and end the circumstances out of which Wright insisted Bigger emerged. Here environment is all—and interestingly enough, environment conceived solely in terms of the physical, the non-conscious. Well, cut off my legs and call me Shorty! Kill my parents and throw me on the mercy of the court as an orphan! Wright could imagine Bigger, but Bigger could not possibly imagine Richard Wright. Wright saw to that.

But without arguing Wright's right to his personal vision, I would say that he was himself a better argument for my approach than Bigger was for his. And so, to be fair and as inclusive as Howe, is James Baldwin. Both are true Negro Americans, and both affirm the broad possibility of personal realization which I see as a saving aspect of American life. Surely, this much can be admitted without denying the injustice which all three of us have protested.

Howe is impressed by Wright's pioneering role and by the ". . . enormous courage, the discipline of self-conquest required to conceive Bigger Thomas. . . ." And earlier: "If such younger novelists as Baldwin and Ralph Ellison were able to move beyond Wright's harsh naturalism toward more supple modes of fiction, that was only possible because Wright had been there first, courageous enough to release the full weight of his anger."

It is not for me to judge Wright's courage, but I must ask just why it was possible for me to write as I write "only" because Wright released his anger? Can't I be allowed to release my own? What does Howe know of my acquaintance with violence, or the shape of my courage or the intensity of my anger? I suggest that my credentials are at least as valid as Wright's, even though he began writing long before I did, and it is possible that I have lived through and committed even more violence than he. Howe must wait for an autobiography before he can be responsibly certain. Everybody wants to tell us what a Negro is, yet few wish, even in a joke, to be one. But if you would tell me who I am, at least take the trouble to discover what I have been.

Which brings me to the most distressing aspect of Howe's thinking: his Northern white liberal version of the white Southern myth of absolute separation of the races. He implies that Negroes can only aspire to contest other Negroes (this at a time when Baldwin has been taking on just about everyone, including Hemingway, Faulkner and the U.S. Attorney General!), and must wait for the appearance of a Black Hope before they have the courage to move. Howe is so committed to a sociological vision of society that he apparently cannot see (perhaps because he is dealing with Negroes—although not because he would suppress us socially or politically, for in fact he is anxious to end such suppression) that whatever the efficiency of segregation as a socio-political arrangement, it has been far from absolute on the level of *culture*. Southern whites cannot walk, talk, sing, conceive of laws or justice, think of sex, love, the family or freedom without responding to the presence of Negroes.

Similarly, no matter how strictly Negroes are segregated socially and politically, on the level of the imagination their ability to achieve freedom is limited only by their individual aspiration, insight, energy and will. Wright was able to free himself in Mississippi because he had the imagination and the will to do so. He was as much a product of his reading as of his painful experiences, and he made himself a writer by subjecting himself to the writer's discipline—as he understood it. The same is true of James Baldwin, who is not the product of a Negro storefront church but of the library, and the same is true of me.

Howe seems to see segregation as an opaque steel jug with the Negroes inside waiting for some black messiah to come along and blow the cork. Wright is his hero and he sticks with him loyally. But if we are in a jug it is transparent, not opaque, and one is allowed not only to see outside but to read of what is going on out there; to make identifications as to values and human quality. So in Macon County, Alabama, I read Marx, Freud, T. S. Eliot, Pound, Gertrude Stein and Hemingway. Books which seldom, if ever, mentioned Negroes were to release me from whatever "segregated" idea I might have had of my human possibilities. I was freed not by propagandists or by the example of Wright—I did not know him at the time and was earnestly trying to learn enough to write a symphony and have it performed by the time I was 26, because Wagner had done so and I admired his music—but by composers, novelists and poets who spoke to me of more interesting and freer ways of life.

These were works which, by fulfilling themselves as works of art, by being satisfied to deal with life in terms of their own sources of power, were able to give me a broader sense of life and possibility. Indeed, I understand a bit more about myself as Negro because literature has taught me something of my identity as Western man, as political being. It has also taught me something of the cost of being an individual who aspires to conscious eloquence. It requires real poverty of the imagination to think that this can come to a Negro *only* through the example of *other Negroes*, especially after the performance of the slaves in recreating themselves, in good part, out of the images and myths of the Old Testament Jews.

No, Wright was no spiritual father of mine, certainly in no sense I recognize—nor did he pretend to be, since he felt that I had started writing too late. It was Baldwin's career, not mine, that Wright proudly advanced by helping him attain the Eugene Saxton Fellowship, and it was Baldwin who found Wright a lion in his path. Being older and familiar with quite different lions in quite different paths, I simply stepped around him.

But Wright was a friend for whose magazine I wrote my first book review and short story, and a personal hero in the same way Hot Lips Page and Jimmy Rushing were friends and heroes. I felt no need to attack what I considered the limitations of his vision because I was quite impressed by what he had achieved. And in this, although I saw with the black vision of Ham, I was, I suppose, as pious as Shem and Japheth. Still I would write my own books and they would be in themselves, implicitly, criticisms of Wright's; just as all novels of a given historical moment form an argument over the nature of reality and are, to an extent, criticisms each of the other.

While I rejected Bigger Thomas as any *final* image of Negro personality, I recognized *Native Son* as an achievement; as one man's essay in defining the human condition as seen from a specific Negro perspective at a given time in a given place. And I was proud to have known Wright and happy for the impact he had made upon our apathy. But Howe's ideas notwithstanding, history is history, cultural contacts ever mysterious, and taste exasperatingly personal. Two days after arriving in New York I was to read Malraux's *Man's Fate* and *The Days of Wrath,* and after these how could I be impressed by Wright as an ideological novelist? Need my skin blind me to all other values? Yet Howe writes:

> When Negro liberals write that despite the prevalence of bias there has been an improvement in the life of their people, such statements are reasonable and necessary. But what have these to do with the way Negroes feel, with the power of the memories they must surely retain? About this we know very little and would be well advised not to nourish preconceptions, for their feelings may well be closer to Wright's rasping outbursts than to the more modulated tones of the younger Negro novelists. *Wright remembered,* and what he remembered other Negroes must also have remembered. And in that way he kept faith with the experience of the boy who had fought his way out of the depths, to speak for those who remained there.

Wright, for Howe, is the genuine article, the authentic Negro writer, and his tone the only authentic tone. But why strip Wright of his individuality in order to criticize other writers. He had his memories and I have mine, just as I suppose Irving Howe has his—or has Marx spoken the final word for him? Indeed, very early in *Black Boy* Wright's memory and his contact with literature come together in a way revealing, at least to the eye concerned with Wright the literary man, that his manner of keeping faith with the Negroes who remained in the depths is quite interesting:

(After I had outlived the shocks of childhood, after the habit of reflection had been born in me, I used to mull over the strange absence of real kindness in Negroes, how unstable was our tenderness, how lacking in genuine passion we were, how void of great hope, how timid our joy, how bare our traditions, how hollow our memories, how lacking we were in those intangible sentiments that bind man to man and how shallow was even our despair. After I had learned other ways of life I used to brood upon the unconscious irony of those who felt that Negroes led so passional an existence! I saw that what had been taken for our emotional strength was our negative confusions, our flights, our fears, our frenzy under pressure.

Whenever I thought of the essential bleakness of black life in America, I knew that Negroes had never been allowed to catch the full spirit of Western civilization, that they lived somehow in it but not of it. And when I brooded upon the cultural barrenness of black life, I wondered if clean, positive tenderness, love, honor, loyalty, and the capacity to remember were native with man. I asked myself if these human qualities were not fostered, won, struggled and suffered for, preserved in ritual from one generation to another.)

Must I be condemned because my sense of Negro life was quite different? Or because for me keeping faith would never allow me to even raise such a question about any segment of humanity? *Black Boy* is not a sociological case history but an autobiography, and therefore a work of art shaped by a writer bent upon making an ideological point. Doubtlessly, this was the beginning of Wright's exile, the making of a decision which was to shape his life and writing thereafter. And it is precisely at this point that Wright is being what I would call, in Howe's words, "literary to a fault."

For just as *How Bigger was Born* is Wright's Jamesian preface to *Native Son,* the passage quoted above is his paraphrase of Henry James' catalogue of those items of a high civilization which were absent from American life during Hawthorne's day, and which seemed so necessary in order for the novelist to function. This, then, was Wright's list of those items of high humanity which he found missing among Negroes. Thank God, I have never been quite that literary.

How awful that Wright found the facile answers of Marxism before he learned to use literature as a means for discovering the forms of American Negro humanity. I could not and cannot question their existence, I can only seek again and again to project that humanity as I see it and feel it. To me Wright as *writer* was less interesting than the enigma he personified; that he could so dissociate himself from the complexity of his background while trying so hard to improve the condition of black men everywhere; that he could be so wonderful an example of human possibility but could not for ideological reasons depict a Negro as intelligent, as creative or as dedicated as himself.

In his effort to resuscitate Wright, Irving Howe would designate the role which Negro writers are to play more rigidly than any Southern politician—and for the best of reasons. We must express "black" anger and "clenched militancy"; most of all we should not become too interested in the problems of the art of literature, even though it is through these that we seek our individual identities. And between writing well and being ideologically militant, we must choose militancy.

Well, it all sounds quite familiar and I fear the social order which it forecasts more than I do that of Mississippi. Ironically, during the 1940s it was one of the main sources of Wright's rage and frustration.

Native Son: A Novel of Social Protest

ROBERT A. BONE

BY WAY OF PRELIMINARY REMARKS, THREE IMPORTANT INFLUENCES ON *Native Son* should be considered. In terms of literary lineage the novel derives from the early American naturalists, by way of Dos Passos, Farrell, Steinbeck, and the late Dreiser. *An American Tragedy* (1925) in particular seems to have been a model for *Native Son*. Both novels make use of criminality as their chief dramatic device, and in each case the crime is the natural and inevitable product of a warped society. Both authors draw the data for their trial scenes, in classic naturalist fashion, from authentic court records: Dreiser from a murder case in upstate New York, and Wright from the famous Leopold and Loeb kidnap-murder in Chicago. Both novels, through their titles, make the point that Clyde Griffiths and Bigger Thomas are native American products, and not, as Wright remarks, imported from Moscow or anywhere else. Both authors advance a guilt-of-the-nation thesis as a corollary to their environmentalist view of crime.

Much of the raw material for *Native Son* was provided by Wright's personal experience in metropolitan Chicago. For several hard-pressed years he worked at all kinds of jobs, from porter and dishwasher to ditch-digger and post office clerk. One job as agent for a burial society took him inside the south-side tenement houses, where he saw the corrosive effects of ghetto life on the Negro migrant. During the depression a relief agency placed him in the South Side Boys' Club, where he met the live models from whom he was to sketch Bigger Thomas: "They were a wild and homeless lot, culturally lost,

---

From *The Negro Novel in America,* by Robert A. Bone (New Haven: Yale University Press, revised edition, 1965), pp. 142–152.

spiritually disinherited, candidates for the clinics, morgues, prisons, reformatories, and the electric chair of the state's death house."[1] Meanwhile, even as his empirical knowledge of urban life increased, Wright was introduced to the theoretical concepts of Marxism through the John Reed Club and the Communist party.

Wright joined the party in 1934, breaking decisively about ten years later. The extent of his involvement has been, to put it as kindly as possible, modestly understated in *The God That Failed* (1949). For several years, Wright acted as a dependable wheel horse in a wide variety of party activities. To his credit, however, a stubborn and uncorruptible individualism kept him in constant conflict with the party bureaucracy, leading eventually to his break and expulsion. Of his main motive for joining the party Wright has written in retrospect: "[The party] did not say 'Be like us and we will like you, maybe.' It said: 'If you possess enough courage to speak out what you are, you will find that you are not alone.' "[2] As an excluded Negro and an alienated intellectual, Wright needed above all to feel this sense of belonging. That he was able to find it, however fleetingly, only within the ranks of the Communist party is a commentary on the failure of the democratic left.

Wright's debt to Marxism is quite a different matter from his personal history in the Communist party. The party, it must be understood, manipulates Marxism for its own ends, which are the ends of the Russian ruling class. Yet the basic ideas of Karl Marx, like those of Sigmund Freud, are capable of effecting so vast a revolution in the consciousness of an individual that he may never recapture his former state of innocence. For Richard Wright, Marxism became a way of ordering his experience; it became, in literary terms, his unifying mythos. It provided him with a means of interpreting the urban scene which the Harlem School had lacked. Above all, it provided him with an intellectual framework for understanding his life as a Negro.

Wright, more than any Negro author who preceded him, has a sense of the presentness of his racial past. This sense of history, which was part and parcel of his Marxist outlook, has been recorded in *Twelve Million Black Voices* (1941), published hard on the heels of *Native Son*. In this folk history of the American Negro, Wright sees the black ghetto as the end product of a long historical process (p. 93):

Perhaps never in history has a more utterly unprepared folk wanted to go to the city; we were barely born as a folk when we headed for the tall and sprawling centers of steel and stone. We who were landless on the land; we who had barely managed to live in family groups; we who needed the ritual and guidance of established institutions to hold our atomized lives

[1] Richard Wright, "I Tried to Be a Communist," *Atlantic Monthly, 174* (Aug. 1944), p. 68.

[2] Ibid., p. 62.

together in lines of purpose . . . we who had had our personalities blasted with 200 years of slavery had been turned loose to shift for ourselves.

It was in this perspective that Wright saw the life of Bigger Thomas.

The most impressive feature of *Native Son* is its narrative drive. From the outset the novel assumes a fierce pace which carries the reader breathlessly through Bigger's criminal career. Wright allows as little interruption of the action as possible, with no chapter divisions as such and only an occasional break to mark a swift transition or change of scene. At the same time, he writes with great economy, breaking with the comprehensive and discursive tradition of the naturalistic novel. He provides only three brief glimpses of Bigger's life prior to the main action of the novel: his relationship with his family, with his gang, and with his girl, Bessie. The reader must supply the rest, for Wright's presentation is not direct but metaphorical.

On a literal level *Native Son* consists of three Books, dealing with a murder, a flight and capture, and a trial. But the murder and the circumstances which surround it are in reality an extended metaphor, like the whale hunt in *Moby Dick*. The novel is not to be read merely as the story of a gruesome crime, though it is that. It is the hidden meaning of Bigger's life, as revealed by the murder, which is the real subject of *Native Son*. The novel is a modern epic, consisting of action on the grand scale. As such, it functions as a commentary on the more prosaic plane of daily living.

Book I is called "Fear." Its structure pulsates in mounting waves of violence, beginning with the opening rat scene, increasing during Bigger's fight with Gus, and culminating in murder. Each successive wave of violence is a means of reducing fear, for great fear automatically produces great violence in Bigger. He has been so conditioned that being found in a white girl's room is the ultimate fear-inspiring situation. When the blind Mrs. Dalton appears as a white blur in the doorway of Mary's room, Bigger is seized with hysterical terror, and he murders. It is both an accident and not an accident, for the first characteristic of Bigger's life which the murder reveals is his uncontrollable fear of whites.

The second aspect of Bigger's normal life to receive thematic stress is his bitter sense of deprivation: "We black and they white. They got things and we ain't. They do things and we can't. It's just like living in jail. Half the time I feel like I'm on the outside of the world peeping in through a knot-hole in the fence" (p. 17). Living on the margin of his culture, Bigger is constantly tormented by the glitter of the dominant civilization. "The Gay Woman," a movie which he watches while waiting to rob a neighborhood store, is emblematic of that world of cocktail parties, golf, and spinning roulette wheels from which he is forever excluded. To fill the intolerable void in his life he seeks "something big"—the "job" at Blum's which never comes off, his real job as chauffeur and handyman for the Daltons. He finally breaks through the confines of his daily life by committing murder.

Book II, "Flight," opens with a recapitulation of Bigger's relations with family and gang, to show how they have changed as a result of the murder. Bigger has now achieved heroic stature: "He had murdered and created a new life for himself." This is the dominant irony of Book II—that Bigger finds fulfillment only by the most violent defiance of the legal and moral precepts of the society which oppresses him. As a criminal, Bigger achieves a sense of purpose, a feeling of elation which is a measure of the meaninglessness of his former existence.

After the fact of Bigger's rebirth is established, the narrative proceeds with a series of interrogations by Peggy, by the Daltons, and finally by the police. Bigger's conduct throughout is determined by the heightened perceptions which he enjoys as a result of the murder: "The whole thing came to him in the form of a powerful and simple feeling; there was in everyone a great hunger to believe that made him blind, and if he could see while others were blind, then he could get what he wanted and never be caught at it" (p. 91). Bigger learns to exploit the blindness of others, "fooling the white folks" during his interrogation, and this is again something deep in his racial heritage, springing from a long tradition of telling whites whatever they want to hear.

At last comes discovery, flight, and capture. Once again the action of the novel serves as an oblique comment on Bigger's "normal" way of life: "But it was familiar, this running away. All his life he had been knowing that sooner or later something like this would come to him" (p. 187). No such fear-ridden sequence as Bigger's flight and capture is possible without a proportionate act of violence. Bessie's murder, compounding horror upon grisly horror, serves to dispel any lingering doubt concerning Bigger's guilt. Learning from Dreiser's mistake, Wright takes no chances that his audience may be diverted from his main point by quibbling over the "accidental" nature of Mary Dalton's death. At the same time, the audience knows intuitively that it is Mary's murder, and not Bessie's, for which society will demand Bigger's life.

The successful fusion of narrative and metaphorical levels in *Native Son* is only a sample of Wright's craftsmanship. Not the least of his problems is to induce his readers to identify with Bigger in spite of his monstrous crimes. This he accomplishes by a tone which subtly controls and defines the reader's attitude toward Bigger. It is a tone of anguish and despair, established at the outset by Wright's epigraph from the Book of Job: "Even today is my complaint rebellious; my stroke is heavier than my groaning." Thus the stark horror of *Native Son* is balanced by the spiritual anguish which, in a sense, produced it. This note of anguish, which emphasizes Bigger's suffering, is so intense as to be almost physical in character. It is sustained by a style which can only be called visceral. The author writes from his guts, describing the emotional state of his characters in graphic psychosomatic terms. It is a characteristic device which has its source in Wright's aching memory of the deep South.

Notwithstanding Wright's professed naturalism, the symbolic texture of *Native Son* is exceptionally rich. The whole novel is contained in the first few pages when Bigger, in unconscious anticipation of his own fate, corners a huge black rat and kills him with a skillet. Much of Wright's meaning is conveyed by appropriate "objective correlatives" for Bigger's inner feelings and emotions. The icy gales and heavy snowfalls of Books I and II represent a hostile white environment: "To Bigger and his kind, white people were not really people; they were a sort of great natural force, like a stormy sky looming overhead" (p. 97). Throughout Book II the red glow of the furnace appears as a projection of Bigger's guilt. A series of breathing and choking images anticipates the manner of the murder, linking it symbolically to Bigger's choked and stifled life. There is a constant play on blindness, focused around the figure of Mrs. Dalton but aimed ultimately at the reader, who is expected to grope his way to an understanding of Bigger's life.

A lesser artist would have directed Bigger's symbolic revolt against a brutal oppressor, but Wright understands that such an approach would only make his audience feel smug and superior. He chooses as Bigger's victim a girl who is "friendly to Negroes," but whose kindness under the circumstances is a bitter mockery. By this device, Wright means to suggest that Bigger's sickness is too deep to be reached by kindness, and at the same time to involve his audience in responsibility for Bigger's crime. The Daltons, who are people of good will, hire Bigger because they "want to give Negroes a chance." But they also own real estate on the South side, and have thus helped to make the black ghetto what it is. They are, in short, just as innocent and just as guilty as we.

Book I portrays the old Bigger; Book II, the new; Book III, the Bigger who might have been. The bare narrative is concerned with Bigger's fight for his life, but the dramatic tension of Book III is centered elsewhere. The important question is not whether Bigger will be spared, but whether he will be saved. Bigger's impending death in the electric chair is simply the crisis which forces a resolution of his inner conflict, thus revealing what is basic in his personality. After his talk with the lawyer, Max—the most intimate of his life—Bigger feels that he must make a decision: "In order to walk to that chair he had to weave his feelings into a hard shield of either hope or hate. To fall between them would mean living and dying in a fog of fear" (p. 305). On what terms will Bigger die; in hope or in hate? This is the tension of Book III.

Bigger's basic problem is to find someone or something he can trust. Kardiner and Livesey have written of the lower-class Negro family: "The result of the continuous frustration in childhood is to create a personality devoid of confidence in human relations, of an eternal vigilance and distrust of others. This is a purely defensive maneuver, which purports to protect the individual against the repeatedly traumatic effects of disappointment and frustration. He must operate on the assumption that the world is hostile."[3] This lack of relatedness appears above all in Bigger's relationship with Bessie. As Max points out, "His relationship to this poor black girl reveals his relationship to the world." It is a mutually exploitative affair, devoid of devotion, loyalty, or trust—luxuries which are denied to Bigger and Bessie by the circumstances of their lives.

Bigger's lack of relatedness is presented symbolically at the end of Book II, just before his capture: "Under it all some part of his mind was beginning to stand aside; he was going behind his curtain, his wall, looking out with sullen stares of contempt." This retreat, amounting almost to a catatonic trance, sets the stage for the dominant conflict in Book III. As Bigger slowly awakens from his trance, his fierce life-drive, set off perfectly by the death cell which he occupies, struggles toward some sort of relatedness with his fellows: "If he reached out his hands, and if his hands were electric wires, and if his heart were a battery giving life and fire to those hands, and if he reached out with his hands and touched other people, if he did that, would there be a reply, a shock?" (p. 307).

The structure of Book III is essentially a series of attempts by Bigger to realize this vision. He seeks desperately for a basis for hope but discards one alternative after another. He rejects his family ("Go home, Ma"); his fellow prisoners ("Are you the guy who pulled the Dalton job?"); the race leaders ("they almost like white folks when it comes to guys like me"); and religion. The old preacher tempts Bigger with the Christian explanation of suffering, but when the mob burns a fiery cross outside the jail, the cross of love turns to a cross of hate. Bigger finds it hardest to reject Jan and Max. These are the last symbols of relatedness to which he clings, and the main conflict of the novel occurs between them and Bigger's deepest experience as a Negro—his distrust of whites, his Negro nationalism.

Bigger's relations with Jan and Max cannot be understood apart from the context of Wright's experience in the Communist party. Most Negro Communists—and Wright was no exception—are Negro nationalists, for it is precisely the most embittered, anti-white Negroes to whom the party offers the possibility of revenge. But the vast majority of American Communists, after all, are white. Paradoxically, the most white-hating Negro is thrust, by his membership in the party, into what is surely, whatever else it may be, one of the freest arenas of interracial contact in America. The result is an agonizing psychological

[3] Abram Kardiner and Lionel Livesey, *The Mark of Oppression* (New York, Norton, 1951), p. 308.

conflict, as the Negro nationalist, newly won to Communism, struggles to relate to his white comrades. This is the conflict which is bothering Wright in Book III of *Native Son*, expressed on a somewhat primitive level through Bigger's relations with the white Communists, Jan and Max.

To Bigger, Communism is a matter not of ideology but of relatedness. Jan and Max are the flimsy base on which he tries to erect his shield of hope. Jan, through an act of understanding and forgiveness, evokes what is almost a religious response from Bigger, where the old colored preacher had failed: "The word had become flesh. For the first time in his life a white man became a human being to him." The resolution of the novel, however, comes in terms of Bigger's relationship with Max. Max serves as Bigger's father confessor as well as his lawyer, and Bigger comes closest to establishing a human contact with him.

After Max's speech fails, and after all avenues have been closed to Bigger, Max makes a final visit to Bigger's cell. Bigger seeks to recapture their former intimacy, but Max is too concerned with comforting him in the face of death. Max then tries to communicate his vision of Communism to Bigger, but fails. As his shield of hope slips from his grasp, Bigger takes up the shield of hate which is his destiny. The impact comes through Max's reactions: "Bigger saw Max back away from him with compressed lips. . . . Max lifted his hand to touch Bigger, but did not. . . . Max's eyes were full of terror. . . . He felt for the door, keeping his face averted. . . . He did not turn around. . . . Max paused, but did not look" (pp. 358–59). What terrifies Max is that Bigger, re-possessed by hate, ends by accepting what life has made him: a killer. Bigger's real tragedy is not that he dies, but that he dies in hatred. A tragic figure, he struggles for love and trust against a hostile environment which defeats him in the end.

Book III, and therefore the novel, suffers from a major structural flaw, flowing from the fact that Wright has failed to digest Communism artistically. The Communist party is simply not strong enough as a symbol of relatedness; Bigger's hatred, firmly anchored in his Negro nationalism, is hardly challenged. The contest is unequal, because there is nothing in Bigger's life that corresponds to "Communism." As a result, the conflict between love and hate, between universal brotherhood and Negro nationalism, cannot be successfully internalized. Wright is forced to go outside of Bigger, to Jan and Max, both of whom are more the mouthpieces for a thesis than credible characters in their own right. Wright is sure of Bigger, but Jan and Max elude him. In noting his failure to realize Communism artistically, it is not irrelevant to recall that for Wright himself, the party was no shield of hope.

Since Bigger is unable to bear the weight of political symbolism intended for him, Wright is forced to resort to rhetoric. The first two books of *Native Son* contain two levels of meaning; the bare action, and a running account of Bigger's feelings at the time. Now a third level is introduced: an interpretation of the action, undertaken by the author through the medium of Max's speech. This speech, with its guilt-of-the-nation thesis, throws the novel badly out of focus. The reader is likely to come away thinking that Bigger committed a horrible crime to which he was driven by a still more horrible environment, which I, the reader, have helped to create. Fictionally, however, the novel makes a different point: Bigger is a human being whose environment has made him incapable of relating meaningfully to other human beings except through murder.

Not satisfied with interpreting his own novel through Max, Wright tries again in his article "How Bigger Was Born": "Bigger, an American product, a native son of this land, carries within him the potentialities of either fascism or communism."[4] But Wright can only attempt in retrospect to impose a political symbolism on the novel which he fails to realize fictionally. He simply cannot fit the ideas of Bigger into those of the Communist party. A white Bigger could be a fascist; a colored Bigger with trade-union experience could be a Communist. But Bigger is a Negro without fellow workers and is therefore only Bigger, a memorable figure in contemporary literature whom Wright created in spite of his own political ideology.

Of the Negro novelists who wrote during the Great Depression, Richard Wright came closest to expressing the essential spirit of the decade. At bottom, the Depression years witnessed a continuation of the cultural dualism of the Negro Renaissance. During the thirties the Negro novelist maintained an active interest in his Negro heritage, systematically exploring the racial past in his search for distinctive literary material. Upon this base, in accordance with the climate of the times, was superimposed the formula of "proletarian art." Wright's contribution to the Negro novel was precisely his fusion of a pronounced racialism with a broader tradition of social protest.

The Red Decade was brought to an abrupt close by America's entry into World War II. As the unemployed workers were gradually absorbed into war industry, and as New Dealers and Communists alike raised the slogan of "national unity," the radicalism of the thirties faded into oblivion. The intelligentsia's brief excursion into proletarian art was over. During the war years, in any case, literary activity became a luxury and like so many aspects of the national life was laid aside for the duration. The Negro novel entered a period of wartime quiescence, from which it emerged into a vastly altered postwar world.

[4] *Saturday Review, 22* (1940), 1–4, 17–20.

Fever and Feeling: Notes on the Imagery in *Native Son*

JAMES A. EMANUEL

WAS [LIFE] SIMPLY FEVER, FEELING WITHOUT KNOWING, SEEKING WITHOUT finding? . . . He grew thin and his eyes held the red blood of his body" (315).[1] After this anguished question felt by Bigger Thomas, and this vivid expression of the failure and turning inward of his sensory yearnings, *Native Son* closes with an interchange between the condemned man and his lawyer, Max, that has never been completely analyzed. A close comparison with Albert Camus' existentialist novelette *The Stranger*—including such related images as droning and stuttering, such related characters as Camus' priest and Wright's preacher, and such related themes as knowledge-through-death and the artificiality of all courtroom trials—would advance the critical Establishment toward a professionally full understanding of Book Three, especially.

Native Son has had many admirers for thoroughly defensible reasons. Its racial passion and sociological and psychological richness so complement Wright's other signal achievements—*Black Boy* and *Uncle Tom's Children,* among others—that none of a succeeding generation of black novelists has been able to replace him in the esteem of his fellow writers. The excellence of Wright's work, however, still needs to be minutely analyzed. The phrase "protest literature," no matter what adjectives surround it, reveals almost nothing of the permament virtues of *Native Son*—although those virtues are profoundly anchored in blackness, in racial oppression, and in the militant spirit of the author. *Native Son* is a novel of remarkable agony, individualized in Bigger Thomas, yet universalized in ways grievously recognizable over a quarter of a century later, on almost every page, by Negro readers especially.

The question of how the author transmitted such power and truth should have been perfectly answered by now. To observe that Wright suffered keenly from racism and wrote feelingly about his experiences is merely to repeat what might equally be said of many black writers.

[1] All such page numbers refer to the first edition of *Native Son* (New York: Harper & Brothers, 1940).

From *Negro Digest,* 18 (December 1968), pp. 16–26.

Wright's racial fire is widely known, and it has long warmed a race in need of strong voices. The still challenging question, however, is literary: by what verbal techniques did the author help Bigger Thomas make the reader peep through his "knot-hole in the fence" and understand his feelings about his existence? Bigger did not want to die without being understood by somebody. And Richard Wright has bequeathed one large means of understanding each Bigger Thomas among us, the very thing that Bigger hungered for after his capture: that "vast configuration of images and symbols whose magic and power could lift him up and make him live so intensely that the dread of being black and unequal would be forgotten . . ." (234).

It is more than aestheticism that argues the value of images and symbols in Bigger's life. Largely existential in his perceptions, Bigger knows himself and his environment most surely through images. When despairing, he sees his life as "an obscene joke happening amid a colossal din of siren screams and white faces and circling lances of light under a cold and silken sky" (235). When Bigger is walking with Bessie, his "*mind* could *feel* the soft swing of her body" (119). A young man "consumed always with a body hunger" (128), sensitive Bigger is vulnerable even to a ray of sunshine: in his cell near the end of the novel, a "shaft of yellow sun cut across his chest with as much weight as a beam forged of lead. With a convulsive gasp, he bent forward and shut his eyes" (383). He yearns for wholeness of experience—made possible only when his feelings merge with some equivalent object around him—a yearning graphically portrayed when, lying on his cot in jail, Bigger's "hands were groping fumblingly through the city of men for something to match the feelings smoldering in him . . ." (350). Viewed internally as a conflict of forces, he is physically a centrally expanding "impulse always throbbing" but seldom countered by anything "outside of him to meet it and explain it" (350). The symbolic cast of Bigger's mind is often made clear; for example, while he hides in an empty building, a chunk of bread in his pocket and his gun nestled under his shirt against his chest are described as symbolic of his rejection of folk religion. Bigger's tragedy, his abortive "sense of power, a power born of a latent capacity to live" (140), is made palpable to the reader primarily through the sharing of his many "images charged with terror" (214).

Native Son, then, enables the reader to live with a black "man of feeling" in the truest sense of the phrase, a young American whose specific ambition is "to merge himself with others and be a part of this world, to lose himself in it so he could find himself, to be allowed a chance to live like others, even though he was black" (204). The constant frustration of that simple ambition and of the feelings supporting it is the psychological substance of the novel. The network of images that most authentically attend that daily frustration—and their personal, racial, and national significance—is the Jamesian "stuff of consciousness" to be conveyed.

A few miscellaneous techniques serving that end might be briefly mentioned. Images of light and dark, as expected, recur frequently, without special emphasis. The light in the Dalton house is hardly ever natural: it is a bright flood in the kitchen (a room important in racial history), is dim elsewhere in the home, and is hallucinatory and glaring in the semihuman furnace. Images of snow often suggest Bigger's complex connections—including aesthetic ones—with the "white world." When he leaps from the Daltons' window after the discovery of Mary's bones, for example, the "shock of [his fall] went through him, up his back to his head and he lay buried in a cold pile of snow, dazed. Snow was in his mouth, eyes, ears; snow was seeping down his back" (187). A related type of imagery, temperature contrasts (such as Bigger's despairing wonder about the "warm red blood here and cold blue sky there" [351]), marks the protagonist's awareness of paradox in his surroundings. Natural images of those surroundings used for the sake of sensory appeal unrelated to Bigger's mood of the moment occur fewer than five times in the whole novel. Other images of nature are even more rarely thematic; and the exception is interesting: after Bessie's murder, Bigger "lifted her, feeling the wind screaming a protest against him" (202). Finally, what might be called "intestinal imagery" is skillfully used: the repeated image of Mary's severed head, urgent in Bigger's feelings rather than merely sensational on the page, catches fully the ambivalence and sensory horror that drive him. Similarly effective are pictures of the demonic furnace, with its "muffled breathing of the fire" (165).

The furnace, emphatically described about 10 times, stands in the middle range of key images found in *Native Son*. That almost living, demanding-to-be-fed gorge whispers and sucks in its air (as Bigger sucks in air during his many moments of fearful tension). And no air can "get through" the furnace (183) while Bigger stands breathless before the imminent discovery of Mary's bones, her earring, and the hatchet blade. The full identification of the furnace activities with Bigger's own bodily sensations was incipient earlier when he neared collapse after sticking his ransom note under the Daltons' door: "A wave of numbness spread fanwise from his stomach over his entire body . . . making his mouth gap" (157). Here the furnace mouth that Bigger has often peeked anxiously into becomes his own mouth, and the fan-shaped grate of glowing coals becomes his burning stomach. Later, as the incredulous newsman pokes at the bones in the furnace ashes, "[Bigger] himself was a huge furnace now through which no air could go; and the fear that surged into his stomach . . . was like the fumes of smoke that had belched from the ash bin" (185). And as Bigger runs from the house, "the inside of his stomach glowed white-hot" (187). The identification persists as Bigger notices newspaper headlines while walking to Bessie's room, resenting the failure of newsmen to take any interest in "*his* story"—meaning his very life—"as long as it had remained buried and burning in his own heart" (188).

A rather peculiar image (reminiscent of its striking usage by

Chekhov in *Ward No. 6*) occurs slightly more often than that of the furnace: the picture of an excited Bigger standing "in the middle of the floor." He leaps to this position at Bessie's when he wonders if he can trust her (116) and when he wonders if the police are questioning his family at that very moment (194). He takes the same stance in his own room when he discovers that he has forgotten to burn his incriminating gloves, pencil, and paper (157); and he moves to the center of his jail cell when he is excited about the revelations of his first long talk with his lawyer, Max (305) and, again minutes later, when he first tries "to see himself in relation to other men" (306). The meaning of these postures is specified when Bigger, fearfully embarrassed by the addition of his servile family and friends to the ranks of staring white people (the whole cast of the novel) already standing in his cell, "was so tense in body and mind that when the door swung in he bounded up and stood in the middle of the room" (251). This peculiar image, then, pictorially frames some of Bigger's moments of maximum tension and freezes him at the point of maximum flight within areas that restrict his movement or thought. Daily trapped in corners and pockets on Chicago's South Side, at crucial instants Bigger needs space—at least that semblance of it represented by equidistance and centrality.

A subtler geometric pattern, comparable to effects achieved by Nathaniel Hawthorne in *The Marble Faun,* emerges when Bigger appears at the center of another figure, the Christian cross. At the inquest, with one policeman on each side of him and with two in front and two behind (totaling six, and therefore matching the number of jurors), Bigger moves ironically at the center of a cross. Afterwards, speeding through the streets toward the Dalton home for a bullying interrogation, Bigger rides with one officer seated on each side of him and with six police cars in front and a similar string behind, carried thus is the middle of an elongated crucifix (realistically adjusted to the spatial restrictions of traffic). While Bigger is resisting in the Dalton home the imposition of a false charge of rape, he confuses a cross being burned atop a building on the other side of the street with the cross recently hung around his neck by his mother's minister, Reverend Hammond. Thinking that a holy cross should not be burned, but hearing outside the cries "Burn 'im!" and "Kill 'im!", Bigger suddenly knows that he is not looking at "the cross of Christ, but the cross of the Ku Klux Klan. He had a cross of salvation round his throat and they were burning one to tell him that they hated him" (287). Just as his body had metaphorically become the furnace, it becomes the cross when a jailer attributes his rebellion against the religious symbol to Communist dogma: " 'That's a goddamn lie!' Bigger shouted. His body seemed a flaming cross as words boiled hysterically out of him" (288). After Bigger throws his cross away three times, the author's condensed metaphor shows the meaning of these several pages in Book Three: Bigger reflects that "the cross the preacher had hung round his throat had been burned in front of his eyes" (289).

Wright takes pains with less noticeable images. Such is the case with his depiction of eyes as emblems of blindness and guilt (exclusive of his many pictures of the blind Mrs. Dalton). Strangely liberated by his accidental murder of Mary, Bigger thinks about nearby people waiting for street cars:

> He did not look at them; they were simply blind people, blind like his mother, his brother, his sister, Peggy, Britten, Jan, Mr. Dalton, and the sightless Mrs. Dalton and the quiet empty houses with their black gaping windows (148).

Those "blind" houses in the ghetto, according to Bigger's feelings, have stares like that of the Dalton's white cat that leaped upon his shoulder in front of photographers in the basement when Mary's bones were discovered, "its big round black eyes twin pools of secret guilt" (190), and like that of the murdered Bessie, "staring at him with those round large black eyes, her bloody mouth open in awe and wonder and pain . . ." (201). To a person like Bigger, his life reduced to occasional sensory joys snuffed out by a constant overbalance of pain, images of the corruption of the eye—his only receptor of magnitude—would disturbingly crowd his mind.

Two kinds of images are thematically as well as numerically impressive in *Native Son,* each found in various passages between fifteen and twenty times. The type discernible slightly less often, the "blot-out" image, shares the powers of physical violence upon its initial appearance, the day Bigger first comes to 4605 Drexel Boulevard and wants "to wave his hand and blot out" Mr. Dalton for making him feel embarrassed, or, failing in that, "to blot himself out" (41). Using the same or quite similar words, Bigger wants to "blot out" a number of people and things before the novel ends. This list of people includes Negroes because they never act in unity, catching "the mind and body in certainty and faith" (98); whites because they are "measuring every inch of his weakness" (252); and all the people at the inquest because they look at and cause him to look at Bessie's corpse. But Bigger's destructive impulse as made known through this kind of image is usually aimed elsewhere. It is aimed, for example, at inactivity: planning the ransom note, he does not "need to dance and sing and clown over the floor in order to blot out a day and night of doing nothing" (120). It is aimed at sound, blotted out by the "roaring noise in his ears," for instance, when he hates Britten "so hard and hot" for being a bigot (138); at fear, "blotted out" by his sudden confidence when he eats breakfast with his family and thinks of "how blind they were" (127); and at death itself, "a different and bigger adversary" than "the white mountain" of vengeful society (350).

In a reversal of this variety of imagery, white society itself becomes an arbitrary agent of the blotting-out impulse surrounding Bigger, for it feels "that nothing short of a quick blotting out of his life would make the city safe again" (281). All of society colludes in such destruction, points out Max: "Your Honor, injustice blots out one form of life, but another grows up in its place with its own rights, needs, and aspirations" (330). Max himself, however, his hat "jammed" on his head in that subtle last scene of the novel (358), has in effect blotted out of his head all the words from Bigger that he did not want to hear, those expressions of the black prisoner's superior humanity that outdistanced Communist dogma.

The other kind of image thematic in *Native Son* with about equal frequency is the "white blur" and its variant forms. Bigger's certainty of the color and his uncertainty regarding the substance of these sense impressions invest them with a degree of pathos and irony. Blind Mrs. Dalton, always dressed in white, both a victim and an object of faulty external perception, is typically a "white blur . . . standing by the door, silent, ghostlike" (73). Other people pictorially share her color and meaning: while Bigger stands bewildered by his discovery that he has killed Mary, a "vast city of white people" blurs the reality of the room (75); while viewing his picture in the newspaper, in which the white cat perches accusingly on his shoulder, Bigger feels that the "whole vague white world . . . would track him down . . ." (190); and while he is being cruelly dragged and cursed and stamped in the snow, he dimly sees around him "an array of faces, white and looming" (229). An implicit image of the "white blur"—and a source of monumental frustration in Bigger Thomas and in many of his progeny —is voiced by Max, who tells the judge that the prisoner "had no notion before he murdered, and he has none now, of having been wronged by any specific individuals" (332). Material objects in the "white world" also appear as blurs. The reader slowly realizes that the white-owned cars that "whirred over the smooth black asphalt" (13), "shot past them at high speed" (19), and "zoomed past on swift rubber tires" (37) early in the novel have been varicolored forerunners of the white blur. When images like "the white flash of a dozen silver bulbs" (171) occur, the mass image of the newsmen in the basement has a manifold significance.

A reversal like that observed in the blot-out images appears in the use of the white blur. State's Attorney Buckley, himself part of the white blur, urges the death penalty to enable whites "to sleep in peace tonight, to know that tomorrow will not bring the black shadow of death over the homes and lives" (341). The sentence of death brings another reversal, a counter image, to Bigger's perception as he understands "every word" while reacting only to "the judge's white face, his eyes not blinking" (348). The "blur" now disappears from the language of the novel, clarified by its own revealed deadliness—to recur implicitly and indirectly only once, transformed into a "new adversary" for Bigger: the opaqueness in the mind of Max that blurs his "deeper awareness" of his client (353).

By far the most numerous and the most meaningful, Wright's closely related images of the wall and the curtain, widely distributed in over fifty separate passages in *Native Son*, deserve a closer study than is possible here. But their categories (thirteen in number), at least, can be indicated. When ranked according to frequency of usage, the wall-curtain as a shield of indifference and detachment, emphasized in eleven different passages, is predominant. On the first morning of the novel, Bigger has "lurked behind his curtain of indifference . . . snapping and glaring at whatever had tried to make him come out into the open" (24). Several such images cluster on the pages describing Bigger's capture, where the reader sees him trapped on the icy water tank, "going behind his curtain, his wall, looking out with sullen stares of contempt" (226), "behind his curtain now, looking down at himself freezing under the impact of water in sub-zero winds" (227); and when his fingers are too stiff to pick up his gun, "Something laughed in him, cold and hard; he was laughing at himself" (228). The final such image in the novel is especially interesting: "Bigger's eyes were wide and unseeing; his voice rushed on" (355) as he explains to Max important things about his life and recent actions that Max really does not want to hear. Bigger is walling Max out of his perceptions, so that he, Bigger, can better gauge with his feelings whether his own *tone* is carrying his meaning (it had been Max's tone in court, not his words, that had made him believe "that Max knew how he felt" [350]).

A category of wall-curtain images used somewhat less often, and used negatively, is one reflecting on the artificial separation of certain classes of people: Bigger, for example, rides in the front seat of the Dalton car "between two vast white looming walls [Mary and Jan]" (59). The suggestion of protectiveness in this kind of image disappears from the novel after white but "honest" Jan has approached Bigger, "flung aside the curtain and walked into the room of his life" (246)—a passage important also for its metaphor showing Bigger's life as a room, and therefore enhancing the meaning of every wall-curtain image. Thus reversed, the image later pictures Bigger trying to break down walls to reach other people. One of the most gratifying passages in the novel employs such an image when the prisoner wonders whether, if his hands were electric wires and his heart a battery, and if he

> reached out through these stone walls and felt other hands . . . would there be a reply, a shock? Not that he wanted those hearts to turn their warmth to him; . . . But just to know that they were there and warm! . . . And in that touch, response of recognition, there would be union, identity; . . . a wholeness which had been denied him all his life (307).

Similarly moved by his new insight, Bigger wonders how he can "break down this wall of isolation" between him and Max, whom he now sees "upon another planet, far off in space" (353); and he apprehensively tells Max that maybe the wall between him and other men will still be there when he is executed: "I'll be feeling and thinking that they didn't see me and I didn't see them" (355)—an early expression of Ralph Ellison's "invisible man" theme.

The remaining 11 subdivisions of the wall-curtain image, spread throughout approximately 35 passages, need not be illustrated by more excerpts to document the variety and authenticity in this area of Wright's style. Nevertheless, the following list of the subdivisions, ranked again according to their frequency of use, should be informative. The other figurative walls and curtains, then, vividly represent (1) the suppression of certain feelings; (2) hatred, resentment, and mistrust; (3) the stunting or perversions of intelligence and imagination; (4) the withering of familial and friendly affection; (5) the ineffectiveness of certain barriers; (6) the deprivation of fundamental human needs; (7) natural barriers; (8) entrapment; (9) deceit; (10) defensive counterfeelings; and (11) the acceptance of certain isolation.

A knowledge of all the images in *Native Son* does not produce automatically a knowledge of Bigger Thomas. And Bigger himself feels more than he thinks, concluding at last, existentially, that his feelings are the surest guide to truth and to morality. "But when I think of why all the killing was," he says (apparently including all the fancied killings of his life), "I begin to feel what I wanted, what I am" (358). To know what and why a man desires, and to know what he is, is the deepest human engagement of our faculties. The furnace, the trembling poise in the middle of the room, the crucifix, the haunting blind eyes, the wish to blot out, the "white blur" of the hater and avenger, and the looming wall so massively effective and yet so useless and wrong—all these images metaphorically dramatize part of the black man's American experience; and *Native Son* preserves them for us to feel and to believe.

Richard Wright: Complexes and Black Writing Today

CECIL M. BROWN

So notoriously void of honesty is White Society in this country that any writer made famous by it is an immediate suspect, and if he is a Negro writer, double suspect. Black writers, who are of extreme value to the Black Community, for example, cannot, by definition, be of much value to White Society (I am thinking of such writers as LeRoi Jones and Eldridge Cleaver); and conversely, white writers of national popularity are the Black Community's enemy. One might say that a writer of Richard Wright's status is an exception, but let me hasten to add that, as a chronic, black reader of literature, I have felt, in reading Wright's books, a strange uneasiness, not about the sub-human puppets dangled before me, but about the man controlling, these puppets—who is, really, the Booker T. Washington of American letters. (And is it not the messianic urge for another B. T. Washington that haunts the white critic like Irving Howe, who can so swiftly conclude that Wright is Ralph Ellison's and James Baldwin's "spiritual father"?)

Because I had barely survived the dirt farms of North Carolina myself, I stayed away from Wright as long as I could; and even after I broke down and read *Native Son* and enjoyed it and was surprised, even then I felt I was patronizing "Negro Literature." When I read Baldwin, Ellison, Jones, or Cleaver, however, I read for myself; I feel I understand something about myself as a black man and a writer; I feel involved with these writers' lives because they, themselves, are involved in explaining to themselves and to all who listen to their weird position in White America; Wright, in contrast, spent his life explaining someone *else* (*i.e.* the Bigger Thomases) to white people who were anxious to believe that, indeed, Bigger existed, but not Wright himself.

It is not that the social reality portrayed by Wright is false, but that, insofar as it represents Wright's own life, it is . . . (I do not wish to use the word "lie" so let's say simply that Wright availed himself of a literary convention). Anyone wishing to view the distance between the benighted Bigger Thomas and the enlightened Richard Wright with more accurate measurement should compare, for example, Wright's attitude towards white women in his fiction and his attitude towards them in his biography and his autobiographical works. By insisting on the disparity between Wright's life and the social reality he created, I am not saying that Wright was dishonest and that he betrayed (however unwittingly) the values of the black community; rather, to emphasize the extent to which literature is dependent, for its impetus and impact, on literary fashions and conventions. One should avoid the implication of Wright's social reality, that South Chicago was worse in the 40's than it is now. Wright wrote about Chicago in the manner that he did because that was what white America was ready to accept (in terms of literary fashion and social imagery), or more accurately, *needed* to accept.

White America branded Wright the Official Negro Protester, the genuine article; to reject him was to reject official, genuine Negro protest, no matter what your own experience as a Negro might have been. In terms of popularity, Wright was the Great American Writer, and in Europe even more so—and probably for the same reason that *Patch of Blue* was so popular in Denmark. I remember walking out of that movie in Copenhagen trying to explain to sympathetic Danish friends ("It's not *that* simple; I mean it's more *complex*") why I rejected the movie's reality.

To reject Wright's art is not to reject protest; it is to reject negative protest, to reject the white man's concept of protest, which is that of a raging, ferocious, uncool, demoralized black boy banging on the immaculate door of White Society, begging, not so much for political justice as for his own identity, and in the process, consuming himself, so that in the final analysis, his destiny is at the mercy of the White Man. No, to reject Wright is not to reject protest, it is to reject negative protest. Every black person who realizes how sick American white society is, by the logic of this awareness, makes a protest, a positive protest. This is a delicate point which the oversimplification of Wright's social reality has obscured.

Positive protest that creates as it eliminates: it deals with the opposition's ugliness by concentrating on its own beauty. LeRoi Jones' prose is positive protest, because it is witty and beautiful to black people—which means simply white people cannot understand it; black children in the doorways of the ghetto doing the James Brown or the Uptight are positive protest directed against white people, because white people can't dance; NEGRO DIGEST is positive protest against the Reader's Digest; every ghetto—I do not mean slum—is positive protest against white insipid suburbs; black people together, involved with their lives, carrying on with their black and bluesy culture, is positive protest against the simpleness and the uninterestedness that haunt the abstracted lives of middle-class whites.

The argument that the value in Richard Wright's work lies in how well it describes the "specific social climate" that produced it is nothing more than a rationalization for the man's success, and an erroneous one at that; for it misses the point that it was Wright's attitude towards the Negro writer and Negro literature that led him to believe there was a gold mine in explaining to White America the lives of Black People; it was his definition of "Negro Writer" that led him to select from his own vast and rich experiences those horrifying scraps from which emerged a dozen or so unbelievably dumb Negroes. Just as the monster was created not by Frankenstein but by Mary Shelley, so Wright's creation cannot be foisted off on society; if we want to get to the key to Wright's work, we would do best by examining the theories of fiction Wright accepted during his day. A crucial question in Wright's definition of the Negro writer had to do with subject-matter, which stated simply that a Negro writer was someone who wrote about Negro life (Jesus, this would make Jessie Hill Ford, Nat Hentoff, Robert Penn Warren and William Faulkner Negro writers!) and, as though this was not enough, there was a definite itemized catalog (*i.e.* set-pieces) of what constituted "Negro life"—this, of course, was a much easier way out than saying "Negro life" is anything that a Negro does, because this leaves a definition of "Negro" too open and, baby, white people weren't having that just yet! An intellectual life, literary success, marriage to a white woman, for example, did not constitute "Negro life" (at least not for the white reading public), which explains why Wright published not one scratch about *this* aspect of his life. (In order to see how Black Writing handles this, compare, for example, the manner in which LeRoi Jones handles these aspects of his life in plays *Dutchman* and *The Slave*.)

Wright believed, as far too many people still do, that there are certain categories which constitute black experience and others white experience, that these white and black categories are (and this is a shame) ascribed, with you when you are born, and cannot be shaken by individual will. For Wright, it was his damnation to be born black, and his will to achieve whiteness—*i.e.* to pull himself up to the literary standards of white America.

The tenets of Black Writing today are the reverse of what Wright believed. For Black Writing, a black writer is first of all black, which means simply that he accepts the standards of black people OVER those of White America. Every Negro baby in America is born white, born, that is, into a world of white values, and if he is to survive that world, he has to *achieve* blackness; somewhere in the marrow of his youth must be that experience, that awakening, that *rebirth* Jesus talked so much about, which must carry him over to accept the reality of blackness. This journey is ultimately an achievement of both grace and one's own will. One must, as Ellison so strongly insists upon, *will* to be a Negro: ". . . being a Negro American involves a *willed* (who wills to be a Negro? *I* do!) affirmation of self against all outside pressures." But the Irving Howe types ("Freedom can be fought for, but it cannot always be willed or asserted into existence") wishes this weren't so.

So then, a Black Writer is not just some colored person trying to prove to White Society that he is not a "nigger," or/and that if he is, White Society is to blame. No, when we meet the Black Writer in the pages of his work, we encounter someone who has *achieved* and *willed* an identity of blackness, someone who has accepted Negro life not as a burden, as Ellison puts it, but as a discipline.

Subject-matter, then, is not part of the criteria in determining a Black Writer, but quality of life, will, discipline and moral courage are. A Black Writer can write about anything, I mean this literally, and what he has to say will still be said by a black man. As LeRoi Jones puts it:

> If I say, "I am a black man. All my writing is done by a black man," whether I label each thing I write, "Written by a black," it's still written by a black man, so that if I point out a bird, a black man has pointed out that bird, and it is the weight of that experience in me and the way I get it from where it is to you that says whether or not I am a writer. (*Anger and Beyond*, p. 56.)

The tragedy of Richard Wright's life is that he subscribed to a definition of the Negro Writer that was perniciously paradoxical: on the one hand the role of the Negro Writer, as Wright saw it, allowed him the potent power of the raging satirist, while at the very same time rendered him, in the last years of his life, impotent and exiled. It was near impossible for Wright to change his ideas about the function of the writer, because such ideas were, as always, intricately woven into the writer's definition of his *self*. "To me Wright as *writer* was less interesting than the enigma he personified," Ellison can say, "that he could so dissociate himself from the complexity of his background while trying so hard to improve the condition of black men everywhere; that he could be so wonderful an example of human possibility but could not for ideological reasons depict a Negro as intelligent, as creative or as dedicated as himself" (*Anger and Beyond,* p. 26). Wright's idea of a Negro Writer was extremely middle-class, which means that he believed that what white society thought to be Negro reality was more important than what Negroes knew to be their reality.

Wright was exiled because his definition of "Negro life" was too narrow, too confining, too puny, and too dependent on White Society. Wright was afraid to define "Negro life" too broadly for fear it would cease to be Negro. A weird kind of insecurity.

It was Wright's conception of what he thought his function as a Negro Writer should be that is primarily responsible for his style (*i.e.* his attitude towards his reader and his characters).

The Negro world that Wright wrote about was so strange, so far from the lives of his white audience, that Wright indulged, too often, in the explanatory. The Negro Characters that he created are usually so sub-human, so dumb that, for the most part, Wright was forced to stand in the pages of his fiction as a kind of "Negro Spokesman." In order for a work of fiction to mean anything, it must first of all involve the reader. For a Black Reader, it is difficult to become involved—I mean really involved—with Wright's characters because he is always there intruding with his commentary, explaining, as it were, what to a Black Reader needs no apologetic explanation. This explanatory mood of Wright's resulted, finally, in a dull, dessicated, prosaic sentence structure that leaves nothing to the reader's imagination.

It is not, as some critics have stated, that Wright doesn't have a sense of humor in his fiction; it is simply that his prose style strangles his humor, which, like most elements of black culture, has nuances that are difficult to grasp with discursive prose. It is only after we have laid the story aside for some time and have allowed our minds to rearrange the images, the setting, the tone, of Wright's stories, only after that methodical and plodding rhythm of his prose has ceased to reverberate in our minds, that we appreciate his humor.

One of the reasons, incidentally, that LeRoi Jones is such a funny writer ("The Alternative" has to be one of the funniest stories ever written in America) is that his style is essentially poetic; and this is why, too, in *Tales* he can convey so much of Negro life. Poetry, rather than prose, seems to be the tool that is best for conveying the subtleties, the nuances, the complexity of Negro Culture. Wright's style is about as close to poetry as, say, Booker T. Washington's or Richard Nixon's.

With the exception of two stories, "Man of All Work," and "Man, God Ain't like That . . . ," both of which were written in dialogue, which was Wright's forte, the book, *Eight Men,* is the dullest I have ever read. Everywhere the reader turns in the book there is the dumb, sub-human, animal-like nigger, and his eloquent interpreter who, possessing some smattering of sociological theories, usually has the responsibility of forging the animal's actions into some acceptable "universal" or "literary" theme.

Take, for instance, the first few lines of the very first story, "The Man Who Was Almost a Man":

> Dave struck out across the fields, looking homeward through paling light. Whut's the use talkin wid'em niggers in the field? Anyhow, his mother was putting supper on the table. Them niggers can't understan' nothing. One of these days he was going to get a gun and practice shooting, then they couldn't talk to him as though he were a little boy (p. 11).

The first sentence is by the intelligent, objective, omniscient narrator whom we may presume is also the author; the second that of some Negro who seems to be thinking to himself, and I say *seems* because Wright's Negroes *never* think (although, Wright will *tell* you they do), this is left up to Wright—as Ellison said, "Wright could imagine Bigger, but Bigger could not possibly imagine Richard Wright. Wright saw to that"; the third is by the narrator (*i.e.* Wright), but it is—and this is important—only an interpretation of what presumably the character is thinking; the fourth, which is Dave speaking again, is fused with the narrator's interpretation; and finally, the fifth sentence, although written in the language of the narrator, is the thoughts of the boy—or, is it the narrator putting words into the boy's mouth? The problem is this: we believe we know something about the boy's mind, but we can't be sure, for after all, it was *reported* to us by the narrator. We can never really know the boy, the narrator stands between us, such that, at the end of the story our feeling towards the boy are ambivalent and anxious. This anxiety builds up to disastrous proportions if in the course of the story, the protagonist is the victim of violence, because one is forced to feel great sympathy for someone one does not know, and does not know why. Maybe this is why upon finishing each of these stories, I felt, a bit frustrated and unsatisfied.

The long, short story, "The Man Who Lived Underground," collected in *Eight Men,* suffers greatly from Wright's dumb Negro-eloquent spokesman device. The story cites the adventures of a Negro murderer, Fred, who lives in a man-hole, making Robinson Crusoe-type discoveries; Fred is quite childish, and when he finds a stack of money, unlike Crusoe with his mature sense of what money can do in English society, Fred is only "intrigued with the form and color of [it]." He steals a typewriter and radio upon which he literally spends hours, tinkering like a 10-year-old; but it is not of a child Wright wants us to think; he is imagining Fred as a sub-human, as some human who has become less human because he has been shut out of White Society, and this is what is behind Wright's statement about Fred: ". . . never in [Fred's] life had he used [a typewriter]. It was a queer instrument of business, *something beyond the rim of his life*" (italics added)—as though using a typewriter is going to add something to the quality of one's life! (One is reminded, of course, of the demoralized Bigger Thomas who wants "to do things," "to fly airplanes" like white boys. A cryin shame.)

Yet this sub-human who has no humanity to speak of, or at least one is not convinced of it, is transformed into an intellectual before the story ends—because Wright has to give the thing a universal theme. He selects the theme of Orestes and the furies. Fred, then, marches out of his man-hole into the police station and confesses he is "guilty." The police try to convince him that they have already caught the murderer of the woman whom Fred claims he killed.

The story ends when Fred finally persuades two policemen to go down into the underground to witness what he had experienced, so that "At last he would be free of his burden"; when they are deep in the tunnel, one of the police shoots him, with the explanation, "You've got to shoot his kind. They'd wreck things." Wright not only ended up with the "universal theme" but he even achieved a bit of a tear-jerker. What Black Writing has come to realize is that meaning (*i.e.* theme) is always implied in the image. One has only to paint the metaphor of blackness—the whole community, despite its pretense to the contrary, knows what the meaning is. And again, the history of black people in this country is within itself a universal theme—the most universal of themes. (What "Universal Theme" means, that is in Wright, is to write so white people can understand—*i.e.* without really understanding.)

In the few stories in which Wright left off the discursive prose, and let his characters do their own explaining, he created masterpieces; in *Lawd Today*, for example, the dialogue gets as close to poetry as Wright ever got. In this novel the dialogue is fascinating, because it is used to provoke the atmosphere, the mood of black people that the most skilled prose writer would have difficulty in capturing. The last fourth of the book is the best piece of writing Wright accomplished, the proof of this being in the fact that one can return to it and re-read it again and again. The novel depicts one day in the life of a postal clerk, and in order to give the events his inevitable commentary, Wright has that day happen on February 12, Abraham Lincoln's birthday. Throughout the novel, there are brief reminders of the Civil War, reminders that are so planted in the novel as to remind the reader that these Negroes, although wrapped in their own black culture, are not free yet. If this novel, in its celebration of Negro life, could shake itself free of Wright's commentary device it would rival *Native Son* as being Wright's most valuable book.

I have been talking about technique and style and how they were influenced by Wright's definition of the Negro writer. Let me now deal with the treatment of theme, which in Wright's work was as subject to being dictated by White Society as well as style. Let us take for example the theme of the white woman and her relationship with the black man. There is only one kind of interaction between these two, and that is one of unadulterated violence inflicted by the black male, who is imaged as an animal. This relationship is as rigid and codified as any element of medieval symbolism. The idea that a white woman is only a human being and one to whom it is possible to feel something other than hate is an idea that Wright's blacks are incapable of; this, despite the fact that Wright's own experience taught him otherwise.

When Max is questioning Bigger Thomas about his alleged rape and murder of the white girl, Mary Dalton, he suggests that Bigger might have liked Mary. Bigger's reaction is depicted as that of an animal's:

> "Did you like her?" Max asked.
> "*Like* her?"
> Bigger's voice *boomed so suddenly from his throat* that Max started. Bigger *leaped to his feet;* his *eyes widened* and his hands *lifted* midway to face, *trembling*. (Italics added.)
> "No! No! Bigger . . ." Max said (p. 323).

Thus, Bigger, the prototype nigger, in his attitude towards the White Woman, is more of a creation of White Society (which is why White Men like Irving Howe can so eagerly lay claim to him) than he is of any black man's: and so are those other black males in the pages of Wright's fiction whose only response to White Women is to chop off their heads.

Concerning this, Baldwin has written:

> In most of the novels by Negroes until today . . . there is a great space where sex ought to be; and what usually fills this space is violence. This violence, as in so much of Wright's work, is gratuitous and compulsive. It is one of the severest criticisms that can be leveled against his work. The violence is never examined.

I do not believe that Wright did not examine that violence, if it existed, in his personal life; what seems to be the case is that Wright subscribed to a literary convention that had as much to do with life as, say, menthol cigarettes, a convention responsible only to White Society. One could look, for example, at the treatment of the theme of the White Woman in an autobiographical story called "The Man Who Went to Chicago," in which the hero is an intelligent young man whom we must recognize as none other than the author; and his attitude towards White Women is, simply, normal. It is only when Wright had to create fictional characters that he insisted on gratuitous violence.

Bigger Thomas, like Othello, another victim of White Society, is dumb, but whereas Othello's error lies in Othello, in his perception, Bigger's lies in bad style, in Richard Wright. Bigger's dumbness is only a thematic device. Wright is not so much interested in the character of Bigger as he is in using whatever literary conventions to make an ideological point. Thus, at the beginning of the novel, it is convenient to have Bigger extremely stupid, for purposes of motivation; and after the murder, again it is convenient to give Bigger some awareness of his crime, thus adding to the significance of the crime as a theme. So that on page 35, Bigger is so stupid that he doesn't know what a communist is (when his friend helps him with "a communist is a red" he dumbly asks, "What's a red?"); yet, on page 109, he is suddenly ruminating on world issues:

> Of late he had liked to hear tell of men who could rule others, for in actions such as these he felt that here was an escape from his tight morass of fear and shame that sapped at the base of his life. He liked to hear of how Japan was conquering China; of how Hitler was running the Jews to the ground; of how Mussolini was invading Spain.

One ceases to believe in Bigger as a character, and there are moments when the reader grasps at Bigger's action and the ideas behind them with the same awe and lack of understanding that his own family did. And this happens because one feels he does not know Bigger, which is because he doesn't exist as a human being.

A rebel without a brain, Bigger's tragedy is a personal one, and it exists in the fact that he simply refuses to (cannot) see; Wright's tragedy is that he fails to condemn this blindness. Though, it may be that Bigger's demoralization is Wright's, *i.e.* Wright as artist. Bigger, for instance, prides himself on the knowledge that no one would ever think that a black timid Negro like himself was responsible (or is this Wright putting words in his mouth?): ". . . for he felt that they [white people] ruled him, even when they were far away and not thinking of him, ruled him by conditioning him in his relations to his own people" (p. 110). Bigger is only embodying a fantasy White Society created for him long ago, and this is why he feels that the murder is an act of creation; he talks about the murder bringing out the "hidden meaning of his life." This has to be taken ironically, because what is really meant is that Bigger, a kind of racial correlative objective, was created to serve White Society.

Bigger wanted to be white, but he wasn't smart enough to see that what can be had in whiteness can most certainly be had in blackness. Why couldn't Wright see this?

The distance between Bigger Thomas and Richard Wright, even after the publication of *Black Boy,* was so notoriously great that Ellison, in his famous essay, "Richard Wright's Blues," set out to explain it: "By discussing some of its cultural sources I hope to answer those critics who would make of the book a miracle and of its author a mystery." One of those "cultural sources" Ellison took to be the blues, and so began his essay with a much quoted paragraph on the function of the blues; after this insightful opening, Ellison dwindles into some well-stated sociology about the southern rural family, and has nothing else to say about the blues, except in the last paragraph.

Despite its title and general intent, Ellison's essay, in retrospect, sheds much doubt on whether Wright ever really understood the blues. In another essay, "A Rejoinder," published 19 years later, Ellison disparages Wright's knowledge of blues, and says "Hemingway was more important to me than Wright. Not because he was white, or more 'accepted' but because he appreciated the things of this earth which I love and which Wright was too driven or deprived or inexperienced to know." Hemingway's love for life, Ellison says in counterdistinction, "was very close to the feeling of the Blues." In terms of "explaining" Wright, I think Ellison was much closer when he said recently that Wright "was as much a product of his reading as of his painful experiences, and he made himself a writer by subjecting himself to the writer's discipline—as he understood it."

This changing critical attitude of Ellison's toward Wright I cite as an example of how critical theory has changed in the last 20 years. It is interesting, too, that during the writing of his essay, Ellison's criticism was about as equally imbued with sociological theories as was Wright's writing. Baldwin's criticism of the protest novel ("Everybody's Protest Novel") in general, and his essay, "Alas, Poor Richard," in particular, is very good critically on Wright, and precisely because Baldwin stayed clear of theories—well, at least sociological ones.

Irving Howe is typical of the white critics who harbor a vested interest in Richard Wright's Negroes. In his now famous essay, "Black Boys and Native Sons," Howe claims his disagreement with Ellison and Baldwin has something to do with protest, but Howe's real objection is that these writers, unlike Wright, refuse to create demoralized, unintelligible, sub-humans whose sole life-time concern is consumed in hating the invincible force (as Howe likes to imagine it) of the White World; rather, these writers have given us humane, courageous, profound, aware, conscious heroes, who are really more concerned with themselves and their own realities than with those of White Jewish intellectuals like Howe, whom Wright, apparently, was so respectful of; Howe accuses Baldwin and Ellison of not protesting, but what he refuses to acknowledge is that Baldwin and Ellison, for all their faults, by virtue of their existence as excellent, moral craftsmen, are protesting; their protest is positive protest because, in addition to blasting the White World (*i.e.* not letting White people get to them), they erect black positive images.

Richard Wright begged; Baldwin, Ellison, LeRoi Jones, Eldridge Cleaver are not begging, and this upsets the Howe-types, because they need to hear the rasping rage of groveling, demoralized Bigger Thomases at the door of White Society in order to be assured themselves that White Society still exists as the only possible alternative for the Negro personality.

Howe writes, for example, that in *Native Son,* Wright struggles to "transcend" violence. "That he did not fully succeed seems obvious; one may doubt that any Negro writer could." Now this cracker must be kidding, because almost every Black Writer I know of has "transcended" violence, at least that violence of Bigger's. Howe, like Wright, believes that "violence" is the Negro writer's lot; not to write about violence is to avoid writing about Negro life. This is why he finds *Giovanni's Room* "a flat failure," because "it abandons Negro Life entirely."

Finally, Howe assigns Wright as spiritual father to both Ellison and Baldwin—Ellison, because he didn't come around to protest, is suffering as a result; but Baldwin has come around: "Baldwin's most recent novel, *Another Country,* is a protest novel quite as much as *Native Son* . . . No longer is Baldwin's prose so elegant or suave as it once was; in this book it is *harsh, clumsy, heavy-breathing* with the pant of *suppressed bitterness.*" Obviously, this White Man is speaking of negative protest, demoralized protest, and not the protest of James Brown or LeRoi Jones. In other words, positive protest that asserts its own beauty, if you will, *its own elegance* as it protests is not viable? Well, Howe and his buddies had better wake up. Or not wake up, as they wish.

Richard Wright: Beyond Nihilism

ADDISON GAYLE, JR.

RICHARD WRIGHT'S REVEALING STATEMENT CONCERNING THE LITERATURE that he wrote had little to do with literature at all. In his autobiography, *Black Boy,* Wright recorded:

> There are some elusive, profound, recondite things that men find hard to say to other men; but with the Negro it is the little things of life that become hard to say, for these tiny items shape his destiny. A man will seek to express his relations to the stars; but when a man's consciousness has been riveted upon obtaining a loaf of bread, that loaf of bread is as important as the stars.

Metaphorically speaking, the choice was one between the abstract and the pragmatic, between a literature which did not, in the words of critic Stanley Braithwaite, "hover over the race question," but instead, "owed its highest allegiance to poetry," and a realistic art which dealt with the fundamental problem of being Negro in America—art which refused to either ignore or subsume the problem through adherence to critical standards acceptable to the American academic community.

Having made his choice, Richard Wright refused to compromise. Believing always that words were weapons, he dared to probe levels of experience which more timid writers by-passed. Like Goethe's Faust, he was obsessed by an insatiable desire to delve into the pits of darkness and despair in an attempt to reveal the inferno of human discontent, fear, hatred, and violence which is the most telling characteristic of twentieth century man. Having himself undergone experiences which can only be called Kafkaesque in their grotesqueness, like Coleridge's Ancient Mariner, he was ravished with a passion to tell his story, to inform the naive of the malady of terror with which "everyman," trapped in a brutal, oppressive environment, is inflicted.

For this reason, his earliest fiction was naturalistic, and there was certainly a great deal of truth in his admonition that, "All my life had shaped me for the realism, the naturalism of the modern novel . . ." Yet, neither his writings nor his experiences can be so narrowly categorized. "The Negro," writes Saunders Redding, "lives on two planes of awareness," which is close to saying that the Negro's experiences are likely to be at one and the same time both realistic and existential. To be sure, the Negro lives in a society in which his outlook upon life, his personality, and his psychological make-up are predetermined to a great degree; however, each Negro (despite the disclaimers) envisions a coming *Götterdämmerung*, when, like the existential hero, he undertakes the establishment of his own identity by destroying in total the oppressive, restrictive societal apparatus which he secretly loathes.

It is not true therefore, as Ralph Ellison, among others, has intimated, that Wright was stifled and restricted by the form of the naturalistic novel; for in the light of his myriad experiences, Wright could not completely adhere to the naturalistic formula. Despite his indebtedness to Emile Zola, the father of the naturalistic novel, or to Theodore Dreiser whose *Sister Carrie* had a "tremendous effect" upon him; unlike his counterparts, for Wright there was always the insurmountable barrier of color which constituted a wedge of such fortitude between reality and illusion as to produce a fiction vastly different from that of other naturalistic adherents.

But insofar as a black writer could be true to any formula, Wright was true to the naturalistic code. Yet, he never forgot his earlier injunction that a "loaf of bread is as important as the stars." His literature, therefore, would always contain a schizophrenic quality, wavering, as did the lives of those whom he wrote about, between pragmatism and transcendence. He never lost sight of the pull of "those tremendous forces upon the individual"; yet, he took cognizance of the individual's obsession to crush those forces. He never ceased to marvel at "how smoothly the black boys acted out the roles that the race had mapped out for them. Most of them were not conscious of living a special, separate, stunted way of life. Yet . . . in some period of their growing —a period they had no doubt forgotten—there had been developed in them a delicate sensitive controlling mechansim that shut off their minds and emotions from all that the white race said was taboo."

Yet, he knew, and perhaps he was his own best example, that the personality had not been totally destroyed, that all emotions had not been channeled into a predetermined direction, that the social institutions had not completely transformed 20 million people into non-thinking, non-sensitive, non-feeling robots. And never mind that men wore masks. Never mind that men refused to articulate the truth; never mind that men practiced the art of mimetics—and American Negroes have made a profession of the art—the atmosphere of hatred and fear which created Bigger Thomas is still present in modern day America, goading and pushing each Negro across the nihilistic brink where, in one transcendent moment, he is lifted above his predetermined state, gaining a sense of manhood, identity, and social worth, through the only means possible in an oppressive society—the medium of violence.

This is the reality of Bigger Thomas ignored by white and black critics alike. There can, however, be no doubt of Bigger's transcendence. In Book One of *Native Son*, Bigger Thomas is, indeed, the mechanical robot, the prototype of the naturalistic character:

> [He] had the feeling that the robbing of Blum's would be a violation of ultimate taboo; it would be a trespassing into territory where the full wrath of an alien white world would be turned loose upon [him;] it would be a symbolic challenge of the white world's rule over [him;] a challenge which [he] yearned to make, but [was] afraid.

The Bigger Thomas of Book Two, however, transcends this fear. This section is appropriately labelled "Flight"—for it signifies not only Bigger's flight from the law, but also his flight from the frightened, unsure boy of Book One to whom "white folks formed a kind of superworld." "The thought of what he had done," Wright elaborates after Bigger murders Mary Dalton

> The awful horror of it, the daring associated with such actions, formed for him for the first time in his fear-ridden life a barrier of protection between him and a world he feared. He had murdered and created a new life for himself.

"Americans," Wright was to record much later—referring to *Native Son*—"have not been able to accept my vision," which is not completely true—Americans were capable of accepting the vision in part. Critics admit to the sanctity of the sociological argument, agree that the institutions of the American society have been repressive in regard to its black minority; indeed, few would disagree with the indictment of the American social system leveled by Bigger's lawyer, Max. That part of the vision which Americans have not been able to accept—despite the recent yearly insurrections in the ghettos—is a nation of Bigger Thomases for whom no hope can be found, for whom no peace can come, for whom no transcendence is possible save through the flaming Armageddon of violent revolution. But on another level, as James Baldwin has pointed out, Americans have little to fear from Bigger Thomas. The underlying thesis of *Native Son* offers hope to the American society if that society will come to the unmistakable conclusion that men live despicable lives of continuous desperation, and undertake those programs which, by resurrecting Bigger Thomas, will grant salvation to the nation as a whole. It is on this level, Baldwin's critique to the contrary, that Bigger Thomas serves as the Christ figure, the martyr to the hopes of desperate men everywhere, the catalytic agent by which a society can be redeemed.

But "Hope," writes Matthew Arnold, "once crushed is less quick to spring anew," and the Bigger Thomas of the 1940's is the embryo of the Bigger Thomas of the 50's and 60's. This is not to maintain, as Wright has been accused of doing, that blacks have not made progress in the American society since the 1940's; but rather to suggest that progress must be measured not in terms of civil rights, material wealth, or governmental appointments but, instead, in terms of level of consciousness and the awareness by black people of those tremendous forces of which Bigger could only conjecture—a realization that the human spirit must be free, unrestricted by either demagogic men or demagogic institutions. Wright was among the first to recognize such progress, and to create a character who serves as a footnote to black men today—those for whom all hope has been dissipated, all optimism subsumed under the weight of constant rejection; men who see salvation not in terms of resurrecting the society, but in dismantling it *in toto* to produce a social order in which each individual will be the architect of his own destiny.

The Outsider, written 12 years after *Native Son*, is the archetype of the new spirit—the first black character in American fiction to "dare all" in an existential attempt to stave off personal dehumanization. In Damon, the bridge from Bigger Thomas to nihilistic man is traversed, for

> by the nature of things such a man sooner or later [was] bound to appear. Modern man sleeps in the myths of the Greeks and Jews. Those myths are now dying in his head and in his heart. They can no longer serve him. When they are really gone, those myths, *man* returns . . . and what's to guide him? Nothing at all but his own desires, which would be his only values.

Such a vision was totally rejected by Americans, both black and white. A nation of men clutching a dream which has long since become a nightmare for most of its citizens, a nation whose people are daily tranquilized by the rhetoric of its leaders portraying a land of freedom, promise and opportunity while one tenth of its population knows only misery, despair, and frustration—is it any wonder that such a nation would be incapable of accepting the existence of a character for whom the society is so degenerate as to produce a savage obsession to destroy everything that society has constructed?

Even Wright, himself, was ambivalent towards this vision. He could not accept Cross Damon as readily as he accepted Bigger Thomas, for it is Damon, not Bigger, who is the real monster, that "aberration," as one unkind critic has remarked, "upon humankind." Bigger blunders into murder, Cross skillfully executes it. Bigger's motives are guided by urges beyond his control; Damon's are premeditated, each step well calculated. Bigger desired to create a new identity; Cross desired no less than to create a new world. Bigger wants to share in the Protestant Ethic; Cross will settle only for an ethic devised by himself. Bigger is the disgruntled reformer; Cross is closer to being a nihilist, in the Camus sense, than any character in American fiction.

A "nihilist is not one who believes in nothing," writes Albert Camus, "he simply does not believe in what exists at the moment." And Wright's creation, but not Wright himself, could adhere to this philosophy. Wright believed wholeheartedly in the ethics and values which Damon—theoretically at least—wanted to destroy; and thus, Wright's most complex character got out of hand, refusing to allow his master to resurrect him even at the end of the novel. Damon remains the prophetic portrait of modern-day black men who are putting forth the most nihilistic of questions—whether a nation which continues to physically and mentally murder and maim one-tenth of its people has any valid reason for existing.

Wright, himself, had asked a similar question before. In the short story, "Bright and Morning Star," Aunt Sue is forced to choose between saving her life and that of her son or protecting the movement which is to eventually usher in the new Jerusalem over the dying corpse of the old. Her hatred of the old system is so intense that she chooses in favor of the movement despite the tenuous position upon which the movement rests.

Wright never made such a choice. Despite periods of overwhelming doubt, he remained wedded to the theoretical concepts of Western democracy. Despite his brief excursion into the Communist party, despite his self-imposed exile, he remained convinced—as he argued in *Black Power*—that the survival of Western Civilization rested upon the co-existence and co-recognition of multi-cultures in which the sanctity of all would be inviolate.

His vision, though often varied, remained true to the theme of his earlier writings. He saw the possibility of transcendence in the Bigger Thomases of the nation, and he warned America that a nation incapable of putting its ideals into practice would produce Cross Damons seeking their manhood through a nihilistic attempt to negate the very structure of democracy itself. He reaffirmed this thesis in *White Man, Listen!*, projecting his vision onto the world arena. Here he admonished the world powers, East and West, that at present the wretched of the earth could transcend their conditions only through violence, and if this remained the price that men would have to pay for individual freedom, then pay it they would.

This was Wright's final message to white men, and in light of the turbulence of the past years, the message is, perhaps, already outdated. For Wright is the last black writer to admonish men to listen. Today, the representatives of that third force which Frantz Fanon envisioned as moving beyond existentialism to create a world order out of many varied identities no longer seek to communicate with those who continue the oppression begun by their ancestors. Each day, the lines of communication between black man and white man in particular, and man and man in general, drift wider apart; and perhaps the telling mark of the twentieth century is the inability of one man to communicate with another.

This, Wright would not have liked. He believed always in the "community of man," and he realized that complete dedication to nihilism would make impossible the building of such a community. True, then, to his basic ideals—to those ethics and values hewn out of the violence and terror of "those most darkest of Southern nights"—he would still believe, even at the time of his death, with André Malraux that "every man is a mad man; but what is a human destiny for if not to unite the mad man with the universe."

The Social Significance of Bigger Thomas

DAN MCCALL

In his essay on Bigger's birth, Wright said that "life had made the plot over and over again, to the extent that I knew it by heart." Repeatedly he had seen black boys picked off the streets to be charged with an unsolved case of "rape." "This thing happens so often that to my mind it had become a representative symbol of the Negro's un-

---

certain position in America." Robert Nixon was apprehended and sent sprawling across the front page of the *Tribune* while Wright was in mid-passage with Bigger Thomas. The actual case is a part of history—as the novel is part of the literary history—of the thing itself. In Chicago in 1938 two black men were testifying to the myth, one with a brick and the other with a book.

Richard, like Bigger, lived in a Chicago slum with his mother. As an insurance agent Wright had visited various black kitchenettes like the one with which his book would begin. In the opening scene the people driven so closely together are driven violently apart. Wright would say the following year, in *12 Million Black Voices*, "The kitchenette throws desperate and unhappy people into an unbearable closeness of association, thereby increasing latent friction, giving birth to never-ending quarrels of recrimination, accusation, and vindictiveness, producing warped personalities." The full recognition of how the "kitchenette" (which refers to the cramped apartment itself, not just the cooking area) forms Bigger's sensibility—or how it deprived him of what we could call a "sensibility"—was one of Wright's most daring and significant choices.

In "Many Thousands Gone," Baldwin saw that "Bigger has no discernible relationship to himself, to his own life, to his own people, nor to any other people" and because of that "a necessary dimension has been cut away." But that was surely Wright's point; he knew that he was cutting away a dimension. He said in "How Bigger Was Born" that he planned for his black boy to be "estranged from the religion and the folk culture of his race"—a statement that shows that Wright was consciously pulling things away and not, as the criticism against Wright might lead one to believe, that Wright just didn't know how to show them. In *12 Million Black Voices* he summarized:

> Perhaps never in history has a more utterly unprepared folk wanted to go to the city; we were barely born as a folk when we headed for the tall and sprawling centers of steel and stone. We, who were landless on the land; we, who had barely managed to live in family groups; we, who needed the ritual and guidance of institutions to hold our atomized lives together in lines of purpose; we, who had known only relationships to people and not relationships to things; we, who had never belonged to any organizations except the church and burial societies; we, who had had our personalities blasted with two hundred years of slavery and had been turned loose to shift for ourselves. . . .

In the figure of Bigger Thomas, Wright was trying to show the ultimate sense of horror: unpreparedness set loose in a metropolis. Bigger has nothing to hold him back and nothing to define his responses other than the blackness of his skin. He is, as his mother wails, "black crazy"; his mind is crazed by his color. He is incapable of a nonracial thought. His obsession produces what Wright would later call, "The State of

Exaggeration." In *White Man, Listen!*, Wright says that "one of the aspects of life of the American Negro that has amazed observers is the emotional intensity with which he attacks ordinary, daily problems." How can the mind ever relax or grow when its defining problem is always and unbearably one thing? Wright offers as an example the problem a Negro has in renting a place to live; the overriding question, the one that gathers all the usual questions of whether the place is clean, whether it is well-made, whether it's near a school, whether it's near stores, is only one question: can a black person live there? And as the great migration moved northward in the twenties and thirties the black folk found their answer. They would live in the kitchenette.

This "state of exaggeration" that Wright speaks of is most clearly seen in the kitchenette by an overwhelming fear of being looked at. The kitchenette means lack of privacy. On the first page of *Native Son*, when people get out of bed, the first words are "Turn your heads so I can dress." Day after day in the ghetto that is the call to society; and on the second day of Wright's story, in the center section of his book, Vera repeats the line "Turn your head so I can dress." Even when one is dressed, the fear continues at the breakfast table, this horror of being seen.

> "Stop looking at me, Bigger!"
> "Aw, shut up and eat your breakfast!"
> "Ma, make 'im stop looking at me!"
> "I ain't looking at her, Ma!"
> "You *is!*" Vera said.

And so it goes, on into the night where children are given their sexual education because the mother and father cannot not give it to them. After his murders Bigger roams the ghetto apartment houses, climbing them and peering into windows where he sees

> through a window without shades . . . a room in which were two small iron beds with sheets dirty and crumpled. In one bed sat three naked black children looking across the room to the other bed on which lay a man and woman, both naked and black. . . . There were quick, jerky movements on the bed where the man and woman lay, and the three children were watching.

Bigger sees it as a memory, for he, too, had often "awakened and watched his father and mother." He climbs on up with one last look in at "the man and woman moving jerkily in tight embrace, and the three children watching."

Wright's point is not to deny the Negro's "folk culture." He was trying to show that for these urban slum dwellers the folk culture was swallowed in unbearable closeness. This emptiness and fear of being looked at Bigger carries with him all the day long. The scene which begins the book is present at the very center of the crime where Bigger is hysterical at not being able to get the full human form into a tight place. He has to cut off the head. Bigger's head, his sensibility, was cut off in the kitchenette. (And the severed head appears in his dream as his own.) At the end of the book Max keeps asking Bigger what Mary Dalton had done to him that made Bigger say, "I ain't sorry she's dead." Bigger struggles for the answer; all he knows is that he hated her. He stammers and tries to find it and then vaguely he gets an image of his sister

> Vera, sitting on the edge of a chair crying because he had shamed her by "looking" at her; he saw her rise and fling her shoe at him. He shook his head confused.

That is it: racial misery is indecent exposure.

And so Wright would tell us at the beginning of his story that Bigger's relationship to his family was that "he lived with them, but behind a wall, a curtain." When he relates to black people he takes his violence out on them. His hate bottles up and has to get out; since it cannot reach its stimulus, the white man, it is expelled on blacks. He corners his pal, Gus, and holds a knife blade at his mouth, saying, "Lick it." What he wants to do, of course, is hold it at the white man's lips, draw blood from the white man's tongue. But he can't get at him. Bigger "had heard it said that white people felt it was good when one Negro killed another; it meant that they had one Negro less to contend with." When a Negro says he is afraid to go to Mississippi because "down there they'd as soon kill you as look at you" he does not refer merely to the white race. Bigger cannot feel "guilt" about his murders. His is a mind in which "guilt" plays as negligible a part as it did in the whites who set fire to Bobo. Bigger cannot say, "I have killed a *human being*," for there are no human beings on his planet. Bessie was not at all his "sweetheart," only the "girl" he had because other boys had them. His relationship to her is his relationship to the black community; he will use and enjoy her when he can and strike out when she gets in his way. "The black girl was merely 'evidence.' And under it all he knew that the white people did not really care about Bessie's being killed."

Bigger is, then, one of the Negro's "roles" (in spite of the continuing objection that he is not) and the white reader can see it more clearly now as black voices from the ghetto begin to come out with verification of how accurate Bigger was. Anyone who has read *The Autobiography of Malcolm X* or *Manchild in the Promised Land* or Eldridge Cleaver's remarkable *Soul on Ice* can see Biggers in the characters the authors draw around them and explore, with considerable courage, in themselves. Wright does not, as Baldwin said, "cut a necessary dimension away." Again, white America beat him to it. Had Wright not portrayed Bigger in this way he would have been cutting a "necessary dimension away" not from his figure but from the importance of the forces that would make him what he was. To create a "folk tradition" in the slum—that is, to create whole human beings in a brutally fragmented world—would not be to take that world seriously. It would be a gross underestimation of how massive the damage is. Wright saw that if people do not have any chance to get culture it is rather unlikely that they will have its blessings.

When Bigger goes out onto the street he sees a poster for Buckley's campaign: "IF YOU BREAK THE LAW, YOU CAN'T WIN!" And, as Bigger knows, if you don't break it, you keep losing. This is the white man's law. What Bigger has available to him is no "folk tradition" but the glittery expression of the white civilization. He goes to a movie, *The Gay Woman,* in which he gets that tradition in "scenes of cocktail drinking, dancing, golfing, swimming, and spinning roulette wheels, a rich young white woman kept clandestine appointments with her lover while her millionaire husband was busy in the offices of a vast paper mill." If Bigger went to that world of money and fancy sex, the white folks would run—thinking, as Bigger's chum says, "a gorilla broke loose from the zoo and put on a tuxedo."

When Bigger actually goes into the white mansion where "the gay woman" lives, he goes as a chauffeur. His position behind the wheel is a gross parody of his deepest wish: to be behind the stick of the airplane. Passionate to get out of his prison, to roam the skies, he is only a "driver." Bigger is constantly assuming such poses that are emblematic stances of the Negro. When he puts the white maiden in the trunk and carries her down to the furnace he is frozen for a moment as the jolly redcap at the station. The black destroyer is a porter. Climbing buildings he is the giant darky we blew up onto the screen, the "Bigger" black man; he stands roaring on the rooftops until white technology sends him plummeting to the street below. And *King Kong* ends with the assertion that "beauty killed the beast" just as *Native Son* shows how the beast—if given a chance—will kill the beauty.

The scene with Jan and Mary is one of gross comedy. In order to make Bigger feel at home Jan says first of all in the restaurant, "You like fried chicken?" (And decades later Lenny Bruce would begin his sketch, "How to Make a Negro Feel Comfortable at a Party" with the white host going over to the black guest—"Can I get you something? Piece of watermelon? Chicken leg?") Jan and Mary are locked almost as tightly in stereotypes as is Bigger. The drunker they get the more they retreat into those stereotypes, and Mary asks Bigger to sing "Swing low, sweet chariot, Coming fer to carry me home. . . ." Fer, she says. All of it is torture for Bigger, who at the beginning was so impressed with them and so upset that he couldn't stop saying "*yessuh* and *yessum* to white people in one night when he had been saying it all his life long." In the early hours he could not eat with them because under the pressure of their openness he could not chew; it seemed to him "that the very organic functions of his body had altered." As the game goes on he cannot escape the suspicion that they are playing a dreadful game with him, cheating him of the stability, the certainty, that he has learned.

When the Daltons wanted to "give the negroes a chance," they never reckoned with just how well Bigger would take it. The game that Jan and Mary play throws off his timing. He never wanted to know people like Jan ("He didn't want to meet any Communists. They didn't have any money.") and now he has known for too long that whites are not people. "He was sitting between two vast white looming walls." When the walls talk, and ask him, "We seem strange to you, don't we, Bigger?" he replies, "Oh, no'm," and the female wall gets mad. Bigger keeps using the language that's supposed to work, he keeps trying not to be noticed. These whites are cheating; they made up the game and now they're not sticking to the rules. "These people made him feel things he did not want to feel." He has a right to be suspicious; when she gets enough rum, Mary begins to hold him up for amusement. Come, driver, do your tricks.

When he kills, his only way of apprehending that death is: "She was dead; she was white; she was a woman; he had killed her; he was black. . . ." It is part of the general stunting of his emotional growth. He later enjoys reports of Japan's war on China and the news that Hitler is "running the Jews to the ground" and Mussolini's troops are slaughtering Spain. There is never any "moral" question for him; aggressions and atrocities are a way of getting out of racial pain. All he wants is some day some black man "who would whip the black people into a tight band and together they would act and end fear and shame." He lives in a world where guilt can only be "a white blur" of blind Mrs. Dalton.* Guilt is no more than terror; when he sees "the awesome white blur floating toward him" he kills the whiteness.

The murder is an act of creation. It is a way of escaping all the negatives in his life: "The knowledge that he had killed a white girl they loved and regarded as their symbol of beauty made him feel the equal of them, like a man who had been somehow cheated, but had now evened the score." He has had *The Gay Woman,* the pretty white girl who gets drunk. He has taken her out of her high room, brought her down to his own level. He has had her on his bed of coals. Bigger had "committed rape every time he looked into a white face" and now he has done it in a way that the white face would have to cry out in pain. He creates by making whole, by severing the perpetual discon-

* David B. Davis has suggested to me an interesting version, possibly a source, for this central dramatic scene involving Bigger, Mary, and the blind mother. In Thomas Dixon's *The Clansman,* 1905 (on which *Birth of a Nation,* the first Hollywood spectacular, was based), the insufferable blond virgin, Marion, is raped by the young black man, Gus (the name of Bigger Thomas's best buddy). The rapist's identity is later discovered by a "scientific" study of his image in the eye of the mother, who watched her daughter's violation.

tinuity between his two worlds, his aspirations and his abilities to attain their satisfaction; "never had he felt a sense of wholeness" until he introduced Mary Dalton to the furnace.

Murder is a recapitulation of suffering. Bigger hides in empty houses the way Big Boy hid in empty kilns. Bigger wants to know "the right way" to behave when he is captured, "the right way being the way that would enable him to die without shame"—as in *Uncle Tom's Children* Brother Mann and especially Silas in "Long Black Song" and the Negro mother in "Bright and Morning Star" wanted to die. In this sense *Native Son* becomes a way of retrieving the pain of *Uncle Tom's Children,* hurtling that pain into the white community.

But Bigger's act is as futile as was any of the acts in *Uncle Tom's Children* and can bring only the same results. As soon as the newspaper can run the headlines "AUTHORITIES HINT SEX CRIME," Bigger knows it is all over. He has blown the fuse in the white mind. Immediately the police are able to gather three thousand volunteers. "The Negro rapist and murderer" the papers call him before he gets a chance. Massive reprisals come immediately and hundreds of black employees are fired from their jobs, Negro men are beaten on the streets, and all the ghetto hotspots are raided and closed down. The triumph must yet again remain in the mind.

Wright's novel begins to fall slightly out of focus as he tries to show how that triumph registers in his hero's mind. Bigger is smart. The problem Wright did not adequately solve was the nature of Bigger's intelligence. For the most part we see it as a strategic, military mind; he feels power and knows how to use it. But he has no "ideas"—just the vast obsession. He can see the world only as "iron palms" and "fiery furnaces" and a "sea of white faces," blurs of motion and sound and racial horrors. Yet Wright begins to dress up Bigger's "act of creation" in a prose that rings false. Bigger had "accepted the moral guilt and responsibility for that murder"—but he had not; he could not think in terms of "moral guilt and responsibility," let alone "accept" them. When "a supreme act of will springing from the essence of his being" drove him into crime he "looked wistfully upon the dark face of ancient waters upon which some spirit had breathed and created him." The language is all wrong, and so is Bigger. Preparing for the forensics in the courtroom, Wright begins to lose his grasp on his great character. Able to "look wistfully upon the dark face of ancient waters" Bigger can see a gavel in the courtroom only as a "hammerlike piece of wood."

The problem had been with Wright from the beginning, and all along he had been wrestling with it. In the second section, "Even though Mr. Dalton gave millions of dollars for Negro education, he would rent houses to Negroes only in this prescribed area, the corner of the city tumbling down from rot. In a sullen way Bigger was conscious of this." Wright wants to make his point, then suddenly realizes how important it is that we see it only through Bigger's eyes, and so he leans on "a sullen way" of consciousness. As Bigger climbs in the abandoned house "he remembered that bombs had been thrown by whites into houses like these when Negroes had first moved into the South Side"—yet while Bigger might know that, he does not "remember" it as he climbs inside the old wreck.

The fuzziness in Bigger's characterization is part of a general falling off in the third part as the terms of the book begin to change. Bigger is undergoing a psychic rehabilitation, and too often we see him in his Sunday best: "He lay on the cold floor sobbing; but really he was standing up strongly with contrite heart. . . ."

Margaret Butcher has summed up the usual objection voiced against the third part of Wright's novel. "Ideological commitment cheated him of a classic." The Party had interrupted Wright's project and falsified the message of "the bad nigger." Wright himself said in "How Bigger Was Born":

> Two items of my experience combined to make me aware of Bigger as a meaningful and prophetic symbol. First, being free of the daily pressure of the Dixie environment, I was able to come into possession of my own feelings. Second, my contact with the labor movement and its ideology made me see Bigger clearly and feel what he meant. I made the discovery that Bigger Thomas was not black all the time; he was white, too, and there were literally millions of him, everywhere.

Wright seems to want Bigger to stand for any colorless slum kid; his problems are the problems of any impoverished group. Yet in the last section of *Native Son* this idea is only presented briefly and parenthetically in Boris Max's speech. When it makes its second appearance, in the very last scene in the prison cell, Max draws Bigger to the little barred window, shows him the skyscrapers, and says that *that* is what killed you, Bigger, the capitalist economy; the men in those buildings "want to keep what they own, even if it makes others suffer." But Bigger rejects all that. He knows the problems of his life cannot be explained by economics or the class system. Bigger knows, however crudely, what kind of skull he is in.

For the most part, in his lengthy courtroom address, Max takes the terms for granted and speaks solely to the problem of race. What is wrong in the courtroom is not this evasion of the problem by an assertion that "Bigger was not black all the time." Something more generally is wrong with the entire idea of a courtroom confrontation itself. The name "Bigger Thomas" carries us back to the name in that other famous novel which had achieved such immediate and large sales almost a century before. Bigger Thomas is "bigger" than Uncle Tom, but he is part of the family, a son, just as Tom was an uncle. And Wright will use some of Mrs. Stowe's imagery for the Negro in America. The black man is Christ; he is Christ in the complicated way that Buckley, State's Attorney, impulsively feels when he cries, "O suffering Christ, there are no words to tell of a deed so black and awful!" (that is, an inverted Christ). When Bigger is captured, "two men stretched his arms out, as though about to crucify him." The black Christ is nailed by white America. James Baldwin saw *Native Son* as "a continuation, a complement of that monstrous legend it was written to destroy," for in Wright's book

> Bigger is Uncle Tom's descendant, flesh of his flesh, so exactly opposite a portrait that, when the books are placed together, it seems that the contemporary Negro novelist and the dead New England woman are locked together in a deadly, timeless battle; the one uttering merciless exhortations, the other shouting curses.

Mrs. Stowe often sacrificed her characters to the moral crusade; the fictional personages became mere pawns in the propagandistic enterprise. The figure of St. Clare is well drawn in the first part of the book, but he tends to disintegrate into merely a mouthpiece for high-sounding morals. That is what begins to happen in Wright's courtroom. Max's speech falls into the category. Mrs. Stowe wrote her book, she said, "to awaken sympathy for the African race as they exist among us," and what else is Boris Max trying to do? Mrs. Stowe showed it by Uncle Tom's gigantic loveliness, concluding we should not do horrid things to people like that. Max shows Bigger's enormous sickness, concluding he is sick because the society is. From exactly opposite directions the two avenues come to the same destination: the crusader tells white America to stop ruining black people.

In the first two parts of the book Wright had been doing something intensely more complicated. We were not seeing Bigger as an object; we were participating with him as a subject. No white man could have written that part of the book, no white man could have stayed so resolutely and utterly in Bigger's brain. But a white man could have written all the courtroom speeches (and it is a white man who gives them). In the last section we are no longer in Bigger's mind. He continues to be the zero he was at the beginning of that third book, a brute in a chair, only listening. Max asks, "Let me, Your Honor, explain further the meaning of Bigger Thomas' life." That is exactly the flaw. I have said the chief virtue of the novel is that it is an exorcism, a calling up of mysterious disasters; the chief error of the third part of the novel is that it is only explanation, no longer a vital artistic effort at a full understanding. What Max is saying is surely true, but it is a truth of a far less demanding kind, the lesser truth that Mrs. Stowe herself achieved.

> Your Honor, consider the mere physical aspect of our civilization. How alluring, how dazzling it is! How it excites the senses! How it seems to dangle within easy reach of everyone the fulfillment of happiness! How constantly and overwhelmingly the advertisements, radios, newspapers and

movies play upon us! But in thinking of them remember that to many they are tokens of mockery. These bright colors may fill our hearts with elation, but to many they are daily taunts. Imagine a man walking amid such a scene, a part of it, and yet knowing that it is *not* for him!"

All of this is certainly true, not at all an extraneous interpretation of the action. It is a perfectly accurate description of what the action can show us. That is what is wrong. It is an "interpretation." It is part of Wright's flaw of overwriting, a consequence of his fear that we will not see Bigger's meaning, and he must rush in to point it out to us. The third section of the book, all the rhetoric in the courtroom, is the architectural equivalent of the local failures all through the book sentence by sentence, in the unnecessary adverbs and stereotypic figures of speech.

When Bigger is attacked in court, beaten in the head, he is going through a torture that Wright had read about in the Robert Nixon case. On June 8, 1938, Elmer Johnson, the husband of Florence, smashed his fists into Nixon's face at the inquest. Later Nixon rushed Johnson on the stand and tried to strangle him. Thus, at Nixon's trial, and at Bigger's, the courtroom is ringed with uniformed guards to keep the people apart. All of this Wright is able to convey convincingly. But the performance of the lawyer is incredibly stupid—if he is supposed to be a lawyer concerned with getting his man off, and not just a mouthpiece.

The relationship between the Thomas family and the Dalton family was that of renter to landlord, customer–merchant, employee to employer. The Thomas family got poor and the Dalton family got rich. And Mr. Dalton, a decent man, tried to salve his feelings by giving money. But, my friend, gold was not enough! Corpses cannot be bribed! Say to yourself, Mr. Dalton, "I offered my daughter as a burnt sacrifice and it was not enough to push back into its grave this thing that haunts me."

How Bigger is going to be assisted by this line is utterly unclear. Those people in the jury box, staring at the father of the lost child, hear her described as a burnt offering; to see Dalton browbeaten will not impel them to leniency. The passage also distracts us and exposes as obtrusive and mechanical the symbols we had lived through with Bigger. It is "poetic justice"—and no other kind—that the Thomas house should be owned by the Daltons. All perfectly true, of course—the philanthropist gouged the rent out of the Negroes and paid them back with ping-pong tables—but we could get that on the pages of the *Daily Worker* and it is an insane tactic in a courtroom. The lawyer turns to the poor blind mother: "And to Mrs. Dalton, I say: 'Your philanthropy was as tragically blind as your sightless eyes!'" Again, the defense attorney is publicly badgering a defenseless *blind* parent weeping for the lost child. The "blindness" of Mrs. Dalton had been a great dramatic touch, for we felt Bigger's fear of it, his sense that she was compensating for it with some supersensory perception that saw into him as other whites could not. Her blindness had been an important key in the plot; she had to be in the room, but unable to see, for the accidental murder to take place. But the critic who praises the book for its symbols ("a constant play on blindness, focused around the figure of Mrs. Dalton but aimed ultimately at the reader") is taking the least demanding of Wright's terms.

When we are pulled up out of the nightmare to this reflection upon it, we begin to ask all the wrong questions. The rum bottle—how does it suddenly appear in court when Jan had left it in the gutter and there was no reason for anyone to start looking for it until several days and several garbage trucks had passed? When the judge calls the lawyers forward and they have a conference at "the railing" for "over an hour" surely in any courtroom the conference would be in the judge's chambers. These are silly little details, hardly worth mention, but they bother us in the third part because we are "shedding daylight" on the problem—we have gone out of Bigger's mind to look back on it—and the book comes to a standstill, where we look at the landscape to see everything out of place. Max is not defending Bigger; Wright is using Max to point Bigger's tragedy out.

Bigger has, as one critic has said, an "incurable neurosis." Or, as Wright himself said, Bigger is "an obscene joke happening." In one sense the courtroom scene is in a line of the finest detective stories and murder mysteries, Wright's attempt to take the step that will lead to greatness. He is trying to expose communal guilt. He is entering on a question of judgment that will judge the whole stucture of his work and the moral views we hold of it. We know the community is not going to let Bigger go. Buckley cries, "Your Honor, in the name of Almighty God, I plead with you to be merciful to us!" He is facing an inescapable fact: to say that we may have "made" Bigger what he is, that may be true. But the damage has been done. It has been accumulating and maiming for centuries. But what are the people in that room, facing that Bigger, supposed to do about it? They face a boy who killed twice in twenty-four hours, killed black and white. It becomes a question for the reader. Given the fact that the society into which Bigger would ultimately re-enter is not going to be changed, and given the present sad state of psychiatric tools to rehabilitate him wholly, what is to be done? Perhaps the most humane course, though it is a wretched one, is to allow him to live out his life in prison. And this is what Boris Max asks.

But that isn't what *Native Son* is all about. Again the courtroom scene only distracts us from Wright's central vision. Max says, "In a certain sense, every Negro in America's on trial out there today." But that "certain sense" is terribly important, and here in part three of his novel Wright has it wrong.

He said in "How Bigger Was Born" that "what Bigger meant had claimed me because I felt with all of my being that he was more important than what any person, white or black, would say or try to make of him, more important than any political analysis designed to explain or deny him, more important even, than my own sense of fear, shame, and diffidence." But "what Bigger meant" had not sufficiently "claimed" him so that he could resist the impulse to "try to make" an explanatory rhetoric that would "deny him." Or, to be fully fair, Bigger had "claimed" Richard Wright in the first two sections of the book to the point of utter possession.

PART FOUR: RELATED ESSAYS

Growing up in the Streets of Harlem

CLAUDE BROWN

I WANT TO TALK ABOUT THE FIRST NORTHERN URBAN GENERATION OF Negroes. I want to talk about the experiences of a misplaced generation, of a misplaced people in an extremely complex, confused society. This is a story of their searching, their dreams, their sorrows, their small and futile rebellions, and their endless battle to establish their own place in America's greatest metropolis—and in America itself.

The characters are sons and daughters of former Southern sharecroppers. These were the poorest people of the South, who poured into New York City during the decade following the Great Depression. These migrants were told that unlimited opportunities for prosperity existed in New York and that there was no "color problem" there. They were told that Negroes lived in houses with bathrooms, electricity, running water, and indoor toilets. To them, this was the "promised land" that Mammy had been singing about in the cotton fields for many years.

Going to New York was good-bye to the cotton fields, good-bye to "Massa Charlie," good-bye to the chain gang, and, most of all, good-bye to those sunup-to-sundown working hours. One no longer had to wait to get to heaven to lay his burden down; burdens could be laid down in New York.

So, they came, from all parts of the South, like all the black chillun o' God following the sound of Gabriel's horn on that long-overdue Judgment Day. The Georgians came as soon as they were able to pick train fare off the peach trees. They came from South Carolina where the cotton stalks were bare. The North Carolinians came with tobacco tar beneath their fingernails.

They felt as the Pilgrims must have felt when they were coming to America. But these descendants of Ham must have been twice as happy as the Pilgrims, because they had been catching twice the hell.

Reprinted by permission of The Macmillan Company from *Manchild in the Promised Land,* by Claude Brown.

Even while planning the trip, they sang spirituals as "Jesus Take My Hand" and "I'm On My Way" and chanted, "Hallelujah, I'm on my way to the promised land!"

It seems that Cousin Willie, in his lying haste, had neglected to tell the folks down home about one of the most important aspects of the promised land: it was a slum ghetto. There was a tremendous difference in the way life was lived up North. There were too many people full of hate and bitterness crowded into a dirty, stinky, uncared-for closet-size section of a great city.

Before the soreness of the cotton fields had left Mama's back, her knees were getting sore from scrubbing "Goldberg's" floor. Nevertheless, she was better off; she had gone from the fire into the frying pan.

The children of these disillusioned colored pioneers inherited the total lot of their parents—the disappointments, the anger. To add to their misery, they had little hope of deliverance. For where does one run to when he's already in the promised land?

"Run!"

Where?

Oh, hell! Let's get out of here!

"Turk! Turk! I'm shot!"

I could hear Turk's voice calling from a far distance, telling me not to go into the fish-and-chips joint. I heard, but I didn't understand. The only thing I knew was that I was going to die.

I ran. There was a bullet in me trying to take my life, all thirteen years of it.

I climbed up on the bar yelling, "Walsh, I'm shot. I'm shot." I could feel the blood running down my leg. Walsh, the fellow who operated the fish-and-chips joint, pushed me off the bar and onto the floor. I couldn't move now, but I was still completely conscious.

Walsh was saying, "Git outta here, kid. I ain't got no time to play."

A woman was screaming, mumbling something about the Lord, and saying, "Somebody done shot that poor child."

Mama ran in. She jumped up and down, screaming like a crazy woman. I began to think about dying. The worst part of dying was thinking about the things and the people that I'd never see again. As I lay there trying to imagine what being dead was like, the policeman who had been trying to control Mama gave up and bent over me. He asked who had shot me. Before I could answer, he was asking me if I could hear him. I told him that I didn't know who had shot me and would he please tell Mama to stop jumping up and down. Every time Mama came down on that shabby floor, the bullet lodged in my stomach felt like a hot poker.

Another policeman had come in and was struggling to keep the crowd outside. I could see Turk in the front of the crowd. Before the cops came, he asked me if I was going to tell them that he was with me. I never answered. I looked at him and wondered if he saw who shot me. Then his question began to ring in my head: "Sonny, you gonna tell 'em I was with you?" I was bleeding on a dirty floor in a fish-and-chips joint, and Turk was standing there in the doorway hoping that I would die before I could tell the cops that he was with me. Not once did Turk ask me how I felt.

Hell, yeah, I thought, I'm gonna tell 'em.

It seemed like hours had passed before the ambulance finally arrived. Mama wanted to go to the hospital with me, but the ambulance attendant said she was too excited. On the way to Harlem Hospital, the cop who was riding with us asked Dad what he had to say. His answer was typical: "I told him about hanging out with those bad-ass boys." The cop was a little surprised. This must be a rookie, I thought.

The next day, Mama was at my bedside telling me that she had prayed and the Lord had told her that I was going to live. Mama said that many of my friends wanted to donate some blood for me, but the hospital would not accept it from narcotics users.

This was one of the worst situations I had ever been in. There was a tube in my nose that went all the way to the pit of my stomach. I was being fed intravenously, and there was a drain in my side. Everybody came to visit me, mainly out of curiosity. The girls were all anxious to know where I had gotten shot. They had heard all kinds of tales about where the bullet struck. The bolder ones wouldn't even bother to ask: they just snatched the cover off me and looked for themselves. In a few days, the word got around that I was in one piece.

On my fourth day in the hospital, I was awakened by a male nurse at about 3 A.M. When he said hello in a very ladyish voice, I thought that he had come to the wrong bed by mistake. After identifying himself, he told me that he had helped Dr. Freeman save my life. The next thing he said, which I didn't understand, had something to do with the hours he had put in working that day. He went on mumbling something about how tired he was and ended up asking me to rub his back. I had already told him that I was grateful to him for helping the doctor save my life. While I rubbed his back above the beltline, he kept pushing my hand down and saying, "Lower, like you are really grateful to me." I told him that I was sleepy from the needle a nurse had given me. He asked me to pat his behind. After I had done this, he left.

The next day when the fellows came to visit me, I told them about my early-morning visitor. Dunny said he would like to meet him. Tito joked about being able to get a dose of clap in the hospital. The guy with the tired back never showed up again, so the fellows never got a chance to meet him. Some of them were disappointed.

After I had been in the hospital for about a week, I was visited by another character. I had noticed a woman visiting one of the patients on the far side of the ward. She was around fifty-five years old, short and fat, and she was wearing old-lady shoes. While I wondered who this woman was, she started across the room in my direction. After she had introduced herself, she told me that she was visiting her son. Her son had been stabbed in the chest with an ice pick by his wife. She said that his left lung had been punctured, but he was doing fine now, and that Jesus was so-o-o good.

Her name was Mrs. Ganey, and she lived on 145th Street. She said my getting shot when I did "was the work of the Lord." My gang had been stealing sheets and bedspreads off clotheslines for months before I had gotten shot. I asked this godly woman why she thought it was the work of the Lord or Jesus or whoever. She began in a sermonlike tone, saying, "Son, people was gitting tired-a y'all stealing all dey sheets and spreads." She said that on the night that I had gotten shot, she baited her clothesline with two brand-new bedspreads, turned out all the lights in the apartment, and sat at the kitchen window waiting for us to show.

She waited with a double-barreled shotgun.

The godly woman said that most of our victims thought that we were winos or dope fiends and that most of them had vowed to kill us. At the end of the sermon, the godly woman said, "Thank the Lord I didn't shoot nobody's child." When the godly woman had finally departed, I thought, Thank the Lord for taking her away from my bed.

Later on that night, I was feeling a lot of pain and couldn't get to sleep. A nurse who had heard me moaning and groaning came over and gave me a shot of morphine. Less than twenty minutes later, I was deep into a nightmare.

I was back in the fish-and-chips joint, lying on the floor dying. Only, now I was in more pain than before, and there were dozens of Mamas around me jumping up and screaming. I could feel myself dying in a rising pool of blood. The higher the blood rose the more I died.

I dreamt about the boy who Rock and big Stoop had thrown off that roof on 149th Street. None of us had stayed around to see him hit the ground, but I just knew that he died in a pool of blood too. I wished that he would stop screaming, and I wished that Mama would stop screaming. I wished they would let me die quietly.

As the screams began to die out—Mama's and the boy's—I began to think about the dilapidated old tenement building that I lived in, the one that still had the words "pussy" and "fuck you" on the walls where I had scribbled them years ago. The one where the super, Mr. Lawson, caught my little brother writing some more. Dad said he was going to kill Pimp for writing on that wall, and the way he was beating Pimp with that ironing cord, I thought he would. Mama was crying, I was crying, and Pimp had been crying for a long time. Mama said that he was too young to be beaten like that. She ran out of the house and came back with a cop, who stopped Dad from beating Pimp.

I told Pimp not to cry any more, just to wait until I got big: I was going to kill Dad, and he could help me if he wanted to.

This was the building where Mr. Lawson had killed a man for peeing in the hall. I remembered being afraid to go downstairs the morning after Mr. Lawson had busted that man's head open with a baseball bat. I could still see blood all over the hall. This was the building where somebody was always shooting out the windows in the hall. They were usually shooting at Johnny D., and they usually missed. This was the building that I loved more than anyplace else in the world. The thought that I would never see this building again scared the hell out of me.

I dreamt about waking up in the middle of the night seven years before and thinking that the Germans or the Japs had come and that the loud noises I heard were bombs falling. Running into Mama's room, I squeezed in between her and Dad at the front window. Thinking that we were watching an air raid, I asked Dad where the sirens were and why the street lights were on. He said, "This ain't no air raid—just a whole lotta niggers gone fool. And git the hell back in that bed!" I went back to bed, but I couldn't go to sleep. The loud screams in the street and the crashing sound of falling plate-glass windows kept me awake for hours. While I listened to the noise, I imagined bombs falling and people running through the streets screaming. I could see mothers running with babies in their arms, grown men running over women and children to save their own lives, and the Japs stabbing babies with bayonets, just like in the movies. I thought, Boy, I sure wish I was out there. I bet the Stinky brothers are out there. Danny and Butch are probably out there having all the fun in the world.

The next day, as I was running out of the house without underwear or socks on, I could hear Mama yelling, "Boy, come back here and put a hat or something on your head!" When I reached the stoop, I was knocked back into the hall by a big man carrying a ham under his coat. While I looked up at him, wondering what was going on, he reached down with one hand and snatched me up, still holding the ham under his coat with his other hand. He stood me up against a wall and ran into the hall with his ham. Before I had a chance to move, other men came running through the hall carrying cases of whiskey, sacks of flour, and cartons of cigarettes. Just as I unglued myself from the wall and started out the door for the second time, I was bowled over again. This time by a cop with a gun in his hand. He never stopped, but after he had gone a couple of yards into the hall, I heard him say, "Look out, kid." On the third try, I got out of the building. But I wasn't sure that this was my street. None of the stores had any windows left, and glass was everywhere. It seemed that all the cops in the world were on 145th Street and Eighth Avenue that day. The cops were telling everybody to move on, and everybody was talking about the riot. I went over to a cop and asked him what a riot was. He told me to go on home. The next cop I asked told me that a riot was what had happened the night before. Putting two and two together I decided that a riot was "a whole lotta niggers gone fool."

I went around the corner to Butch's house. After I convinced him that I was alone, he opened the door. He said that Kid and Danny were in the kitchen. I saw Kid sitting on the floor with his hand stuck way down in a gallon jar of pickled pigs' ears. Danny was cooking some bacon at the stove, and Butch was busy hiding stuff. It looked as though these guys had stolen a whole grocery store. While I joined the feast, they took turns telling me about the riot. Danny and Kid hadn't gone home the night before; they were out following the crowds and looting.

My only regret was that I had missed the excitement. I said, "Why don't we have another riot tonight? Then Butch and me can get in it."

Danny said that there were too many cops around to have a riot now. Butch said that they had eaten up all the bread and that he was going to steal some more. I asked if I could come along with him, and he said that I could if I promised to do nothing but watch. I promised, but we both knew that I was lying.

When we got to the street, Butch said he wanted to go across the street and look at the pawnshop. I tagged along. Like many of the stores where the rioters had been, the pawnshop had been set afire. The firemen had torn down a sidewall getting at the fire. So Butch and I just walked in where the wall used to be. Everything I picked up was broken or burned or both. My feet kept sinking into the wet furs that had been burned and drenched. The whole place smelled of smoke and was as dirty as a Harlem gutter on a rainy day. The cop out front yelled to us to get out of there. He only had to say it once.

After stopping by the seafood joint and stealing some shrimp and oysters, we went to what was left of Mr. Gordon's grocery store. Butch just walked in, picked up a loaf of bread, and walked out. He told me to come on, but I ignored him and went into the grocery store instead. I picked up two loaves of bread and walked out. When I got outside, a cop looked at me, and I ran into a building and through the backyard to Butch's house. Running through the backyard, I lost all the oysters that I had; when I reached Butch's house, I had only two loaves of bread and two shrimp in my pocket.

Danny, who was doing most of the cooking, went into the street to steal something to drink. Danny, Butch, and Kid were ten years old, four years older than I. Butch was busy making sandwiches on the floor, and Kid was trying to slice up a loaf of bologna. I had never eaten shrimp, but nobody seemed to care, because they refused to cook it for me. I told Butch that I was going to cook it myself. He said that there was no more lard in the house and that I would need some grease.

I looked around the house until I came up with some Vaseline hair pomade. I put the shrimp in the frying pan with the hair grease, waited until they had gotten black and were smoking, then took them out and made a sandwich. A few years later, I found out that shrimp were supposed to be shelled before cooking. I ate half of the sandwich and hated shrimp for years afterward.

The soft hand tapping on my face to wake me up was Jackie's. She and Della had been to a New Year's Eve party. Jackie wanted to come by the hospital and kiss me at midnight. This was the only time in my life that I ever admitted being glad to see Jackie. I asked them about the party, hoping that they would stay and talk to me for a while. I was afraid that if I went back to sleep, I would have another bad dream.

The next thing I knew, a nurse was waking me up for breakfast. I didn't recall saying good night to Jackie and Della, so I must have fallen asleep while they were talking to me. I thought about Sugar, how nice she was, and how she was a real friend. I knew she wanted to be my girl friend, and I liked her a lot. But what would everybody say if I had a buck-toothed girl friend. I remembered Knoxie asking me how I kissed her. That question led to the first fight I'd had with Knoxie in years. No, I couldn't let Sugar be my girl. It was hard enough having her as a friend.

The next day, I asked the nurse why she hadn't changed my bed linen, and she said because they were evicting me. I had been in the hospital for eleven days, but I wasn't ready to go home. I left the hospital on January 2 and went to a convalescent home in Valhalla, New York. After I had been there for three weeks, the activity director took me aside and told me that I was going to New York City to see a judge and that I might be coming back. The following morning, I left to see that judge, but I never got back to Valhalla.

I stood there before Judge Pankin looking solemn and lying like a professional. I thought that he looked too nice to be a judge. A half hour after I had walked into the courtroom, Judge Pankin was telling me that he was sending me to the New York State Training School for Boys. The judge said that he thought I was a chronic liar and that he hoped I would be a better boy when I came out. I asked him if he wanted me to thank him. Mama stopped crying just long enough to say, "Hush your mouth, boy."

Mama tried to change the judge's mind by telling him that I had already been to Wiltwyck School for Boys for two and a half years. And before that, I had been ordered out of the state for at least one year. She said that I had been away from my family too much; that was why I was always getting into trouble.

The judge told Mama that he knew what he was doing and that one day she would be grateful to him for doing it.

I had been sent away before, but this was the first time I was ever afraid to go. When Mama came up to the detention room in Children's Court, I tried to act as though I wasn't afraid. After I told her that

Warwick and where I was going were one and the same, Mama began to cry, and so did I.

Most of the guys I knew had been to Warwick and were too old to go back. I knew that there were many guys up there I had mistreated. The Stinky brothers were up there. They thought that I was one of the guys who had pulled a train on their sister in the park the summer before. Bumpy from 144th Street was up there. I had shot him in the leg with a zip gun in a rumble only a few months earlier. There were many guys up there I used to bully on the streets and at Wiltwyck, guys I had sold tea leaves to as pot. There were rival gang members up there who just hated my name. All of these guys were waiting for me to show. The word was out that I couldn't fight any more—that I had slowed down since I was shot and that a good punch to the stomach would put my name in the undertaker's book.

When I got to the Youth House, I tried to find out who was up at Warwick that I might know. Nobody knew any of the names I asked about. I knew that if I went up to Warwick in my condition, I'd never live to get out. I had a reputation for being a rugged little guy. This meant that I would have at least a half-dozen fights in the first week of my stay up there.

It seemed the best thing for me to do was to cop out on the nut. For the next two nights, I woke up screaming and banging on the walls. On the third day, I was sent to Bellevue for observation. This meant that I wouldn't be going to Warwick for at least twenty-eight days.

While I was in Bellevue, the fellows would come down and pass notes to me through the doors. Tito and Turk said they would get bagged and sent to Warwick by the time I got there. They were both bagged a week later for smoking pot in front of the police station. They were both sent to Bellevue. Two weeks after they showed, I went home. The judge still wanted to send me to Warwick, but Warwick had a full house, so he sent me home for two weeks.

The day before I went back to court, I ran into Turk, who had just gotten out of Bellevue. Tito had been sent to Warwick, but Turk had gotten a walk because his sheet wasn't too bad. I told him I would probably be sent to Warwick the next day. Turk said he had run into Bucky in Bellevue. He told me that he and Tito had voted Bucky out of the clique. I told him that I wasn't going for it because Bucky was my man from short-pants days. Turk said he liked him too, but what else could he do after Bucky had let a white boy beat him in the nutbox? When I heard this, there was nothing I could do but agree with Turk. Bucky had to go. That kind of news spread fast, and who wanted to be in a clique with a stud who let a paddy boy beat him?

The next day, I went to the Youth House to wait for Friday and the trip to Warwick. As I lay in bed that night trying to think of a way out, I began to feel sorry for myself. I began to blame Danny, Butch, and Kid for my present fate. I told myself that I wouldn't be going to

Warwick if they hadn't taught me how to steal, play hookey, make homemades, and stuff like that. But then I thought, aw, hell, it wasn't their fault—as a matter of fact, it was a whole lotta fun.

I remembered sitting on the stoop with Danny, years before, when a girl came up and started yelling at him. She said that her mother didn't want her brother to hang out with Danny any more, because Danny had taught her brother how to play hookey. When the girl had gone down the street, I asked Danny what hookey was. He said it was a game he would teach me as soon as I started going to school.

Danny was a man of his word. He was my next-door neighbor, and he rang my doorbell about 7:30 A.M. on the second day of school. Mama thanked him for volunteering to take me to school. Danny said he would have taught me to play hookey the day before, but he knew that Mama would have to take me to school on the first day. As we headed toward the backyard to hide our books, Danny began to explain the great game of hookey. It sounded like lots of fun to me. Instead of going to school, we would go all over the city stealing, sneak into a movie, or go up on a roof and throw bottles down into the street. Danny suggested that we start the day off by waiting for Mr. Gordon to put out his vegetables; we could steal some sweet potatoes and cook them in the backyard. I was sorry I hadn't started school sooner, because hookey sure was a lot of fun.

Before I began going to school, I was always in the streets with Danny, Kid, and Butch. Sometimes, without saying a word, they would all start to run like hell, and a white man was always chasing them. One morning as I entered the backyard where all the hookey players went to draw up an activity schedule for the day, Butch told me that Danny and Kid had been caught by Mr. Sands the day before. He went on to warn me about Mr. Sands, saying Mr. Sands was that white man who was always chasing somebody and that I should try to remember what he looked like and always be on the lookout for him. He also warned me not to try to outrun Mr. Sands, "because that cat is fast." Butch said, "When you see him, head for a backyard or a roof. He won't follow you there."

During the next three months, I stayed out of school twenty-one days. Dad was beating the hell out of me for playing hookey, and it was no fun being in the street in the winter, so I started going to school regularly. But when spring rolled around, hookey became my favorite game again. Mr. Sands was known to many parents in the neighborhood as the truant officer. He never caught me in the street, but he came by my house many mornings to escort me to class. This was one way of getting me to school, but he never found a way to keep me there. The moment my teacher took her eyes off me, I was back on the street. Every time Dad got a card from Mr. Sands, I got bruises and welts from Dad. The beatings had only a temporary effect on me. Each time, the beatings got worse; and each time, I promised never to play hookey again. One time I kept that promise for three whole weeks.

The older guys had been doing something called "catting" for years. That catting was staying away from home all night was all I knew about the term. Every time I asked one of the fellows to teach me how to cat, I was told I wasn't old enough. As time went on, I learned that guys catted when they were afraid to go home and that they slept everywhere but in comfortable places. The usual places for catting were subway trains, cellars, unlocked cars, under a friend's bed, and in vacant newsstands.

One afternoon when I was eight years old, I came home after a busy day of running from the police, truant officer, and storekeepers. The first thing I did was to look in the mailbox. This had become a habit with me even though I couldn't read. I was looking for a card, a yellow card. That yellow card meant that I would walk into the house and Dad would be waiting for me with his razor strop. He would usually be eating and would pause just long enough to say to me, "Nigger, you got a ass whippin' comin'." My sisters, Carole and Margie, would cry almost as much as I would while Dad was beating me, but this never stopped him. After each beating I got, Carole, who was two years older than I, would beg me to stop playing hookey. There were a few times when I thought I would stop just to keep her and Margie, my younger sister, from crying so much. I decided to threaten Carole and Margie instead, but this didn't help. I continued to play hookey, and they continued to cry on the days that the yellow card got home before I did.

Generally, I would break open the mailbox, take out the card, and throw it away. Whenever I did this, I'd have to break open two or three other mailboxes and throw away the contents, just to make it look good.

This particular afternoon, I saw a yellow card, but I couldn't find anything to break into the box with. Having some matches in my pockets, I decided to burn the card in the box and not bother to break the box open. After I had used all the matches, the card was not completely burned. I stood there getting more frightened by the moment. In a little while, Dad would be coming home; and when he looked in the mailbox, anywhere would be safer than home for me.

This was going to be my first try at catting out. I went looking for somebody to cat with me. My crime partner, Buddy, whom I had played hookey with that day, was busily engaged in a friendly rock fight when I found him in Colonial Park. When I suggested that we go up on the hill and steal some newspapers, Buddy lost interest in the rock fight.

We stole papers from newsstands and sold them on the subway trains until nearly 1 A.M. That was when the third cop woke up and put us off the train with the usual threat. They would always promise to beat us over the head with a billy and lock us up. Looking back, I think the cops took their own threats more seriously than we did. The third cop put us off the Independent Subway at Fifty-ninth Street and Columbus Circle. I wasn't afraid of the cops, but I didn't go back into the subway—the next cop might have taken me home.

In 1945, there was an Automat where we came out of the subway. About five slices of pie later, Buddy and I left the Automat in search of a place to stay the night. In the center of the Circle, there were some old lifeboats that the Navy had put on display.

Buddy and I slept in the boat for two nights. On the third day, Buddy was caught ringing a cash register in a five-and-dime store. He was sent to Children's Center, and I spent the third night in the boat alone. On the fourth night, I met a duty-conscious cop, who took me home. That ended my first catting adventure.

Dad beat me for three consecutive days for telling what he called "that dumb damn lie about sleeping in a boat on Fifty-ninth Street." On the fourth day, I think he went to check my story out for himself. Anyhow, the beatings stopped for a while, and he never mentioned the boat again.

Before long, I was catting regularly, staying away from home for weeks at a time. Sometimes the cops would pick me up and take me to a Children's Center. The Centers were located all over the city. At some time in my childhood, I must have spent at least one night in all of them except the one on Staten Island.

The procedure was that a policeman would take me to the Center in the borough where he had picked me up. The Center would assign someone to see that I got a bath and was put to bed. The following day, my parents would be notified as to where I was and asked to come and claim me. Dad was always in favor of leaving me where I was and saying good riddance. But Mama always made the trip. Although Mama never failed to come for me, she seldom found me there when she arrived. I had no trouble getting out of Children's Centers, so I seldom stayed for more than a couple of days.

When I was finally brought home—sometimes after weeks of catting—Mama would hide my clothes or my shoes. This would mean that I couldn't get out of the house if I should take a notion to do so. Anyway, that's how Mama had it figured. The truth of the matter is that these measures only made getting out of the house more difficult for me. I would have to wait until one of the fellows came around to see me. After hearing my plight, he would go out and round up some of the gang, and they would steal some clothes and shoes for me. When they had the clothes and shoes, one of them would come to the house and let me know. About ten minutes later, I would put on my sister's dress, climb down the back fire escape, and meet the gang with the clothes.

If something was too small or too large, I would go and steal the right size. This could only be done if the item that didn't fit was not the shoes. If the shoes were too small or large, I would have trouble running in them and probably get caught. So I would wait around in the backyard while someone stole me a pair.

Mama soon realized that hiding my clothes would not keep me in the house. The next thing she tried was threatening to send me away until I was twenty-one. This was only frightening to me at the moment of hearing it. Ever so often, either Dad or Mama would sit down and have a heart-to-heart talk with me. These talks were very moving. I always promised to mend my bad ways. I was always sincere and usually kept the promise for about a week. During these weeks, I went to school every day and kept my stealing at a minimum. By the beginning of the second week, I had reverted back to my wicked ways, and Mama would have to start praying all over again.

The neighborhood prophets began making prophecies about my life-span. They all had me dead, buried, and forgotten before my twenty-first birthday. These predictions were based on false tales of policemen shooting at me, on truthful tales of my falling off a trolley car into the midst of oncoming automobile traffic while hitching a ride, and also on my uncontrollable urge to steal. There was much justification for these prophecies. By the time I was nine years old, I had been hit by a bus, thrown into the Harlem River (intentionally), hit by a car, severely beaten with a chain. And I had set the house afire.

While Dad was still trying to beat me into a permanent conversion, Mama was certain that somebody had worked roots on me. She was writing to all her relatives in the South for solutions, but they were only able to say, "that boy musta been born with the devil in him." Some of them advised Mama to send me down there, because New York was no place to raise a child. Dad thought this was a good idea, and he tried to sell it to Mama. But Mama wasn't about to split up her family. She said I would stay in New York, devil or no devil. So I stayed in New York, enjoying every crazy minute.

Mama's favorite question was, "Boy, why you so bad?" I tried many times to explain to Mama that I wasn't "so bad." I tried to make her understand that it was trying to be good that generally got me into trouble. I remember telling her that I played hookey to avoid getting into trouble in school. It seemed that whenever I went to school, I got into a fight with the teacher. The teacher would take me to the principal's office. After I had fought with the principal, I would be sent home and not allowed back in school without one of my parents. So to avoid all that trouble, I just didn't go to school. When I stole things, it was only to save the family money and avoid arguments or scoldings whenever I asked for money.

Mama seemed silly to me. She was bothered because most of the parents in the neighborhood didn't allow their children to play with me. What she didn't know was that I never wanted to play with them. My friends were all daring like me, tough like me, dirty like me, ragged like me, cursed like me, and had a great love for trouble like me. We took pride in being able to hitch rides on trolleys, buses, taxicabs and in knowing how to steal and fight. We knew that we were the only kids in the neighborhood who usually had more than ten dollars in their pockets. There were other people who knew this too, and that was often a problem for us. Somebody was always trying to shake us down or rob us. This was usually done by the older hustlers in the neighborhood or by storekeepers or cops. At other times, older fellows would shake us down, con us, or Murphy us out of our loot. We accepted this as the ways of life. Everybody was stealing from everybody else. And sometimes we would shake down newsboys and shoeshine boys. So we really had no complaints coming. Although none of my sidekicks was over twelve years of age, we didn't think of ourselves as kids. The other kids my age were thought of as kids by me. I felt that since I knew more about life than they did, I had the right to regard them as kids.

Hustler

MALCOLM X

I CAN'T REMEMBER ALL THE HUSTLES I HAD DURING THE NEXT TWO YEARS in Harlem, after the abrupt end of my riding the trains and peddling reefers to the touring bands.

Negro railroad men waited for their trains in their big locker room on the lower level of Grand Central Station. Big blackjack and poker games went on in there around the clock. Sometimes five hundred dollars would be on the table. One day, in a blackjack game, an old cook who was dealing the cards tried to be slick, and I had to drop my pistol in his face.

The next time I went into one of those games, intuition told me to stick my gun under my belt right down the middle of my back. Sure enough, someone had squealed. Two big, beefy-faced Irish cops came in. They frisked me—and they missed my gun where they hadn't expected one.

The cops told me never again to be caught in Grand Central Station unless I had a ticket to ride somewhere. And I knew that by the next day, every railroad's personnel office would have a blackball on me, so I never tried to get another railroad job.

There I was back in Harlem's streets among all the rest of the

---

From *The Autobiography of Malcolm X*, by Malcolm X, with the assistance of Alex Haley (New York: Grove Press, Inc., 1965), pp. 109–118. Reprinted by permission of Grove Press, Inc.

hustlers. I couldn't sell reefers; the dope squad detectives were too familiar with me. I was a true hustler—uneducated, unskilled at anything honorable, and I considered myself nervy and cunning enough to live by my wits, exploiting any prey that presented itself. I would risk just about anything.

Right now, in every big city ghetto, tens of thousands of yesterday's and today's school drop-outs are keeping body and soul together by some form of hustling in the same way I did. And they inevitably move into more and more, worse and worse, illegality and immorality. Full-time hustlers never can relax to appraise what they are doing and where they are bound. As is the case in any jungle, the hustler's every waking hour is lived with both the practical and the subconscious knowledge that if he ever relaxes, if he ever slows down, the other hungry, restless foxes, ferrets, wolves, and vultures out there with him won't hesitate to make him their prey.

During the next six to eight months, I pulled my first robberies and stick-ups. Only small ones. Always in other, nearby cities. And I got away. As the pros did, I too would key myself to pull these jobs by my first use of hard dope. I began with Sammy's recommendation—sniffing cocaine.

Normally now, for street wear, I might call it, I carried a hardly noticeable little flat, blue-steel .25 automatic. But for working, I carried a .32, a .38 or a .45. I saw how when the eyes stared at the big black hole, the faces fell slack and the mouths sagged open. And when I spoke, the people seemed to hear as though they were far away, and they would do whatever I asked.

Between jobs, staying high on narcotics kept me from getting nervous. Still, upon sudden impulses, just to play safe, I would abruptly move from one to another fifteen- to twenty-dollar-a-week room, always in my favorite 147th-150th Street area, just flanking Sugar Hill.

Once on a job with Sammy, we had a pretty close call. Someone must have seen us. We were making our getaway, running, when we heard the sirens. Instantly, we slowed to walking. As a police car screeched to a stop, we stepped out into the street, meeting it, hailing it to ask for directions. They must have thought we were about to give them some information. They just cursed us and raced on. Again, it didn't cross the white men's minds that a trick like that might be pulled on them by Negroes.

The suits that I wore, the finest, I bought hot for about thirty-five to fifty dollars. I made it my rule never to go after more than I needed to live on. Any experienced hustler will tell you that getting greedy is the quickest road to prison. I kept "cased" in my head vulnerable places and situations and I would perform the next job only when my bankroll in my pocket began to get too low.

Some weeks, I bet large amounts on the numbers. I still played with the same runner with whom I'd started in Small's Paradise. Playing my hunches, many a day I'd have up to forty dollars on two numbers, hoping for that fabulous six hundred-to-one payoff. But I never did hit a big number full force. There's no telling what I would have done if ever I'd landed $10,000 or $12,000 at one time. Of course, once in a while I'd hit a small combination figure. Sometimes, flush like that, I'd telephone Sophia to come over from Boston for a couple of days.

I went to the movies a lot again. And I never missed my musician friends wherever they were playing, either in Harlem, downtown at the big theaters, on 52nd Street.

Reginald and I got very close the next time his ship came back into New York. We discussed our family, and what a shame it was that our book-loving oldest brother Wilfred had never had the chance to go to some of those big universities where he would have gone far. And we exchanged thoughts we had never shared with anyone.

Reginald, in his quiet way, was a mad fan of musicians and music. When his ship sailed one morning without him, a principal reason was that I had thoroughly exposed him to the exciting musical world. We had wild times backstage with the musicians when they were playing the Roxy, or the Paramount. After selling reefers with the bands as they traveled, I was known to almost every popular Negro musician around New York in 1944–1945.

Reginald and I went to the Savoy Ballroom, the Apollo Theater, the Braddock Hotel bar, the nightclubs and speakeasies, wherever Negroes played music. The great Lady Day, Billie Holiday, hugged him and called him "baby brother." Reginald shared tens of thousands of Negroes' feelings that the living end of the big bands was Lionel Hampton's. I was very close to many of the men in Hamp's band; I introduced Reginald to them, and also to Hamp himself, and Hamp's wife and business manager, Gladys Hampton. One of this world's sweetest people is Hamp. Anyone who knows him will tell you that he'd often do the most generous things for people he barely knew. As much money as Hamp has made, and still makes, he would be broke today if his money and his business weren't handled by Gladys, who is one of the brainiest women I ever met. The Apollo Theater's owner, Frank Schiffman, could tell you. He generally signed bands to play for a set weekly amount, but I know that once during those days Gladys Hampton instead arranged a deal for Hamp's band to play for a cut of the gate. Then the usual number of shows was doubled up—if I'm not mistaken, eight shows a day, instead of the usual four—and Hamp's pulling power cleaned up. Gladys Hampton used to talk to me a lot, and she tried to give me good advice: "Calm down, Red." Gladys saw how wild I was. She saw me headed toward a bad end.

One of the things I liked about Reginald was that when I left him to go away "working," Reginald asked me no questions. After he came to Harlem, I went on more jobs than usual. I guess that what influenced me to get my first actual apartment was my not wanting Reginald to be knocking around Harlem without anywhere to call "home."

That first apartment was three rooms, for a hundred dollars a month, I think, in the front basement of a house on 147th Street between Convent and St. Nicholas Avenues. Living in the rear basement apartment, right behind Reginald and me, was one of Harlem's most successful narcotics dealers.

With the apartment as our headquarters, I gradually got Reginald introduced around to Creole Bill's, and other Harlem after-hours spots. About two o'clock every morning, as the downtown white nightclubs closed, Reginald and I would stand around in front of this or that Harlem after-hours place, and I'd school him to what was happening.

Especially after the nightclubs downtown closed, the taxis and black limousines would be driving uptown, bringing those white people who never could get enough of Negro *soul*. The places popular with these whites ranged all the way from the big locally famous ones such as Jimmy's Chicken Shack, and Dickie Wells', to the little here-tonight-gone-tomorrow-night private clubs, so-called, where a dollar was collected at the door for "membership."

Inside every after-hours spot, the smoke would hurt your eyes. Four white people to every Negro would be in there drinking whisky from coffee cups and eating fried chicken. The generally flush-faced white men and their makeup-masked, glittery-eyed women would be pounding each other's backs and uproariously laughing and applauding the music. A lot of the whites, drunk, would go staggering up to Negroes, the waiters, the owners, or Negroes at tables, wringing their hands, even trying to hug them, "You're just as good as I am—I want you to know that!" The most famous places drew both Negro and white celebrities who enjoyed each other. A jam-packed four-thirty A.M. crowd at Jimmie's Chicken Shack or Dickie Wells' might have such jam-session entertainment as Hazel Scott playing the piano for Billie Holiday singing the blues. Jimmy's Chicken Shack, incidentally, was where once, later on, I worked briefly as a waiter. That's where Redd Foxx was the dishwasher who kept the kitchen crew in stitches.

After a while, my brother Reginald had to have a hustle, and I gave much thought to what would be, for him, a good, safe hustle. After he'd learned his own way around, it would be up to him to take risks for himself—if he wanted to make more and quicker money.

The hustle I got Reginald into really was very simple. It utilized the psychology of the ghetto jungle. Downtown, he paid the two dollars, or whatever it was, for regular city peddler's license. Then I took him to a manufacturers' outlet where we bought a supply of cheap imperfect "seconds"—shirts, underwear, cheap rings, watches, all kinds of quick-sale items.

Watching me work this hustle back in Harlem, Reginald quickly caught on to how to go into barbershops, beauty parlors, and bars acting very nervous as he let the customers peep into his small valise of "loot." With so many thieves around anxious to get rid of stolen good-quality merchandise cheaply, many Harlemites, purely because of this conditioning, jumped to pay hot prices for inferior goods whose sale was perfectly legitimate. It never took long to get rid of a valiseful for at least twice what it had cost. And if any cop stopped Reginald, he had in his pocket both the peddlers's license and the manufacturers' outlet bills of sale. Reginald only had to be certain that none of the customers to whom he sold ever saw that he was legitimate.

I assumed that Reginald, like most of the Negroes I knew, would go for a white woman. I'd point out Negro-happy white women to him, and explain that a Negro with any brains could wrap these women around his fingers. But I have to say this for Reginald: he never liked white women. I remember the one time he met Sophia; he was so cool it upset Sophia, and it tickled me.

Reginald got himself a black woman. I'd guess she was pushing thirty; an "old settler," as we called them back in those days. She was a waitress in an exclusive restaurant downtown. She lavished on Reginald everything she had, she was so happy to get a young man. I mean she bought him clothes, cooked and washed for him, and everything, as though he were a baby.

That was just another example of why my respect for my younger brother kept increasing. Reginald showed, in often surprising ways, more sense than a lot of working hustlers twice his age. Reginald then was only sixteen, but, a six-footer, he looked and acted much older than his years.

All through the war, the Harlem racial picture never was too bright. Tension built to a pretty high pitch. Old-timers told me that Harlem had never been the same since the 1935 riot, when millions of dollars worth of damage was done by thousands of Negroes, infuriated chiefly by the white merchants in Harlem refusing to hire a Negro even as their stores raked in Harlem's money.

During World War II, Mayor LaGuardia officially closed the Savoy Ballroom. Harlem said the real reason was to stop Negroes from dancing with white women. Harlem said that no one dragged the white women in there. Adam Clayton Powell made it a big fight. He had successfully fought Consolidated Edison and the New York Telephone Company until they had hired Negroes. Then he had helped to battle the U.S. Navy and the U.S. Army about their segregating of uniformed Negroes. But Powell couldn't win this battle. City Hall kept the Savoy closed for a long time. It was just another one of the "liberal North" actions that didn't help Harlem to love the white man any.

Finally, rumor flashed that in the Braddock Hotel, white cops had shot a Negro soldier. I was walking down St. Nicholas Avenue; I saw all of these Negroes hollering and running north from 125th Street. Some of them were loaded down with armfuls of stuff. I remember it was the bandleader Fletcher Henderson's nephew "Shorty" Henderson who told me what had happened. Negroes were smashing store windows, and taking everything they could grab and carry—furniture, food, jewelry, clothes, whisky. Within an hour, every New York City cop seemed to be in Harlem. Mayor LaGuardia and the NAACP's then Secretary, the famed late Walter White, were in a red firecar, riding around pleading over a loud-speaker to all of those shouting, milling, angry Negroes to please go home and stay inside.

Just recently I ran into Shorty Henderson on Seventh Avenue. We were laughing about a fellow whom the riot had left with the nickname of "Left Feet." In a scramble in a women's shoe store, somehow he'd grabbed five shoes, all of them for left feet! And we laughed about the scared little Chinese whose restaurant didn't have a hand laid on it, because the rioters just about convulsed laughing when they saw the sign the Chinese had hastily stuck on his front door: "Me Colored Too."

After the riot, things instantly got very tight in Harlem. It was terrible for the night-life people, and for those hustlers whose main income had been the white man's money. The 1935 riot had left only a relative trickle of the money which had poured into Harlem during the 1920's. And now this new riot ended even that trickle.

Today the white people who visit Harlem, and this mostly on weekend nights, are hardly more than a few dozen who do the twist, the frug, the Watusi, and all the rest of the current dance crazes in Small's Paradise, owned now by the great basketball champion "Wilt the Stilt" Chamberlain, who draws crowds with his big, clean, All-American-athlete image. Most white people today are physically afraid to come to Harlem—and it's for good reasons, too. Even for Negroes, Harlem night life is about finished. Most of the Negroes who have money to spend are spending it downtown somewhere in this hypocritical "integration," in places where previously the police would have been called to haul off any Negro insane enough to try and get in. The already Croesus-rich white man can't get another skyscraper hotel finished and opened before all these integration-mad Negroes, who themselves don't own a tool shed, are booking the swanky new hotel for "cotillions" and "conventions." Those rich whites could afford it when they used to throw away their money in Harlem. But Negroes can't afford to be taking their money downtown to the white man.

Sammy and I, on a robbery job, got a bad scare, a very close call.

Things had grown so tight in Harlem that some hustlers had been forced to go to work. Even some prostitutes had gotten jobs as domestics, and cleaning office buildings at night. The pimping was so poor, Sammy had gone on the job with me. We had selected one of those situations considered "impossible." But wherever people think that, the guards will unconsciously grow gradually more relaxed, until sometimes those can be the easiest jobs of all.

But right in the middle of the act, we had some bad luck. A bullet grazed Sammy. We just barely escaped.

Sammy fortunately wasn't really hurt. We split up, which was always wise to do.

Just before daybreak, I went to Sammy's apartment. His newest woman, one of those beautiful but hot-headed Spanish Negroes, was in there crying and carrying on over Sammy. She went for me, screaming and clawing; she knew I'd been in on it with him. I fended her off. Not able to figure out why Sammy didn't shut her up, I did . . . and from the corner of my eye, I saw Sammy going for his gun.

Sammy's reaction that way to my hitting his woman—close as he and I were—was the only weak spot I'd ever glimpsed. The woman screamed and dove for him. She knew as I did that when your best friend draws a gun on you, he usually has lost all control of his emotions, and he intends to shoot. She distracted Sammy long enough for me to bolt through the door. Sammy chased me, about a block.

We soon made up—on the surface. But things never are fully right again with anyone you have seen trying to kill you.

Intuition told us that we had better lay low for a good while. The worst thing was that we'd been seen. The police in that nearby town had surely circulated our general descriptions.

I just couldn't forget that incident over Sammy's woman. I came to rely more and more upon my brother Reginald as the only one in my world I could completely trust.

Reginald was lazy, I'd discovered that. He had quit his hustle altogether. But I didn't mind that, really, because one could be as lazy as he wanted, if he would only use his head, as Reginald was doing. He had left my apartment by now. He was living off his "old settler" woman—when he was in town. I had also taught Reginald how he could work a little while for a railroad, then use his identification card to travel for nothing—and Reginald loved to travel. Several times, he had gone visiting all around, among our brothers and sisters. They had now begun to scatter to different cities. In Boston, Reginald was closer to our sister Mary than to Ella, who had been my favorite. Both Reginald and Mary were quiet types, and Ella and I were extroverts. And Shorty in Boston had given my brother a royal time.

Because of my reputation, it was easy for me to get into the numbers racket. That was probably Harlem's only hustle which hadn't slumped in business. In return for a favor to some white mobster, my new boss and his wife had just been given a six-months numbers banking privilege for the Bronx railroad area called Motthaven Yards. The white mobsters had the numbers racket split into specific areas. A designated area would be assigned to someone for a specified period of time. My boss' wife had been Dutch Schultz's secretary in the 1930's, during the time when Schultz had strong-armed his way into control of the Harlem numbers business.

My job now was to ride a bus across the George Washington Bridge where a fellow was waiting for me to hand him a bag of numbers betting slips. We never spoke. I'd cross the street and catch the next bus back to Harlem. I never knew who that fellow was. I never knew who picked up the betting money for the slips that I handled. You didn't ask questions in the rackets.

My boss' wife and Gladys Hampton were the only two women I ever met in Harlem whose business ability I really respected. My boss' wife, when she had the time and the inclination to talk, would tell me many interesting things. She would talk to me about the Dutch Schultz days—about deals that she had known, about graft paid to officials—rookie cops and shyster lawyers right on up into the top levels of police and politics. She knew from personal experience how crime existed only to the degree that the law cooperated with it. She showed me how, in the country's entire social, political and economic structure, the criminal, the law, and the politicians were actually inseparable partners.

It was at this time that I changed from my old numbers man, the one I'd used since I first worked in Small's Paradise. He hated to lose a heavy player, but he readily understood why I would now want to play with a runner of my own outfit. That was how I began placing my bets with West Indian Archie. I've mentioned him before—one of Harlem's really *bad* Negroes; one of those former Dutch Schultz strong-arm men around Harlem.

West Indian Archie had finished time in Sing Sing not long before I came to Harlem. But my boss' wife had hired him not just because she knew him from the old days. West Indian Archie had the kind of photographic memory that put him among the elite of numbers runners. He never wrote down your number; even in the case of combination plays, he would just nod. He was able to file all the numbers in his head, and write them down for the banker only when he turned in his money. This made him the ideal runner because cops could never catch him with any betting slips.

I've often reflected upon such black veteran numbers men as West Indian Archie. If they had lived in another kind of society, their exceptional mathematical talents might have been better used. But they were black.

Anyway, it was status just to be known as a client of West Indian Archie's, because he handled only sizable bettors. He also required integrity and sound credit: it wasn't necessary that you pay as you played; you could pay West Indian Archie by the week. He always carried a couple of thousand dollars on him, his own money. If a client came up to him and said he'd hit for some moderate amount, say a fifty-cent or one dollar combination, West Indian Archie would peel off the three or six hundred dollars, and later get his money back from the banker.

Every weekend, I'd pay my bill—anywhere from fifty to even one hundred dollars, if I had really plunged on some hunch. And when, once or twice, I did hit, always just some combination, as I've described, West Indian Archie paid me off from his own roll.

The six months finally ended for my boss and his wife. They had done well. Their runners got nice tips, and promptly were snatched up by other bankers. I continued working for my boss and his wife in a gambling house they opened.

Bigger in Wonderland

LERONE BENNETT, JR.

Bigger Thomas stood on a Southside street corner. Around him swirled the sound of the slums and, high above, an airplane dipped in and out of the clean white fluffs of clouds. Bigger watched the plane for a moment and, of a sudden, all the horror of his life bubbled to the surface.

"Goddamit!" he said, focusing his anxieties on the faraway symbol of white power and white control—"Goddamit!" "They won't let us do nothing."

These words, spoken in the 1940 novel *Native Son,* seemed, to some anyway, oddly unrealistic in the early fifties. By that time, "they" were "letting" Negroes do a great many things no one dreamed of in the forties. Negroes were flying airplanes and making them. There was a black general in the Air Force, a black star with the Brooklyn Dodgers, and a black administrative assistant in the White House. The Myth of Negro Progress, which is the only thing that stands between the Negro and revolt, seemed real enough in those days. The myth was tangible, the myth was palpable. You could see it, you could touch it—the brass ring was gold.

As the midcentury mark passed, Negro Americans thought they could see the beginning of the end. The great burst of reform projects of the thirties and forties lost their savor, and the ghetto surrendered to what C. Wright Mills called the optative mood. In this mood, men speak of things hoped for as though they existed, and the substance of things dreamed of becomes the evidence of things not seen. Racial strife in America is punctuated by such periods of relative calm during which the greater fury of the next phase silently gathers itself. Coming, as it always does, between two periods of acute tension, the optative mood bridges past and future, giving men time to count their winnings, leading them on to absurd exaggerations of their gains, preparing them, unwittingly, for the next period of excruciating disappointment. When the optative mood seizes the ghetto, when dreams become things, and mirages, realities, protest organizations lapse into somnolence, activists become clerks, and paper work replaces demonstrations.

The period between 1950 and 1954 was a classic example of optative evasion. Some men announced, with incredible optimism, the imminent disappearance of Negroes. The *Detroit News* spoke of "the

---

From *Confrontation: Black and White,* by Lerone Bennett, Jr. (Chicago: Johnson Publishing Company, 1965), pp. 199–205. Reprinted by permission of Johnson Publishing Company.

eventual disappearance" of all-white neighborhoods in that city. The Colored Methodist Church and several other organizations met and solemnly removed the word "colored" from their titles. In keeping with the spirit of racial ecumenicity, some Negro writers announced that they would henceforth write about people—and not Negroes. At least one prominent novelist said publicly that he was through with the race struggle, and several of his colleagues resigned, insofar as that was possible, from the race. Charles S. Johnson, an eminent Negro sociologist who was then president of Fisk University, sounded the dominant note of the period in a 1953 speech. "We are changing," he said, "from a racial society in many respects to a human relations society."

So it went everywhere, men dreaming dreams and seeing them.

How explain this?

First of all, by the spirit of the age. This was a time of fierce affirmation, of frenetic and sometimes ludicrous attempts on the part of all Americans to accentuate the positive. This mood was linked to disturbing changes in the world, to the contraction of the European ego abroad, the explosion of the atom bomb, the rise of Afro-Asia, and the red clouds over Europe.

Another factor in the damping down of discontent was fatigue. Men cannot live forever at fever heat. The ghetto had been in almost constant turmoil now for some twenty years. Negroes were tired; they stopped now on the ledge of the mountain to catch their breath and consolidate their gains. Finally, and most significantly, there was the simple and unalterable fact of progress. *The brass ring was gold or, at least, gold-plated.*

Negro gains were more apparent than real, but they were real enough for all that. Negro workers were making four times as much as they made in 1940. By 1953, Negroes owned almost a third of the dwellings they occupied, a two-thirds rise over 1940. Negro college enrollment was up 2,500 per cent over 1930. Negroes, moreover, were receiving unprecedented recognition. There was a new sensitivity to Negro demands at the national level. The "great experiment" of integration in the armed forces was initiated and ripples from this great wave spread, beneficently. The Eisenhower Administration continued the postwar policy of appointing Negroes to highly visible posts, naming J. Ernest Wilkins assistant secretary of labor and E. Frederic Morrow administrative assistant in the White House. There was, additionally, a bumper crop of new Negro judges on the federal, state, and local level.

The North just then was beginning the open-city leap the South would make ten years later. As a result of direct-action probes (sit-ins and stand-ins) by CORE and other organizations, and litigation or the threat of litigation by local NAACP chapters, public facilities (lunch counters, restaurants, hotels, recreational facilities) in downtown sections in Chicago and other Northern cities opened their doors to Negro citizens. The most dramatic change was the integration of Washington,

D.C., as a result of court orders and prodding by the Eisenhower Administration. Some public facilities were also desegregated in Baltimore, St. Louis and other Border State areas.

Tangible gains were also evident in the old states of the Confederacy. By 1953, almost one million Negroes were voting in the South. Negroes had been elected or appointed to boards, commissions, and public offices in Atlanta, Richmond, Nashville, Winston-Salem and other urban areas in the South. After a trip through Dixie, Roi Ottley, the Negro author, reported an air of expansiveness in the Negro sections of urban areas. Some Negro matrons, Ottley reported, believed cities like Nashville and Atlanta were making more progress than Chicago and New York. According to these informants, department store clerks were addressing Negro customers as "Mr." and "Mrs." and were permitting them to try on clothes and other articles before purchasing them. Ottley also reported a big building boom. With one eye on the Supreme Court and the other on Thurgood Marshall and the NAACP legal staff, mayors were feverishly building schools and hospitals for "our Negro citizens."

In both the South and North, Negroes were holding on to their war gains and breaking new ground. Department stores and public utilities (telephone companies, bus companies) were hiring a small number of Negroes. The Korean War added to the climate of general prosperity by keeping the labor market tight. As a result, money flowed freely and credit was easy to get. Negro-owned businesses, especially savings and loan associations, reported record earnings. By the early fifties, there were some fifty thousand Negro-owned businesses, including about fifty insurance companies and fourteen banks.

The net result of all this was an enormous expansion of the Negro middle class. The proliferation of clerks, technicians, secretaries, and professional people changed the tone of life in the ghetto and paved the way for the confrontation of the sixties. Middle-class groups are generally useless in a social revolution, but, paradoxically, a middle-class core seems to be a prerequisite, in the West anyway, for a social revolution. The children of the new Negro middle class and some of the more sensitive adults found the fruit rotten on the vine; and their despair, and the despair of the deprived underclass, would be decisive in the upheaval of the sixties. But none of this could be foreseen in the halcyon days of the fifties. The new middle class, pitilessly described in E. Franklin Frazier's *Black Bourgeoisie,* inherited the hand-me-down brownstones and Georgians of whites who were fleeing the city. Gilded ghettos sprang up in Chicago, Atlanta, Detroit, New Orleans and other urban areas. With new grass to mow, with shiny new gadgets to explore (hi-fi sets and washing machines and power mowers), the Black Bourgeoisie became desperately serious Babbitts. *Time* magazine reported in 1953 that the number of Negro golfers in Chicago "had gone up from 25, a few years ago, to more than 2,000." On Lenox Avenue in Harlem, the magazine reported, "Cadillacs are so commonplace that nobody turns around to look at them anymore." Some of the "Cadillac prosperity," *Time* concluded, "is obviously false or forced." Still, the magazine said, coming dangerously close to a provocative quote of Marie-Antoinette, "for most Negroes, the problem is no longer jobs, but better jobs; for many, it is no longer bread, but cake."

A great deal of this progress stemmed from impersonal changes in the world: the increasing industrialization of the South, the artificial expansion of the Cold War economy, and the changing tone and texture of power relations in the world beyond the Atlantic. Even more persuasive was negative democratization, the wooing of Negroes by white men of power who needed their voices or, at least, their silence in the ideological struggle against Russia. Nor does the chain of causation end there. The Negro revolts of the thirties and forties were major causative factors; so, to be sure, were Negro radicals like Paul Robeson who frightened America into a course of action that would have come with better grace from an internal consciousness of the acute need for change.

For all these reasons, and for others, America began to cash the blue chips of Negro citizens. The Supreme Court—signaling the beginning of the era of integration as it signaled in the Reconstruction era the beginning of the era of segregation—began in the late forties to define with greater precision the equal part of the "separate-but-equal" myth. What was more important were several hints from the Court that it was ready to go beyond "separate-but-equal" and rule on segregation per se. The Court's drift toward truth was, in part, a result of the changing climate of the age; but it was also a tribute to the patient, plodding, persistent efforts of Thurgood Marshall and the staff of the NAACP Legal and Educational Fund. The grand outcome was a series of decisions that doomed the white primary, restrictive covenants, and segregation in colleges, graduate schools, and interstate travel.

All of this—the increasing sensitivity of the federal government, the series of Supreme Court decisions—reflected a new level of concern in white America. In this period, there was a rash of books and movies (*Home of the Brave*, *Pinky*, *Lost Boundaries*) and a paroxysm of organizational activity. It was estimated that there were some one hundred official and some four hundred unofficial race relations committees in the North by 1950. By that time, according to press reports, white people were expending voluntarily nearly one hundred million hours a year in organized efforts to improve the climate of race relations.

Most of this activity was busy work which merely scratched the surface. It seems, in retrospect, that most Americans were engaged in a huge conspiracy to deny the reality of their eyes. The "gains" most people praised were confined almost entirely to the Negro middle- and upper-classes. Some of the "progress," moreover, masked dangerous setbacks. Negro "gains" in the housing markets, for instance, solidified housing and school segregation. As whites fled to the new bedroom dormitories in the suburbs, the ghetto expanded enormously. More ominous yet was the crystallization, in the wake of the suburban boom, of the new idea of one-color, one-class, one-kind neighborhoods. Robert Weaver, almost alone among the social commentators, noted that this idea, in and of itself, was a clear and present danger to American democracy. But it would take time to see this—time and the polarization of the American community. In the fifties, Negroes did not look gift horses in the mouth. As whites moved out, they moved in. House by house, block by block, the ghetto marched toward the city limits of scores of municipalities. This was not, all things considered, an unmixed blessing but it was not a clear-cut gain.

Beyond the horizon were other dark clouds. White fear, as expressed in the resurgence of the Ku Klux Klan in the South and the growth of property owners associations in the North, was growing. This fear bubbled to the surface periodically in violent episodes like the bomb-murder of Harry Sims, the Florida NAACP official, in 1951, and the Cicero (1951) and Trumbull Park (1953–56) housing riots in Chicago. Although 1952 was the first year without a single reported lynching, terrorism and intimidation, often under the color of law, was common in the South. And to all this must be added the obvious fact that almost everyone was dealing with symptoms not causes. Segregation was not decreasing; it was growing. The South was still spending five, six and seven dollars for white education for every one dollar spent on the education of Negro children. There were more books in the Oklahoma state penitentiary than in the state's Negro university. In progressive Atlanta, there was not a single kindergarten for Negroes in the early fifties, not one community center and only one Negro park. In Chicago and other Northern cities, schools were segregated, dilapidated and transparently unequal.

Deep in the heart of the ghetto, unnoticed by most commentators, things were going from bad to worse. Nearly a third of all Negro homes were dilapidated, as compared with less than 10 per cent for the nation as a whole. Worse, more than 20 per cent of all Negro homes were overcrowded. Although the citizens of *this* America shared to an extent in the general prosperity of the period (via easy credit plans), they were, on the whole, sitting ducks for the series of recessions which began in 1952 and became progressively worse as the years wore on. The full impact of all this, and of the hidden threat of automation, would not be felt until years later, but the signs of impending disaster were clear to some men.

Acquiring Manhood

WILLIAM H. GRIER AND PRICE M. COBBS

Jimmy was a twelve-year-old boy whose rapid growth had left him gawky and uncomfortable. He sat slumped in a chair, trying to conceal his ill-fitting clothes. His face was jet-black, and his expressions ranged from somber to sad. Whether relating stories of home, school, or the streets, he disguised his true feelings. At twelve he had learned one of his first lessons—always play it cool. As much as possible, he worked to hide his inner life.

One day he stared long and hard at his fist and said: "I want to hit a white man." For once, the therapist could sense an uncensored outpouring of feelings. Then Jimmy frowned, started another sentence, and began to cry.

The anger was welcome, if unexpected, but the comment was surprising. In over three months of weekly visits, the boy had never directly mentioned white people. There had been allusions to trouble at school with boys who were not "bloods" and once he talked of his father's job at a can factory, where there were few Negroes. But Jimmy had never spoken in terms of racial feelings or problems. He had never directly felt antagonism from a white person, but when his anger spilled over, he chose that target.

He was a quiet, introverted boy who found it difficult to talk for fifty minutes. He would smile in acknowledging something pleasant, but generally he seemed to feel despair. His emotions were expressed in terms of stubbornness and obstinacy. If he felt threatened, he became passive and silent and in this manner opposed anything he did not want to do or say. This was his means of dealing with any authority, whether a teacher in school or a parent. Though he had an above-average intelligence, he was doing poorly in school. There were important things he would not do or forgot to do, and his grades suffered. In talking about his life, Jimmy was vague. He had trouble seeing anything in his life as definite, with any form or shape.

One thing in his life was clear. He saw his father as weak and powerless. However much his father threatened, cajoled, or beat him, Jimmy always knew that the man was playing a role.

His father was a large man, lighter in color than his son, and grossly overweight. He dressed in rumpled suits, wrinkled shirts, and greasy ties. In some of the early family sessions, he would interrupt to complain of his various ailments. He spoke of an ulcer that was always "acting up." Mr. B. "played at" (this was Jimmy's phrase) being the minister of a storefront church, in addition to his full-time job at the factory. From an early age, Jimmy was aware that his father could never "stand up." He had heard his mother say it and he observed it himself. One of the boy's few delights was in recalling an occasion when his father cringed and sent his wife to the door to handle a bill collector. Many of Jimmy's friends did not have their fathers living at home, but he was certain that those fathers, in the same situation, would have acted the same way.

Mrs. B. was a short, dark woman with an attractive but worried face. She was neat and "fixed up" and openly compared her appearance with her husband's usually disheveled state. She did not hide her contempt for him. She constantly undermined his feeble attempts to relate to Jimmy. She was the dominant figure in the house, and she assumed this position as an unwanted burden, as something about which she had no choice. She would alternate between understanding Jimmy and dramatically washing her hands of everything.

In terms of individual psychopathology, Jimmy can be matched with thousands of teenage boys of every race and ethnic background. He is responding to his puberty with restlessness and feelings he cannot articulate directly. He is angry with his father and alternately attracted to and repelled by his mother. Every therapist has seen many Jimmys. What is different about him is that he is black and is experiencing what every black boy in this country must undergo. His personality and character structure, his emotional assets and liabilities, are being shaped as much by his blackness as by his personal environment.

Jimmy is beginning to realize that he has no power and, like his father, will not get it. At his age the concepts are misty, but he realizes that his father and the fathers of his friends are lacking something. He has had few, if any, traumatic incidents with whites. There have been no overt acts of discrimination. The family has lived in a ghetto, and all their socialization has been within that framework. But Jimmy is part of a historical legacy that spans more than three hundred years. He lives in a large city but he shares his insight with every black child in every city in this country. He must devise individual ways to meet group problems. He must find compensations, whether healthy or unhealthy. There must be a tremendous expenditure of psychic energy to cushion the shock of learning that he is denied what other men around him have. When he states his desire to attack a white man, he consciously acknowledges his wish to attack those who keep him powerless.

Both theories of personality development and clinical experience attest to the troubled path from childhood to manhood. The young man must have developed a fine expertise in making his way in a complex and ambiguous social organization. Under the most favorable signs it is a difficult task and society must turn its most benign and helping face to the young aspirant. And once the game is mastered a certain flexible readiness is required because the rules are constantly being changed.

Thus the black boy in growing up encounters some strange impediments. Schools discourage his ambitions, training for valued skills is not available to him, and when he does triumph in some youthful competition he receives compromised praise, not the glory he might expect. In time he comes to see that society has locked arms *against* him, that rather than help he can expect opposition to his development, and that he lives not in a benign community but in a society that views his growth with hostility.

For the black man in this country, it is not so much a matter of acquiring manhood as it is a struggle to feel it his own. Whereas the white man regards his manhood as an ordained right, the black man is engaged in a never-ending battle for its possession. For the black man, attaining any portion of manhood is an active process. He must penetrate barriers and overcome opposition in order to assume a masculine posture. For the inner psychological obstacles to manhood are never so formidable as the impediments woven into American society. By contrast, for a white man in this country, the rudiments of manhood are settled at birth by the possession of a penis and a white skin. This biological affirmation of masculinity and identity as master is enough to insure that, whatever his individual limitations, this society will not systematically erect obstructions to his achievement.

Throughout his life, at each critical point of development the black boy is told to hold back, to constrict, to subvert and camouflage his normal masculinity. Male assertiveness becomes a forbidden fruit, and if it is attained, it must be savored privately.

Manhood must always be defined for the setting in which it occurs. A man in a Siberian village may be very different from a man in a Chicago suburb. Biologically they share the same drives and limitations, but their societies may decree totally different roles. Manhood in this country has many meanings, but a central theme is clear. Men are very early taught that they have certain prerogatives and privileges. They are encouraged to pursue, to engage life, to attack, rather than to shrink back. They learn early that to express a certain amount of aggression and assertion is manly. Every playground, every schoolyard is filled with boys fighting and attacking, playing at being grown up. The popular heroes in this country are men who express themselves aggressively and assertively.

As boys approach adulthood, masculinity becomes more and more bound up with money making. In a capitalistic society economic wealth is inextricably interwoven with manhood. Closely allied is power—power to control and direct other men, power to influence the course of one's own and other lives. The more lives one can influence, the greater the power. The ultimate power is the freedom to understand and alter one's life. It is this power, both individually and collectively, which has been denied the black man.

Under slavery, the black man was a psychologically emasculated and totally dependent human being. Times and conditions have changed, but black men continue to exhibit the inhibitions and psychopathology that had their genesis in the slave experience. It would seem that for masculine growth and development the psychological conditions have not changed very much. Better jobs are available, housing is improving, and all the external signs of progress can be seen, but the American heritage of racism will still not allow the black man to feel himself master in his own land. Just as Jimmy is beset by forces larger than his individual experiences, so is the black man in this society, more than other men, shaped by currents more powerful than the course of his own life. There are rules which regulate black lives far more than the lives of white men.

The simplistic view of the black family as a matriarchy is an unfortunate theme repeated too often by scholars who should know better. If a man is stripped of his authority in the home by forces outside that home, the woman naturally must assume the status of head of household. This is the safety factor inherent in a household which includes two adults and it by no means suggests that the woman prefers it that way. If a woman is widowed she may assume many masculine functions, but the household may be a patriarchy without a patriarch.

In the black household the man faces greater than usual odds in making his way. The care and rearing of children falls even more heavily on the wife; she is the culture bearer. She interprets the society to the children and takes as her task the shaping of their character to meet the world as she knows it. This is every mother's task. But the black mother has a more ominous message for her child and feels more urgently the need to get the message across. The child must know that the white world is dangerous and that if he does not understand its rules it may kill him.

When black men recall their early life, consistent themes emerge. For example, the mother is generally perceived as having been sharply contradictory. She may have been permissive in some areas and punitive and rigid in others. There are remembrances of stimulation and gratification coexisting with memories of deprivation and rejection. There is always a feeling that the behavior of the mother was purposeful and deliberate.

The black man remembers that his mother underwent frequent and rapid shifts of mood. He remembers the cruelty. The mother who sang spirituals gently at church was capable of inflicting senseless pain at home. These themes of gratification and cruelty are consistent enough to suggest that they played a critical role in preparing the boy for adulthood. It would seem that the boy had to experience the polarities of ambivalence so that he could understand his later role in a white society. He must be adequately prepared.

The black mother shares a burden with her soul sisters of three centuries ago. She must produce and shape and mold a unique type of man. She must intuitively cut off and blunt his masculine assertiveness and aggression lest these put the boy's life in jeopardy.

During slavery the danger was real. A slave boy could not show too much aggression. The feelings of anger and frustration which channeled themselves into aggression had to be thwarted. If they were not, the boy would have little or no use as a slave and would be slain. If any feelings, especially those of assertive manhood, were expressed too strongly, then that slave was a threat, not only to himself and his master but to the entire system as well. For that, he would have to be killed.

The black mother continues this heritage from slavery and simultaneously reflects the world she now knows. Even today, the black man cannot become too aggressive without hazard to himself. To do so is to challenge the delicate balance of a complex social system. Every mother, of whatever color and degree of proficiency, knows what the society in which she lives will require of her children. Her basic job is to prepare the child for this. Because of the institutionalization of barriers, the black mother knows even more surely what society requires of *her* children. What at first seemed a random pattern of mothering has gradually assumed a definite and deliberate, if unconscious, method of preparing a black boy for his subordinate place in the world.

As a result, black men develop considerable hostility toward black women as the inhibiting instruments of an oppressive system. The woman has more power, more accessibility into the system, and therefore she is more feared, while at the same time envied. And it is her lot in life to suppress masculine assertiveness in her sons.

Mr. R. was a writer who presented himself for treatment in his mid-fifties. In his younger days he had enjoyed success and a certain amount of adulation in white society. Throughout the course of treatment he presented a picture of culture and refinement. His trouble was that several years earlier he had lost the spark of creativity and his writing ceased. He made frequent resolutions to resume writing, but his motivation never matched his ambition.

It developed that he was afraid to compete with white men as a writer. Whatever he wrote, his obsessional fears dictated that somewhere someone who was white had written something better. He was a defeated and despairing man when he entered treatment. He had, however, a delicious secret which he used as comfort when he was most depressed.

His face would crease with a smile when he recounted his numerous affairs as a young man. In all his life he never doubted his ability to outperform a white man sexually. He told how he had "banged many white women." He sometimes spoke of himself as a deformed man or as a cripple, but sex was the one area in which he felt completely adequate.

The mythology and folklore of black people is filled with tales of sexually prodigious men. Most boys grow up on a steady diet of folk heroes who have distinguished themselves by sexual feats. It is significant that few, if any, of these folk heroes are directing armies or commanding empires. Dreams must in some way reflect reality, and in this country the black man, until quite recently, had not been in positions of power. His wielding of power had been in the privacy of the boudoir.

To be sure, black men have sexual problems. They may have impotence, premature ejaculation, and the entire range of pathology which limits and distorts sexual life. Such ailments have the same dynamic origins in men of all races. But where sex is employed as armament and used as a conscious and deliberate means of defense, it is the black man who chooses this weapon. If he cannot fight the white man openly, he can and does battle him secretly. Recurrently, the pattern evolves of black men using sex as a dagger to be symbolically thrust into the white man.

A black man who was an orderly in a hospital had an eighth-grade education and felt himself inadequate in most endeavors. If called upon to perform a new duty, he would reflect for a moment and feel dumbstruck. One evening an attractive young nurse made seductive overtures to him. At first he was not convinced that she was serious but thought she was playing a game. When he discovered that she meant it, he took her to bed with a vengeance. During the weekly therapy hour he would elaborate and expand on his feats. One central fact became more and more clear. He was able to state very directly that every time he possessed the girl sexually, he was making up for having sat in the back of the bus and having endured numberless humiliations. He was getting revenge for generations of slavery and degradation.

One of the constant themes in black folklore is the "bad nigger." It seems that every community has had one or was afraid of having one. They were feared as much by blacks as by whites. In the slave legends there are tales of docile field hands suddenly going berserk. It was a common enough phenomenon to appear in writings of the times and to stimulate the erection of defenses against this violent kind of man.

Today black boys are admonished not to be a "bad nigger." No description need be offered; every black child knows what is meant. They are angry and hostile. They strike fear into everyone with their uncompromising rejection of restraint or inhibition. They may seem at one moment meek and compromised—and in the next a terrifying killer. Because of his experience in this country, every black man harbors a potential bad nigger inside him. He must ignore this inner man. The bad nigger is bad because he has been required to renounce his manhood to save his life. The more one approaches the American ideal of respectability, the more this hostility must be repressed. The bad nigger is a defiant nigger, a reminder of what manhood could be.

Cultural stereotypes of the savage rapist-Negro express the fear that the black man will turn on his tormentors. Negro organizations dread the presence of the bad nigger. White merchants who have contact with black people have uneasy feelings when they see a tight mouth, a hard look, and an angry black face. The bad nigger in black men no doubt accounts for more worry in both races than any other single factor.

Granting the limitations of stereotypes, we should nevertheless like to sketch a paradigmatic black man. His characteristics seem so connected to employment that we call it "the postal-clerk syndrome." This man is always described as "nice" by white people. In whatever integrated setting he works, he is the standard against whom other blacks are measured. "If they were all only like him, everything would be so much better." He is passive, nonassertive, and nonaggressive. He has made a virtue of identification with the aggressor, and he has adopted an ingratiating and compliant manner. In public his thoughts and feelings are consciously shaped in the direction he thinks white people want them to be. The pattern begins in childhood when the mother may actually say: "You must be this way because this is the only way you will get along with Mr. Charlie."

This man renounces gratifications that are available to others. He assumes a deferential mask. He is always submissive. He must figure out "the man" but keep "the man" from deciphering him. He is prevalent in the middle and upper-middle classes, but is found throughout the social structure. The more closely allied to the white man, the more complete the picture becomes. He is a direct lineal descendant of the "house nigger" who was designed to identify totally with the white master. The danger he poses to himself and others is great, but only the surface of passivity and compliance is visible. The storm below is hidden.

A leading Negro citizen came to a therapy session with his wife, who was suffering from a severe and intractable melancholia. She had several times seriously attempted suicide. The last attempt was particularly serious. She was angry with her husband and berated him for never opening up and exposing his feelings.

For his part, the husband remained "nice." He never raised his voice above a murmur. His wife could goad him, but he was the epitome of understanding. He was amenable to all suggestions. His manner and gestures were deliberate, studied, and noninflammatory. Everything was understated. During the course of treatment he was involved in several civil rights crises. His public life was an extension of his private one, and he used such words as "moderation" and "responsibility." His entire life was a study in passivity, in how to play at being a man without really being one.

It would be easy to write off this man as an isolated passive individual, but his whole community looks upon his career as a success story. He made it in the system to a position of influence and means. And it took an aggressive, driving, determined man to make it against the odds he faced. We must ask how much energy is required for him to conceal his drive so thoroughly. And we wonder what would happen if his controls ever failed.

Starting with slavery, black people, and more particularly black men, have had to devise ways of expressing themselves uniquely and individually and in a manner that was not threatening to the white man. Some methods of giving voice to aggressive masculinity have become institutionalized. The most stylized is the posture of "playing it cool."

The playing-it-cool style repeats itself over and over again in all aspects of black life. It is an important means of expression and is widely copied in the larger white culture. A man may be overwhelmed with conflict, threatened with an eruption of feelings, and barely maintaining his composure, but he will present a serene exterior. He may fear the eruption of repressed feelings if they bring a loss of control, but an important aspect of his containment is the fear that his aggression will be directed against the white world and will bring swift punishment. The intrapsychic dynamics may be similar in a white man, but for the black man it is socially far more important that the façade be maintained.

Patients have come for treatment who have had one or two visits with a variety of psychiatrists, psychologists, and social workers. In many cases they were written off as having no significant pathology or as being "poor patients." The importance of the cool style is apparent when one realizes the cost and suffering required to maintain it. Those who practice it have raised to a high art a life style which seems a peculiarly black contribution to adaptation in this society.

Several decades ago, observers were impressed by the black community's adulation of Joe Louis. They were a starved and deprived group, but, even so, their deification of him seemed all out of proportion. In retrospect, there is an explanation. In the ring he was the picture of fury. As he demolished foe after foe, every black man could vicariously taste his victory. If his victims were white, the pleasure was even greater. He symbolized assertiveness and unbridled aggression for the black man. In watching him or reading about him, an entire community could find expression through him of inhibited masculine drives. As others have entered professional sports in later years, the heroes have served a similar purpose. Educated and sophisticated Negroes also participate in this hero worship, since all black men swim in the same sea.

A black man in treatment kept reaching for a memory. He finally recalled watching a fight on television, at a time when a black coed, Authurine Lucey, was integrating the University of Alabama. The contest was between a black and white fighter. During the bout he kept hearing someone shout: "Hit him one for Authurine." Even after he had forgotten the fight, the phrase kept returning to his mind, "Hit him one for Authurine." It became his battle cry. Whenever he was pressed, the thought would come again and again in an obsessional fashion. He then began to talk of his own repressed aggression and the pieces of the puzzle began to fit, and the obsession receded.

When all the repressive forces fail and aggression erupts, it is vital that we ask the right questions. The issue is not what caused the riots of the past few years—that is clear to any man who has eyes. Rather, we must ask: What held this aggression in check for so long and what is the nature of this breached barrier? Dare anyone try to reconstruct it?

During recent riots there was a wry saying in the ghetto. "Chuck can't tell where it's going to hit next because we don't know ourselves." And it was a fact. The most baffling aspect to rioting in Newark, Detroit, and Watts was the complete spontaneity of the violence. Authorities turned to "responsible" Negro leaders to calm the black rebels and the Negro leaders did not know where to start. They were confronted with a leaderless mob which needed no leader. Every man was a leader—they were of one mind.

The goods of America, piled high in the neighborhood stores, had been offered to them with a price tag that made work slavery and made balancing a budget a farce. The pressure was ever on parents to buy a television set, to buy kitchen appliances and new cars. The available jobs paid so poorly and the prices (plus interest) of goods were so high that if one made a purchase he was entering upon years of indebtedness.

The carrot held in front of the ghetto laborer is the consumer item—the auto, the TV, and the hi-fi set. If the poor black man falls into place in America, he takes whatever job is offered, receives minimal pay, purchases hard goods at harder prices, and teeters from insolvency to bankruptcy in the ghetto.

Exhausted, he was offered a stimulant in the form of the civil rights laws. When it become clear that they were nothing more than words from Washington, he kicked over the traces. He took a short cut. Instead of working for a lifetime to buy a piece of slum property which might fall at any moment and which he would likely never own anyway—instead of this treadmill, he burned it down. Instead of working for years to pay three times the usual cost of a television set, he broke a window and stole it. Instead of the desperate, frustrating search to find out which white man was friendly and which was hostile, he simply labeled them all the enemy. There never seemed to be a great deal of difference between friends and enemies anyway. So in a spontaneous blast he burned up the ghetto. And the wrong question continued to be asked: Why a riot in Detroit, where conditions were so good?

The worst slum and the best slum are very close together compared with the distance separating the world of black men and the world of whites. At bottom, America remains a slave country which happens to have removed the slave laws from the books. The question we must ask is: What held the slave rebellion in check for so long?

The racist tradition is pervasive and envelops every American. For black men it constitutes a heavy psychological burden. From the unemployed, illiterate ghetto dweller to the urbanized man living in an integrated setting, careful examination shows psychological scars. Black men fight one another, do violence to property, do hurtful things to themselves while nursing growing hatred for the system which oppresses and humiliates them. Their manhood is tested daily. As one patient expressed it: "The black man in this country fights the main event in Madison Square Garden every day."

A reflective and cautious man relates some episode of irrational and aggressive behavior. He has spent a lifetime suppressing his feelings, and now he is frightened and wants reassurance that what has happened will not recur.

Another man erupts and attacks a neighbor who knocks on his door.

These incidents, like the regular Saturday-night brawls that have been characteristic of the black ghetto, are the short bursts of rage which find broader expression in Watts, Newark, and Detroit.

Many black men show a curious symptom—weeping without feeling. The tears come without warning and may be quite embarrassing. It is seen frequently in our patient population of black men of above-average achievement. We can only speculate on the basis of a small sample, but it would seem that it also occurs, though with less frequency, among black men of lower socioeconomic levels. Clinical experience indicates that the symptom is relatively rare among white men of all classes.

A man watching a football game on television sees a Negro star take the ball on a long downfield run and as he crosses the goal line in triumph the viewer is aware of tears in his eyes.

Another patient recalls attending a civil rights meeting at which Martin Luther King spoke eloquently. He was suddenly aware of tears.

Another man attended a business meeting at which a successful white businessman was being extolled, and as the guest of honor's unbroken series of business triumphs was told, the patient found himself wiping away tears.

Common to all these incidents is a black man passively viewing another man, black or white, triumphant over odds and standing supreme in a moment of personal glory. Further, the patients were struck by the fact that the tears seemed to come of their own accord, unsummoned and unaccompanied by any emotional feeling or any thought which might cause them to weep. The event was too simple: witnessing another triumphant man, and tears, no feelings, no thoughts.

In the course of treatment, attention was focused on the lack of feeling, and the associations which came gradually made it clear that it was important for the viewer not to allow himself feelings. The obvious forbidden feelings were ones of sadness. And for what? For what he might have been. He might have been the victor receiving the roar of the crowd. The tears are for what he might have achieved if he had not been held back. He was held back by some inner command not to excel, not to achieve, not to become outstanding, not to draw attention to himself. Even at the price of achievement, he felt bound to follow a command to remain anonymous.

Once he sees the compelling nature of this inner rule of behavior, he can trace it to his mother. Only she was so concerned with his behavior and she was most concerned that he be modest and self-effacing. And when he sees that his grief is over lost achievement, relinquished at the behest of his mother, he becomes enraged with her. This was the reason he had to suppress all feeling connected with the tears, because it led too directly to his mother as the inhibiting factor in his development.

Upon reaching this point many patients immediately displace the rage onto society, saying they were not inhibited early in life by parents, but later, upon encountering a restrictive and inhibiting social system where the cards were stacked against them. With some patients the first object of their anger was white society and the second the mother, but always the mother was close to the surface. It was her closeness to the symptom which made necessary the inhibition of feeling associated with the tears.

Finally, there comes later a deeper understanding of the mother as a concerned mediator between society and the child. The patient comes to recognize that, while the larger society imposes a harsh inhibition on his development and a threat to any aggressivity, this hostility of society is communicated to him by his mother, whose primary concern is that he survive. For if he does not realize that his aggressiveness puts him in grave danger from society generally, he may *not* survive. With this recognition his hostility toward his mother lessens and is directed toward white society.

This symptom, seen so frequently, is like an isolated sentinel suggesting deeper layers of interaction between impulse and inhibition, individual drive and the stone wall of external reality.

How much of this finds its roots in history? How did the mother come to systematically drive out manliness from her sons under the sign of love? And does our patient weep only for himself?

We are certain that the answers lie in the past.

Concerning Violence

FRANTZ FANON

A WORLD DIVIDED INTO COMPARTMENTS, A MOTIONLESS, MANICHEISTIC world, a world of statues: the statue of the general who carried out the conquest, the statue of the engineer who built the bridge; a world which is sure of itself, which crushes with its stones the backs flayed by whips: this is the colonial world. The native is a being hemmed in; apartheid is simply one form of the division into compartments of the colonial world. The first thing which the native learns is to stay in his place, and not to go beyond certain limits. This is why the dreams of the native are always of muscular prowess; his dreams are of action and of aggression. I dream I am jumping, swimming, running, climbing; I dream that I burst out laughing, that I span a river in one stride, or that I am followed by a flood of motor-cars which never catch up with me. During the period of colonisation, the native never stops achieving his freedom from nine in the evening until six in the morning.

The colonised man will first manifest this aggressiveness which has been deposited in his bones against his own people. This is the period when the niggers beat each other up, and the police and magistrates do not know which way to turn when faced with the astonishing waves of crime in North Africa. We shall see later how this phenomenon should be judged.* When the native is confronted with the colonial order of things, he finds he is in a state of permanent tension. The settler's world is a hostile world, which spurns the native, but at the same time it is a world of which he is envious. We have seen that the native never ceases to dream of putting himself in the place of the settler—not of becoming the settler but of substituting himself for the settler. This hostile world, ponderous and aggressive because it fends off the colonised masses with all the harshness it is capable of, represents not merely a hell from which the swiftest flight possible is desirable, but also a paradise close at hand which is guarded by terrible watchdogs.

The native is always on the alert, for since he can only make out with difficulty the many symbols of the colonial world, he is never sure

* See chap. V: *Colonial war and mental disorders.*

From *The Wretched of the Earth,* by Frantz Fanon (New York: Grove Press, Inc., 1966), pp. 41–50. Translated from the French by Constance Farrington. Reprinted by permission of Grove Press, Inc.

whether or not he has crossed the frontier. Confronted with a world ruled by the settler, the native is always presumed guilty. But the native's guilt is never a guilt which he accepts; it is rather a kind of curse, a sort of sword of Damocles, for, in his innermost spirit, the native admits no accusation. He is overpowered but not tamed; he is treated as an inferior but he is not convinced of his inferiority. He is patiently waiting until the settler is off his guard to fly at him. The native's muscles are always tensed. You can't say that he is terrorized, or even apprehensive. He is in fact ready at a moment's notice to exchange the *rôle* of the quarry for that of the hunter. The native is an oppressed person whose permanent dream is to become the persecutor. The symbols of social order—the police, the bugle-calls in the barracks, military parades and the waving flags—are at one and the same time inhibitory and stimulating: for they do not convey the message "Don't dare to budge"; rather, they cry out "Get ready to attack." And, in fact, if the native had any tendency to fall asleep and to forget, the settler's hauteur and the settler's anxiety to test the strength of the colonial system would remind him at every turn that the great show-down cannot be put off indefinitely. That impulse to take the settler's place implies a tonicity of muscles the whole time; and in fact we know that in certain emotional conditions the presence of an obstacle accentuates the tendency towards motion.

The settler-native relationship is a mass relationship. The settler pits brute force against the weight of numbers. He is an exhibitionist. His preoccupation with security makes him remind the native out loud that there he alone is master. The settler keeps alive in the native an anger which he deprives of outlet; the native is trapped in the tight links of the chains of colonialism. But we have seen that inwardly the settler can only achieve a pseudo petrification. The native's muscular tension finds outlet regularly in bloodthirsty explosions—in tribal warfare, in feuds between septs, and in quarrels between individuals.

Where individuals are concerned, a positive negation of common sense is evident. While the settler or the policeman has the right the live-long day to strike the native, to insult him and to make him crawl to them, you will see the native reaching for his knife at the slightest hostile or aggressive glance cast on him by another native; for the last resort of the native is to defend his personality *vis-à-vis* his brother. Tribal feuds only serve to perpetuate old grudges deep buried in the memory. By throwing himself with all his force into the *vendetta*, the native tries to persuade himself that colonialism does not exist, that everything is going on as before, that history continues. Here on the level of communal organisations we clearly discern the well-known behaviour patterns of avoidance. It is as if plunging into a fraternal blood-bath allowed them to ignore the obstacle, and to put off till later the choice, nevertheless inevitable, which opens up the question of armed resistance to colonialism. Thus collective autodestruction in a very concrete form is one of the ways in which the native's muscular tension is set free. All these patterns of conduct are those of the death reflex when faced with danger, a suicidal behaviour which proves to the settler (whose existence and domination is by them all the more justified) that these men are not reasonable human beings. In the same way the native manages to by-pass the settler. A belief in fatality removes all blame from the oppressor; the cause of misfortunes and of poverty is attributed to God; He is Fate. In this way the individual accepts the disintegration ordained by God, bows down before the settler and his lot, and by a kind of interior restabilization acquires a stony calm.

Meanwhile, however, life goes on, and the native will strengthen the inhibitions which contain his aggressiveness by drawing on the terrifying myths which are so frequently found in underdeveloped communities. There are maleficent spirits which intervene every time a step is taken in the wrong direction, leopard-men, serpent-men, six-legged dogs, zombies—a whole series of tiny animals or giants which create around the native a world of prohibitions, of barriers and of inhibitions far more terrifying than the world of the settler. This magical superstructure which permeates native society fulfils certain well-defined functions in the dynamism of the libido. One of the characteristics of under-developed societies is in fact that the libido is first and foremost the concern of a group, or of the family. The feature of communities whereby a man who dreams that he has sexual relations with a woman other than his own must confess it in public and pay a fine in kind or in working days to the injured husband or family is fully described by ethnologists. We may note in passing that this proves that the so-called prehistoric societies attach great importance to the unconscious.

The atmosphere of myth and magic frightens me and so takes on an undoubted reality. By terrifying me, it integrates me in the traditions and the history of my district or of my tribe, and at the same time it reassures me, it gives me a status, as it were an identification paper. In underdeveloped countries the occult sphere is a sphere belonging to the community which is entirely under magical jurisdiction. By entangling myself in this inextricable network where actions are repeated with crystalline inevitability, I find the everlasting world which belongs to me, and the perenniality which is thereby affirmed of the world belonging to us. Believe me, the zombies are more terrifying than the settlers; and in consequence the problem is no longer that of keeping oneself right with the colonial world and its barbed-wire entanglements, but of considering three times before urinating, spitting or going out into the night.

The supernatural, magical powers reveal themselves as essentially personal; the settler's powers are infinitely shrunken, stamped with their alien origin. We no longer really need to fight against them since what counts is the frightening enemy created by myths. We perceive that all is settled by a permanent confrontation on the phantasmic plane.

It has always happened in the struggle for freedom that such a people, formerly lost in an imaginary maze, a prey to unspeakable terrors yet happy to lose themselves in a dreamlike torment, such a people becomes unhinged, reorganises itself, and in blood and tears gives birth to very real and immediate action. Feeding the *moudjahidines,** posting sentinels, coming to the help of families which lack the bare necessities, or taking the place of a husband who has been killed or imprisoned: such are the concrete tasks to which the people is called during the struggle for freedom.

In the colonial world, the emotional sensitivity of the native is kept on the surface of his skin like an open sore which flinches from the caustic agent; and the psyche shrinks back, obliterates itself and finds outlet in muscular demonstrations which have caused certain very wise men to say that the native is a hysterical type. This sensitive emotionalism, watched by invisible keepers who are however in unbroken contact with the core of the personality, will find its fulfilment through eroticism in the driving forces behind the crisis' dissolution.

On another level we see the native's emotional sensibility exhausting itself in dances which are more or less ecstatic. This is why any study of the colonial world should take into consideration the phenomena of the dance and of possession. The native's relaxation takes precisely the form of a muscular orgy in which the most acute aggressivity and the most impelling violence are canalised, transformed and conjured away. The circle of the dance is a permissive circle: it protects and permits. At certain times on certain days, men and woman come together at a given place, and there, under the solemn eye of the tribe, fling themselves into a seemingly unorganised pantomime, which is in reality extremely systematic, in which by various means—shakes of the head, bending of the spinal column, throwing of the whole body backwards—may be deciphered as in an open book the huge effort of a community to exorcise itself, to liberate itself, to explain itself. There are no limits—inside the circle. The hillock up which you have toiled as if to be nearer to the moon; the river bank down which you slip as if to show the connection between the dance and ablutions, cleansing and purification—these are sacred places. There are no limits—for in reality your purpose in coming together is to allow the accumulated libido, the hampered aggressivity to dissolve as in a volcanic eruption. Symbolical killings, fantastic rites, imaginary mass murders—all must be brought out. The evil humours are undammed, and flow away with a din as of molten lava.

One step further and you are completely possessed. In fact, these are actually organised *séances* of possession and exorcism; they include vampirism, possession by djinns, by zombies, and by Legba, the famous god of the Voodoo. This disintegrating of the personality, this splitting and dissolution, all this fulfils a primordial function in the

* Highly-trained soldiers who are completely dedicated to the Moslem cause. (Transl.)

organism of the colonial world. When they set out, the men and women were impatient, stamping their feet in a state of nervous excitement; when they return, peace has been restored to the village; it is once more calm and unmoved.

During the struggle for freedom, a marked alienation from these practices is observed. The native's back is to the wall, the knife is at his throat (or, more precisely, the electrode at his genitals): he will have no more call for his fancies. After centuries of unreality, after having wallowed in the most outlandish phantoms, at long last the native, gun in hand, stands face to face with the only forces which contend for his life—the forces of colonialism. And the youth of a colonised country, growing up in an atmosphere of shot and fire, may well make a mock of, and does not hesitate to pour scorn upon the zombies of his ancestors, the horses with two heads, the dead who rise again, and the djinns who rush into your body while you yawn. The native discovers reality and transforms it into the pattern of his customs, into the practice of violence and into his plan for freedom.

We have seen that this same violence, though kept very much on the surface all through the colonial period, yet turns in the void. We have also seen that it is canalised by the emotional outlets of dance and possession by spirits; we have seen how it is exhausted in fratricidal combats. Now the problem is to lay hold of this violence which is changing direction. When formerly it was appeased by myths and exercised its talents in finding fresh ways of committing mass suicide, now new conditions will make possible a completely new line of action.

Nowadays a theoretical problem of prime importance is being set, on the historical plane as well as on the level of political tactics, by the liberation of the colonies: when can one affirm that the situation is ripe for a movement of national liberation? In what form should it first be manifested? Because the various means whereby decolonisation has been carried out have appeared in many different aspects, reason hesitates and refuses to say which is a true decolonisation, and which a false. We shall see that for a man who is in the thick of the fight it is an urgent matter to decide on the means and the tactics to employ: that is to say, how to conduct and organise the movement. If this coherence is not present there is only a blind will towards freedom, with the terribly reactionary risks which it entails.

What are the forces which in the colonial period open up new outlets and engender new aims for the violence of colonised peoples? In the first place there are the political parties and the intellectual or commercial *élites*. Now, the characteristic feature of certain political structures is that they proclaim abstract principles but refrain from issuing definite commands. The entire action of these nationalist political parties during the colonial period is action of the electoral type: a string of philosophico-political dissertations on the themes of the rights of peoples to self-determination, the rights of man to freedom from hunger and human dignity, and the unceasing affirmation of the principle: "One man, one vote." The national political parties never lay stress upon the necessity of a trial of armed strength, for the good reason that their objective is not the radical overthrowing of the system. Pacifists and legalists, they are in fact partisans of order, the new order—but to the colonialist bourgeoisie they put bluntly enough the demand which to them is the main one: "Give us more power." On the specific question of violence, the *élite* are ambiguous. They are violent in their words and reformist in their attitudes. When the nationalist political leaders *say* something, they make quite clear that they do not really *think* it.

This characteristic on the part of the nationalist political parties should be interpreted in the light both of the make-up of their leaders and the nature of their followings. The rank-and-file of a nationalist party is urban. The workers, primary schoolteachers, artisans and small shop-keepers who have begun to profit—at a discount, to be sure—from the colonial set-up, have special interests at heart. What this sort of following demands is the betterment of their particular lot: increased salaries, for example. The dialogue between these political parties and colonialism is never broken off. Improvements are discussed, such as full electoral representation, the liberty of the press, and liberty of association. Reforms are debated. Thus it need not astonish anyone to notice that a large number of natives are militant members of the branches of political parties which stem from the mother country. These natives fight under an abstract watchword: "Government by the workers", and they forget that in their country it should be *nationalist* watchwords which are first in the field. The native intellectual has clothed his aggressiveness in his barely veiled desire to assimilate himself to the colonial world. He has used his aggressiveness to serve his own individual interests.

Thus there is very easily brought into being a kind of class of affranchised slaves, or slaves who are individually free. What the intellectual demands is the right to multiply the emancipated, and the opportunity to organise a genuine class of emancipated citizens. On the other hand, the mass of the people have no intention of standing by and watching individuals increase their chances of success. What they demand is not the settler's position of status, but the settler's place. The immense majority of natives want the settler's farm. For them, there is no question of entering into competition with the settler. They want to take his place.

The peasantry is systematically disregarded for the most part by the propaganda put out by the nationalist parties. And it is clear that in the colonial countries the peasants alone are revolutionary, for they have nothing to lose and everything to gain. The starving peasant, outside the class system, is the first among the exploited to discover that only violence pays. For him there is no compromise, no possible coming to terms; colonisation and decolonisation are simply a question of relative strength. The exploited man sees that his liberation implies the use of all means, and that of force first and foremost. When in 1956, after the capitulation of Monsieur Guy Mollet to the settlers in Algeria, the *Front de Libération Nationale,* in a famous leaflet, stated that colonialism only loosens its hold when the knife is at its throat, no Algerian really found these terms too violent. The leaflet only expressed what every Algerian felt at heart: colonialism is not a thinking machine, nor a body endowed with reasoning faculties. It is violence in its natural state, and it will only yield when confronted with greater violence.

At the decisive moment, the colonialist bourgeoisie, which up till then has remained inactive, comes into the field. It introduces that new idea which is in proper parlance a creation of the colonial situation: non-violence. In its simplest form this non-violence signifies to the intellectual and economic *élite* of the colonised country that the bourgeoisie has the same interests as them and that it is therefore urgent and indispensable to come to terms for the public good. Non-violence is an attempt to settle the colonial problem around a green baize table, before any regrettable act has been performed or irreparable gesture made, before any blood has been shed. But if the masses, without waiting for the chairs to be arranged around the baize table, listen to their own voice and begin committing outrages and setting fire to buildings, the *élites* and the nationalist bourgeois parties will be seen rushing to the colonialists to exclaim "This is very serious! We do not know how it will end; we must find a solution—some sort of compromise."

This idea of compromise is very important in the phenomenon of decolonisation, for it is very far from being a simple one. Compromise involves the colonial system and the young nationalist bourgeoisie at one and the same time. The partisans of the colonial system discover that the masses may destroy everything. Blown-up bridges, ravaged farms, repressions and fighting harshly disrupt the economy. Compromise is equally attractive to the nationalist bourgeoisie, who since they are not clearly aware of the possible consequences of the rising storm, are genuinely afraid of being swept away by this huge hurricane and never stop saying to the settlers: "We are still capable of stopping the slaughter; the masses still have confidence in us; act quickly if you do not want to put everything in jeopardy." One step more, and the leader of the nationalist party keeps his distance with regard to that violence. He loudly proclaims that he has nothing to do with these Mau-Mau, these terrorists, these throat-slitters. At best, he shuts himself off in a no-man's-land between the terrorists and the settlers and willingly offers his services as go-between; that is to say, that as the settlers cannot discuss terms with these Mau-Mau, he himself will be quite willing to begin negotiations. Thus it is that the rear-guard of the national struggle, that very party of people who have never ceased to be on the other side in the fight, find themselves somersaulted into the van of negotiations and compromise—precisely because that party has taken very good care never to break contact with colonialism.

Before negotiations have been set on foot, the majority of nationalist parties confine themselves for the most part to explaining and excusing this "savagery". They do not assert that the people have to use physical force, and it sometimes even happens that they go so far as to condemn, in private, the spectacular deeds which are declared to be hateful by the press and public opinion in the mother country. The legitimate excuse for this ultra-conservative policy is the desire to see things in an objective light; but this traditional attitude of the native intellectual and of the leaders of the nationalist parties is not, in reality, in the least objective. For in fact they are not at all convinced that this impatient violence of the masses is the most efficient means of defending their own interests. Moreover, there are some individuals who are convinced of the ineffectiveness of violent methods; for them, there is no doubt about it, every attempt to break colonial oppression by force is a hopeless effort, an attempt at suicide, because in the innermost recesses of their brains the settler's tanks and aeroplanes occupy a huge place. When they are told "Action must be taken", they see bombs raining down on them, armoured cars coming at them on every path, machine-gunning and police action . . . and they sit quiet. They are beaten from the start. There is no need to demonstrate their incapacity to triumph by violent methods; they take it for granted in their everyday life and in their political manoeuvres.

Notes on a Native Son

ELDRIDGE CLEAVER

After reading a couple of James Baldwin's books, I began experiencing that continuous delight one feels upon discovering a fascinating, brilliant talent on the scene, a talent capable of penetrating so profoundly into one's own little world that one knows oneself to have been unalterably changed and *liberated,* liberated from the frustrating grasp of whatever devils happen to possess one. Being a Negro, I have found this to be a rare and infrequent experience, for few of my black brothers and sisters here in America have achieved the power, which James Baldwin calls his revenge, which outlasts kingdoms: the power of doing whatever cats like Baldwin do when combining the alphabet with the volatile elements of his soil. (And, like it or not, a black man,

---

unless he has become irretrievably "white-minded," responds with an additional dimension of his being to the articulated experience of another black—in spite of the universality of human experience.)

I, as I imagine many others did and still do, lusted for anything that Baldwin had written. It would have been a gas for me to sit on a pillow beneath the womb of Baldwin's typewriter and catch each newborn page as it entered this world of ours. I was delighted that Baldwin, with those great big eyes of his, which one thought to be fixedly focused on the macrocosm, could also pierce the microcosm. And although he was so full of sound, he was not a noisy writer like Ralph Ellison. He placed so much of my own experience, which I thought I had understood, into new perspective.

Gradually, however, I began to feel uncomfortable about something in Baldwin. I was disturbed upon becoming aware of an aversion in my heart to part of the song he sang. Why this was so, I was unable at first to say. Then I read *Another Country,* and I knew why my love for Baldwin's vision had become ambivalent.

Long before, I had become a student of Norman Mailer's *The White Negro,* which seemed to me to be prophetic and penetrating in its understanding of the psychology involved in the accelerating confrontation of black and white in America. I was therefore personally insulted by Baldwin's flippant, schoolmarmish dismissal of *The White Negro.* Baldwin committed a literary crime by his arrogant repudiation of one of the few gravely important expressions of our time. *The White Negro* may contain an excess of esoteric verbal husk, but one can forgive Mailer for that because of the solid kernel of truth he gave us. After all, it is the baby we want and not the blood of afterbirth. Mailer described, in that incisive essay, the first important chinks in the "mountain of white supremacy"—important because it shows the depth of ferment, on a personal level, in the white world. People are feverishly, and at great psychic and social expense, seeking *fundamental and irrevocable liberation*—and, what is more important, *are succeeding in escaping*—from the big white lies that compose the monolithic myth of White Supremacy/Black Inferiority, in a desperate attempt on the part of a new generation of white Americans to enter into the cosmopolitan egalitarian spirit of the twentieth century. But let us examine the reasoning that lies behind Baldwin's attack on Mailer.

There is in James Baldwin's work the most grueling, agonizing, total hatred of the blacks, particularly of himself, and the most shameful, fanatical, fawning, sycophantic love of the whites that one can find in the writings of any black American writer of note in our time. This is an appalling contradiction and the implications of it are vast.

A rereading of *Nobody Knows My Name* cannot help but convince the most avid of Baldwin's admirers of the hatred for blacks permeating his writings. In the essay "Princes and Powers," Baldwin's antipathy toward the black race is shockingly clear. The essay is Baldwin's interpretation of the Conference of Black Writers and Artists which met in Paris in September 1956. The portrait of Baldwin that comes through his words is that of a mind in unrelenting opposition to the efforts of solemn, dedicated black men who have undertaken the enormous task of rejuvenating and reclaiming the shattered psyches and culture of the black people, a people scattered over the continents of the world and the islands of the seas, where they exist in the mud of the floor of the foul dungeon into which the world has been transformed by the whites.

In his report of the conference, Baldwin, the reluctant black, dragging his feet at every step, could only ridicule the vision and efforts of these great men and heap scorn upon them, reserving his compliments—all of them left-handed—for the speakers at the conference who were themselves rejected and booed by the other conferees because of their reactionary, sycophantic views. Baldwin felt called upon to pop his cap pistol in a duel with Aimé Césaire, the big gun from Martinique. Indirectly, Baldwin was defending his first love—the white man. But the revulsion which Baldwin felt for the blacks at this conference, who were glorying in their blackness, seeking and showing their pride in Negritude and the African Personality, drives him to self-revealing sortie after sortie, so obvious in "Princes and Powers." Each successive sortie, however, becomes more expensive than the last one, because to score each time he has to go a little farther out on the limb, and it takes him a little longer each time to hustle back to the cover and camouflage of the perfumed smoke screen of his prose. Now and then we catch a glimpse of his little jive ass—his big eyes peering back over his shoulder in the mischievous retreat of a child sneak-thief from a cookie jar.

In the autobiographical notes of *Notes of a Native Son*, Baldwin is frank to confess that, in growing into his version of manhood in Harlem, he discovered that, since his African heritage had been wiped out and was not accessible to him, he would appropriate the white man's heritage and make it his own. This terrible reality, central to the psychic stance of all American Negroes, revealed to Baldwin that he hated and feared white people. Then he says: "This did not mean that I loved black people; on the contrary, I despised them, possibly because they failed to produce Rembrandt." The psychic distance between love and hate could be the mechanical difference between a smile and a sneer, or it could be the journey of a nervous impulse from the depths of one's brain to the tip of one's toe. But this impulse in its path through North American nerves may, if it is honest, find the passage disputed: may find the leap from the fiber of hate to that of love too taxing on its meager store of energy—and so the long trip back may never be completed, may end in a reconnaissance, a compromise, and then a lie.

Self-hatred takes many forms; sometimes it can be detected by no one, not by the keenest observer, not by the self-hater himself, not by his most intimate friends. Ethnic self-hate is even more difficult to detect. But in American Negroes, this ethnic self-hatred often takes the bizarre form of a racial death-wish, with many and elusive manifestations. Ironically, it provides much of the impetus behind the motivations of integration. And the attempt to suppress or deny such drives in one's psyche leads many American Negroes to become ostentatious separationists, Black Muslims, and back-to-Africa advocates. It is no wonder that Elijah Muhammad could conceive of the process of controlling evolution whereby the white race was brought into being. According to Elijah, about 6300 years ago all the people of the earth were Original Blacks. Secluded on the island of Patmos, a mad black scientist by the name of Yacub set up the machinery for grafting whites out of blacks through the operation of a birth-control system. The population on this island of Patmos was 59,999 and whenever a couple on this island wanted to get married they were only allowed to do so if there was a difference in their color, so that by mating black with those in the population of a brownish color and brown with brown—but never black with black—all traces of the black were eventually eliminated; the process was repeated until all the brown was eliminated, leaving only men of the red race; the red was bleached out, leaving only yellow; then the yellow was bleached out, and only white was left. Thus Yacub, who was long since dead, because this whole process took hundreds of years, had finally succeeded in creating the white devil with the blue eyes of death.

This myth of the creation of the white race, called "Yacub's History," is an inversion of the racial death-wish of American Negroes. Yacub's plan is still being followed by many Negroes today. Quite simply, many Negroes believe, as the principle of assimilation into white America implies, that the race problem in America cannot be settled until all traces of the black race are eliminated. Toward this end, many Negroes loathe the very idea of two very dark Negroes mating. The children, they say, will come out ugly. What they mean is that the children are sure to be black, and this is not desirable. From the widespread use of cosmetics to bleach the black out of one's skin and other concoctions to take Africa out of one's hair, to the extreme, resorted to by more Negroes than one might wish to believe, of undergoing nose-thinning and lip-clipping operations, the racial death-wish of American Negroes—Yacub's goal—takes its terrible toll. What has been happening for the past four hundred years is that the white man, through his access to black women, has been pumping his blood and genes into the blacks, has been diluting the blood and genes of the blacks—i.e., has been fulfilling Yacub's plan and accelerating the Negroes' racial death-wish.

The case of James Baldwin aside for a moment, it seems that many Negro homosexuals, acquiescing in this racial death-wish, are outraged and frustrated because in their sickness they are unable to have a baby by a white man. The cross they have to bear is that, already bending over and touching their toes for the white man, the fruit of their miscegenation is not the little half-white offspring of their dreams but an increase in the unwinding of their nerves—though they redouble their efforts and intake of the white man's sperm.

In this land of dichotomies and disunited opposites, those truly concerned with the resurrection of black Americans have had eternally to deal with black intellectuals who have become their own opposites, taking on all of the behavior patterns of their enemy, vices and virtues, in an effort to aspire to alien standards in all respects. The gulf between an audacious, bootlicking Uncle Tom and an intellectual buckdancer is filled only with sophistication and style. On second thought, Uncle Tom comes off much cleaner here because usually he is just trying to survive, choosing to pretend to be something other than his true self in order to please the white man and thus receive favors. Whereas the intellectual sycophant does not pretend to be other than he actually is, but hates what he is and seeks to redefine himself in the image of his white idols. He becomes a white man in a black body. A self-willed, automated slave, he becomes the white man's most valuable tool in oppressing other blacks.

The black homosexual, when his twist has a racial nexus, is an extreme embodiment of this contradiction. The white man has deprived him of his masculinity, castrated him in the center of his burning skull, and when he submits to this change and takes the white man for his lover as well as Big Daddy, he focuses on "whiteness" all the love in his pent up soul and turns the razor edge of hatred against "blackness"—upon himself, what he is, and all those who look like him, remind him of himself. He may even hate the darkness of night.

The racial death-wish is manifested as the driving force in James Baldwin. His hatred for blacks, even as he pleads what he conceives as their cause, makes him the apotheosis of the dilemma in the ethos of the black bourgeoisie who have completely rejected their African heritage, consider the loss irrevocable, and refuse to look again in that direction. This is the root of Baldwin's violent repudiation of Mailer's *The White Negro*.

To understand what is at stake here, and to understand it in terms of the life of this nation, is to know the central fact that the relationship between black and white in America is a power equation, a power struggle, and that this power struggle is not only manifested in the aggregate (civil rights, black nationalism, etc.) but also in the interpersonal relationships, actions, and reactions between blacks and whites where taken into account. When those "two lean cats," Baldwin and Mailer, met in a French living room, it was precisely this power equation that was at work.

It is fascinating to read (in *Nobody Knows My Name*) in what terms this power equation was manifested in Baldwin's immediate reaction to that meeting: "And here we were, suddenly, circling around each other. We liked each other at once, but each was frightened that the other would pull rank. He could have pulled rank on me because he was more famous and *had more money* and also *because he was white;* but I could have pulled rank on him precisely because I was black and knew more about that periphery he so helplessly maligns in *The White Negro* than he could ever hope to know." [Italics added.]

Pulling rank, it would seem, is a very dangerous business, especially when the troops have mutinied and the basis of one's authority, or rank, is devoid of that interdictive power and has become suspect. One would think that for Baldwin, of all people, these hues of black and white were no longer armed with the power to intimidate—and if one thought this, one would be exceedingly wrong: for behind the structure of the thought of Baldwin's quoted above, there lurks the imp of Baldwin's unwinding, of his tension between love and hate—love of the white and hate of the black. And when we dig into this tension we will find that when those "two lean cats" crossed tracks in that French living room, one was a Pussy Cat, the other a Tiger. Baldwin's purr was transmitted magnificently in *The Fire Next Time.* But his work is the fruit of a tree with a poison root. Such succulent fruit, such a painful tree, what a malignant root!

It is ironic, but fascinating for what it reveals about the ferment in the North American soul in our time, that Norman Mailer, the white boy, and James Baldwin, the black boy, encountered each other in the eye of a social storm, traveling in opposite directions; the white boy, with knowledge of white Negroes, was traveling toward a confrontation with the black, with Africa; while the black boy, with a white mind, was on his way to Europe. Baldwin's nose, like the north-seeking needle on a compass, is forever pointed toward his adopted fatherland, Europe, his by intellectual osmosis and in Africa's stead. What he says of Aimé Césaire, one of the greatest black writers of the twentieth century, and intending it as an ironic rebuke, that "he had penetrated into the heart of the great wilderness which was Europe and stolen the sacred fire . . . which . . . was . . . the assurance of his power," seems only too clearly to speak more about Peter than it does about Paul. What Baldwin seems to forget is that Césaire explains that fire, whether sacred or profane, burns. In Baldwin's case, though the fire could not burn the black off his face, it certainly did burn it out of his heart.

I am not interested in denying anything to Baldwin. I, like the entire nation, owe a great debt to him. But throughout the range of his work, from *Go Tell It on the Mountain,* through *Notes of a Native Son, Nobody Knows My Name, Another Country,* to *The Fire Next Time,* all of which I treasure, there is a decisive quirk in Baldwin's vision which corresponds to his relationship to black people and to masculinity. It was this same quirk, in my opinion, that compelled Baldwin to slander Rufus Scott in *Another Country,* venerate André Gide, repudiate *The White Negro,* and drive the blade of Brutus into the corpse of Richard Wright. As Baldwin has said in *Nobody Knows My Name,*

"I think that I know something about the American masculinity which most men of my generation do not know because they have not been menaced by it in the way I have been." O.K., Sugar, but isn't it true that Rufus Scott, the weak, craven-hearted ghost of *Another Country,* bears the same relation to Bigger Thomas of *Native Son,* the black rebel of the ghetto and a man, as you yourself bore to the fallen giant, Richard Wright, a rebel and a man?

Somewhere in one of his books, Richard Wright describes an encounter between a ghost and several young Negroes. The young Negroes rejected the homosexual, and this was Wright alluding to a classic, if cruel, example of a ubiquitous phenomenon in the black ghettos of America: the practice by Negro youths of going "punk-hunting." This practice of seeking out homosexuals on the prowl, rolling them, beating them up, seemingly just to satisfy some savage impulse to inflict pain on the specific target selected, the "social outcast," seems to me to be not unrelated, in terms of the psychological mechanisms involved, to the ritualistic lynchings and castrations inflicted on Southern blacks by Southern whites. This was, as I recall, one of Wright's few comments on the subject of homosexuality.

I think it can safely be said that the men in Wright's books, albeit shackled with a form of impotence, were strongly heterosexual. Their heterosexuality was implied rather than laboriously stated or emphasized; it was taken for granted, as we all take men until something occurs to make us know otherwise. And Bigger Thomas, Wright's greatest creation, was a man in violent, though inept, rebellion against the stifling, murderous, totalitarian white world. There was no trace in Bigger of a Martin Luther King-type self-effacing love for his oppressors. For example, Bigger would have been completely baffled, as most Negroes are today, at Baldwin's advice to his nephew (*The Fire Next Time*), concerning white people: "You must accept them *and accept them with love.* For these innocent people have no other hope." [Italics added.]

Rufus Scott, a pathetic wretch who indulged in the white man's pastime of committing suicide, who let a white bisexual homosexual fuck him in his ass, and who took a Southern Jezebel for his woman, with all that these tortured relationships imply, was the epitome of a black eunuch who has completely submitted to the white man. Yes, Rufus was a psychological freedom rider, turning the ultimate cheek, murmuring like a ghost, *"You took the best so why not take the rest,"* which has absolutely nothing to do with the way Negroes have managed to survive here in the hells of North America! This all becomes very clear from what we learn of Erich, the arch-ghost of *Another Country,* of the depths of his alienation from his body and the source of his need:

And it had taken him almost until this very moment, on the eve of his departure, to begin to recognize that part of Rufus' great power over him had to do with the past which Erich had buried in some deep, dark place; was connected with himself, in Alabama, *when I wasn't nothing but a child;* with the cold white people and the warm black people, warm at least for him. . . .

So, too, who cannot wonder at the source of such audacious madness as moved Baldwin to make this startling remark about Richard Wright, in his ignoble essay "Alas, Poor Richard": "In my own relations with him, I was always exasperated by his notions of society, politics, and history, for they seemed to me utterly fanciful. I never believed that he had any real sense of how a society is put together."

Richard Wright is dead and Baldwin is alive and with us. Baldwin says that Richard Wright held notions that were utterly fanciful, and Baldwin is an honorable man.

> *"O judgment; thou art fled to*
> *brutish beasts,*
> *And men have lost their reason!"*

Wright has no need, as Caesar did, of an outraged Antony to plead his cause: his life and his work are his shield against the mellow thrust of Brutus' blade. The good that he did, unlike Caesar's, will not be interred with his bones. It is, on the contrary, only the living who can be harmed by Brutus.

Baldwin says that in Wright's writings violence sits enthroned where sex should be. If this is so, then it is only because in the North American reality hate holds sway in love's true province. And it is only through a rank perversion that the artist, whose duty is to tell us the truth, can turn the two-dollar trick of wedding violence to love and sex to hate—if, to achieve this end, one has basely to transmute rebellion into lamblike submission—*"You took the best,"* sniveled Rufus, *"so why not take the rest?"* Richard Wright was not ghost enough to achieve this cruel distortion. With him, sex, being not a spectator sport or a panacea but the sacred vehicle of life and love, is itself sacred. And the America which Wright knew and which *is,* is not the Garden of Eden but its opposite. Baldwin, embodying in his art the self-flagellating policy of Martin Luther King, and giving out falsely the news that the Day of the Ghost has arrived, pulled it off in *Another Country.*

Of all black American novelists, and indeed of all American novelists of any hue, Richard Wright reigns supreme for his profound political, economic, and social reference. Wright had the ability, like Dreiser, of harnessing the gigantic, overwhelming environmental forces and focusing them, with pinpoint sharpness, on individuals and their acts as they are caught up in the whirlwind of the savage, anarchistic sweep of life, love, death, and hate, pain, hope, pleasure, and despair across the face of a nation and the world. But, ah! "O masters," it is Baldwin's work which is so void of a political, economic, or even a social reference. His characters all seem to be fucking and sucking in a vacuum. Baldwin has a superb touch when he speaks of human beings, when he is inside of them—especially his homosexuals—but he flounders when he looks beyond the skin; whereas Wright's forte, it seems to me, was in reflecting the intricate mechanisms of a social organization, its functioning as a unit.

Baldwin's essay on Richard Wright reveals that he despised—not Richard Wright, but his masculinity. He cannot confront the stud in others—except that he must either submit to it or destroy it. And he was not about to bow to a *black* man. Wright understood and lived the truth of what Norman Mailer meant when he said ". . . for being a man is the continuing battle of one's life, and one loses a bit of manhood with every stale compromise to the authority of any power in which one does not believe." Baldwin, compromised beyond getting back by the white man's *power,* which is real and which has nothing to do with *authority,* but to which Baldwin has ultimately succumbed psychologically, is totally unable to extricate himself from that horrible pain. It is the scourge of his art, because the only way out for him is psychologically to embrace Africa, the land of his fathers, which he utterly refuses to do. He has instead resorted to a despicable underground guerrilla war, waged on paper, against black masculinity, playing out the racial death-wish of Yacub, reaching, I think, a point where Mailer hits the spot: "Driven into defiance, it is natural if regrettable, that many homosexuals go to the direction of assuming that there is something intrinsically superior in homosexuality, and carried far enough it is a viewpoint which is as stultifying, as ridiculous, and as anti-human as the heterosexual's prejudice."

I, for one, do not think homosexuality is the latest advance over heterosexuality on the scale of human evolution. Homosexuality is a sickness, just as are baby-rape or wanting to become the head of General Motors.

A grave danger faces this nation, of which we are as yet unaware. And it is precisely this danger which Baldwin's work conceals; indeed, leads us away from. We are engaged in the deepest, the most fundamental revolution and reconstruction which men have ever been called upon to make in their lives, and which they absolutely cannot escape or avoid except at the peril of the very continued existence of human life on this planet. The time of the sham is over, and the cheek of the suffering saint must no longer be turned twice to the brute. The titillation of the guilt complexes of bored white liberals leads to doom. The grotesque hideousness of what is happening to us is reflected in this remark by Murray Kempton, quoted in *The Realist:* "When I was a boy Stepin Fetchit was the only Negro actor who worked regularly in the movies. . . . The fashion changes, but I sometimes think that Malcolm X and, to a degree even James Baldwin, are *our* Stepin Fetchits."

Yes, the fashion does change. "Will the machinegunners please step forward," said LeRoi Jones in a poem. "The machine gun on the corner," wrote Richard Wright, "is the symbol of the twentieth century." The embryonic spirit of kamikaze, real and alive, grows each day in the black man's heart and there are dreams of Nat Turner's legacy. The ghost of John Brown is creeping through suburbia. And I wonder if James Chaney said, as Andrew Goodman and Michael Schwerner stood helplessly watching, as the grizzly dogs crushed his bones with savage blows of chains—did poor James say, after Rufus Scott—"*You took the best, so why not take the rest?*" Or did he turn to his white brothers, seeing their plight, and say, after Baldwin, "That's your problem, baby!"

I say, after Mailer, "There's a shit-storm coming."

PART FIVE: APPENDICES

Chronology: Richard Wright (1908–1960)

THE ONLY BIOGRAPHY OF WRIGHT TO APPEAR THUS FAR IS CONSTANCE Webb's *Richard Wright: A Biography* (1968). The primary source of information about Wright's early years is his classic autobiography, *Black Boy,* which covers his life up to his departure for Chicago in 1927. Wright described his early experiences in Chicago in "The Man Who Went to Chicago," included in his volume of stories *Eight Men.* He contributed numerous pieces—many of them containing biographical information—to newspapers, journals, and books. Besides those reprinted in this volume, the most important is the account of his experiences as a member of the Communist party, published in the *Atlantic Monthly* (August and September 1944) under the title "I Tried to Be a Communist" and reprinted in Richard Crossman's *The God That Failed* (1949).

1908 Wright was born September 4 on a farm near Natchez, Mississippi, to Nathaniel Wright, an illiterate sharecropper, and Ella Wright, a country schoolteacher.

1912 Wright accidentally set fire to his grandmother's home, for which he was beaten so severely by his mother that he lay seriously ill for several weeks. The fire and the beating he received because of it remained a vivid recollection throughout his life.

1914 Like thousands of other sharecroppers, Nathaniel Wright was forced off the land when the cotton exchanges closed and the price of cotton plummeted. Nathaniel moved the family to Memphis, Tennessee, and shortly thereafter deserted them, leaving Ella, Richard, and his younger brother Alan (born in 1910) destitute. Ella found work as a cook and the boys were left to shift for themselves. Wright began hanging around the neighborhood saloon, where patrons found it amusing to give him drinks. As a result, in Wright's words, "I was a drunkard in my sixth year, before I had begun school" (*Black Boy*).

1916–1918 Wright entered Howard Institute, a grammar school, for his first formal education, although Ella had by this time taught him to read. But school had hardly begun when Ella fell ill and Wright had to drop out of school to care for her. Unable to find work after recovering from her illness, Ella was forced to place the boys in an orphanage. After six weeks, Ella and the boys went to live with her sister in Elaine, Arkansas. There, for the first time in his life, Richard had enough food to eat. This happy interlude ended abruptly in terrifying flight when the uncle was murdered for refusing to sell his profitable saloon to whites. After a brief stay in West Helena, Arkansas, the Wrights went to live with Ella's mother in Jackson, Mississippi. The grandmother's insistence that everyone in her home observe the strict religious routine of Seventh Day Adventism made life so difficult that Ella and her widowed sister Maggie finally moved back to West Helena, where Wright once again entered school. During this period, Wright received his second memorable beating from his mother, this time for fighting with white boys. After his mother suffered a paralytic stroke, Wright was sent to live with an uncle in Greenwood, Mississippi, and his brother to Detroit to live with Aunt Maggie, while Ella returned to her mother's home to be cared for. After a few unhappy months in Greenwood, Wright rejoined his mother in Jackson.

1920–1921 In September, Wright was enrolled in the Seventh Day Adventist school in near-by Huntsville where one of his aunts was a teacher (at this point he had not yet had a full year's schooling). After a year of contending with the hostility of his severely religious aunt, Wright refused to attend the school any longer. The following year he was transferred to the Jim Hill Public School, where he was placed in the fifth grade. After two weeks of diligent study, he was promoted to the sixth grade and quickly distinguished himself as an extraordinarily bright and eager student. The tension he felt in his grandmother's house and his growing sense of alienation from his family were exacerbated by his grandmother's refusal to allow him to work on Saturday, the Adventist Sabbath, even though there was never enough food in the house and Wright suffered constantly from gnawing hunger. The issue was finally resolved shortly after Wright began the seventh grade, when his grandmother yielded to his threat that either he be allowed to work on Saturdays or he would leave home.

1923–1924 Wright entered the Smith-Robertson Public School. His brilliance soon brought him to the attention of the principal, who encouraged him to consider going on to college. In 1924 (exact date of publication is unknown), the editor of the Jackson, Mississippi, *Southern Register,* a Negro newspaper, printed Wright's first story, "The Voodoo of Hell's Half Acre," and gave the young writer his first encouragement. The editor offered Wright a summer job as news collector, but he had to turn it down because the pay was uncertain and the family was counting on his summer income.

1925 Wright graduated from Smith-Robertson on May 29 as class valedictorian. He worked at a variety of odd jobs, but as his realization grew that he could not possibly continue his education and that his inability to play the role of a humble nigger might well result in his death, he determined to save enough money to leave Jackson and the South. The impossibility of saving enough money from his meager earnings for train fare led Wright to stealing. By the end of the year, he had enough money for a ticket to Memphis, Tennessee, where he arrived in November.

1926 After a short period as dishwasher, Wright went to work for the American Optical Company and was able to save enough money to send for his mother and brother. In the course of his wide reading, he discovered H. L. Mencken, whose writings showed Wright that one could fight with words and introduced him to the names of many great contemporary writers. His creative impulses were stirred by his reading, especially of novelists like Sinclair Lewis and Theodore Dreiser. Of this period, Wright later wrote: "All my life had shaped me for the realism, the naturalism of the modern novel, and I could not read enough of them" (*Black Boy*). Getting books was the most difficult problem Wright faced, since the Memphis library could not be used by black men. With the help of a sympathetic white co-worker, however, Wright began checking out books on the pretext that he was borrowing them for the white man.

1927–1928 In December 1927, Wright moved to Chicago, where his mother and brother joined him somewhat later. After working as a helper in a grocery store and as a waiter, Wright passed a Civil Service examination for postal clerk. He worked nights at the post office and spent his days reading and writing.

1929–1930 As a result of the stock market crash, the volume of mail dropped so low that Wright lost his job. After weeks of unsuccessful searching, he found work with a Negro burial society as an insurance agent, a job that took him into the homes of many poor blacks. The ignorance and abject poverty he witnessed daily kept him in a state of nervous exhaustion that became even more severe when he learned that the burial society was defrauding its clients.

1931 The job with the burial society gave out and Wright went on relief. His caseworker, Mary Wirth, became interested in him and sent him to see her husband, Dr. Louis Wirth, the famous University of Chicago sociologist. Through the Wirths, Wright got a job as an orderly in the Michael Reese Hospital; when this job ended, he was assigned by the relief office to the South Side Boys' Club, where he came to know and understand the ghetto youths. He was then transferred to a job as publicity agent for the Federal Negro Theatre (a WPA project) and later to the Illinois Writers' Project for his first assignment as a professional writer. Wright's second story, "Superstition," was published in the April issue of *Abbot's Monthly Magazine.*

1932 Wright began attending meetings of the John Reed Club, a club organized by the Communists to foster new literary talent in the service of revolution. Through the John Reed Club, Wright began publishing stories, poems, and essays in *New Masses, Left Front,* and other left-wing journals sponsored by the John Reed Club. Wright joined the Communist party because "here at last," he explained, "in the realm of revolutionary expression, Negro experiences could find a home, a functioning value, and role" ("I Tried to Be a Communist").

1933–1936 Wright worked assiduously for the John Reed Club and was elected its executive secretary. He wrote steadily but during this period began to experience difficulties with party leaders and discipline that were ultimately to lead to his break with the party. His article "Joe Louis Uncovers Dynamite" (*New Masses,* October 8, 1935), a political interpretation of the Joe Louis–Max Baer fight, brought him to the favorable attention of the highest party leaders, who decided that his talents could be better used in organizing activities on the South Side. Wright protested that this would leave him too little time to write, but he submitted to party discipline. Despite organizing activities, Wright finished a story, "Big Boy Leaves Home," which was published in 1936 in *New Caravan,* an anthology of Negro writing.

1937 In May, Wright moved to New York to assume the position of Harlem editor of the *Daily Worker.* Shortly after his arrival in New York, the party appointed him associate editor of *New Challenge,* a short-lived Negro literary quarterly. During this year, his short story "Fire and Cloud" won the *Story Magazine* prize, and "The Ethics of Living Jim Crow" was published in the WPA writers' anthology, *American Stuff.* A well-known writer by this time, Wright was sought out by the young Ralph Ellison for advice and encouragement.

1938 Wright continued working and writing for the Communist party. He began seeing two white women—Ellen Poplar, an organizer for the Party, and Rose Dhima Meadman, a modern dancer. Wright published *Uncle Tom's Children: Four Novellas,* which won the $500 *Story Magazine* prize for the best work from the Federal Writers' Project.

1939 Wright received a Guggenheim Fellowship, which gave him the freedom to complete *Native Son.* "Bright and Morning Star," published the previous year in *New Masses,* was selected by the eminent anthologist Edward O'Brien as one of the two best short stories of the year and as one of the fifty best short stories published in America since 1915. Wright married Rose Dhima Meadman.

1940 Wright published *Native Son,* which received immediate critical and popular acclaim (it was the March selection of the Book-of-the-Month Club). Distressed by the growing tension in America over the international scene, Wright and his wife moved to Cuernavaca, Mexico. Restless and dissatisfied with life in Mexico after a few months, and increasingly estranged from his wife, Wright returned alone to New York, stopping in Jackson and Natchez, Mississippi, and Memphis, Tennessee, to renew old feelings preparatory to writing his autobiography. In Mississippi, he visited his family and saw his father, who had returned to Natchez and resumed sharecropping. Of this meeting, Wright wrote, "When I tried to talk to him I realized that, though ties of blood made us kin, though I could see a shadow of my face in his face, though there was an echo of my voice in his voice, we were forever strangers, speaking a different language, living on vastly different planes of reality" (*Black Boy*).

1941 In New York, Wright resumed his friendship with Ellen Poplar, whom he married on March 12 despite the objection of Ellen's parents to her marrying a Negro. With Paul Green, Wright wrote a dramatic version of *Native Son* that was produced on Broadway by Orson Welles's Mercury Theater. Wright received the Spingarn Medal, awarded annually to an outstanding Negro by the National Association for the Advancement of Colored People.

1942–1944 Wright's daughter Julia was born in 1942. After years of strained relations, Wright quit the Communist party in 1944. The immediate cause was his disillusionment when the party turned away from the Negro question to devote all its energies to supporting the war against the fascists.

1945 Early in the year, Wright published *Black Boy,* an autobiography covering the first nineteen years of his life. Like *Native Son,* the book was selected by the Book-of-the-Month Club and instantly achieved enormous popularity. Wright met the aspiring young writer James Baldwin, who called at the home of the older writer for advice and encouragement.

1946 Wright bought a home in Greenwich Village, an attorney friend acting as a front because the owner would not sell to Negroes. In April, Wright received an invitation to visit France for three months as a guest of the French government. After unaccountable delays in receiving a passport (Wright was convinced the State Department did not want him to leave the country because he had written so critically of the U.S.), Wright completed arrangements and sailed for France, arriving in May. In France, Wright felt the burden of his race drop from him and knew for the first time what it was to be a free man. After some months in France, during which time he became a close friend of Gertrude Stein and made arrangements for foreign editions of his work, Wright decided to return to the United States.

1947 Wright stopped off in London, where he met George Padmore, an ex-Communist member of the African Bureau, an organization working on behalf of Pan-Africanism. Shortly after returning to his Greenwich Village home, however, Wright became discouraged with the treatment of black men in America, especially as he thought of what his young daughter would have to face. In the middle of the year, he sold his house and by August was again in France, determined that he would not live in America again. He established himself in Paris and quickly was accepted into Parisian intellectual and artistic circles, becoming a close friend of the existentialist Jean-Paul Sartre and Simone de Beauvoir. In the uncertain atmosphere of postwar Europe, with the fierce jockeying for power between the left and the right, Wright concluded in disillusionment that the two great powers, Russia and America, were moving in the same direction. Wright grew increasingly interested in Africa and the Third World, and he helped Alioune Diop, the Senegalese intellectual, found *Presence Africaine*, a journal devoted to the values and causes of black men everywhere.

1949 Wright's second daughter, Rachel, was born on January 17. Toward the end of the year, Wright signed a contract with Argentina Sono Film to do a screen version of *Native Son,* with Wright writing the shooting script and playing the leading role of Bigger Thomas. By August, Wright had concluded business arrangements for the film in New York and went to Chicago to film the exterior shots. He was shocked and dismayed that the South Side had changed so little since he had left (Wright described his reactions in an essay, "The Shame of Chicago," published in the December 1951 issue of *Ebony* magazine). Wright and the film company arrived in Buenos Aires in November to begin filming.

1950 Wright spent most of the year in Buenos Aires working on the film, returning to Paris in August. In spite of the severe editing unilaterally undertaken by the American distributor of the film (which Wright felt was done out of political fear) and the poor reviews in America, the film received great praise in Europe.

1951–1952 Wright wrote a few essays for French journals but spent most of his time working on two novels, *The Outsider* and *Savage Holiday.*

1953 Wright published *The Outsider,* which was poorly received in America but highly praised in Europe. Through George Padmore, Wright received an invitation from Kwame Nkhrumah to visit the Gold Coast (which four years later became Ghana). Wright's growing interest in Africa as a potential third force in the world, as well as his curiosity about the land of his ancestors and his personal relationship to it, made the offer irresistible. With an advance from his publisher for a book to be based on his visit, Wright sailed for Africa, arriving in June. He traveled extensively in the Gold Coast for three months, impressed both by the social and political awakening occurring in Africa and by the discovery that he was much more a Westerner than an African.

1954 Wright published *Black Power: A Record of Reactions in a Land of Pathos,* based on his travels in the Gold Coast. He also published a novel with all white characters, *Savage Holiday,* as a paperback original. During three visits, Wright spent almost three months in Spain, gathering material for a book.

1955 Wright bought an old farm near Ailly in Normandy in order to have a quiet place to write whenever he wished to escape the interruptions of Paris life. He traveled to Jakarta and Bandung, Indonesia, to attend a conference on Asian-African problems.

1956 Wright published *The Color Curtain: A Report on the Bandung Conference* and *Pagan Spain,* a book based on his visits to Spain. To ease financial problems, he made a lecture tour to Germany, Switzerland, Norway, Denmark, and Sweden.

1957 Wright published *White Man, Listen!,* a collection of the lectures he had written for the tour of the preceding year. He spent a good deal of time at his farm in Ailly working on a new novel, *The Long Dream.*

1958 Wright published *The Long Dream,* the story of a young Mississippi black who is forced to leave his home town or face murder at the hands of white men. The novel was generally attacked by American reviewers on the grounds that Wright had lost touch with America and had greatly exaggerated the plight of black people.

1959 Wright received a visit from Dr. Martin Luther King. Julia graduated with honors from the Sorbonne and was accepted as a student by both Oxford and Cambridge. With Julia going to England and the political situation in France extremely unstable, Wright sold his farm in Ailly and moved to London, with the intention of settling there permanently. For reasons never disclosed, even when the issue was raised in Parliament, the British government refused to issue Wright a permanent visa. Leaving his family in London, Wright returned to Paris.

1960 A dramatic version of *The Long Dream* ran briefly on Broadway. Wright became interested in Japanese haiku and wrote a great number of these poems, with the intention of eventually publishing a book. In

September, Julia visited her father in Paris and decided to give up Cambridge to remain with him. Wright's health began to decline, and he became seriously ill in November. Wright died on November 28 of a heart attack. His body was cremated and the ashes buried in the *Cimitier Du Pere Lachaise* in Paris.

Bibliography

The following bibliography is confined, with few exceptions, to American publications. I have attempted to be inclusive in listing books and articles on Richard Wright and periodical essays devoted to *Native Son.* The section on reviews includes all major periodical and newspaper reviews. Scores of books mention Wright briefly or in passing; the section on books that include discussions of Wright is limited to works that deal with him at some length. Significant discussion of Wright and of the tradition of black literature is the criterion I have used in compiling the section on essays including discussions of Richard Wright.

The December 1968 issue of the *Negro Digest* and the June 1969 issue of the *CLA Journal* are special Richard Wright numbers; the essays from these issues are listed separately under the authors' names in the appropriate sections. An annotated list of critical material on Wright, including reviews of all Wright's books, is to be found in Jackson R. Bryer's "Richard Wright (1908–1960): A Selected Checklist of Criticism," *Wisconsin Studies in Contemporary Literature,* I (Fall 1960), 22–33. A comprehensive bibliography of Wright's writings, including his contributions to books and foreign periodicals, is available in Michel Fabré and Edward Margolies' "Richard Wright (1908–1960): A Bibliography," *Bulletin of Bibliography,* XXIV (January–April 1965), 131–133, 137 (reprinted in Constance Webb's *Richard Wright: A Biography* and in the December 1968 *Negro Digest*).

BOOKS ABOUT RICHARD WRIGHT

Bone, Robert. *Richard Wright.* Minneapolis: University of Minnesota Press, 1969.

Brignano, Russell Carl. *Richard Wright: An Introduction to the Man and His Works.* Pittsburgh: University of Pittsburgh Press, 1970.

Margolies, Edward. *The Art of Richard Wright.* Carbondale: Southern Illinois University Press, 1969.

McCall, Dan. *The Example of Richard Wright.* New York: Harcourt, Brace & World, 1969.

Webb, Constance. *Richard Wright: A Biography.* New York: G. P. Putnam's Sons, 1968.

BOOKS INCLUDING DISCUSSIONS OF RICHARD WRIGHT

Barton, Rebecca Chalmers. *Witnesses for Freedom: Negro Americans in Autobiography.* New York: Harper & Brothers, 1948. Pp. 254–268.

Blake, Nelson Manfred. *Novelists' America: Fiction as History, 1910–1940.* New York: Syracuse University Press, 1969. Pp. 226–253.

Bone, Robert. *The Negro Novel in America.* Revised edition. New Haven, Conn.: Yale University Press, 1965. Pp. 140–152.

Cruse, Harold. *The Crisis of the Negro Intellectual.* New York: William Morrow & Company, 1967. Pp. 181–189.

Embree, Edwin R. *Thirteen Against the Odds.* New York: Kennikat Press, 1944. Pp. 25–46.

Gloster, Hugh M. *Negro Voices in American Fiction.* New York: Russell & Russell, 1948. Pp. 222–234.

Hughes, Carl Milton. *The Negro Novelist.* New York: Citadel Press, 1953. Pp. 197–206.

Littlejohn, David. *Black on White: A Critical Survey of Writing by American Negroes.* New York: Grossman Publishers, 1966. Pp. 102–110.

Slochower, Harry. *No Voice Is Wholly Lost.* London: Denis Dobson Limited, 1946. Pp. 84–88.

Weitz, Morris. *Philosophy of the Arts.* New York: Russell & Russell, 1950. Pp. 137–141.

ESSAYS ON RICHARD WRIGHT

Algren, Nelson. "Remembering Richard Wright." *Nation,* CXCII (January 28, 1961), 85.

Baldwin, James. "Alas, Poor Richard." In *Nobody Knows My Name.* New York: Dial Press, 1961.

Berry, Faith. "On Richard Wright in Exile: Portrait of a Man as Outsider." *Negro Digest,* XVIII (December 1968), 27–37.

Breit, Harvey. "Wright You Are." *New York Times* (March 22, 1953), 8.

Brown, Cecil. "Richard Wright: Complexes and Black Writing Today." *Negro Digest,* XVIII (December 1968), 78–82.

Burns, Ben. "Return of the Native Son." *Ebony,* VII (December 1951), 100.

————. "They're Not Uncle Tom's Children." *Reporter,* XIV (March 8, 1956), 21–23.

Cayton, Horace. "The Curtain." *Negro Digest,* XVIII (December 1968), 11–15.

Charney, Maurice. "James Baldwin's Quarrel with Richard Wright." *American Quarterly,* XV (Spring 1963), 65–75.

Davis, Arthur P. "*The Outsider* as a Novel of Race." *Midwest Journal,* VII (Winter 1955–1956), 320–326.

Delpech, Jeanine. "An Interview with Native Son." *Crisis,* CVII (November 1950), 625–626, 678.

Faris, Kenneth. "A Small Portrait of Richard Wright." *Negro History Bulletin,* XXV (April 1962), 155–156.

Ford, Nick Aaron. "The Ordeal of Richard Wright." *College English,* XV (November 1953), 87–94.

————. "Richard Wright: A Profile." *Chicago Jewish Forum,* XXI (Fall 1962), 26–30.

Fuller, Hoyt. "On the Death of Richard Wright." *Southwest Review,* XLVI (Autumn 1961), vi–vii, 334–337.

————. Review-article of Dan McCall's *The Example of Richard Wright.* In *New York Times Book Review* (May 18, 1969), 8, 10.

Gayle, Addison, Jr. "Richard Wright: Beyond Nihilism." *Negro Digest,* XVIII (December 1968), 5–10.

Gibson, Donald B. "Richard Wright: A Bibliographical Essay." *CLA Journal,* XII (June 1969), 360–365.

————. "Richard Wright and the Tyranny of Convention." *CLA Journal,* XII (June 1969), 344–357.

Harrington, Ollie. "The Last Days of Richard Wright." *Ebony,* XVI (February 1961), 83–86, 88, 90, 92–94.

Hill, Herbert, ed. "Reflections on Richard Wright: A Symposium on an Exiled Native Son." In *Anger, and Beyond.* New York: Harper & Row, 1966. (Other participants are Arna Bontemps, Horace Cayton, and Saunders Redding.)

Hughes, Langston. "Richard Wright's Last Guest at Home." *Ebony,* XVI (February 1961), 94.

Isaacs, Harold. "Five Writers and Their African Ancestors." *Phylon,* XXI (Fall 1960), 254–273.

Jackson, Blyden. "Richard Wright: Black Boy from America's Black Belt and Urban Ghettos." *CLA Journal,* XII (June 1969), 287–309.

Kent, George E. "On the Future Study of Richard Wright." *CLA Journal,* XII (June 1969), 366–370.

————. "Richard Wright: Blackness and the Adventure of Western Culture." *CLA Journal,* XII (June 1969), 322–343.

Kinnamon, Keneth. "The Pastoral Impulse in Richard Wright." *Midcontinent American Studies Journal,* X (Spring 1969), 41–47.

Prescott, Orville. "The Power of Environment: Wright, Motley, Wolff, Betty Smith." In *In My Opinion: An Inquiry into the Contemporary Novel.* New York: Bobbs-Merrill Company, 1952.

Redding, Saunders. "The Alien Land of Richard Wright." In Herbert Hill, ed., *Soon, One Morning: New Writing by American Negroes, 1940–1952.* New York: Alfred A. Knopf, Inc., 1965.

Riesman, David. "Marginality, Conformity, and Insight." *Phylon,* XIV (Third Quarter 1953), 241–257.

Sanders, Ronald. "Richard Wright and the Sixties." *Midstream,* XIV (August–September 1968), 28–40.

Scott, Nathan A. "Search for Beliefs: Fiction of Richard Wright." *University of Kansas City Review,* XXIII (October 1956), 19–24.

————. "Search for Beliefs: Richard Wright." *University of Kansas City Review,* XXIII (December 1956), 129–138.

Smith, William Gardner. "Black Boy in France." *Ebony,* VIII (July 1953), 32–36, 39–42.

Turner, Darwin T. "The Outsider: Revision of an Idea." *CLA Journal,* XII (June 1969), 310–321.

Vogel, Albert W. "The Education of the Negro in Richard Wright's *Black Boy.*" *Journal of Negro History,* XXXV (Spring 1966), 195–198.

Webb, Constance. "What Next for Richard Wright?" *Phylon,* X (Second Quarter 1949), 161–166.

White, Ralph K. "*Black Boy:* A Value Analysis." *Journal of Abnormal and Social Psychology,* XLII (October 1947), 440–461.

Widmer, Kingsley. "The Existential Darkness of Richard Wright's *The Outsider.*" *Wisconsin Studies in Literature,* I (Fall 1960), 13–21.

Williams, John A. "On Wright, Wrong, and Black Reality." *Negro Digest,* XVIII (December 1968), 25.

ESSAYS INCLUDING DISCUSSIONS OF RICHARD WRIGHT

Baldwin, James. "Everybody's Protest Novel." *Partisan Review,* XVI (June 1949), 578–585. Reprinted in Baldwin's *Notes of a Native Son.* Boston: Beacon Press, 1955.

Ford, Nick Aaron. "Four Popular Negro Novelists." *Phylon,* XV (First Quarter 1954), 29–39.

Gayle, Addison, Jr. "A Defense of James Baldwin." *CLA Journal,* X (March 1967), 201–208.

———. "Cultural Nationalism: The Black Novel and the City." *Liberator,* IX (July 1969), 14–17.

Glicksberg, Charles I. "The Alienation of Negro Literature." *Phylon,* XI (First Quarter 1950), 49–58.

———. "The Furies in Negro Fiction." *Western Review,* XIII (Winter 1949), 107–114.

———. "Negro Fiction in America." *South Atlantic Quarterly,* XLV (October 1946), 478–488.

Green, Gerald. "Back to Bigger." *Kenyon Review,* XXVIII (September 1966), 521–539.

Gross, Theodore. "The Idealism of Negro Literature in America." *Phylon,* XXX (Spring 1969), 5–10.

Jackson, Esther Merle. "The American Negro and the Image of the Absurd." *Phylon,* XXIII (Winter 1962), 359–371.

Jarrett, Thomas. "Recent Fiction by Negroes." *College English,* XVI (November 1954), 85–91.

Lehan, Richard. "Existentialism in Recent American Fiction: The Demonic Quest." *Texas Studies in Literature and Language,* I (Summer 1959), 181–202.

Locke, Alain. "From Native Son to Invisible Man: A Review of the Literature of the Negro for 1952." *Phylon,* XIV (First Quarter 1953), 34–44.

Marcus, Steven. "The American Negro in Search of Identity." *Commentary,* XVI (November 1953), 456–463.

Maund, Alfred. "The Negro Novelist and the Contemporary Scene." *Chicago Jewish Forum,* XIII (Fall 1954), 28–34.

Mayfield, Julian. "And Then Came Baldwin." *Freedomways,* III (Spring 1963), 143–155.

Redding, J. Saunders. "American Negro Literature." *American Scholar,* XVIII (Spring 1949), 137–148.

———. "The Problems of the Negro Writer." *Massachusetts Review,* VI (Autumn–Winter 1964–1965), 57–70.

Scott, Nathan A. "Judgment Marked by a Cellar: The American Negro Writer and the Dialectic of Despair." *University of Denver Quarterly,* II (Summer 1967), 5–35.

REVIEWS OF *Native Son*

The reviewer's name is given in parentheses.

American Mercury, L (May 1940), 113–116. (Burton Rascoe)

Atlantic Monthly, CLXV (May 1940), 659-661. (David Cohn)

Book-of-the-Month Club News (February 1940), 2–3. (Henry Seidel Canby)

Boston Transcript (March 2, 1940), 1. (Howard Mumford Jones)

Canadian Forum, XX (May 1940), 60. (Marguerite Wyke)

Catholic World, CLI (May 1940), 243–244. (Reverend Joseph McSorley)

Chicago Defender (March 16, 1940), 22.

Chicago Tribune (March 6, 1940), 19. (Fanny Butcher)

Commonweal, XXXI (March 8, 1940), 438. (Edward Skillen, Jr.)

Crisis, XLVII (April 1940), 122. (James W. Ivy)

Des Moines Register (March 3, 1940), 9.

Interracial Review, XIII (April 1940), 64–65. (Theophilus Lewis)

Journal of Negro History, XXV (April 1940), 251–252. (J. D. Jerome)

Los Angeles Times (March 10, 1940), Section Three, 7. (Wilbur Needham)

Louisville Courier-Journal (March 10, 1940), Sunday Magazine, 7.

Memphis Commercial Appeal (March 10, 1940), Section Four, 10. (Jack Lockhart)

Nation, CL (March 16, 1940), 367–368. (Margaret Marshall)

New Bedford Standard Times (March 3, 1940), 19.

New Masses, XXXIV (March 5, 1940), 24–25. (Samuel Sillen)

———, XXXV (April 30, 1940), 13–21. (Samuel Sillen). Second part of a two-part review.

———, XXXV (April 23, 1940), 25–27. (Samuel Sillen). Analysis of the novel's reception by the press.

———, XXXV (May 21, 1940), 23–26. (Samuel Sillen). Comments by *New Masses* readers on the novel.

New Orleans Times-Picayune (March 3, 1940), Section Two, 9.

New Republic, CII (March 18, 1940), 382–383. (Malcolm Cowley)

New Statesman and Nation, XIX (April 20, 1940), 542. (Anthony West)
New York Herald Tribune Books (March 3, 1940), 5. (Milton Rugoff)
New York Sunday Worker (April 14, 1940), Section Two, 4, 6. (Ben Davis, Jr.)
New York Times (March 1, 1940), 19. (Charles Poore)
New York Times Book Review (March 3, 1940), 2, 20. (Peter Monro Jack)
New Yorker, XVI (March 2, 1940), 52–53. (Clifton Fadiman)
Opportunity, XVIII (June 1940), 185–186. (Sterling A. Brown)
Partisan Review, VII (May–June 1940), 245. (David Daiches)
Phylon, I (Second Quarter 1940), 195–197. (Joseph H. Jenkins, Jr.)
St. Louis Globe Democrat (March 9, 1940), 1B. (James E. Daugherty)
San Francisco Chronicle (March 11, 1940), 15. (Joseph Henry Jackson)
San Francisco People's World (April 2, 1940), 5. (Ben Burns)
Saturday Review of Literature, XXI (March 2, 1940), 5. (Jonathan Daniels)
Spectator, CLXIV (April 19, 1940), 574. (Rosamond Lehmann)
Time, XXXV (March 4, 1940), 72.
Times (London) *Literary Supplement* (April 27, 1940), 205.
Virginia Quarterly Review (Summer 1940), 462. (Wallace Stegner)
Washington, D.C. Star (March 3, 1940). Section Five, F-6.
Yale Review, XXIX (Summer 1940), x. (Robert Littell)
Introduction to first edition of *Native Son*. New York: Harper & Brothers, 1940. (Dorothy Canfield Fisher)

ESSAYS ON *Native Son*

Baldwin, James. "Many Thousands Gone." *Partisan Review*, XVIII (November–December 1951), 665–680. Reprinted in Baldwin's *Notes of a Native Son*. Boston: Beacon Press, 1955.
Burgum, Edwin Berry. "The Promise of Democracy in Richard Wright's *Native Son*." In *The Novel and the World's Dilemma*. New York: Russell & Russell, 1963. Published originally in 1947 by Oxford University Press.
Canby, Henry Seidel. "The Right Questions." *Saturday Review of Literature*, XXI (March 23, 1940), 8.
Creekmore, Hubert. "Social Factors in *Native Son*." *University Review*, VIII (Winter 1941), 136–143.
Ellison, Ralph. "The World and the Jug." *New Leader*, XLVI (December 9, 1963), 22–26. A considerably longer version of this essay, written as a rejoinder to Irving Howe's "Black Boys and Native Sons," is included in Ellison's *Shadow and Act*. New York: Random House, 1964.
Emanuel, James A. "Fever and Feeling: Notes on the Imagery of *Native Son*." *Negro Digest*, XVIII (December 1968), 16–26.

Howe, Irving. "Black Boys and Native Sons." In *A World More Attractive.* New York: Horizon Press, 1963.

————. "A Reply to Ralph Ellison." *New Leader,* XLVII (February 3, 1964), 12–14.

Kinnamon, Keneth. "*Native Son:* The Personal, Social, and Political Background." *Phylon,* XXX (Spring 1969), 66–72.

————. "Richard Wright's Use of *Othello* in *Native Son.*" *CLA Journal,* XII (June 1969), 358–359.

Lewis, Theophilus. "The Saga of Bigger Thomas." *Catholic World,* CLIII (May 1941), 201–206.

Margolies, Edward. "Richard Wright: *Native Son* and Three Kinds of Revolution." In *Native Sons: A Critical Study of Twentieth-Century Negro American Authors.* Philadelphia: J. B. Lippincott Company, 1968.

Owens, William A. Introduction to *Native Son.* New York: Harper's Modern Classics, 1957.

Wertham, Fredric. "An Unconscious Determinant in *Native Son.*" In H. M. Ruitenbeek, ed., *Psychoanalysis and Literature.* New York: E. P. Dutton, 1964.